UNIX® FOR THE MAINFRAMER

The Essential Reference for Commands, Conversions, and TCP/IP

DAVID B. HORVATH

To join a Prentice Hall PTR Internet mailing list, point to:
http://www.prenhall.com/mail_lists/

Prentice Hall PTR
Upper Saddle River, NJ 07458

Library of Congress Cataloging-in-Publication Data
Horvath, David B.
Unix for the mainframer: the essential reference for commands, conversions, and TCP/IP / David B. Horvath
p. cm.
Includes bibliographical references and index.
ISBN 0-13-632837-7 (alk. paper)
1. UNIX (Computer file) 2. Operating systems (Computers) 3. TCP/IP (Computer network protocol) 4. IBM computers--Programming. I. Title.
QA76.76.O63H6744 1998 97-14545
005.4'32--dc21 CIP

Editorial/production supervision: *Jane Bonnell*
Cover design director: *Jayne Conte*
Cover design: *Kiwi Designs*
Cover illustration: *David B. Horvath*
Composition: *MacQuistan Consulting*
Manufacturing manager: *Alexis R. Heydt*
Acquisitions editor: *Michael Meehan*
Editorial assistant: *Tara Ruggiero*
Marketing manager: *Stephen Solomon*

Published by Prentice Hall PTR
Prentice-Hall, Inc.
A Simon & Schuster Company
Upper Saddle River, New Jersey 07458

Prentice Hall books are widely used by corporations and government agencies for training, marketing, and resale.

The publisher offers discounts on this book when ordered in bulk quantities. For more information, contact Corporate Sales Department, Phone: 800-382-3419; FAX: 201- 236-7141;
E-mail: corpsales@prenhall.com
Or write: Prentice Hall PTR, Corporate Sales Dept., One Lake Street, Upper Saddle River, NJ 07458.

Printed in the United States of America
10 9 8 7 6 5 4 3 2 1

ISBN 0-13-632837-7

Prentice-Hall International (UK) Limited, *London*
Prentice-Hall of Australia Pty. Limited, *Sydney*
Prentice-Hall Canada Inc., *Toronto*
Prentice-Hall Hispanoamericana, S.A., *Mexico*
Prentice-Hall of India Private Limited, *New Delhi*
Prentice-Hall of Japan, Inc., *Tokyo*
Simon & Schuster Asia Pte. Ltd., *Singapore*
Editora Prentice-Hall do Brasil, Ltda., *Rio de Janeiro*

DEDICATION

I dedicate this book to my wife, Mary.
Ten years of marriage and she still puts up with the time
spent at the keyboard—working, playing, writing,
and talking to people over the net.
Especially for not screaming every time I said,
"I'll be working on the book..."

TABLE OF CONTENTS

PREFACE

YOU HAVE JUST PICKED UP YAUB (YET ANOTHER UNIX BOOK). AND YOU MAY BE ASKING yourself why you should read this one instead of any of the other ones. The answer is simple: If you are a mainframe professional (programmer, analyst, project leader, DBA, etc.) and find yourself having to use the operating system generically known as UNIX, this book is for you.

The idea for this book came when I was working on a conversion project from the IBM mainframe to a UNIX machine. In addition to moving the code, we were supposed to help the staff learn the UNIX system. There were other departments in the same organization that were making similar transitions. Their mainframe professionals were very competent using the mainframe to get their job done, but were having trouble with the new operating system.

Because I am comfortable in both the mainframe and UNIX environments, I was called to help these people out. After they took training courses from outside vendors, they returned to their desks and were immediately hit with questions like "How do I do this?" They wanted to do something under UNIX that they were very quick and familiar with on the mainframe but had difficulty figuring out what to do in the new environment. While helping them solve their problems, one person remarked that he wished there was a book written for what he was going through.

I recommended several books that I had read and others that were on the market, such as *UNIX for Dummies* for example. The people with whom I was working, however, were no dummies and felt insulted at the idea of buying a book by that title. The introductory books were too simple, assuming little or no computer knowledge. But the more advanced books assumed that the reader knew certain things about UNIX already. Besides these problems, the books simply did not answer the question these people were asking: "I do X on the mainframe this way, how do I do it under UNIX?"

At about the same time, a new staff member joined the project, a person who was familiar with UNIX and another interactive operating system known as VMS, but did not know the mainframe. Fortunately, I gave a seminar a few years prior for VMS professionals on how to use the mainframe, so I made a copy of the handouts for the mainframe novice. The mainframe professionals remarked that they wished they could find a book that explained the UNIX operating system in terms with which they were familiar—much as the seminar materials did. That was the beginning of the idea to write this book. What you hold in your hands is the final result.

If you have questions about this book, you can contact me at UNIX_MF@COBS.COM. My Web page is at http://www.cobs.com/~dhorvath

ACKNOWLEDGMENTS

I WOULD LIKE TO INDIVIDUALLY THANK ALL THE PEOPLE WHO WERE INVOLVED IN THE development of this book and in my career leading to a point where I could produce it. But there have been so many people, I know I will forget at least one person—for that I apologize in advance.

I want to thank my wife, Mary, first of all, for putting up with me, my computers, my room of scattered materials, and all the time I have spent on this project.

I very much want to thank Laura Derr at Cardinal Business Media, and all the other people involved in bringing this project to market. They were willing to take a risk on a book that existed as an idea only. Unfortunately, they ceased book publication, which led me to Prentice Hall; thanks to Mike Meehan and the other people there!

Many thanks to Rob Slade (author of Robert Slade's *Guide to Computer Viruses*, 1994 edition ISBN 0-387-94311-0 or 3-540-94311-0 in Europe, 1996 edition ISBN 0-387-94663-2) who offered me advice and suggestions on the business of producing a book. He helped me avoid some of the mistakes that first-time authors make.

Scott A. McMullan, reviewer and proofreader, as well as friend; another UNIX and mainframe professional. Many thanks for the help!

Thanks to Robert A. Larkin of IBM, and Janet Halbert Alvarez, who, in addition to Scott, reviewed this book before the publisher saw it. Tough reading needing many corrections. Both Bob and Janet had to work through the mainframe-to-UNIX transition the hard way (without this book). All three are from the Philadelphia area.

This would not be complete without acknowledging some of the other people who have helped along the way including Ken Hair, the teacher of the summer school computer course, my Granny who paid for that first course (and made me take typing, "... just in case computers turn out to be a fad like comptometers."), my parents, and the rest of my family (even if they can't understand why I spend so much time in front of the PC).

TRADEMARKS AND COPYRIGHT ACKNOWLEDGMENTS

UNIX, X/Open are registered trademarks or trademarks of X/Open Company Limited, part of The Open Group (did belong to Novell, UNIX System Laboratories, Inc., and AT&T).

Enterprise Control Station (ECS), Control-M are registered trademarks or trademarks of 4th Dimension Software, Inc.

ACU-COBOL is a registered trademark or trademark of Acucobol, Inc.

UTS is a registered trademark or trademark of Amdahl Corporation

AT&T, Bell Labs, AT&T UNIX System V, Top End, and NCR are registered trademarks or trademarks of American Telephone and Telegraph Corporation

FOUNDATION is a registered trademark or trademark of Anderson Consulting

AUX, Macintosh are registered trademarks or trademarks of Apple Corporation

AutoSys is a registered trademark or trademark of Autosystems Corporation

Bachman is a registered trademark or trademark of Bachman Information Systems, Inc.

BSD is a registered trademark or trademark of Berkeley Systems Division, Inc.

Ensign is a registered trademark or trademark of Boole & Babbage

Omegacenter, Omegamon are registered trademarks or trademarks of Candle, Inc.

PacBase is a registered trademark or trademark of CGI Systems, Inc.

AD/Advantage, Mantis, Supra, Supra Server are registered trademarks or trademarks of Cincom Systems Inc.

Powerhouse is a registered trademark or trademark of Cognos

CA-ADS, CA-Ideal, CA-Ramis, CA-Telon, CA-PAN/LCM, CA-PAN, CA-DB:Star, CA-Datacom/DB, CA-IDMS for VAX and UNIX, CA-IDMS, CA-TOP SECRET, CA-ACF2, CA-Unicenter, CA-Archival, CA are registered trademarks or trademarks of Computer Associates, Inc.

Select* is a registered trademark or trademark of Computer Corporation Of America

Aviion, DG/UX are registered trademarks or trademarks of DataGeneral Corporation

DEC, PDP, PDP-7, PDP-11, ULTRIX, DSR (Digital Standard Runoff), OSF/1, Digital UNIX, VAX, Alpha, VMS, VT, VT-100, VT-200 series, VT-300 series, VT-400 series are registered trademarks or trademarks of Digital Equipment Corporation

Parts CICS Wrapper is a registered trademark or trademark of Digitalk, Inc.

CICS spII, COBOL spII are registered trademarks or trademarks of Flexus International Corp.

Forté Development Environment is a registered trademark or trademark of Forté Software, Inc.

Q Master is a registered trademark or trademark of GD Associates, Ltd.

HP, HP-UX, MPE, HP-9000 are registered trademarks or trademarks of Hewlett-Packard Company

Art Enterprise is a registered trademark or trademark of Inference Corporation

FOCUS, EDA/SQL are registered trademarks or trademarks of Information Builders, Inc.

Informix is a registered trademark or trademark of Informix Software Inc.

Cosort is a registered trademark or trademark of Innovative Routines International

POSIX is a registered trademark or trademark of Institute of Electrical and Electronic Engineers (IEEE)

IBM, DOS/VS, DOS/VSE, DOS/VSE/XA, DOS/VSE/ESA, OS/MFT, OS/MVT, OS/VS1, OS/VS2, OS/SVS, OS/MVS, MVS/XA, MVS/ESA, MVS, VM/370, VM/SP, VM/HPO, VM/XA, VM/ESA, CMS, VM/CMS, VM, AIX, AIX/370, PROFS, Office Vision, PR/SM (Processor Resource/Systems Manager), RS/6000, ES/9000, TSO, TSO/E, ISPF, ISPF/PDF, PC-DOS, REXX, VSAM (Virtual Sequential Access Method), SMS (System Managed Storage), CICS (Customer Information Control System), CICS/6000, IMS/DC (Information Management System/Data Communications), IMS (Information Management System), SDSF, IOF, DB2, DB2/6000, VS/COBOL, COBOL II, VTAM (Virtual Terminal Access Method), SCRIPT, OS/2, BookManager, InfoExplorer, SNA, ASM/370, BAL, ADSTAR Distributed Storage Manager (ADSM), Enterprise Performance Data Manager (EPDM), IBM Job Scheduler, NetView/6000, NetView, Operations Planning and Control (OPC), IMS TM are registered trademarks or trademarks of International Business Machines Corporation

CorVision is a registered trademark or trademark of International Software Group

PVCS is a registered trademark or trademark of Intersolv, Inc.

MVS/NFS is a registered trademark or trademark of J. Frank & Associates

ADW is a registered trademark or trademark of KnowledgeWare

ADW Repository is a registered trademark or trademark of KnowledgeWare and R&O Inc.

Endevour is a registered trademark or trademark of Legent Corp.

Open PL/I is a registered trademark or trademark of Liant

Erwin is a registered trademark or trademark of Logic Works

Microfocus COBOL, MTS are registered trademarks or trademarks of Microfocus, Ltd.

MS-DOS, Microsoft Windows, Xenix are registered trademarks or trademarks of Microsoft

MKS, MKS Toolkit are registered trademarks or trademarks of Mortice Kern Systems, Inc.

Nomad is a registered trademark or trademark of Must Software International

TransAccess is a registered trademark or trademark of Netwise, Inc.

Novell, Netware are registered trademarks or trademarks of Novell, Inc.

Express is a registered trademark or trademark of Operations Control Systems

Opt-Tech Sort is a registered trademark or trademark of Opt-Tech Data Processing

Oracle and SQL*Connect are registered trademarks or trademarks of Oracle Corporation

Pipes Platform is a registered trademark or trademark of Peerlogic, Inc.

Platinum is a registered trademark or trademark of Platinum Technology Inc.

UniQBatch is a registered trademark or trademark of Primary Ltd.

Lights Out is a registered trademark or trademark of Relational Data Systems

SCO, SCO UNIX, UnixWare are registered trademarks or trademarks of Santa Cruz Operations, Inc.

SAS is a registered trademark or trademark of SAS Institute, Inc.

SecurID Card is a registered trademark or trademark of Security Dynamics, Inc.

Sinix is a registered trademark or trademark of Siemens/Nixdorf

Slackware is a registered trademark or trademark of Slackware, Inc.

CCC/Harvest, CCC/Manager are registered trademarks or trademarks of Softool Corp.

Adabas, Natural2 are registered trademarks or trademarks of Software AG

Hierarchy is a registered trademark or trademark of Software Partners/32

EasyReporter is a registered trademark or trademark of Speedware Corp.

NDM, Connect:DIRECT are registered trademarks or trademarks of Sterling Software

INTRODUCTION

THE TARGET READER FOR THIS BOOK IS SOMEONE WHO IS FAMILIAR WITH THE IBM mainframe environment as a programmer, analyst, database analyst, consultant, etc.—one who uses the mainframe in a professional capacity. The intent is to present the UNIX operating system in a form that builds on your existing knowledge base of the mainframe. Building on what you already know and are comfortable with will ease the transition to the new environment.

I freely admit that this is not the definitive book on UNIX, any editor, any of the extensive toolsets available (sed, awk, grep, and others), or even a comprehensive command reference. There are other books to fill those needs. This is not written for the technically inexperienced, although I try to keep the concepts and examples simple. There are also other books to fill those needs. This book is intended to assist the mainframe professional move to the new environment. When you are comfortable there and want to explore more, then the more advanced books come to mind.

Throughout this book, you will find comparisons between UNIX systems and mainframe systems. I am not one of those who bash mainframes—they have a purpose in the business organization. UNIX systems also have a place in many organizations. The mainframe is clearly better at processing large amounts of data and allowing some access to many users. A UNIX system is clearly better at processing smaller amounts of data and allowing better, more friendly, access to a smaller number of users. The mainframe and mainframe skills are far from extinct, but there is a movement toward more friendly systems.

The examples in this book have been tried under AIX, AT&T UNIX System V Releases 3 and 4, Solaris, and the MKS Toolkit (tools & Korn). The examples will work using the Korn shell, which provides many advanced functions. Many, but not all, of the examples will also work with the Bourne and C shells. See Appendix E (C Shell—An Overview), if you are using that shell. I strongly suggest you use the Korn shell though.

This book is organized into eight chapters, seven appendices, and a glossary. It starts out with some background, compares ways of doing things in both environments, compares the command or job control languages, and moves into advanced topics of editor usage, setting up your own environment, and finishes up with lesser used commands.

Chapter 1 is Operating Systems and Environments. It compares and contrasts the ways of doing things on the mainframe and under UNIX. It delves into the history of both and how their general philosophy (or paradigms) differ. It starts to show the new terminology that you will be learning. UNIX, like French, has been accused of having a different word for everything.

Chapter 2 is Files and Data. The way files are handled is different from what you are used to. The way they are organized, specified, retrieved, and named is very different from the mainframe. Tape handling and special filenames are described.

Chapter 3 is Utilities and Commands. This is the part of the book that quickly answers one of the many questions my unfortunate friends had: "How can I do Y under UNIX? On the mainframe I did A, B, and then C." The major mainframe batch and interactive utilities are presented with their closest UNIX replacements. Direct replacements for ISPF/PDF and command equivalents to menu choices are presented. This is the chapter to jump to if you need to figure out how to do something quickly. But please do read the other chapters, because the background they provide is very important.

Chapter 4 is JCL, PROCs, and CLIST's Become Shell Scripts. Replacements for mainframe job control and command procedures are reviewed. Like the mainframe with JCL, CLIST, and REXX, UNIX has multiple scripting languages, which are reviewed.

Chapter 5 is Advanced Shell Scripts and Commands. This chapter shows some of the more advanced and less frequently used UNIX commands. It also shows advanced scripting features that may not have a mainframe JCL equivalence. These are the commands that will make you more comfortable and productive in the new environment, but you can live without them.

Chapter 6 is Editors. I explain how to use them under UNIX and how to do the familiar ISPF commands in the new editors.

Chapter 7 is Account Configuration. Setting up your personal environment is one of the ways of becoming more productive in the new environment because you can change things to your own preferences.

Chapter 8 is Third-Party Tools. Some of the familiar software tools are available, most are not. This chapter surveys the equivalent tools between the two environments.

Appendix A is Common Error Messages, Codes, and UNIX Signals. This is a short summary of the most common errors that you will see in the new environment along with explanations of what they really mean.

Appendix B is Hints and Techniques. Special ideas, commands, and procedures that may be helpful.

Appendix C is Data Conversion, ASCII and EBCDIC Charts. Methods and techniques of moving data between the environments and character code systems can be difficult to understand. A background and discussion of issues is included.

Appendix D is Hardware Comparisons. I examine how the machines compare to each other in terms of disk, memory, other peripherals, and performance.

Appendix E is C Shell—An Overview. It is a short overview of the C shell building on the information learned about the Korn shell in the rest of the book.

Appendix F is Using TCP/IP Networks. Connectivity between machines is important, and UNIX has a number of facilities that promote networking.

Appendix G is References, Reading List, Other Sources. This section contains listings of books, magazines, and other training sources that I found helpful and interesting.

The Glossary explains UNIX terms. It also provides a cross reference of mainframe and UNIX terms.

CONVENTIONS

Throughout the book, certain typographical and textual conventions are used:

Commands, filenames, and directories under UNIX will appear in `Courier`. All examples are case sensitive.

Menus and full-screen examples under UNIX will appear in `Courier`.

Mainframe commands, filenames, directories, and menus will appear in uppercase `COURIER`. In general, these examples are not case sensitive.

Full-screen examples will be in a smaller font size to allow for a full 80 character width.

In any example where the position of the cursor is important, it will be shown with an underscore (_).

In examples where your input is shown, it will be in `Courier` and highlighted through the use of **`bolding`**. Any place that you are expected to press the enter key, it will be shown as ↵. The computer's response will be shown in `Courier`.

Special keys will be shown using two methods. Keys with special names, such as the enter key, will be referred to as the <ENTER> key and shown in examples as (↵). The <BACKSPACE> key is sometimes called the <DELETE> key—under either name, it is usually above the <ENTER> key. The escape key will be shown as <ESC> since that is the common form on most keyboards. The other method of describing keys are those that require a combination of keys: a <CTRL-Z> is produced by pressing the <CTRL> key (also known as the <CONTROL> key) and then pressing the Z key. When describing control keys in text, the form <CTRL-Z> will be used. In examples, the circumflex (^) will be used to show control keys as this is the most common form under UNIX. <CTRL-Z> in an example will be shown as ^Z.

CHAPTER 1

Operating Systems and Environments

IN THE BEGINNING, THERE WAS THE HARDWARE. THE HARDWARE DID NOT DO VERY MUCH. Then came the software. Suddenly, the hardware started doing something—solving problems. The original software was programmed using boards and connecting wires; soon someone figured out how to store programs in the hardware, and the program was invented.

With the earlier computers, the programmers had to write every line of code: application, floating-point division, and direct control of the devices. The common code, input/output control, and floating-point arithmetic were things needed by every computer installation. Packaging and distributing the common code were the first beginnings of an operating system. With the introduction of assemblers and compilers that allowed the programmer to write in languages higher than machine ones and zeroes, the contents of the operating system grew.

The early operating systems were card-based, meaning that the operating system and all its components were stored on punched cards and each had to be loaded through the card-reader in order to be used. As tape and disk drives became available, the operating systems moved to those mediums. At one time, a Tape Operating System (TOS) was available for the IBM 360 mainframe. Disk Operating Systems (DOS) stored their components on disk and read them into memory as needed. When IBM developed a replacement for DOS/360, the company named it OS/360. It too was primarily disk-based but retained more and more components in memory.

Figure 1.1 shows the family lines and progression of the operating systems for the IBM mainframes. The acronyms can be found in the glossary. The most commonly used mainframe production operating system is MVS, although smaller installations still run DOS/VSE. Many installations run VM, often at the same time as MVS or DOS/VSE. The capability of concurrently running multiple operating systems on the same hardware is unique to the IBM mainframe and is possible through several different mechanisms.

On multiple-CPU (Central Processor Unit) systems, the box can be logically split such that each CPU behaves like a separate computer. A software package known as Processor Resource/Systems Manager (PR/SM) is another method that logically divides one processor into several smaller ones. A complex of CPUs can also be divided into multiple smaller CPUs. Each processor under PR/SM is known as a Logical Partition (LPAR).

Independent on the number of CPUs and PR/SM, the VM operating system allows other operating systems to run under it. The term for these operating systems under VM is guest operating systems. The name VM refers to the ability of this operating system to present each user (including guest operating systems) the appearance of having his or her own machine. The VM operating

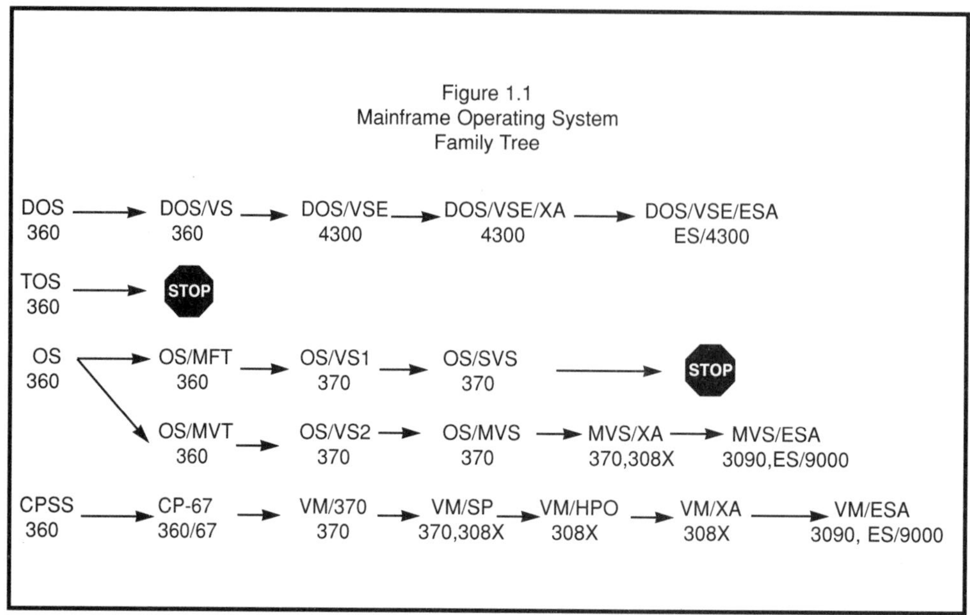

Figure 1.1
Mainframe Operating System
Family Tree

system imposes a considerable amount of overhead, however, which is why installations typically do not run their production MVS operating systems under it.

One of the primary uses of VM is as a migration tool because of its ability to run different operating systems and different versions of the same operating system. It is also used with the CMS (Code Management System) operating system, often referred to as VM/CMS, as an interactive user interface. IBM's electronic mail system, PROFS (Professional Office System) is an application that runs under VM/CMS. PROFS is also known as OfficeVision. Most of the IBM operating systems were developed by IBM to control the IBM mainframes and marketed for that purpose.

UNIX HISTORY

UNIX was originally developed at AT&T Bell Laboratories by Ken Thompson and Dennis Ritchie beginning in 1969 on a Digital Equipment Corporation (DEC) PDP-7 computer. (Ritchie later wrote the C language with Brian Kernighan.) Apparently the machine was unused and Thompson decided to develop an operating system to his personal liking, so he built on the concepts of the MULTICS operating system developed at MIT. In 1971, the operating system was moved to a DEC PDP-11, which was one of the most popular and inexpensive minicomputers from the early 1970s to mid-1980s. In 1973, the operating system was rewritten in the C language and announced publicly as a paper in the Communications of the ACM.

Distribution of UNIX outside of AT&T began shortly after the 1973 public announcement as research versions. These versions were unsupported and as-is. They were also free or priced to cover distribution costs. Source code was included that allowed outsiders to modify and enhance the operating system. The last research distribution was Version 7, which occurred in 1979. Commercial distribution began with System III; System V is the current benchmark of the UNIX operating system.

Figure 1.2
Brief UNIX History

Year	Event
1969	UNIX development begins on a DEC PDP-7.
1974	Paper on UNIX by Thompson and Ritchie published by ACM.
1975	AT&T Bell Labs begins licensing UNIX to Universities.
1977	SCO and Interactive Systems founded.
	BSD Version 1 flavor of UNIX released.
1978	AT&T UNIX Version 7 released.
	BSD Version 2 released.
1979	BSD Version 3 released.
1980	BSD Version 4 released.
1982	AT&T System III UNIX released.
1983	AT&T System V UNIX released.
	BSD Version 4.2 released.
	Hewlett-Packard HP-UX released.
1984	AT&T System V 2 UNIX released.
	DEC ULTRIX released.
1985	Sun releases NFS (Network File System).
	POSIX founded.
1986	AT&T System V 3 released.
	BSD Version 4.3 released.
	IBM AIX released (for the RT PC).
1987	AT&T System V 3.1 released.
	IBM released IX/370.
1988	AT&T System V 3.2 released.
1989	AT&T System V 4 released.
	IBM AIX/370 and AIX/PS2 released.
	OSF founded.
1990	OSF/1 UNIX released.
	IBM AIX for the RiscSystem/6000 released.
1991	Sun Solaris released.
1992	BSD Version 4.4 released.
1994	Open Edition MVS released by IBM, POSIX compliant (API).
1995	SCO purchases UNIX from Novell.
1996	X/Open Co. and Open Systems Foundation merge into The Open Group.

UNIX is a successful operating system for a number of reasons: because of its low cost, it was widely distributed through academia resulting in a large experience base; it was a minicomputer operating system when those boxes experienced extremely strong growth; it is a simple and coherent operating system that pushes several models and good ideas to their limits; it was developed by a small, enthusiastic, and highly motivated group of professionals; and it had an extremely long gestation period under the control of its developers and not subject to the whims or requirements of perceived market forces.

As Figure 1.2 illustrates, the early development of UNIX (1969–1979) closely parallels the development of the VM operating system for IBM mainframes. From about 1965 to 1974, portions and predecessors to the VM operating system were developed for internal use, not as a

Figure 1.3
Computers That Run UNIX

Vendor	Computer	UNIX Flavor
Amdahl Corporation	Mainframes	UTS
Apple	Macintosh	AUX, FreeBSD
Compaq, IBM, Dell Packard-Bell, and many others	Any Intel CPU-based (PC)	Xenix, SCO UNIX, Linux, AT&T UNIX, FreeBSD esix UNIX, UnixWare
Data General	AViion Workstations	DG/UX
Digital Equipment Corp.	VAX, Alpha	Ultrix, OSF/1, Digital UNIX
Hewlett-Packard	Workstations and HP-9000	HP-UX
IBM	RS/6000, ES/9000 (mainframe)	AIX
NCR (AT&T)	Servers and Workstations	UNIX
Siemens/Nixdorf	RISC Servers	Sinix
Sratus	Servers	FTX
Sun Microsystems	Servers and Workstations	Solaris, SunOS, FreeBSD
Unisys	U6000	UNIX

marketed product. The source code was distributed, and individual organizations made improvements that were introduced back into the formal product. In 1983, IBM went to an Object-code-only (OCO) distribution policy, which eliminated the source code distribution of VM. This change in policy upset many installations because they no longer could modify the operating system. In other words, no longer could they make local improvements, and, as a result, the flow of innovation has declined.

AT&T Bell Laboratories developed UNIX and owned the original trademark to the name "UNIX," which is not an acronym. With the break up of AT&T in the 1980s, however, UNIX was split off into a subsidiary with the name UNIX Systems Laboratories (USL).

A major competitor to AT&T/USL's UNIX System V was known as BSD UNIX, a trademark owned by University of California, Berkeley. The university had developed its own version of UNIX from when AT&T distributed the UNIX source code for research. The group that developed this version was split from the university as Berkeley Systems Division (BSD), and eventually killed off by regents (trustees) of the university. The reason BSD UNIX and BSD itself was discontinued was the belief that the University of California should not be involved in commercial ventures.

AT&T later sold USL to Novell. Since Novell's primary products are PC networking products, Novell released a version of UNIX for the PC known as UnixWare. But in December 1995, Novell sold USL to SCO (Santa Cruz Operations). SCO specializes in UNIX operating systems for the PC. With this change, Hewlett-Packard (HP) is supposed to move its 32-bit operating system to a 64-bit CPU, SCO is to merge UnixWare with its own UNIX, HP is to move its 64-bit operating system to an Intel 64-bit CPU, and finally the HP and SCO UNIX versions will be merged together. All this before the end of the decade.

Since the time that AT&T started distributing UNIX commercially, there have been a number of vendors that distribute their own versions of UNIX for various platforms. SCO sells Xenix for PCs, DEC sells Ultrix and OSF/1 for its VAX and Alpha platforms, Sun Microsystems sells Solaris and SunOS for its workstations and servers, HP sells HP-UX for its workstations and HP-9000 systems, Slackware distributes Linux for PCs (shareware), and there are others. Even IBM sells a UNIX operating system for its mainframes and RS/6000 series known as AIX.

Figure 1.3 shows some of the computers that will run UNIX. Although there may be differences between versions, the basic operating system remains the same.

During the time that AT&T owned UNIX and had a computer hardware division, there was movement in the industry to create a standard for UNIX that was out of AT&T's hands since AT&T was sitting in the dual role of competitor and supplier. The Open Software Foundation (OSF) was the more successful effort and it currently owns the trademark to the name UNIX.

What Is UNIX and How It Is Different from the Mainframe

The name UNIX has two connotations: registered trademark and generic descriptor. For a company to sell its operating system with the name UNIX, it must have permission and pay royalties to the trademark holder. For this and marketing reasons, many companies sell operating systems that behave like UNIX but have other names. The name UNIX is also a generic descriptor for all operating systems that have commands and behavior similar to the original AT&T UNIX. Throughout this book, unless an example is limited to a specific vendor's implementation, they will all be referred to as UNIX. Note that I capitalize the word UNIX; I have seen some publications use "Unix" instead of "UNIX." Although "UNIX" is not an acronym, the proper way of writing it is in all uppercase characters.

As mentioned, there are several standards for UNIX. System V, BSD, COSE, OSF, and finally POSIX. The Common Open Software Environment (COSE) was started by HP, IBM, SCO, Sun, Univel, and USL in an attempt to define a common look and feel. Another standard for the programming interface itself is known as UNIX '95 (formerly known as SPEC 1170) which defines the Application Programming Interfaces (API) administered by X/Open Company. POSIX, originally developed by IEEE, is a suite of standards governing the programming interfaces to any operating system. According to the U.S. government, for an operating system to be considered for a project, it must be open; open is defined by conforming to the POSIX standard. True UNIX systems typically are POSIX compliant, and the standard is so important that many non-UNIX operating systems are POSIX compliant, including Unisys CTOS, DEC VMS, HP MP/E, and last, but certainly not least important, IBM MVS.

UNIX is an interactive operating system. That is, it is designed to run interactive, time-sharing, on-line applications with considerable user interface. Historically, IBM mainframe operating systems were originally designed to run batch jobs; VM/CMS is an exception. A prime example of this is the primary interactive interface for MVS: TSO or TSO/E (Time Sharing Option or Time Sharing Option/Extended). A user's TSO session actually runs like a batch job within MVS and it is as easy to run TSO non-interactively within a batch job as any other program or application. Native TSO is difficult to use and I know of very few programmers who do so. Most TSO professionals use a menu-based development facility known as ISPF/PDF (SPF for short): Interactive System Productivity Facility/Program Development Facility or System Productivity Facility.

UNIX is very good for user and developer interaction, it is not quite as good for batch production processing. This is very important to remember if you are involved in migrating an application from the mainframe to a UNIX machine. It is a great operating system to work with as a developer, but many of the batch facilities and tools that are available on the mainframe are not yet available under UNIX. Although there is a command procedure language (like mainframe JCL—Job Control Language), it does not produce the kind or profusion of messages that the mainframe does. It also does not do automatic condition code checking—that is left to the programmer.

Another interactive operating system is PC-DOS or MS-DOS, the most common operating system for the personal computer. MS-DOS was written and marketed by Microsoft. PC-DOS was written by Microsoft, then modified and marketed by IBM. Both UNIX and MS/PC-DOS were designed to accept input from the keyboard, process the command, and output the result to the screen. If you have used MS/PC-DOS, learning UNIX will be much easier than if you are only familiar with the mainframe. Not only is MS/PC-DOS interactive like UNIX, many of the features are similar because the UNIX features were added to MS/PC-DOS. The similarities will be indicated with the description of individual commands later.

The hardware architectures of most systems running UNIX are different from the IBM mainframe. On the mainframe, the terminal and communications equipment handle the processing of the individual keystrokes of the user. Entering data, erasing mistakes, and moving the cursor around are all handled by the terminal and communications equipment. It is only when a hardware attention key (often called a big key) is pressed (<enter>, <attn>, one of the <pa> or <pf> keys, <clear>) that the CPU processes the data from the screen. This architecture means the CPU is busy running applications while the user is inputting.

On the typical UNIX box, the CPU handles all screen manipulation and input/output. When the user presses a key at his or her terminal, that keystroke is transmitted to the UNIX box, the CPU is interrupted from running applications, and must then process that key. If the key is just data, it is stored in the input buffer, echoed back to the screen, and the CPU resumes processing of applications. If the key has special meaning (<backspace>, <up-arrow>, <enter>, or others), the CPU must perform the special processing specified by that key (erase the previously entered key for a <backspace>, move the cursor up a line <up-arrow>, or begin processing of the input or a new command for the <enter> key).

The difference in hardware architectures is reflected in the operating system and many of the applications. For a typical mainframe application, the user enters all fields on a screen, presses <enter>, and then is informed of any input errors. The typical UNIX interactive application will inform the user of a problem as soon as they exit the data field in error. There also tends to be more of a try-and-see attitude held by the developers under UNIX than on the mainframe—results can be seen quickly, processing canceled if not correct, and corrections made.

The difference in hardware architectures is also reflected in the performance of the system. An IBM mainframe can run more program steps for a given MIPS (Million Instructions Per Second) of the CPU than other architectures. This is because there is other equipment (the communications processors) handling the user keystrokes; on most UNIX systems, CPU intervention is required for each and every keystroke. A mainframe can do more work but is less friendly.

Typically, UNIX has many narrowly focused tools that perform small functions, but together they do lots of work. MVS has fewer tools, but each one does much more. I have seen many humorous comparisons of operating systems with real-world items like airplanes. One way to think about MVS and UNIX is to compare them to automobile repair garages. MVS is a huge garage that takes a while to get things done because it works in a few fixed ways (there are dedicated stations for each step in the repair). UNIX is a smaller garage with lots of equipment available, but sometimes it takes several pieces to do each step in the repair. In fact, you may even have to put the tools together.

UNIX comes with many sophisticated tools that do small jobs, are programmable, and can be joined together to do complex things. Instead of writing a very complex tool, a simpler tool is written with the output fed into another tool to complete processing. There are tools to search files for specific strings, compare two or more files, sort, and even perform generalized text processing. If there were five programs you wanted to compile, instead of coding five separate compilation commands or jobs under MVS, under UNIX you would issue one command to find the five filenames, send its output to another to build the five commands, and then have it automatically issue the five compile commands. The UNIX approach certainly requires more thinking about how to do something the first time, but once you have done it, it is faster than doing the same thing with the individual commands. This is especially true if you save the set of commands that got you your results.

The UNIX philosophy shows us that small is good. There is a vast array of commands that perform small and well-defined functions; also provided are the tools to combine these commands to perform sophisticated functions. This philosophy is also the basis for structured programming: Break a large problem into smaller independent pieces and build a framework to connect those pieces. Build a library of small pieces that can be used over and over again; when needed, they are used together to build some larger functionality.

The stepwise refinement process is frequently used when developing or solving small problems under UNIX. Instead of having to design and build a solution from the beginning, small steps are made. As each step is made, a decision is made: Is the solution any closer? If the answer is yes, the results are used in the next small step. If the answer is no, the results are thrown away and the process refined. Use a command to search for some information, pass the results to another command for manipulation (often creating a series of commands as output), and then some final processing. The results are available quickly and easily passed between commands.

The UNIX operating system also follows this philosophy. It consists of two distinct pieces: the kernel and shell. The kernel handles tasks including memory allocation, device input/output, process allocation, security, and user access. The kernel itself is relatively small; everything else is an add-on: networking, usage accounting, queue control, and even batch scheduling is handled through external programs. In the narrowest sense, UNIX is just the kernel, which is really just an input/output multiplexor. The shell handles the user's input and invokes other programs to run commands. Most of the commands are either part of the shell or are external commands with executable images residing on disk. The shell also includes a command programming language similar to JCL, PROCs, CLISTs, and REXX execs on the mainframe.

On the mainframe, MVS is the kernel and TSO (IKJEFT01) is the shell that handles interactive user requests. MVS is like the UNIX kernel but performs many more functions; it also includes JCL (a batch interface language) processing.

MVS also controls printers. ANSI (also known as FORTRAN or ASA) printer control characters are the common means of controlling printers connected to mainframes. These characters occupy the first byte sent to the printer and are not printed. If the printer does not process these control sequences, the operating system converts them to the proper character codes. In keeping with simplicity, UNIX generally does not concern itself with printer control. The user sends data to the printer and the printer prints it. Each printer is different, but most support ASCII control characters like form feed and line feed. Some of the languages available under UNIX, COBOL for example, do support ANSI print control characters, converting them to the appropriate ASCII control characters.

A key difference between UNIX and mainframe operating systems is the way that running programs are referred to and handled. On the mainframe, a program runs as part of a job and only one program at a time runs as part of a job. Under UNIX, running programs are referred to as processes, and processes are owned by other processes. An interactive session is a process; if the user runs two commands at the same time, then there are two (or even more) subprocesses running in addition to the interactive process. On the mainframe, jobs are limited by the number of initiators (batch job sessions) and TSO is itself effectively a job being limited to one or two (ISPF and another command) programs running at one time. There is a limit to the number of processes running at any one time, which is set by the system administrator in the kernel and usually never reached. A user can also be limited to a certain number of concurrent processes by the system administrator.

You may be asking yourself: "What is the real difference besides terminology? If I need to run more than one program at a time, I just submit more jobs to different queues." To a certain extent, this is true. But the real difference is in how things are done. Under UNIX, one process's output can be the input to another; on the mainframe this is done through temporary intermediate files. But under UNIX, the process creating output can be running at the same time as the one using it as input. The processes run together in parallel. You can start seeing output from the second process before the first process is done. If you do not like the results you are getting, you cancel both processes, make corrections, and start again. This comes back to the interactive nature and philosophy of UNIX: Try something, if it does not produce the results you want, change it and try again.

As you move to UNIX, you will find that there are fewer conditions that cause an abend dump to occur. As a general method, applications written under UNIX tend to contain more code to trap and handle errors instead of relying on the operating system to take care of them. Most UNIX errors are brief messages instead of the mainframe's system error code (like S413-24 when you use a bad blocksize with a tape) or error messages (IDC0361I when unable to find a VSAM dataset). There is an equivalent to a mainframe abend dump, the core file. No one reads a core file directly; there are tools under UNIX to process them (abd and sdb).

IBM mainframes use a character set or code known as EBCDIC, which stands for Extended Binary Coded Decimal Interchange Code, an extension to BCD (Binary Coded Decimal), and is directly related to the holes in punched cards. Most systems by other vendors (personal computers, UNIX systems, workstations, servers, etc.) use ASCII (formally known as USASCII), which is the standard character code for computers in the United States. ASCII stands for American Standard Code for Information Interchange. IBM created EBCDIC and chose to retain it on mainframes for marketing, installed base, and compatibility reasons; personal computers and RISC systems that IBM sells use ASCII.

There is no particular technical advantage to either character code. ASCII is much more common. The primary difficulty with the character sets is having to convert between them. A capital A in ASCII is stored in memory with the decimal value 64; under EBCDIC, the same capital A is stored with the decimal value 193. Conversion between the two character sets will be discussed in Appendix C (Data Conversion, ASCII and EBCDIC Charts).

One more terminology difference between UNIX and the mainframe: The mainframe has systems programmers, UNIX has system administrators or system managers. The function and work performed are the same, just the titles have changed. Within the operating system, the user root has the ability to do anything they want no matter what the security and permissions may indicate. The term for this type of access is super-user; root is a super-user and others can be if so configured by the system administrator.

UNIX is a popular operating system. Because it promotes creativity, problem solving can be fun; instead of trying to find a way around the operating system to get something done, you find yourself figuring out which tools can be combined to build something. It is also popular because the skills learned on one UNIX system are transferable to another. The `ls` command under AT&T UNIX System V behaves a lot like the `ls` command under IBM AIX 4.1.1 (more about `ls` later). They may not produce exactly the same output, but they serve the same purpose. You learn what it does once and you can move to computers from other vendors (hence the name: open systems).

The command languages are different between MVS and VM/CMS; as with the mainframe, there are differences between versions of UNIX. There are two major UNIX family lines: AT&T System V and BSD. The differences are much less than between the mainframe operating systems, but do exist.

Most of the commands covered in this book relate to the UNIX based on the original AT&T versions because it is the common heritage to both family lines. Most of the commands are the same, but you may find that a particular command will not work on your system; a command that works fine on one machine may not work on another; or that command requires different modifiers (switches or options). There are even versions of UNIX that claim (correctly) both AT&T and BSD heritage because they accept commands using the syntax of either. If you have a question about the syntax of a command, you can check the documentation for your system.

At this point, you should be developing an understanding of the background of UNIX and the basic paradigm differences between it and mainframe operating systems. There are great differences in terminology, but you will find that although the words are different, in many cases they are describing concepts already familiar to you from the mainframe. The next step is how disks, files, and data are organized within UNIX.

CHAPTER 2

FILES AND DATA

THE UNIX OPERATING SYSTEM AT THE MOST BASIC LEVEL IS AN INPUT/OUTPUT multiplexor; file handling is central to the behavior of the operating system. The way that files are named, allocated, accessed, controlled, stored, referenced, and deleted are all handled within the kernel. Under UNIX, data is stored in files; on the mainframe, they are datasets. Under both operating systems, they are places to store data, programs, and even the operating system itself.

On the mainframe, the life of files are controlled through the DISP (disposition) parameter on the DD statement in JCL. DISP takes up to three arguments: what to do before the step (program) runs, what to do when the step ends successfully, and what to do when the step fails. These actions occur independently of the program being run. In fact, the program may not even access (open) the file and yet the disposition processing will occur. This leads to the use under MVS of the world's smallest utility: IEFBR14. This utility in reality is one but assembly language instruction long: BR 14. BR 14 is the equivalent to the COBOL STOP RUN or C language exit—it returns control to the operating system. The disposition processing will create or delete files when the DD statements are used with the execution of IEFBR14.

Under UNIX, file creation and deletion is performed explicitly. There is no DD statement under UNIX although there are substitutes. There are commands to create empty files and delete existing files. Programs explicitly name and act on files. Some JCL emulation utilities will perform disposition processing, but these are not perfect (one, for example, does not create a file unless the program opens it). Most of the COBOL compilers under UNIX will allow you to use symbolic names (like the DD on the mainframe):

```
SELECT FD-NAME ASSIGN TO UT-S-DDNAME.
```

or explicitly naming the file:

```
SELECT FD-NAME ASSIGN TO "THE.REAL.FILE.NAME".
```

Beware of this difference. It can lead to certain assumptions that are valid on the mainframe but not under UNIX. Just because a filename is assigned to a symbolic (DDNAME), it does not mean that the file will actually be created unless the program opens it. No longer will the JCL processor catch the fact that a file does not exist for a DISP=SHR or DISP=OLD. A file will not be deleted when your program abends like it did when you used DISP=(something,something,DELETE) on the mainframe. The closest equivalent behavior under UNIX is DISP=(MOD,KEEP,KEEP). If the file already exists, overwrite it; if it does not, create it when the program opens the file. If the program blows up after opening the file, keep it. Programs can change this behavior, but it is not done by the command language.

On the mainframe, information about datasets is stored in two places: the VTOC (Volume Table of Contents) and the system catalog. Each disk device contains a VTOC that automatically lists all the datasets on that disk; each datasetname must be unique on that disk. There is one system catalog that contains information about datasets that are explicitly entered. Each datasetname must be unique in the catalog. The catalog keeps track of which device (disk or tape) each dataset is stored on through the volume serial number. If a datasetname exists in the catalog and an attempt is made to insert it into the catalog again with DISP=(NEW,CATLG,something), the dataset is saved on the device, an entry is made in the VTOC if the device is a disk, the catalog is not changed, and a NOT CATLG 2 message appears in the system output but no error status or condition codes are set. A cataloged dataset is accessed through the datasetname and the operating system determines which disk to access or tape to mount. To access a dataset that is not in the catalog, one must specify the datasetname and the volume serial number.

There is also no system-wide catalog under UNIX. There is a structure that connects multiple disks together, but nothing that keeps track of the device or volume serial number on which a file is stored.

Under UNIX the filename must be unique. Any file on a mounted disk is accessed through the filename and the operating system determines which disk to access. While this might seem restrictive, think about how datasets are used under MVS. Generally, they are cataloged when the run completes, which requires unique names (otherwise you get NOT CATLG 2). Tape handling is more complicated.

Every program opens three standard files automatically: stdin, stdout, and stderr. The operating system automatically connects these files with the keyboard, screen, and screen respectively of the user. Mainframe SYSIN is equivalent to stdin, SYSOUT is equivalent to stdout, and stderr corresponds to mainframe SYSOUT, SYSPRINT, SYSERR, or SYSMSG. The UNIX standard files do not have to be connected to a terminal, they can be redirected to other files. Redirection will be explained in Chapter 3 (Utilities and Commands).

UNIX FILES

The UNIX operating system does not store any information about the internal structure of a file. On the mainframe, the DCB parameter sets file information such as record length (LRECL), blocksize (BLKSIZE), and file structure (record format—RECFM). These are items for the programmer, not the operating system, to remember. To UNIX, all files are a sequential collection of data bytes known as a stream. The operating system imposes no structure on the file, the concept of a record is foreign to UNIX. One of the original authors of UNIX, Brian Kernighan, has remarked that the concept of a record is a holdover from the days of punched cards. Along with the lack of record structure in the operating system, there is no ISAM (Indexed Sequential Access Method), VSAM (Virtual Sequential Access Method), or QDAM/BDAM (Queued Direct Access Method/Basic Direct Access Method, QDAM calls BDAM) format files, and there are no GDG (Generation Data Groups) or PDS (Partition Data Set) files.

Most UNIX utilities are designed to work with line-sequential files. That is, sequential files have a line separator character at the end of each logical unit of data (usually records). The line separator character is also known as the new-line character and is usually the line-feed character. In mainframe terminology, these files would be DCB=RECFM=VB (even if all the records are the same size). Since there is no record structure under UNIX, there is no equivalent to a Record Descriptor Word. The normal sequential file (mainframe DCB=RECFM=FB) does not have a line separator character since it has a fixed size. In COBOL, it is very easy to change an application to use line-sequential files instead of sequential. However, if the file contains binary data (COBOL USAGE IS COMP or USAGE IS COMP-3), the standard UNIX utilities will not work properly because the binary data can have the same bit pattern as the <line feed> character.

At this point you are probably wondering how any real work gets done using UNIX when all that is available is plain sequential files. If you were truly limited to plain sequential files, then it would be very difficult to get any real work done. File access by programmers are not as limited as it appears, however. The kernel does not have advanced file structures, but add-on tools do. You may not be able to work with your files with the standard UNIX tools and editors, but there are third-party editors and sort utilities that can. And you can always build your own tools to fill a need.

Mainframe VSAM is really three different types of file access methods: KSDS (Keyed Sequential Dataset), RRDS (Relative Record Dataset), and ESDS (Entry Sequenced Data Set). KSDS is really an enhancement of the original ISAM that IBM has phased out. RRDS is an enhancement to BDAM, allowing access to records based on their position in the file. ESDS is essentially sequential access. Most versions of COBOL for UNIX have facilities for ISAM and RRDS/QDAM/BDAM files. The UNIX kernel allows sequential files to be treated as RRDS/QDAM/BDAM through calls to the fseek function by the programmer providing direct access to any point in the file. Tools to replicate GDG behavior are easy to create and are contained in Appendix B (Hints and Techniques). The PDS is used on the mainframe to organize or group files together under one main name—files in a PDS are known as members. UNIX provides a means to organize all types of files through the directory structure.

This is keeping with the UNIX philosophy of simplicity. Instead of the operating system deciding when to create a file or imposing a structure on it, the programmer must. This provides more control to the program writer along with more work. In an automobile, an automatic transmission is easier to use but gives poorer gas mileage, poorer performance, and less control when in difficult situations. A manual transmission is more work, harder to learn, and, frankly, a pain in city traffic, but it gives better gas mileage, better performance, and more control.

UNIX physical disk storage is organized in units known as filesystems. A specific amount of space on a disk is allocated to a filesystem by the system administrator, and a disk can contain one or many filesystems. This is done to each disk on a system. These filesystems are mounted (a term referring back to when removable hard disks were used). Each filesystem has an inode table which is similar to the mainframe VTOC: information about where a file is stored, the owner, file size, type of file, access permissions, and other data. The inode does not contain the name of the file. That is stored in the directory.

You will find that many concepts throughout UNIX are consistent. When working with disks, everything is a file. The mainframe operating system knows about many different types of files. To UNIX, there are only three types of files: ordinary, special, and directory. Ordinary files are data, program source, executable, and other files that have no particular meaning to the operating system. Special files are used to access devices and facilitate interprocess communication; there is more information about special files later.

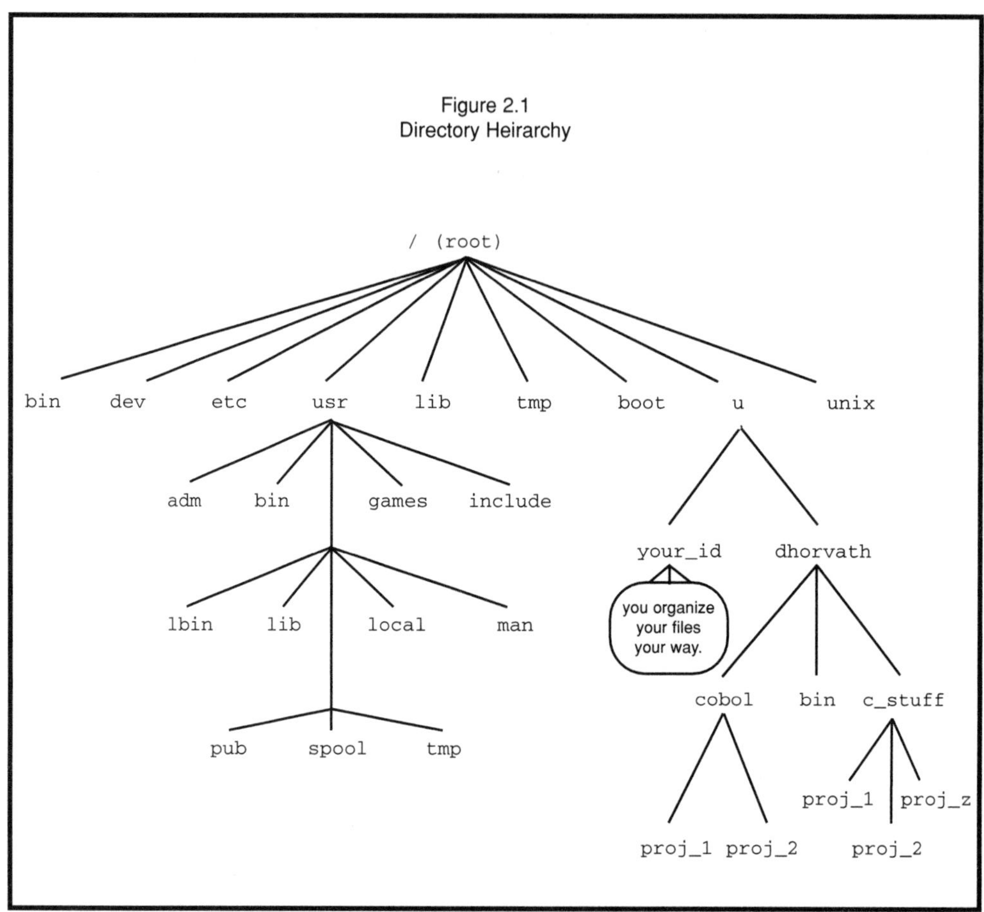

UNIX DIRECTORIES

A directory is a file that contains a list of filenames and their inodes. A directory may have directories under it that are known as subdirectories. The top-level directory is known as the root directory and is similar in some ways to the mainframe VTOC and system catalog because it allows access to files on different disk devices. It is the directory/subdirectory structure that allows the logical grouping of files. As shown in Figure 2.1, I might group all of my COBOL and C code by language and project name.

The directories and subdirectories, as shown in Figure 2.1, are in an upside-down tree structure. The root is shown at the top and the branches move downward. The root directory is said to contain the directories bin, dev, etc, lib, tmp, u, and usr; it also contains the file boot, which is the bootable image of the operating system, and unix, which is a backup of boot. By looking at the names alone, it is not possible to tell if they are directory or filenames.

/bin (for binaries) is the directory where programs reside. These are the programs that are needed for minimal functionality of UNIX. Less important binaries are stored in /usr/bin, which may be in a different filesystem and disk. If the computer will boot, you will have /bin. Even if you cannot mount other disks, you will be able to perform the important functions. This really matters only to the system administrator.

/dev (for devices) is where information about devices are stored. Devices (even terminals) can be treated like they were files on the disk. Even memory can be accessed from a program as if it were a file on disk.

/etc (for et cetera) is where other things are stored, typically administrative files and system programs. The file containing user identification and passwords along with the program that schedules programs to run (similar to a batch queue) are stored in /etc. The specific files contained in this directory vary between versions of UNIX. Some of the more interesting files in this directory are:

/etc/environment	Contains global environmental information (settings for all users).
/etc/profile	Executed once each login. Sets settings for all users.
/etc/filesystems	Describes the filesystems installed on this system.
/etc/group	Describes groups to which users belong.
/etc/passwd	Contains user login information: userid, encrypted password, home directory, and user real name.
/etc/inittab	Lists programs and parameters executed when computer is booted.
/etc/motd	Message of the day.

/lib (for library) is where libraries of functions are stored. Programs written in C, and some other languages use the function libraries stored in this directory.

/tmp (for temporary) is where temporary files are stored. The editor, sort utilities, and application temporary files are stored in this area. The system programs clean up after themselves; your application should also. The system administrator typically has a utility that will clean out this area on a scheduled basis if you do not.

/u (for users) is where user files are stored. When you login, you are connected to this area. Unless you specify otherwise, any file you create will be created in this area. This subdirectory may have a different name: common ones are /usr, /usr1, /usr2, /usrN (when there are many users), and /home. It is up to the system administrator what name is used.

/usr (for user filesystem) is where users' files were originally stored. Now it is much more common to see non-user files stored under this directory. You should note that many of the directories under root are also under /usr. /usr/bin contains executable programs that are less critical to the system. Programs like bc (business calculator) and cal (calendar) are in /usr/bin. Less important libraries are stored in /usr/lib. The definition of "less important" depends on the specific implementation of UNIX. Sometimes the files are stored based on their frequency of use: more frequently used programs in /bin, less in /usr/bin; more frequently used libraries in /lib, less in /usr/lib.

The areas described above are the common locations; by no means are they fixed, just common. I know of one system where the administrator decided to put COBOL under /usr2/cobol. The libraries are under /usr2/cobol/lib and the binaries (compiler and other tools) are under /usr2/cobol/bin. This person decided to install all third-party tools under /usr2 to make it easier to organize and upgrade.

FILESYSTEMS

When filesystems (organized physical disk storage) are connected to the root directory, they are said to be mounted. The mount point looks like a subdirectory; if the filesystem is unmounted, there is an empty directory entry in the root directory. In Figure 2.1, the root directory is part of the root filesystem. The /usr subdirectory could be part of a different filesystem (called /usr). If the /usr filesystem was not mounted, then there would be nothing listed under the /usr subdirectory (no /usr/bin, no /usr/lib). When the operating system starts up, it usually mounts all filesystems that the system administrator has defined. In this case, the /usr filesystem would be mounted over top of the /usr subdirectory and all of the files under it would be usable.

To the programmer, whether a subdirectory is its own filesystem or not is completely transparent. The same commands are used and the space behaves the same way if it is part of the root filesystem or its own filesystem. The only difference is how space is allocated. All files created under a filesystem take up space in that filesystem only. If the filesystem fills up, no other files can be created until space is freed up. By splitting storage up into different filesystems, the system administrator manages the total space available to each area. This may also be done along application lines; if payroll and accounts payable have their own filesystems, one filling up will not impact the other.

MS/PC-DOS also organizes files within a directory structure similar to that under UNIX. The principle difference is that UNIX uses the forward slash (/) and MS/PC-DOS uses the backward slash (\) to separate portions of directory names. Although very few people actually use it, MS/PC-DOS has the ability to connect multiple disks into one directory structure. Instead of accessing each disk by its letter (A:, B:, C:, D:, etc.), the JOIN command connects the disks to a subdirectory. To the user, it looks like there is one large disk with many subdirectories.

On most UNIX versions, the maximum size of a filesystem is 2 GB (2 Gigabytes = 2,147,483,647 bytes). The maximum size of a file on disk is 2 GB. Some versions of UNIX do allow larger filesystems, but I have not seen any that allow an individual file to exceed 2 GB. The limit is due to the kernel using the fseek function to find locations on the disk; fseek only uses a 32-bit integer.

The newer UNIX versions (often referred to as "64-bit") are eliminating this restriction or greatly increasing the limit itself.

On the mainframe, JCL must specify the space required for a sequential file in the SPACE parameter unless a VSAM dataset is being created or SMS (System Managed Storage) is running. VSAM manages its own space within an area set up by the system programmer. SMS will automatically allocate space for files based on groups set up by the system programmer. A filesystem under UNIX is similar to the VSAM space or SMS group. There is no equivalent to the mainframe SPACE parameter under UNIX because space for a file is automatically allocated. The size of a file grows as more data is written. In mainframe terminology, a file starts with one block and grows at the rate of one block per extent with an unlimited number of extents.

On the mainframe, there are two physical disk hardware architectures: CKD and FBA. CKD stands for Count Key Data. Each unit of storage is dependent on the physical attributes of the device: bytes per track and tracks per cylinder. This is the most common. The much less common FBA stands for Fixed Block Architecture, where each unit of storage has a fixed size independent of the physical device.

Most versions of UNIX also use FBA: A typical block is 512 or 1024 bytes long. If a program writes a piece of data that are shorter than a block, then multiple pieces are written in each block. If the data is longer than a block, then multiple blocks are used for each piece. If the length of the data is not an even multiple of the block size, then they will span blocks (part of it will be in two blocks). Since the operating system treats the file as a stream of bytes, the size of a piece of data does not matter.

FILENAME STRUCTURE

A filename under UNIX consists of one or more characters, and a good practice is to use only upper and lowercase letters, numbers, period (.), underscore (_), and some of the other punctuation. In reality, you can use just about any character in filenames, but because many of the characters have special meaning, I avoid them and recommend you do the same. The case of any alphabetic characters are significant: FILE_A is not the same as File_a. The maximum length of a filename depends on the version of UNIX you are using: older versions support up to 14 characters; AIX supports filenames of up to 255 characters; and SunOS up to 511 characters. The length of your filenames can be anywhere from one character (not very useful) to as long as the operating system allows. A filename of 14 characters can get to be ridiculous. Can you imagine one a couple of hundred long? Your system administrator can tell you the maximum length of a filename on your system. You probably do not need to worry about it though, most versions of UNIX after about 1986 support the long filenames. Figure 2.2 shows examples of valid filenames.

Files that begin with a period are generally configuration or setup files for a program, and they are often omitted from directory listings unless you use options to show them. The asterisk has special meaning—it is the wildcard character. The forward slash at the beginning means the root directory. It is also used to separate levels of directories. On the mainframe, periods are used to separate parts (or levels) of a datasetname, that is how they are organized. UNIX provides directories and allows names to be broken into pieces.

DIRECTORY NAME STRUCTURE AND PATHNAMES

Directory names follow the same rules as regular files. When a filename alone is used in a command or within a program, the operating system assumes that the file is in the current directory. If you want to work on a file in another directory, there are several ways of doing so. One way is to specify the pathname as well as the filename.

Using the directory structure in Figure 2.1, there are a number of ways to access files in different places. If I had an executable program in the bin directory of my account with the name of

Figure 2.2
UNIX Filenames

Filename	Valid or Why Not
`This_is_valid`	Valid
`this_is_valid`	Valid but different than This_is_valid
`THIS_IS_VALID`	Valid but different than the two filenames above
`thisisvalid`	Valid but hard to read
`.this_file_is_special`	Files that begin with a period are special
`A.FILE.NAME.LIKE.THE.MAINFR`	You can certainly do this
`A.FILE.NAME.LIKE.GDG(0)`	Valid but bad practice because () are special to the shell
`This is not good`	Valid but bad practice
`this_is*not*a_good_idea`	Valid but bad practice because * is special to the shell
`this/is/not/a/good/filename`	Actually a pathname - directories and filename

asa_to_ascii (to convert from mainframe printer control to normal ASCII printer control) that you wanted to run from your account, you would type:

```
/u/dhorvath/bin/asa_to_ascii
```

This is known as the fully qualified filename. It contains a fully qualified pathname along with the filename. This is sometimes referred to as an absolute path because all of the steps (subdirectories) to the file are included. It tells the operating system to start with the root directory (/), then travel down the subdirectories dhorvath and then bin. Another type of path is the relative path, which gets to the file from where you are now:

```
../dhorvath/bin/asa_to_ascii
```

The .. tells the operating system to go to the parent of your current directory, which is /u in this example, and then travel down the subdirectories dhorvath and then bin. Another way of specifying a path that is a combination of relative and absolute is through the tilde character (~):

```
~dhorvath/bin/asa_to_ascii
```

The tilde character tells the operating system to start at the parent of your home directory (/u). This is different from the previous example because .. is relative to your current directory, which may or may not be your home directory. When you login, you are placed in your home directory; there are commands that allow you to move around (known as navigate or navigating) through the structure.

If I want to get to the same file, I can use any of these methods or another shorthand notation if I am in my home directory:

```
bin/asa_to_ascii
```

Which tells the operating system to go to the bin directory under my current directory for the file. If I want to get to the file when I am in a directory other than my home directory, I can use the form:

```
~/bin/asa_to_ascii
```

Causing the operating system to go to my home directory (~) and then down to the bin directory under it. Notice that ~/ is different from ~dhorvath. ~/ points to my home directory, ~dhorvath points to the home directory of dhorvath. In this example with my account, the two are the same but they are different if you are issuing these commands.

MOVING FROM DATASETNAMES TO UNIX FILE AND PATHNAMES

Using files with absolute and relative paths to directories may seem confusing, but you are already doing something similar under TSO and ISPF. If you want to work with a dataset that has your userid as the high-level qualifier, you do not have to include your userid. If you want to, you can type in the full datasetname if you put it in quotes <'>. If you want to work with my dataset, you must put the datasetname in quotes:

Your Dataset:	`YOURID.PROJ1.PROD.JCL`
Under TSO:	`PROJ1.PROD.JCL`
Or:	`'YOURID.PROJ1.PROD.JCL'`
My Dataset:	`MYID.PROJ1.PROD.JCL`
You type:	`'MYID.PROJ1.PROD.JCL'`
I type:	`PROJ1.PROD.JCL`
Or:	`'MYID.PROJ1.PROD.JCL'`

Using directories and subdirectories to organize files may also seem confusing, but most mainframe installations have conventions that are comparable. The highest level qualifier is the userid for personal files. For data and system files, most installations use a form where the first two or three high-level qualifiers specify file ownership. Depending on the structure of the organization itself (and how billing is done), the highest may be division, the next represents a group or function within that division (such as payroll). Figure 2.3 contains examples of how mainframe dataset names might be implemented as directory and filenames under UNIX.

Instead of separating many parts of a datasetname with periods, you create a series of subdirectories that replace the repetitive information in your datasetname. Upper or lowercase directory and filenames are entirely up to you or your installation. I have seen data filenames from the mainframe in uppercase with directory names and other files usually lowercase. Remember that case is significant for directory and filenames: /DIVISION and /division are two different directories. A mainframe PDS

Figure 2.3
Mainframe Datasetname and
UNIX Equivalents

Mainframe Datasetname	UNIX Equivalent
DIVISION.GROUP.PROGRAM.FILE.MORE	/division/group/program/FILE.MORE
DIVISION.GROUP.PROGRAM.FILE.MORE	/DIVISION/GROUP/PROGRAM/FILE.MORE
YOURID.PANVALET.SOURCE	/u/yourid/panvalet/source/
YOURID.PDS.COBOL.SOURCE	/u/yourid/pds/cobol/source/
YOURID.PDS.JCL	/u/yourid/pds/jcl/
YOURID.LIB.JCL	/u/yourid/lib/jcl/
YOURID.PDS.CLIST	/u/yourid/pds/clist/
YOURID.LOADLIB(PDSMEMBER)	/u/yourid/loadlib/PDSMEMBER
YOURID.PROCLIB(PDSMEMBER)	/u/yourid/proclib/PDSMEMBER
YOURID.JCL.CNTL	/u/yourid/jcl/cntl/
YOURID.PROFILE	/u/yourid/profile/
YOURID.PROJECTS.COBOL	/u/yourid/projects/cobol/
YOURID.PROJECT7.C	/u/yourid/project7/c/
YOURID.PROJECT3.FORT	/u/yourid/project3/fort/
YOURID.PDS.COPYLIB	/u/yourid/pds/copylib/

is implemented as a subdirectory with the PDS member becoming the UNIX file. To replace the PDS, the entire name is converted into subdirectories, and the member of any of the PDS (name inside the <()>) would be placed after the final slash of the UNIX path (as the filename).

UNIX FILENAME CONVENTIONS

Just as there are conventions on the mainframe for filenames and types (LOADLIB for load or executable modules, PROCLIB for procedures, and PDS.JCL for jobs, for example), there are conventions under UNIX. These conventions are shown in Figure 2.4.These suffixes have come from common practices with years of usage and have reached to the point of being unofficial rules.

It is not always possible to tell what kind of file a file is based on its filename. Executable (binary) programs and shell scripts (the UNIX name for jobs containing JCL) may just be a filename without a modifier or extension. One way to determine what is stored in a file is to look at the contents using the editor or other tool. But that does not always help, especially if the file contains binary data. There is also a command known as file that will determine the type of file based on rules stored in /etc/magic.

When converting a mainframe PDS to UNIX directories and files, the filename may not be the same as the PDS member name because of naming conventions like those shown in Figure 2.4. The mainframe convention for a COBOL source program may be:

```
YOURID.COBOL.SOURCE(program)
```

Figure 2.4
UNIX Filename Conventions

UNIX Filename	Convention (Type of File)
`program_name.c`	C language source code
`program_name.cpp`	C++ language source code
`program_name.cbl`	COBOL language source code
`program_name.pc`	C language with embedded SQL
`program_name.pco`	COBOL language with embedded SQL
`include_file.cpy`	COBOL copybook - included into COBOL language programs
`include_file.h`	Header file - included into C and C++ language programs
`.some_name`	Configuration file for application some_name
`program_name.as`	Assembly language source code
`program_name.o`	Compiled program (object module)
`a.out`	Default executable (after link edit) from C compiler
`program_name`	Executable (after link edit) from C or COBOL compiler Could also be shell script (UNIX equivalent of JCL)
`program_name.ksh`	UNIX equivalent to JCL written in Korn (one form of name)
`program_name.sh`	UNIX equivalent to JCL written in Bourne (one form of name)
`program_name.csh`	UNIX equivalent to JCL written in C Shell (one form of name)
`program_name.pl`	UNIX equivalent to JCL written in Perl (one form of name)
`program_name.awk`	UNIX equivalent to JCL written in AWK
`program_name.lst`	Compiler listing from most compilers
`program_name.lst.z`	Compiler listing that has been compressed to save storage space
`program_name.lst.gz`	Compiler listing compressed by GNU zip to save storage space
`program_name.lst.zip`	Compiler listing compressed by zip to save storage space
`datafile.dat`	Data portion of an ISAM file
`datafile.idx`	Index portion of an ISAM file
`job_run_stuff.out`	Log of output from background job
`many_object_modules.a`	Archive file - collection of object modules for link
`some_file_name`	Unknown file type, could be anything
`save_set.tar`	Backup created by tar program
`save_set.cpio`	Archive (often a backup) created by cpio
`my_file.bak`	Backup copy of file in progress
`program_name.v`	RCS (Revision Control System) archive
`this_file.tmp`	Temporary file
`sendmail.cf`	Configuration file (for sendmail program)

A direct conversion to UNIX would be:

```
/u/yourid/cobol/source/program
```

But a conversion that respects the UNIX conventions would actually be:

```
/u/yourid/cobol/source/program.cbl
```

There is nothing mandatory about naming your files as shown in Figure 2.4, but if you want to protect your sanity and that of your co-workers, I strongly suggest you follow them. As you move from being a mainframe to a UNIX professional, you will become more comfortable with the new conventions.

Special UNIX Files

As mentioned previously, there are three types of files that UNIX recognizes: ordinary, directory, and special. You should understand ordinary and directory files. As the name implies, special files have special meaning or purposes. A special file can be a pipe, a link, or a device.

A pipe file looks like a file, has an entry in the directory, but does not store much data on the disk. It acts as a connection between two processes for the flow of data—just like a water pipe connects the water company to a house. The amount of data (and water) actually stored in a pipe is minimal, it is merely a buffer; the real source is a process (or the water company). Typical mainframe applications do not use pipes because of the single-process philosophy of jobs. Under UNIX, however, you may have multiple processes running in parallel feeding each other. To the program, a pipe looks just like any other file. It can be written to and read from and will eventually have an end-of-file (when the writing program closes it).

Pipe files are sometimes referred to as named pipes to distinguish them from other types of pipes within UNIX. Regular or normal pipes are a form of redirection.

Although the mainframe does not have pipes, the concept should not be foreign. In other words, many programs write to files that exist solely to be used as input by other programs. If the reading and writing programs are in the same job, the file might be temporary (automatically deleted when the job is done) or permanent. Even if the file is permanent, it may serve no other purpose than to feed the program in the next job step. UNIX certainly supports temporary and permanent files as feeds between different programs. The advantages to pipes over ordinary files are the reading program does not have to wait for the writer to finish (parallelism); disk usage is minimized (important for large files); and there may be an improvement in efficiency if the operating system is able to buffer the writing and reading such that nothing is actually written to the pipe on disk.

A link file looks like a file, has an entry in the directory, but occupies very little disk space. The link is an alias for another file somewhere on the disk. There are two forms of links: symbolic and hard. A symbolic link is one where the link and the original file are in different filesystems (it has a special entry in the directory that differentiates it from the original file). The symbolic link requires a link file because different filesystems have duplicate inodes since each has its own inode table; the link provides the connection to the other inode and filesystem. A hard link is one between files within the same filesystem. There is no way to determine which is the original file and which is the link.

Links are not completely foreign to the mainframe environment. Within a PDS it is possible to alias one name to another. The member is accessible through either name. UNIX just extends the concept, allowing aliases for any file, not just members in a PDS. In addition, with symbolic links, the files do not have to be on the same physical device.

A hard link occupies no disk space other than the directory entry; a symbolic link uses a directory entry and enough disk space to hold the fully qualified path. To a program, there is no difference between the original file, a symbolic link, and a hard link. All that looks different is the directory listing.

At first glance, it may seem to you that there is little use for file aliases. After all, why not just code the proper name? While the best case would have the proper name coded, aliasing (linking) allows flexibility. There are some programs in UNIX that perform different functions depending on their name. The same program, the same executable, and the same physical file on disk can have different names. When the program runs, the operating system can tell it what its name is. The program then decides what to do based on that name. Again, at first glance this may seem silly to you because it usually makes sense for a program to do one thing and do it well. That is true, but there are programs that do different things that are very similar.

One example is the compress command. In Figure 2.4, there is a file that ends with .Z. That file was created from the original file by the compress program that changed the name from some_program.lst to some_program.lst.Z to show it was the compressed version. There is also an uncompress command to reverse the process. There is only one program: compress. It has three names, three entries in the directory, but only one inode: compress, uncompress, and zcat. The way the program is written, the three main functions are very similar with much code duplication: compress compresses, uncompress reverses the process, and zcat uncompresses to a different filename. Instead of having three copies of the program, there is only one with three different names in the directory, which saves disk space.

Another use for links is when different people need copies of the same file. Instead of duplicating the file, a link is created to the original file. When a file is deleted, the number of links to that file is checked and if there are any, the physical file does not go away. The directory entry is removed by the deletion but not the actual contents. If you link to one of my files and I delete it, you still can access it. To a program, a link to a file looks just like the original file. In reality, every file has at least one link. For example, when a file is created, an entry is made in the inode table and then in the directory where it is created. That entry is technically the first link to a physical file.

Not only can you create hard or symbolic links for individual files, you can link entire directories. This is very useful with third-party tools or utilities. The utility is installed to a directory such as /usr/bin/installed/utility_name/version. Each time you receive and install a new version, the version subdirectory changes. This can be a real bother for users of the utility since it would be stored under a different path (subdirectory) when the version changes. The solution is to create a hard or symbolic link with the path /usr/bin/utility_name that points to the proper /usr/bin/installed/utility_name/version. If a new version is installed, the link is changed. If there is a problem with the new version and falling back to the prior install is needed, the link is changed back.

As you work with UNIX, you will notice the internal consistencies. You can link files to files, directories to directories, pipes to pipes, link files to link files, and files to devices. Remember, UNIX treats all of these as files.

A device file looks like a file, has an entry in the directory, but occupies no disk space. There are two different types of device files: character and block. The type of interface determines the type of file—a terminal is a character device, a disk is a block device. By treating physical devices like files, you can perform many of the same operations on a tape drive, memory, or terminal as a regular disk file. For some devices (disks and the printer), there are two types of access: raw and block. Block mode is the normal method of access (letting the operating system impose its structure on your access). Raw mode gives you total control of the device. When a new disk is installed and formatted, raw mode is used to allow the formatting program complete access. To a program, a device looks just like any other file. It can be written to and read from and will eventually have an end-of-file.

For obvious reasons, you should never create a data file in the /dev directory. There are a number of devices that are common to all UNIX systems, but the actual devices on each system will vary. Figure 2.5 shows common device files and their purpose. Because there can be multiple devices of the same type, there are unit numbers that usually start with zero. The maximum number will be however many of that device are attached to the system; this is shown in Figure 2.5 as ???.

/dev/null is a special device file in that everything written to it is absorbed and all attempts to read from it result in an end-of-file condition. This is equivalent to the mainframe DSN=NULLFILE or DD DUMMY and equivalent to the MS/PC-DOS NUL:. It is useful when a program requires a file exist but not that it contain data. It is also useful if you want to throw away output. /dev/null is the proverbial bit-bucket.

/dev/kmem and /dev/mem allow access to memory as though it were a disk file. The memory used by the kernel is available through kmem and all system memory is available through mem. You must have special permission to access these areas; if you do, your program can access memory as though it were a disk file (without special commands or code). As an application programmer, you may never have need to use these special files, but it is nice knowing they are there should you. A system administrator may write programs and can provide more information if you are interested.

UNIX Tape File Access

Tape access is handled through device files. To access the first tape drive on a system, the name is /dev/rmt0. The next tape drive might be /dev/rmt1. If there are different types of tape drives (reel-to-reel, 3490 cartridge, 8mm cartridge, etc.), the device numbers may be assigned sequentially or with a specific scheme (for example, /dev/rmt0 through /dev/rmt5 are reel-to-reel, /dev/rmt10 through /dev/rmt13 are 3490, /dev/rmt20 through /dev/rmt21 are 8mm cartridge, etc.). The naming convention depends on the system administrator.

To get a file from a tape, the physical mount is performed (by you, an operator, or the system administrator depending on the size of your installation), and a command is issued or program run that accesses the proper device. A plain tape, equivalent to a mainframe LABEL=(,NL), is no problem. Tapes with labels (LABEL=(,SL)—the default) are more difficult to process.

On the mainframe, most tapes have volume labels (describing the tape itself), file labels (describing the file), and end-of-file labels. If a file does not fit on a single tape, an end-of-volume label is written, and the file label on the next tape notes that it is the second tape in the set. The structure of mainframe tapes is detailed in Appendix B (Hints and Techniques). UNIX does not

Figure 2.5
Common UNIX Devices

Device Name	Purpose
/dev/console	System console device. Other names: /dev/syscon and /dev/systty
/dev/dump	Device for system abends
/dev/swap	Device for swap (paging) files. Also /dev/paging00 - ???
/dev/error	Device for error reporting
/dev/dskc0t0d0s0	Disks. Numbers vary depending on controller and disk.
/dev/fp000 - ???	Fixed platter (hard) disks
/dev/hdl - ???	Hard disks.
/dev/hdisk0 - ???	Hard disks.
/dev/rdskc0t0d0s0	Raw disks. Numbers vary depending on controller and disk.
/dev/rfp000 - ???	Raw disks.
/dev/cd0 - ???	CD-ROM
/dev/rcd0 - ???	Raw CD-ROM
/dev/cdrom1 - ???	CD-ROM
/dev/floppy	Floppy disk
/dev/fd0 - ???	Floppy disk
/dev/rfloppy	Raw floppy
/dev/rfd0 - ???	Raw floppy disk
/dev/rmt0 - ???	Tape drives
/dev/kbd	Keyboard attached to workstation
/dev/mouse	Mouse attached to workstation
/dev/sound	Sound device attached to workstation
/dev/video	Screen attached to workstation
/dev/mem	All system memory
/dev/kmem	Memory of current process as seen by Kernel
/dev/kstat	Kernel statistics
/dev/lp	Printer, also /dev/lp0 - ???
/dev/rawlp	Raw printer
/dev/null	NULL device - absorbs all input and returns end-of-file to all reads
/dev/isdn	ISDN networking interface
/dev/rawip	TCP/IP raw IP networking interface
/dev/tcp	TCP/IP networking interface
/dev/udp	UDP (part of TCP/IP protocol suite) networking interface
/dev/ip	IP interface
/dev/ppp	PPP interface
/dev/slip0	SLIP interface
/dev/fddi0 - ???	FDDI Network controller
/dev/tok0 - ???	Token Ring Controller
/dev/term0 - ???	Physically attached terminals
/dev/tty000 - ???	Physically attached terminals
/dev/pts0 - ???	Network connected terminals. Also /dev/pts/0 - ???
/dev/w1 - ???	Windowing terminals. Also /dev/win0 - ???
/dev/window	Windowing terminals

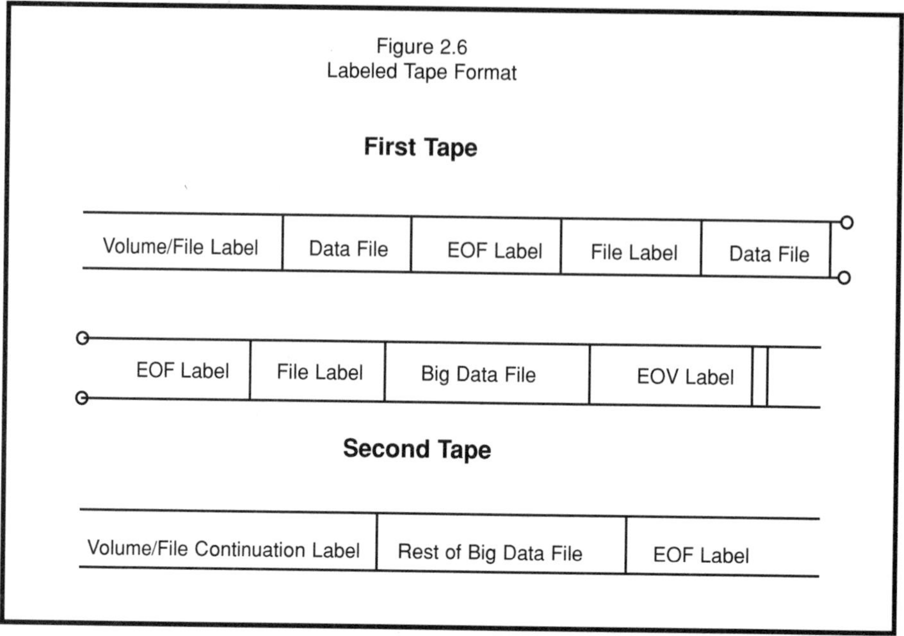

Figure 2.6
Labeled Tape Format

give special meaning to labels. As far as it is concerned, tape labels are just more files on the tape (this is the same as coding LABEL=(,NL) on the mainframe). In processing a labeled tape, multiple files must be read to process the labels and actual data files. Each one of the blocks in Figure 2.6 is a UNIX file. The two pieces of the Big Data File are treated as separate files by UNIX and must be joined by the program reading it. If a tape is changed when in use (file is open) on a UNIX system, the program cannot continue. The device must be closed and then reopened after the tape change in order to continue.

Tapes are treated as a string of characters, but any read or write operation must be a multiple of the block size defined for that device. It is possible to define the tape device for variable block sizes. In that case, any read that handles less than the physical block will return an error since it did not input the full block.

When end-of-file is reached, most commands stop processing the input. Depending on the physical medium (the type of tape device), the end-of-file may be known as a Tape Mark. The Tape Mark is used by the mainframe tape drives to start and stop. Each of the vertical lines in Figure 2.6 is actually an end-of-file or tape mark. The EOF Label (End-of-File) is different from the end of a data file—it is a separate file to UNIX and has its own end-of-file mark. When at the end of the physical device (also known as EOM for End-Of-Media), UNIX treats it as end-of-file.

Creating a plain tape with one file is easy. The appropriate command or program opens the device and writes. When the file is too large to fit on one tape (even a plain tape), the processing is more complex because the program must close the tape device and then reopen it after a new tape is mounted. Creating mainframe labeled tapes requires multiple commands that use the appropriate rmt device that does not rewind when the file is closed.

Figure 2.7
Tape Drive Special File
Characteristics

AIX Tape Characteristics

Device File Name	Rewind when Closed	Retension when Opened	Bytes per Inch
/dev/rmt*	Yes	No	Density setting #1
/dev/rmt*.1	No	No	Density setting #1
/dev/rmt*.2	Yes	Yes	Density setting #1
/dev/rmt*.3	No	Yes	Density setting #1
/dev/rmt*.4	Yes	No	Density setting #2
/dev/rmt*.5	No	No	Density setting #2
/dev/rmt*.6	Yes	Yes	Density setting #2
/dev/rmt*.7	No	Yes	Density setting #2

Where * is the tape unit number
Density settings are defined by the System Administrator

Solaris Tape Characteristics

The format of the Tape special file name is:

/dev/rmt/<tape unit number><Density setting>[<Enable BSD behavior>][<Disable rewind on close>]

Option	Settings
Density setting	l,m,h,u/c (low, medium, high, ultra/compressed)
Enable BSD behavior	b (optional)
Disable rewind	n (optional)

Examples:

`/dev/rmt/0hn`	Unit zero, high density, no rewind. Similar to AIX /dev/rmt0.5
`/dev/rmt/1l`	Unit one, low density, rewind. Similar to AIX /dev/rmt1

Many versions of UNIX have special tape device names with special meanings. For instance, under AIX, /dev/rmt0.1 tells the operating system not to rewind the tape after a file is closed. To get the same behavior under Solaris, you use /dev/rmt/0n. Figure 2.7 provides a summary of the AIX and Solaris special filenames for tape devices. Your system administrator can give you information on the specific names and meaning for your system.

There are security access permissions assigned to all files, including special and directory; these are discussed in the Looking at Directories (the ls command)—Replacement for ISPF Dataset List Utility section of Chapter 3.

The way that files, directories, filesystems, and devices are handled under UNIX may seem a lot to learn and remember. Since many of the concepts are different from the mainframe, there is a lot to get used to, but over time you will become comfortable. As you actually use UNIX, reread the first two chapters, as the background they provide will make more sense. Many of the differences are terminology only; remember that. The next step is getting signed on and actually using UNIX.

CHAPTER 3

UTILITIES AND COMMANDS

This is the chapter that quickly answers the questions many of my unfortunate friends had when they were first learning UNIX: "How can I do Y under UNIX? On the mainframe I did A, B, and then C." After providing some background information on how to get into the UNIX system and how the terminal behaves, the mainframe and closest UNIX equivalents will be presented.

Your system administrator will provide you with a userid and password. Pay close attention to what you are given as upper vs. lower case is significant. Your system administrator will also provide you information on how to connect to the UNIX box. There are three different ways: dial-in via modem, direct connect, and over a network. No matter how you are connected to the computer, you will use a terminal or a PC running terminal emulation software. For simplicity, both will be referred to as a terminal.

With a modem, you instruct it to dial over the telephone lines to the modem connected to the UNIX machine. The answering modem may be connected directly to the UNIX box or may be connected to a terminal server. You may have to hit the <return> key a few times for the equipment to recognize your connection and speed. If you encounter a terminal server, you may have to enter a special login and then tell the terminal server to connect you to the UNIX box. From my experience, only remote connections use a modem. If you are connecting to your company's machine, it will be a direct or network connection.

A direct connection (also known as a RS-232 or serial connection) is easiest to use but very rare these days because it means there is a physical wire from your terminal to the computer. In this case, when you turn your terminal on and hit the <return> key a few times, you will get the login prompt. In some installations, terminal servers have a direct connection to the terminal and a network connection to the UNIX box. If you encounter a terminal server, you may have to enter a special login and then tell the terminal server to connect you to the UNIX box.

The most common method of connecting to a UNIX box is over a network using the telnet protocol. Telnet is part of the TCP/IP networking suite and is used to connect terminals to systems. Most versions of telnet that run on PCs include emulation for ANSI escape sequences (commonly known as the DEC VT-100 command set). Emulation of more advanced DEC terminals is also common: VT-2XX, VT-3XX, or even VT-4XX. Depending on your environment, you may encounter these or other emulations. If you have any doubt, ask your system administrator.

LOGGING IN TO UNIX

Once you are connected to the UNIX box, you will see something similar to Screen 3.1 or 3.2. The actual banner and messages may vary, but you should see something that identifies the system you are logging onto. You enter your userid and then your password. Your password will not show on the screen. Remember to press the <return> or <enter> key (usually above the shift key on the right side) after each entry. You will be reminded of this in all examples with the <↵> symbol. If you type

Screen 3.1 - Example Signon Screen

```
Welcome to The Cooperative Business Solutions UNIX System.

              This system is for authorized users only.

A limited number of guest accounts are available,
login as guest to apply for your own account.

Hey look, this computer has better things to do than being cracked...


Welcome to the System

Please Login: yourid↵
Password: not_your_password↵
Login incorrect
Login: yourid↵
Password: your_real_password↵
```

Screen 3.2 - Example Signon Screen

```
UNIX System V Release 4.0 (mynodeis)

login: yourid↵
Password: not_your_password↵
Login incorrect
Login: yourid↵
Password: your_real_password↵
```

something incorrectly, the <backspace>, <<—>, or <Delete> key will erase the entry. In the first example, if you enter a bad password or bad userid, you will get the message "Login incorrect" and be prompted again. Most systems will disconnect after three failed login attempts.

Once you have entered the correct userid and password, you are signed on. The first time you sign on, you may be prompted to enter a new password and to enter it a second time for confirmation. This is a security feature that ensures no one else, not even the system administrator, knows your password. If implemented by your system administrator, your password can expire after you have used it for a certain number of days. If this feature is enabled, you may get a message and be forced to change your password just like the first time you signed on:

```
Your password has expired.
Choose a new one
Old password: your_real_password↵
New password: your_new_password↵
Re-enter new password: your_new_password↵
```

The first prompt for your password is to verify that you are indeed you. You are then prompted for your new password and if the system likes it, it will prompt you to enter it again. You will not see your password on the screen (character echo is disabled), so the system makes you enter it a second time to be sure you remember it correctly. If the system does not like your new password, it will tell you:

```
Your password has expired.
Choose a new one
Old password: your_real_password↵
New password: your_new_password↵
Your new password must have:
        minimum of 6 alphabetic characters
        minimum of 4 characters not in old password
        maximum of 2 repeated characters
        minimum of 6 characters in length

Your password failed to meet:
        minimum of 4 characters not in old password
```

And you will be prompted for the new password again. The system administrator sets these rules for security reasons, although not all systems have this implemented. If your new password is acceptable but you do not type it exactly the same way the second time, the system will tell you:

```
Your password has expired.
Choose a new one
Old password: your_real_password ↵
New password: your_new_password ↵
Re-enter new password: Your_New_Password ↵
They do not match, try again.
```

And you will be prompted for the new password again.

Screen 3.3 - After ID and Password

```
Please type the terminal name and press RETURN: vt100↵

Last login: Sun Jan 28 10:00:59 from THE.NODE.YOU.USE
Last unsuccessful login: Sun Jan 28, 17:59:59 from THE.NODE.YOU.USE

Welcome to Your Institution's Really Big and Fast Computer System.

The contents of the message of the day file (/etc/motd)
are displayed here.  Watch this space for important announcements
and system status.  They may even tell you when the system is
going to be down or who to call with problems.

You have new mail.

It is now Jan 28 1996 18:01:45
The current number of users is 1
The current disk storage is 5584 /home/yourid

Good Evening, Yourname

[yourid@yournode]: /u/yourid:> _
```

Picking your password under UNIX should be done carefully. Naturally, it must be easy for you to remember and difficult for someone else to guess. UNIX stores passwords in the /etc/password or another hidden file in an encrypted form. The algorithm used to encrypt the password is one-way—that is, it cannot be unencrypted. If you forget your password, the system administrator cannot figure it out for you. The best he or she can do is give you a new one. You can also change your password whenever you want using the passwd command. It will prompt you for your current password (to prevent someone else from changing your password), and then the new password just like it did in the examples above.

But before you get to do any work, a few more things will happen. You may be prompted for your terminal type, which is so UNIX knows what features your terminal supports (is it a dumb terminal that behaves like a printing terminal or is it smart with all kinds of features, graphics, and color?). The system will then provide you with information about its status. Screen 3.3 shows a typical example with the system telling you the last time you logged in, the last time someone failed while attempting to login, a welcoming banner, the message of the day (stored in the file /etc/motd), whether you have mail or not, date, time, number of users, and your disk space usage. The types and amount of information provided vary by version of UNIX and the system administrator.

The final line in Screen 3.3 is the prompt. This shows your userid, which computer you are on (the node or host name), and your current directory. Other prompts may only show your current directory. The prompt is set by each user in his or her profile. However, the system administrator may also set it in the /etc/environment or /etc/profile files. The default prompts for Korn and Bourne shell is the dollar sign <$>; the default prompt for C shell is the percent sign <%>. Except where noted, all further examples will use the <$> prompt.

Figure 3.1
Commonly Used Special Keys

Function Name	AIX	UNIX (AT&T/NCR)	UNIX (System V R3)	Solaris	Key Purpose
intr	^C	<DEL>	<DEL>	^C	Interrupt Program
Quit	^\	^|	^|	^|	Abort - force core dump
erase	^H	^H	^H	<DEL>	Erase one character
kill	^U	^U	@	^U	Erase entire line
eof	^D	^D	^D	^D	End of file (input)
eol	^@	No Default	^`	No Default	End of line
eol2	^@	No Default	Not Supported	No Default	Alternate end of line
start	^Q	^Q	^Q (fixed)	^Q	Communications Xon
stop	^S	^S	^S (fixed)	^S	Communications Xoff
susp	^Z	^Z	Not Supported	^Z	Halt program
dsusp	^Y	^Y	Not Supported	^Y	Resume program
reprint	^R	^R	Not Supported	^R	Redraw line, also rprnt
discard	^O	^O	Not Supported	^O	Discard output, also flush
werase	^W	^W	Not Supported	^W	Erase previous word
inext	^V	^V	Not Supported	^V	Quote next character

TERMINAL AND KEYBOARD BEHAVIOR

You have already seen that the behavior of the terminal and keyboard are different from the mainframe just through the lack of a X-🕓 wait indicator. For a command to take effect, you must press the <return> or <enter> key (usually above the shift key on the right side). To erase any typing errors, you can use the <backspace> or <Delete> key to erase the entry. Which key to use depends on the system you are using and how the keys are configured. You do not want to use the arrow keys (<←>, <→>, <←>, or <←>) to correct typing errors because these keys are translated by the terminal into a sequence of characters that have special meanings. Figure 3.1 shows the commonly used special keys from several versions of UNIX.

To kill (interrupt) a running program or command, you press the intr key defined for your system. The quit key interrupts and forces a core dump of the program's or command's memory. The erase key is used to delete the character to the left of the cursor; pressing the key repeatedly will delete characters repeatedly. The kill key will erase the entire line (the same as pressing the erase key many times). To erase a word, which, to UNIX, is any group of characters separated by spaces, press the werase key—which will erase the word to the left of the cursor. The eof key is used to signal the end of an input file. Used when entering multiple lines of data into a command, it will allow you to exit your current shell process.

The eol and eol2 keys are used to signal the end of a line. The start and stop keys are used to pause and resume output; these are also known as XON and XOFF in communications terminology. The susp (suspend) and dsusp (desuspend) keys are used to halt and resume a running program or command so you can issue other commands without having to interrupt and restart. The discard key causes screen output to cease. In other words, anything that would be displayed is thrown away. The reprint (sometimes referred to as rprnt) key will cause the system to redraw the current line. This is useful if the line becomes corrupted or garbled as you are working with it.

If you have access to a UNIX system, now would be a good time to try logging in. You should see something similar to Screens 3.1 or 3.2 and then 3.3. While signed on, you can try the examples.

The very first thing to do is determine which keys do what. You could ask your system administrator for the specific keys in use on your system, or you could figure them out on your own. The first command to learn is the one that shows and sets terminal characteristics: stty. If you are using the default prompt, you will see:

```
$ ↵                                  Press the enter key
$ stty -a↵                           Set/show terminal characteristics
speed 9600 baud; ; 0 rows; 0 columns
intr = ^C; quit = ^\; erase = ^H; kill = ^U; eof = ^D; eol = ^@
eol2 = ^@; start = ^Q; stop = ^S; susp = ^Z; dsusp = ^Y; reprint = ^R
discard = ^O; werase = ^W; lnext = ^V
```

More lines will print but they are not important now. After the command ends, you will see the prompt again. This example demonstrates how options are used with UNIX commands: The -a on the stty command requests all options be shown.

Remember, the examples in this book will work using the Korn shell, which provides many advanced functions. Many, but not all, of the examples will also work with the Bourne and C shells. See Appendix E (C shell—An Overview), if you are using that shell. I strongly suggest you use the Korn shell though.

This command was executed on a computer running the AIX flavor of UNIX. To erase a mistake, you press the backspace key. If your screen echoes characters like <^?>, your backspace key is actually generating <DEL> or the value of the delete key. You can either change your terminal emulation so the key generates <^H> or tell UNIX to accept a different value:

```
$ stty erase ^?↵        Press the ^ and then ? key or the delete key (prints as ^?)
$ stty -a↵              Set/show terminal characteristics
speed 9600 baud; ; 0 rows; 0 columns
intr = ^C; quit = ^\; erase = ^?; kill = ^U; eof = ^D; eol = ^@
eol2 = ^@; start = ^Q; stop = ^S; susp = ^Z; dsusp = ^Y; reprint = ^R
discard = ^O; werase = ^W; lnext = ^V
```

If your terminal ever appears completely messed up—the keys do not do what they should, nothing is echoed, or it is acting weird—it could be that the last command you executed changed the settings and then did not change them back when it was done. You can force your UNIX terminal settings back to their default values, hopefully making your terminal behave sanely by entering:

```
$ ^j stty sane ^j↵      Control-j is shown as ^j
$
```

You may want to check the actual settings again and make any key function changes again. More detail is provided on the other contents of the show terminal settings in Chapter 7—Account Configuration.

When viewing large amounts of data on your screen, you can get into a situation where the data is flying by on the screen too fast to be of any use. Then you press the intr, quit, stop, susp, or discard keys. The data keeps flying past. Even if you hit those keys repeatedly, nothing seems to stop the screen. This happens because there are large amounts of data buffered in different places. UNIX may buffer the output, the networking software may buffer data on the UNIX box and your PC, the network hardware may have buffers, and finally, your terminal emulator may be buffering the data it receives because it cannot display it fast enough. The system is attempting to respond to your key. It may take effect as soon as you press it, but you do not see this until the buffers in transit complete their journey. It can be frustrating to type in a command that produces much more output than you expected (usually due to incorrect parameters or switches), press <enter>, realize the mistake, react with one of the control keys, and nothing seems to happen. If you press the correct special key, however, it will take effect eventually! (There are commands that present large amounts of data in screens and are covered in the Pipes and Redirection and the more Command section of this chapter.)

UNIX systems tend to be responsive to input. The operating system is optimized for interactive users, not batch. When you get used to UNIX, you will become impatient when back on the mainframe. Response time tends to be much slower on the mainframe. You press <enter> and there is a delay before you see any results while UNIX is much more responsive.

DIRECTORY NAVIGATION (cd AND pwd COMMANDS)

Moving around through directories, also referred to as navigating through directories, is the most frequent single activity in UNIX. The following examples will use the directory hierarchy in Figure 2.1 and assume that when you login, your home directory is /u/yourid. If you are using the default prompt, the first thing to determine is where you are:

```
$ ↵
$ pwd↵
/u/yourid
$
```

The `pwd` command displays your current directory, the name comes from Print Working Directory. The next command is `cd`, which stands for Change Directory. The UNIX `cd` command is similar to MS/PC-DOS `cd` except for the behavior of the `cd` command alone, `cd -`, and `cd ~` behavior. The nice thing about the `cd` command under UNIX is that if you ever get lost and cannot find your way back to your home directory, the command:

```
$ cd↵
$ pwd↵
/u/yourid
$
```

will take you back to your home directory. Under MS/PC-DOS, the cd command alone will just display the current working directory. You can navigate up a level on the tree with:

```
$ cd ..↵
$ pwd↵
/u
$
```

There is a space between the cd and .. above. There is usually a space between a command and its parameters. For example, if you forgot the space in the example above, you would see:

```
$ cd..↵
ksh: cd..:  not found
$
```

Because there was no space, UNIX thinks the .. is part of the command you want to execute and it doesn't recognize that as a command name. You will see a similar message anytime you make a typing mistake or misspell a command name. TSO produces a similar message if you enter an invalid command:

```
READY
THISISNO↵                                An invalid command
 COMMAND THISISNO NOT FOUND
READY
```

You can move back into your home directory with the cd command without any parameters or:

```
$ cd yourid↵
$ pwd↵
/u/yourid
$
```

If you want to move into my home directory or a co-worker's (assuming you have permission), you can do it a few ways. The best way to try this exercise is to use a co-worker's signon wherever you see dhorvath:

```
$ cd ..↵                Move up one level
$ cd dhorvath↵          Move down into my directory.  Relative pathname.
$ pwd↵
/u/dhorvath
$ cd↵                   To get back to your home directory
$ cd ../dhorvath↵       The / separates directories.  Relative pathname.
$ pwd↵
/u/dhorvath
$ cd↵                   To get back to your home directory
$ cd /u/dhorvath↵       The / separates directories.  Absolute pathname.
$ pwd↵
/u/dhorvath
```

```
$ cd↵                          To get back to your home directory
$ cd ~dhorvath↵                Using ~ notation
$ pwd↵
/u/dhorvath
$
```

You can use relative pathnames to move up a level (to /u) and then down into my directory. You can combine the two into one command (../dhorvath). You can specify the absolute pathname (/u/dhorvath) and you can also use the tilde character (~dhorvath), which says go to the dhorvath home directory. You can always change your directory back to where you were before the last cd command:

```
$ pwd↵
/u/dhorvath
$ cd↵                          To get back to your home directory
$ cd - ↵                       Go back to the last place you were
$ pwd↵
/u/dhorvath
$
```

Much of the time you are moving between directories, you go somewhere and then return to where you came from. Anytime you need to know where you are, just use the pwd command.

One of the ISPF options will allow you to change your default dataset prefix (usually your signon id). The cd command essentially does the same thing under UNIX. Neither of these affect the dataset/filename if you specify it completely (within single quotes <'> on the mainframe, a fully qualified path with all directories under UNIX).

LOOKING AT DIRECTORIES (THE ls COMMAND)—REPLACEMENT FOR ISPF DATASET LIST UTILITY

Once you are in a directory, you want to see what files are there by using the ls command:

```
$ pwd↵                         Confirm where you are
/u/dhorvath
$ ls↵                          List the contents of current working directory
bin   c_stuff  cobol_stuff
$ ls -l↵                       Long listing of the contents of current working directory
total 3
drwxr-x---  2 dhorvath users          32 Sep 28 21:17 bin
drwxr-xr-x  2 dhorvath users          96 Oct 18 18:11 c_stuff
drwxr-xr-x  2 dhorvath users          32 Sep 28 09:11 cobol
$
```

The ls command will give you a listing of the files in the directory in a series of columns, similar to the MS/PC-DOS `dir /w` command. The second example shows how to get a listing in the long format. The first line shows the total number of disk blocks used by the files shown. The remaining lines show the selected files broken down into columns: file mode and permission, number of links, the owner id, the group of the file, the number of bytes used by the disk, the creation date and time, and the name of the file. Notice how this information is similar to the ISPF Dataset List Utility, which lets you see a listing of filenames or more detailed information about the files.

The file mode is the first character of the first column and is always one of:

d	file is a directory
p	file is a pipe
l	file is a symbolic link
b	file is a block-type device (in /dev)
c	file is a character-type device (in /dev)
-	file is a plain file

The nine characters that follow are broken down in three sets of three and are indicators of file access permissions. The first set applies to the owner, the second to members of the same group, and the third to all others (the world). The common permission indicators are:

r	file is readable
w	file is writable
x	file is executable
-	this type of access is not allowed

For directories, execute permission is required to be able to search the directory (see the contents). If you have read but not execute permission on a directory, you can access files within the directory but you cannot determine what files are stored there.

Executable programs can have special permissions. In other words, the ability to change its groupid or userid (including that of the super-user, root). A program that is allowed to change its groupid is shown by a group execute permission of <s>. If it is allowed to change its userid, the owner execute permission is <s>. If the owner or members of the group are not allowed to execute the program, the mode will be shown with a capital <S>.

Some programs are run so frequently that the system administrator decides that they should stay in memory when done executing. The first time a program is executed after the system is booted, it is read into virtual memory and remains there after the user is done with it. For the next user of that program, it starts up very quickly because it is already in memory. If there are multiple users of that program, there will still only be one copy of the program in memory (the data portion will be duplicated, one copy for each user). This saves system memory for those programs.

Another term for this type of program is sharable. The last execute permission will be set to <t> for one of these programs. If the world is not allowed to execute the program, the mode will be shown with a capital <T>. This setting is also known as the sticky bit since the program tends to stick around in memory. The sticky bit is also used for directories where access is granted to everyone, like the /tmp directory. This allows any user to create a file in that directory, but no one can remove an existing file owned by another user. Directory files will always have at least two links: the directory file and the subdirectory it contains. The subdirectory contains a connection back to its parent directory.

Looking at the results of the `ls -l` command above, the permissions for each of the files are: /u/dhorvath/bin—file is a directory; the owner (dhorvath) can read, write, and search it; anyone who belongs to the users group can read and search it, other people cannot. /u/dhorvath/c_stuff—file is a directory; the owner (dhorvath) can read, write, and search it; all others can read and search it. /u/dhorvath/cobol—file is a directory; the owner (dhorvath) can read, write, and search it; all others can read and search it. The permissions are changed with the `chmod` command, the owner and group can be changed with the `chown` command, and the group can be changed with the `chgrp` command.

The creation date and time field is varied by the `ls -l` command depending on the values. If the date is within the past 12 months, then the month, day, hours, and minutes of last modification are shown. If the file is older, the hours and minutes are replaced with the year. Many of the commands that output dates and times behave in a similar manner. There are many options to the `ls` command that will be covered later, but the two options I use most often are `-a` and `-l`, which can be combined as `-al`:

```
$ pwd↵                                  Confirm where you are.
/u/dhorvath
$ ls -al↵                               Long listing of all the contents of current working directory
total 19
drwxr-xr-x  5 dhorvath users     464 Jan 28 20:05 .
drwxr-xr-x  9 root     bin       160 Dec  7 19:07 ..
-rw-r--r--  1 dhorvath users     175 Nov  8 19:38 .exrc
-rw-------  1 dhorvath users    4108 Jan 28 12:27 .history
-rw-r--r--  1 dhorvath users     304 Nov  9 21:38 .kshrc
-rw-r--r--  1 dhorvath users     631 Dec 12 21:57 .profile
drwxr-x---  2 dhorvath users      32 Sep 28 21:17 bin
drwxr-xr-x  2 dhorvath users      96 Oct 18 18:11 c_stuff
drwxr-xr-x  2 dhorvath users      32 Sep 28 09:11 cobol
$
```

Normally, any file that begins with a period <.> is suppressed unless the -a option is used. The six files not shown by the ls -l command are:

.	is the current directory. It has at least as many links as there are directories shown.
..	is the parent directory. It has at least as many links as there are directories in it.
.exrc	is the configuration file for the `ex` and `vi` editors.
.history	contains the previously entered commands for retrieval and reuse.
.kshrc	is a Korn shell script run each time a Korn shell is started.
.profile	is a shell script that is executed at login.

Notice that I allow anyone to read my .exrc, .kshrc, and .profile because many people use them as examples. .kshrc and .profile are executed by the shell, not in the normal way (like a command) and therefore do not have the execute permission set. I am the only one allowed to read and write to my command history because I choose to keep other people on the system from seeing what I am doing at any particular moment.

File and directory permissions only apply to users. I could set the permissions on a file so that no one could read it (not even me, the owner), but this will not stop the system administrator. The system administrator has super-user access and can do anything he or she wants. When the computer is shipped, there is one super-user known as root. That account or user (root) owns everything. The operating system runs as though root was sitting at a terminal running it.

As you are entering commands, options (flags), and parameters, remember that UNIX is case sensitive, so the command `ls` will not execute if you type `LS` or `Ls` or `lS`. In general, UNIX commands are lowercase; most options or flags are lowercase but there are those that are upper, usually when there is an option using the same letter in lowercase with a different meaning.

Wildcards and Filenames

Because we did not supply any parameters to the `ls` command, it displayed all files in the directory. By not specifying which files to list, we implied that we wanted to see all files. You can specify a single filename for a command like ls as follows:

```
$ ls -al .profile↵     Display long directory information
-rw-r--r--   1 dhorvath users       631 Dec 12 21:57 .profile
$
```

You can also specify a pattern to be matched. The characters <*> and <?> have special meaning in a filename—they are wildcards. <*> matches any number of characters and <?> matches any single character. ISPF supports the use of <*> and <?> wildcards in the List Dataset Utility (ISPF Screen 3.4) and with PDS member names in the other screens. ISPF and UNIX wildcard behavior is similar. The following command will display information about any file that begins with the lowercase letter c:

```
$ ls -ald c*↵                         Display long directory information
drwxr-xr-x   2 dhorvath users        96 Oct 18 18:11 c_stuff
drwxr-xr-x   2 dhorvath users        32 Sep 28 09:11 cobol
$
```

The `-d` option was added to the `ls` command so it shows the directory files themselves, not the contents. This option is required when you specify or explicitly wildcard the name of a directory. If it was not included, the contents of the /u/dhorvath/c_stuff and /u/dhorvath/cobol directories would have been displayed. The <*> wildcard can be at the beginning, middle, or end of the filename for which you are searching. You can use multiple <*> wildcards in the same search. For example, the following will search for any filename that has the lowercase letter o followed by the lowercase letter l somewhere in the name:

```
$ ls -ald *o*l*↵                             Display long directory information
-rw-r--r--   1 dhorvath users       631 Dec 12 21:57 .profile
drwxr-xr-x   2 dhorvath users        32 Sep 28 09:11 cobol
$
```

Both files match the pattern. Notice that the cobol directory does not have any letters after the lowercase letter l; <*> matches zero to many characters. The <?> matches any single character and can be repeated to match multiple single characters. Like the <*> wildcard, <?> wildcard can be used at the beginning, middle, or end of the filename for which you are searching. You can also use multiple <?> wildcards in the same search. The following will search for any filename that begins with the lowercase letter c and has four characters after it:

```
$ ls -ald c???? ↵                            Display long directory information
drwxr-xr-x   2 dhorvath users          32 Sep 28 09:11 cobol
$
```

The c_stuff directory did not match the pattern because it has six characters after the initial c. These wildcards work with other commands when specifying filenames. MS/PC-DOS supports wildcards and even uses the same characters as UNIX, but the behavior is different. The <*> wildcard can only be used to match zero to many characters to the right. For instance, the pattern *o*l* would be interpreted as just * by MS/PC-DOS. This is because prefix asterisk wildcards are converted to eight question marks (????????) in the directory search routines within the operating system. In addition, the format of a filename on the PC is eight characters, a period, then three characters (EIGHTXXX.123) and is treated as two separate fields for purposes of wildcards. UNIX supports much more complicated pattern matching for filenames. These will be discussed later.

COMMAND BUFFERING

In the preceding examples, if you were not careful, you may have started typing the next command before the computer was finished with the last. Do not worry, UNIX supports command line buffering. That is, you can type ahead of the computer and it will eventually catch up. Your new input may get mixed in with the computer's output, but it is being accepted exactly as you type it. This is much different than the mainframe where you have to wait for the computer to respond (turn the little X-🕑 or X-SYS off). The mainframe refers to command buffering as command stacking under ISPF. The command delimiter is set in the ISPF Terminal Characteristics screen; the default is the semicolon <;>. You can type several edit commands, separate them with <;>, and press enter at the end of the line. The commands will be executed in sequence and control will return to you when done:

```
EDIT --- TOP.NXT.GROUP.PRJ.TEST.JCL ---------------------- ROW 00022 OF 00029
COMMAND ===> DOWN 300;  RIGHT 20;  HEX ON ø                  SCROLL ===> PAGE
```

Issuing these commands will jump you down 300 lines in the file, shift the screen right 20 characters, and then show the lines in hex. UNIX also supports explicit command buffering and it also uses the <;> character to separate commands. The last directory navigation example can be shown as one line:

```
$ pwd; cd ..; pwd; cd ; pwd↵                show and move and show...
/u/dhorvath
/u
/u/dhorvath
$
```

The example does not make much sense now, but this is just to show you what you can do. This is handy if the commands will take a period of time and you want to get coffee while they are running, not sitting at your desk hitting the <return> key when each command is done. There are other ways of automating long running commands or groups of commands that will be covered later.

ISPF BROWSE AND EDIT REPLACEMENT—AN OVERVIEW OF UNIX EDITORS

In the old days when modems were expensive and slow, when video terminals were expensive and printing terminals relatively cheap, most people learned one of the line-oriented editors. When your screen updates at the rate of 30 or 120 characters a second, fullscreen editing was painfully slow; on a printing terminal it is impossible. You edited your programs and developed documentation using a line editor (line-by-line). If you were lucky enough to have a video terminal and were directly connected to your computer, then you learned the visual editor. With cheaper and faster modems, LAN connections, video terminals (or emulation on a PC), the need to learn a line-oriented editor has dropped dramatically.

Learning a new editor is probably the toughest part of learning a new operating system and environment. After you have used an editor or any tool for a long time, you reach the point where the keys you press to perform special functions become ingrained in your brain. Eventually, you do not have to think how to get the screen contents to move up or down and you learn shortcut tricks to perform your common tasks. You go to the new system and after you figure out which command gets you into the editor, you have to figure out the keys to perform the task at hand. Instead of your fingers automatically doing things, you have to actually think about what you are doing.

There are four major classifications of editors under UNIX: native, shareware or public domain, vendor or tool specific, and transitional. Native editors are those that come with the UNIX operating system; shareware or public domain editors are written and distributed non-commercially (typically over the Internet); transitional editors mimic editors from other environments (particularly the mainframe).

Figure 3.2 lists the standard editors under UNIX. Nearly every version or flavor of UNIX will have these editors. There are others but they are not as widely available.

The editors `ed` and `red` are actually the same program with different names, implemented through links. The only difference between the two editors are the restrictions under `red`. `red` restricts the user to editing files in the current directory and prevents him or her from entering UNIX commands (known as executing shell commands). These are known as the standard text editors under UNIX and are the oldest still being supported.

The editors `edit`, `ex`, `vi`, `vedit`, and `view` are actually the same program with different names, implemented through links. The process of editing a file is really the same, all that changes between the editors is the user interface or command language. The `ex` editor is the basis for these four editors and is a superset of the `ed` editor. The full screen editor is `vi`; you can switch from visual mode to the `ex` line mode. While using `ex` in line mode, you can switch to the visual mode of `vi`. `vedit` is the same as `vi` except that some options are set to make it easier to learn. `view` is the same as `vi` except it will not allow you to replace the original file with a changed version.

The stream editor, `sed`, is different from the other standard UNIX editors because it is intended to edit sets of data without direct user interaction. What this really means is that you give sed a series of commands (on the command line or in a command file) and the file to edit. The editing will occur without user interaction. The sed editor can also be used as a filter between two programs, changing the output format of one program and feeding it as the input to another. It can also be used to apply the same changes to a number of files, for example, to change the

Figure 3.2
Standard UNIX Editors

These editors are available under most flavors of UNIX:

`ed`	Line-oriented editor.
`red`	Restricted version of ed.
`edit`	Simple version of ex.
`ex`	Line-oriented editor.
`vi`	Visual editor.
`vedit`	Simple version of vi.
`view`	Read-only (browse) version of vi.
`sed`	Stream editor.

company name in a series of reports after a corporate merger takes place. Sed is one of the tools that helps you work smarter instead of harder.

There are many shareware and public domain editors for UNIX available, and many university computer science curriculum have courses that result in the students writing compilers or editors. One freely available editor that deserves mention is emacs. Originally written by Richard M. Stallman at MIT in the late 1970s, it is available on many platforms and may be installed at your installation. The editor itself is extremely extensible and has its own programming language. The name emacs stands for Editing with Macros.

The editors that I classify as vendor or tool specific are those that third-party software companies sell. Microfocus (a COBOL development environment vendor) sells an editor with an interface similar to their PC based products. These editors have a limited marketplace and, while they may have very good features, are not necessarily portable skills to learn. The product may not be around long enough for you to become productive with it and might not be installed at your next employer.

Transitional editors are created to mimic editors developed by other companies. As the book progresses, you will see examples of uni-SPF and SPF/UX, two editors under UNIX that mimic the mainframe ISPF editor. The primary advantage to this type of editor is that you are already familiar with its features and the sequences of keys to get a task done. Coming from the mainframe and ISPF, these editors allow you to be productive quickly.

The ISPF Browse and Edit screens allow you to review and modify a dataset. They both accept many of the same commands, but Browse does not let you do anything that will modify the dataset. In Browse, you cannot even change something on the screen—it is a completely read-only (view) mode. Either one allows you to look at sequential datasets, GDG datasets, and members of Partitioned Datasets; the dataset can contain binary or text-only data and be formatted fixed or variable record length. There are a few restrictions though, like VSAM datasets and datasets with extremely long records cannot be browsed or edited. Extremely large files cannot be edited but can be viewed with Browse. Binary data can be viewed in browse or changed in edit by replacing them with printable characters or entering hex mode where all characters are shown as their hexadecimal values and the hexadecimal values can be changed.

The native UNIX equivalents are `view` (or `vi -r`) and `vi`. `view` and `vi -r` (read-only) provided exactly the same functionality as the vi editor except that they do not allow you to save the file. The commands are exactly the same whether you are using `vi`, `vi -r`, or `view`; the only difference is that the save command does not work while in read-only mode. The editors under UNIX are limited compared to the mainframe because the file must be line sequential, have a record length less than 2,048 characters, and should not contain binary data. COBOL COMP and COMP-3 fields contain binary data that can cause problems because vi ignores the <NUL> character (binary zeroes) and will treat any character with the value of the line feed in ASCII (hexadecimal 0A) as the end of a record.

The transitional editor uni-SPF can edit data files with binary data, records of up to 4,096 characters in length, and does not require line sequential records; it cannot browse them though. The transitional editor SPF/UX is able to browse and edit text files, but cannot handle sequential records or binary data. Although the UNIX editors are not as capable as ISPF or the transitional editors for working with some data files, they have many more functions and are comparatively very flexible.

The downside to using transitional editors is that you may never learn the more standard UNIX editors like vi. While this really does not make you less capable with UNIX or say that you do not know the UNIX operating system, many UNIX professionals act that way. Learn vi or emacs, because they are much better editors for creating programs than any mainframe editor. It will take an effort to make the transition, but it is necessary if you ever plan on selling yourself for another job with UNIX. Using the native UNIX editors and some of the special features of the transitional editors (differences from ISPF) are discussed in Chapter 6 (Editors).

IEBGENER AND ISPF MOVE/COPY UTILITY REPLACEMENT

The remainder of this chapter presents practical examples showing the UNIX equivalents to mainframe activities. The first is IEBGENER, which is used to copy or move sequential datasets:

```
//GENERA    EXEC PGM=IEBGENER
//SYSUT1    DD DSN=THE.INPUT.FILE,DISP=OLD
//SYSUT2    DD DSN=THE.NEW.FILE,DISP=(NEW,CATLG,DELETE),
//     DCB=(LRECL=80,BLKSIZE=16000,RECFM=FB),UNIT=SYSDA
//     SPACE=(CYL,(10,5),RLSE)
//SYSPRINT DD SYSOUT=*
//SYSOUT    DD SYSOUT=*
//SYSIN     DD DUMMY
/*
```

THE.INPUT.FILE is copied to THE.NEW.FILE. IEBGENER can also be used to print a file by replacing the SYSUT2 DSN with SYSOUT=A. The ISPF Move/Copy utility, shown in Screens 3.4 and 3.5, also performs this function so long as THE.NEW.FILE has already been allocated.

After selecting the copy function, entering the old datasetname, and pressing the <enter> key on Screen 3.4, you will see the results shown on Screen 3.5.

Screen 3.4 - ISPF Move/Copy Utility

```
------------------------------ MOVE/COPY UTILITY ------------------------------

OPTION  ===> C

    C - Copy data set or member(s)           CP - Copy and Print
    M - Move data set or member(s)           MP - Move and Print
    L - Copy and LMF lock member(s)          LP - Copy, LMF lock, and print
    P - LMF Promote data set or member(s)    PP - LMF Promote and print

    SPECIFY "FROM" DATA SET BELOW, THEN PRESS ENTER KEY

    FROM ISPF LIBRARY: ------Options C, CP, L, and LP only ------
       PROJECT ===>     |                                        |
       GROUP   ===>          ===>          ===>          ===>
       TYPE    ===>
       MEMBER  ===>               (Blank or pattern for member selection is
                                   '*' for all members:

    FROM OTHER PARTITIONED OR SEQUENTIAL DATA SET:
       DATA SET NAME  ===> 'THE.INPUT.FILE'
       VOLUME SERIAL ===>          (If not cataloged)

       DATA SET PASSWORD ===>           (If password protected)
```

Screen 3.5 - ISPF Move/Copy Utility - 2

```
COPY --- FROM THE.INPUT.FILE ------------------------------------------
 COMMAND ===>

 SPECIFY "TO" DATA SET BELOW.

  TO ISPF LIBRARY:
    PROJECT ===>
    GROUP   ===>
    TYPE    ===>

  TO OTHER PARTITIONED OR SEQUENTIAL DATA SET:
    DATA SET NAME ===> 'THE.NEW.FILE'
    VOLUME SERIAL ===>        (If not cataloged)

    DATA SET PASSWORD ===>          (If password protected)

  "TO" DATA SET OPTIONS:
    IF PARTITIONED, REPLACE LIKE-NAMED MEMBERS ===> NO  (YES or NO)
    IF SEQUENTIAL, "TO" DATA SET DISPOSITION   ===> OLD (OLD OR MOD)
    SPECIFY PACK OPTION FOR "TO" DATA SET      ===>     (YES, NO, or blank)
```

Screen 3.6 - SPF-UX Move/Copy Utility

```
------------------------------- DATASET COPY/MOVE -------------------------------
OPTION:    ===> c

Valid Options:
       C - Copy datasets             M - Move datasets

ISPF LIBRARY:
   PROJECT ===>
   GROUP   ===>
   TYPE    ===>
   MEMBER  ===>                          (Use * to copy/move all members)

OTHER DATA SET:
   DATA SET NAME  ===> /the/input/FILE


Press [END] to return.
```

Screen 3.7 - SPF-UX Move/Copy Utility - 2

```
---------------------------  COPY/MOVE DESTINATION  ---------------------------
COMMAND ===>


Specify destination dataset:

ISPF LIBRARY:
   PROJECT ===>
   GROUP   ===>
   TYPE    ===>
   MEMBER  ===>

OTHER DATA SET:
   DATA SET NAME: ===> /the/new/FILE


Press [END] to return.
```

The ISPF screens could be replaced with the SPF-UX screens shown in Screens 3.6 and 3.7. Note the change in filename. /the/new/FILE does not have to be allocated first, UNIX performs this function automatically.

Screen 3.8 - Uni-SPF Move/Copy Utility

```
----------------------------      MOVE/COPY UTILITY      ---------------------------
OPTION ===> c

   C - Copy files           CS - Copy files and subdirectories
   M - Move files         (move always moves any subdirectories)

SPECIFY "FROM" FILE BELOW, THEN PRESS ENTER TO SPECIFY "TO" FILE

FROM FILE:
   DIRECTORY PATH ===> /the/input
        FILE NAME ===> FILE                (* for all files, or
                                            blank for selection list)
```

Screen 3.9 - Uni-SPF Move/Copy Utility - 2

```
COPY --- FROM FILE /the/input/FILE ----------------------------------
   COMMAND ==>

SPECIFY "TO" DIRECTORY BELOW.

TO FILE:
   DIRECTORY PATH ===> /the/new
        FILE NAME ===> FILE


PRESS THE ENTER KEY TO DISPLAY THE FILE SELECTION PANEL.
PRESS THE END KEY (NORMALLY PF3) TO CANCEL.
```

The Uni-SPF screens shown in Screens 3.8 and 3.9 perform the same function with a slightly different format. Again, the filename is different from the datasetname of the mainframe and the file does not need to be allocated before putting data in it.

The screens look a little different, but the general functions are still the same. This is a good example of using a transitional editor. You can be productive very quickly under UNIX because you are still using tools that look like the ones you are used to on the mainframe.

COPY, MOVE, AND LINK COMMANDS (cp, mv, AND ln)

Consider trying the commands within UNIX itself. Copying a file is even easier using the `cp` command than moving through multiple levels of menus:

```
$ cp /the/input/FILE /the/new/FILE↵
$
```

The file named as the first parameter to `cp` will be copied to the file named as the second. Instead of two screens and moving through many fields, you enter three things: the command name and the two filenames (parameters). If the action is successful, you will get the prompt back. If there is a problem, you will get an error message like:

```
cp: cannot open /the/input/FILE
cp: cannot create /the/new/FILE
cp: no space on device

ksh: File too large                              followed by:
cp: /the/new/FILE: No such file or directory
```

If you want to copy members of a PDS on the mainframe, you can omit or use a wildcard in the member name field or portion of the datasetname. ISPF will present you with a selection list of members. If you try to copy a subdirectory using SPF/UX or Uni-SPF and omit or use a wildcard for the filename, you will receive a selection list of files in the subdirectory.

Moving a dataset or file using ISPF, SPF/UX, or Uni-SPF is similar to copying a dataset or file. Under UNIX, the syntax for the `mv` command is similar to the `cp` command:

```
$ mv /the/input/FILE /the/new/FILE↵
$
```

The file named as the first parameter to `mv` will be copied to the file named as the second and then the first will be deleted. If the action is successful, you will get the prompt back. If there is a problem, you can get the same error messages as `cp` or an error message like:

```
mv: cannot unlink /the/input/FILE
```

You can use wildcards to copy or move files, but you cannot use them if you are changing the name of the file because of the way wildcards are handled. When copying or moving multiple files, you can use the `-i` option (interactive), which will prompt you before acting on the file.

A third way of manipulating a file, unique to UNIX, is the link. If you want to work with the same file under a different name and are not concerned about the contents changing (that could be a feature—instant synchronization), then you can save disk space and link the files:

```
$ ln /the/input/FILE /the/new/FILE↵
$
```

If you get the error message ln: cannot link across file systems, you must use a symbolic link because the files you want to link are on different filesystems:

```
$ ln -s /the/input/FILE /the/new/FILE↵
$
```

Either command will create a new directory entry called /the/new/FILE, which will be connected to the original /the/input/FILE. The `ln` command produces hard links or just links. Using the `ln` command with the `-s` flag creates symbolic links.

It is possible to create a link to a pipe and to a device. Using a pipe named n_pipe, the command to create a link to it is shown as the first command line below. To create a link to a device, it must be a symbolic link since /dev is not part of the /u directory. The command to do this is shown in the second line below. The final command below shows the files with their inodes:

```
$ ln l_n_pipe n_pipe↵
$ ln -s my_t /dev/pts8↵
$ ls -ail↵
14860 prw-r--r--   2 dhorvath   user    0 Jan 31 11:42 n_pipe
14861 lrwxrwxrwx   1 dhorvath   user    9 Jan 31 11:43 my_t -> /dev/pts8
14860 prw-r--r--   2 dhorvath   user    0 Jan 31 11:42 l_n_pipe
$
```

Both of the files, n_pipe and l_n_pipe, have the same inode (14860) and the same file mode (p for pipe). The symbolic link to the /dev/pts8 shows a file mode of l (for symbolic link). It occupies 9 bytes on the disk, which is the length of the device name string.

Common Errors and Problem Determination

Although the error messages produced by these commands may seem simplistic, they actually contain a lot of information once you understand them. Determining the reason for the error may require additional research, but not an excessive amount.

`cannot access` simply means that the input file or path does not exist, obviously you cannot do anything with it.

`cannot open` means that you do not have permission to read the file. You should contact the owner of the file (use the `ls -l` command to determine the owner) and ask him or her to change the permissions.

`cannot create` suggests that you either do not have permission to write in your current directory or that the file already exists and you do not have write permission (required to replace).

`no space on device` error message is produced when the device (filesystem) is full.

`ksh: File too large` typically followed by `No such file or directory` occurs when you have violated a user limit imposed by the system administrator. For instance, you tried to create a file that was too large.

`cannot unlink` error message is produced when the you do not have permission to remove a link (delete) the existing file when using the mv command.

Problem Determination—Permissions

Most problems are related to permissions, which you can verify a number of different ways. A quick way to see if you are allowed to write in the current directory (you should only need to do this once in a particular directory) is:

```
$ touch /the/new/a.dummy.name↵
$
```

If there is no error message (`touch: /the/new/a.dummy.name cannot create`), you have write permission to the directory. The touch command updates the file's timestamp or creates an empty file if it does not already exist. To be nice, type the following command to get rid of your dummy file:

```
$ rm /the/new/a.dummy.name↵          (more about this command later)
$
```

You can also check the ownership and permissions of the directory itself:

```
$ ls -ald /the/new↵
total 6
dr-xr-xr-x    9 dhorvath users          512 Nov 30 11:05 .
drwxr-xr-x   31 root     system        2048 Feb  6 06:30 ..
drwxr-x---   11 dhorvath users          512 Feb  6 11:01 new
$
```

The options on the list directory command (`-ald`) are actually three options combined together: `-a` (show all files, include those that begin with <.>), `-l` (long format), and `-d` (show subdirectory entry, not the contents of it). Based on this example, the subdirectory now is owned by dhorvath, who has full permissions to it (rwx). Members of the group users can read or execute (r-x) the directory. They cannot write files in the directory but they can access them (read or execute if appropriate) and they can search the directory. The rest of the world can do nothing with this directory (---). Even if your userid belongs to the group users, you cannot write a file in this directory unless you are dhorvath or root.

Assuming that you can write to a directory (group or world permissions of rwx) but encounter the cannot create error message, it may already exist. To verify file existence and check permissions, use the list directory command:

```
$ ls -l /the/new/FILE↵
-rw-r-----    1 dhorvath users           10 Dec 27 21:42 /the/new/FILE
$
```

In this case, you do not have write permission to the file. dhorvath owns the file and can read and write (delete and replace) because of permissions (`rw-`). A member of the group users can read the file (`r--`), and the rest of the world can do nothing (`---`). Now you know why you got the error message in the first place.

Problem Determination—Available Space

When the system administrator creates filesystems, he or she allocates disk space to them. The disk space is fixed; when it is used up, the system will not automatically assign more on the fly. This prevents one user or a rogue application from using up all disk space in the system. It also enforces constraints on all users attempting to create files in that area. The error message `no space on device` tells you that a filesystem is full. The first response to this error should be a check on what files exist and their size. If there are large files that are not needed, they should be deleted, which will free up space. If you need more space allocated to a filesystem, you should discuss those needs with the system administrator.

The following command will show you information about filesystems:

```
$ df .↵                      Display information about this filesystem
Filesystem     Total KB    free %used   iused %iused Mounted on
/dev/fs1         110592   27304   75%    1260     4% /home
$ df /the/new↵               Display information about a particular directory
Filesystem     Total KB    free %used   iused %iused Mounted on
/dev/data1       409600  369328    9%    1159     1% /the
$ df↵                        Display information about all filesystems
Filesystem     Total KB    free %used   iused %iused Mounted on
/dev/fs4          20480    6168   69%    1143    18% /
/dev/fs2         503808  193864   61%   15177    11% /usr
/dev/fs3          32768   21972   32%      98     1% /tmp
/dev/fs1         110592   27304   75%    1260     4% /home
/dev/usr2         65536    7732   88%    1504     9% /usr2
/dev/code          4096    1532   62%     232    22% /code
/dev/data1       409600  369328    9%    1159     1% /the
/dev/data2       102400   99032    3%      16     0% /the/data2
/dev/data3      1003520  971856    3%      16     0% /the/new/stuff
/dev/data4      1003520  971332    3%      18     0% /the/new/other
/dev/sort1      1449984 1404432    3%      22     0% /sort1
/dev/sort2      1449984 1404432    3%      22     0% /sort2
/dev/bkupspc    1024000  991824    3%      16     0% /the/backup
/dev/temp        512000  495768    3%      18     0% /tempspace
$
```

The first column is the name of the filesystem, the name of the disk or pseudo-disk where the space is stored. The second column is the total space available in that filesystem in kilobytes, followed by the amount of free space in kilobytes and percentage used. The number and percentage of i-nodes used follows. The last column is the mount point where the filesystem resides in the directory structure. When you request information on a specific directory (using relative or absolute notation), the command shows the filesystem that contains that directory.

The df command supports a series of options. The default is -i (shown above); each option displays a differently formatted report:

```
$ df -i .↵                        Display information about this file system
Filesystem    Total KB    free %used    iused %iused Mounted on
/dev/fs1        110592   27304   75%     1260     4% /home
$ df -I .↵                        Display space information only, not inodes
Filesystem    Total KB    used     free %used Mounted on
/dev/fs1        110592   83288   27304    75% /home
$ df -M .↵                        Display in slightly different format
Filesystem    Mounted on         Total KB     free %used    iused %iused
/dev/fs1      /home                110592    27304    75%     1260     4%
$ df -v .↵                        Display in verbose form
Filesystem    Total KB    used     free %used    iused    ifree %iused Mounted on
/dev/fs1        110592   83288    27304   75%     1260    27412     4% /home
```

Typically, I just use the default because it provides me with the information I need most of the time. Other versions of UNIX have a different output format where only free space and free inodes are shown by default:

```
$ df .↵                           Default display of free space and inodes
/          (/dev/fp002):    4518 blocks    2071 i-nodes
$ df -t .↵                        Display free and total values
/          (/dev/fp002):    4518 blocks    2071 i-nodes
                  total:   29104 blocks    3632 i-nodes
$ df -k .↵                        Display in kilobytes
Filesystem             kbytes    used    avail capacity  Mounted on
/dev/fp002              14552   12293     2259     84%    /
$
```

The first and second examples show the mount point as /, the filesystem as /dev/fp002 with 4518 blocks and 2071 inodes free. The second example, using the -t (total) flag, shows that the filesystem has a total of 29104 blocks and 3632 inodes assigned to it. The third example, using the -k (display in kilobytes), at least provides headings for the columns; the capacity is percentage used.

Problem Determination—Used Space

No matter what the format, the df command shows how much space is available and may show how much space is used within a filesystem. Another useful command displays the disk usage of a specific file, group of files, directory, or series of subdirectories. The du command is different from the df command because it displays the space usage of specific items instead of the entire filesystem, which can contain thousands of files and directories. The filesystem /dev/fs1 could contain over 28,000 files and subdirectories. If you want information about some grouping, you use the du command. To determine how much space the dhorvath directory and all subdirectories use:

```
$ du -s /u/dhorvath↵              Summary only - total space used
240      /u/dhorvath
```

```
$ du -s -k /u/dhorvath↵          Summary only - total space used in kilobytes
120      /u/dhorvath
$
```

By default, du displays space used in units of disk blocks. Typically a disk block is 512 bytes. The -k option will force display of space used in units of kilobytes (1024 bytes). The -s option forces a summary or total of the space used. Without the -s option, du will display the directory specified and any subdirectories:

```
$ du /u/dhorvath↵                Detail of this and subdirectories
168      /u/dhorvath/subdir
240      /u/dhorvath
$
```

Since the /u/dhorvath directory contains the subdir directory under it, the 168 blocks in /u/dhorvath/subdir are included in the 240 block size of /u/dhorvath. You can also request the usage of specific files through the use of the -a option:

```
$ du -a /u/dhorvath/.profile↵ Detail of this file
8        /u/dhorvath/.profile
$
```

The file occupies eight disk blocks of 512 bytes each. The value shown by the ls -l command may be less since it tracks the actual size of the file based on number of bytes written (position of last byte); the value shown will not be more than du multiplied by 512. Only full blocks are allocated to files but a file may not use a full block.

```
$ du -a /u/dhorvath↵             Detail of files here and below
8        /u/dhorvath/.profile
16       /u/dhorvath/.sh_history
8        /u/dhorvath/change.log
100      /u/dhorvath/subdir/file1
8        /u/dhorvath/subdir/file2
42       /u/dhorvath/subdir/big_file
168      /u/dhorvath/subdir
240      /u/dhorvath/
```

The size of the individual files does not add up to the total for /u/dhorvath/ because the size of the file containing the directory is not shown. The same applies to the subdirectory /u/dhorvath/subdir.

Problem Determination—Limits on Resource Usage

Being informed that your file is too large can be a bit disconcerting but the cause is rather simple: You have created a file larger than the limit assigned by the system administrator. Only the system administrator can increase this value, but you can determine what the current setting is and even lower it. Although it may seem a bit silly to purposely lower the maximum sized file you can create, it does make sense during testing to prevent a runaway program from using all the space in a filesystem or running for a long time. The ulimit command is actually part of the Bourne and Korn command shells and is not an external command. To determine the current limit, enter the following command:

```
$ ulimit↵                              Display maximum file size
4097151
$
```

This value is in disk blocks of 512 bytes, other versions of UNIX will show this number in bytes or kilobytes. In my case, I have a limit of over 4 million disk blocks, which is equivalent to a limit of 2 GB (my system administrator really trusts me). This limit applies to each file as it is being written to; I could have many files each just under 4097151 blocks each. Because I want to keep the administrator's trust, I limit my disk usage when conducting early testing of programs:

```
$ ulimit 1000000↵                      Limit file to 500 MB
$ ulimit↵                              Display maximum file size
1000000
$
```

will prevent my program from using too much space. There is one catch. Once you lower your limit, you cannot raise it again. Do not worry, it is not permanent; it exists only for the current invocation of the shell. If you lowered your limit with your login shell, you will have to logout and back in for the limit to be reset. There are ways to invoke a subshell so your login shell is not affected; see the section on IKJEFT01 (TSO).

When I try to return to my original disk usage limit, it fails:

```
$ ulimit 4097151↵                      Limit file to original maximum
ksh: ulimit: exceeds allowable limit
$ ulimit↵                              Display maximum file size
1000000
$
```

After logging out and back in, my limit is reset to the original value. You can confirm that and determine other usage limits as follows:

```
$ ulimit -a↵                           Show all limits
time(seconds)      unlimited
file(blocks)       4097151
data(kbytes)       2048576
stack(kbytes)      82768
memory(kbytes)     909600
coredump(blocks)   204800
$
```

The C shell uses the limit command for the same purpose (notice the prompt):

```
% limit↵
cputime          unlimited
filesize         unlimited
datasize         2097148 kbytes
stacksize        8192 kbytes
coredumpsize     0 kbytes
descriptors      64
memorysize       unlimited
%
```

Not all versions of the command shells support limits other than maximum file size. In this example, the system administrator can enforce more limits than just maximum file size. The user can lower these other values but not raise them. Time is the maximum number of CPU seconds a single process can use; data is the maximum amount of data area than any one process can have (in memory). It is also the most virtual memory a single process can use; stack is the maximum stack size for a single process; memory is the maximum amount of real (physical) memory a single process can use at any time; and finally, coredump is the maximum number of blocks that a coredump (abend) file can use.

Another way that system administrators limit the use of resources is through disk quotas. By implementing disk quotas, the maximum space that a user can use within a filesystem can be limited. If the limit is exceeded, there is an overdraw allowed (like overdraft protection on a checking account, it gives you a bit more once you run out). You can determine how much space remains using the following command:

```
$ quota -v↵
Disk quotas for dhorvath (uid 6061):
Filesystem      usage  quota  limit    timeleft  files
/dev/fs1          300    200    250      5 days      3
$
```

Shows that my quota on the /dev/fs1 filesystem is 200 blocks with an overdraft of another 250. I have three files that are over the quota and in five days they will be deleted. The output of the quota command will differ on each system; check with your system administrator on how quotas are implemented at your installation. Quota limits are not universally implemented and you may get the message that you have no quotas, which means you can use the entire filesystem.

IEFBR14 AND ISPF LIBRARY AND DATASET UTILITY REPLACEMENT

IEFBR14 is another of the commonly used MVS utilities. All it does when executed is return control to the operating system. Its true value comes from the fact that the JCL controls dataset actions when a program executes, not the program itself. A dataset is created because the DD statement says to, not because the program opens the file and writes to it.

IEFBR14 is typically used to delete or create a dataset. Properly coded, the delete will behave properly and not report an error even if the dataset does not exist.

Screen 3.10 - ISPF Dataset - Delete

```
------------------------------  DATASET UTILITY  ------------------------------
OPTION  ===> D

   A - Allocate new data set                C - Catalog data set
   R - Rename entire data set               U - Uncatalog data set
   D - Delete entire data set               S - Data set information (short)
   blank - Data set information             M - Enhanced data set allocation

   ISPF LIBRARY:
      PROJECT ===>
      GROUP   ===>
      TYPE    ===>

   OTHER PARTITIONED OR SEQUENTIAL DATA SET:
      DATA SET NAME  ===>  'A.FILE.TO.DELETE'
      VOLUME SERIAL  ===>    (If not cataloged, required for option "C")

      DATA SET PASSWORD ===>       (If password protected)
```

```
//SCRATCH  EXEC PGM=IEFBR14
//SYSPRINT DD SYSOUT=*
//SYSOUT   DD SYSOUT=*
//DDNAME   DD DSN=A.FILE.TO.DELETE,DISP=(MOD,DELETE,DELETE),
//    DCB=(LRECL=255,BLKSIZE=2550,RECFM=VB),UNIT=3390,
//    SPACE=(3120,(1,1),RLSE)
//*   DISP USED TO CREATE IF DOESN'T EXIST; DELETE WHEN DONE,
//*   SUCCESS OR FAILURE.
//*
//*   DCB, UNIT, AND SPACE CODED IN CASE FILE DOESN'T EXIST
//*   AND NEEDS TO BE CREATED.  DCB AND UNIT SHOULD MATCH
//*   ACTUAL FILE.
//CREATE   EXEC PGM=IEFBR14
//SYSPRINT DD SYSOUT=*
//SYSOUT   DD SYSOUT=*
//DDNNEW  DD DSN=A.FILE.TO.CREATE,DISP=(NEW,CATLG,DELETE),
//    DCB=(LRECL=255,BLKSIZE=2550,RECFM=VB),UNIT=3390,
//    SPACE=(3120,(200,150))
```

The ISPF Dataset Utility (ISPF Screen 3.2) is used to create, delete, or rename datasets. Partitioned Datasets are created using the ISPF Dataset Utility and then the contents (members) are manipulated using the ISPF Library Utility (ISPF Screen 3.1). Deleting a dataset with ISPF is shown in Screen 3.10.

Screen 3.11 - ISPF Dataset - Allocate (Create)

```
------------------------------  DATASET UTILITY  ------------------------------

OPTION  ===> A

   A - Allocate new data set              C - Catalog data set
   R - Rename entire data set             U - Uncatalog data set
   D - Delete entire data set             S - Data set information (short)
   blank - Data set information           M - Enhanced data set allocation

   ISPF LIBRARY:
      PROJECT ===>
      GROUP   ===>
      TYPE    ===>

   OTHER PARTITIONED OR SEQUENTIAL DATA SET:
      DATA SET NAME  ===> 'A.FILE.TO.CREATE'
      VOLUME SERIAL  ===>     (If not cataloged,  required for option "C")

      DATA SET PASSWORD ===>        (If password protected)
```

Screen 3.12 - ISPF Dataset - Allocate (Create) - 2

```
---------------------------  ALLOCATE NEW DATA SET  ---------------------------
COMMAND ===>

 DATA SET NAME: THE.FILE.TO.CREATE

   VOLUME SERIAL          ===> 3390  (Blank for authorized default volume) *
   GENERIC UNIT           ===>       (Generic group name or unit address) *
   SPACE UNITS            ===> BLOCK (BLKS, TRKS, or CYLS)
   PRIMARY QUANTITY       ===> 200   (In above units)
   SECONDARY QUANTITY     ===> 150   (In above units)
   DIRECTORY BLOCKS       ===> 0     (Zero for sequential data set)
   RECORD FORMAT          ===> VB
   RECORD LENGTH          ===> 255
   BLOCK SIZE             ===> 2550
   EXPIRATION DATE        ===>       (YY/MM/DD, YYYY/MM/DD
                                      YY.DDD, YYYY.DDD in Julian form
                                      DDDD for retention period in days
                                      or blank)

                              (* Only one of these fields may be specified)
```

Creating an empty dataset requires two screens to specify the name and space allocation. These steps using ISPF are shown in Screens 3.11 and 3.12.

Since there is no need to allocate space for files under UNIX and Partitioned Datasets are just subdirectories, there is no direct equivalent to ISPF 3.1 and 3.2 screens in uni-SPF or SPF/UX. The closest equivalent screens are Directory Utility in uni-SPF and Library Utilities in SPF/UX. These screens are shown in the upcoming section, ISPF Dataset List Utility Replacement.

The screens provide a means to delete files, but it takes time to navigate the menu structure. In an interview, do not expect to be asked how to delete a file using one of the transitional editors, You may be asked how to do it in native UNIX though.

DELETE AND CREATE FILE COMMANDS (rm AND touch)

To delete a file under native UNIX, the command syntax is:

```
$ rm /a/file/to/DELETE↵
$
```

The first thing `rm` does is checks permissions to verify you are allowed to remove the file. Then the number of links to the file are decremented. If the link count reaches zero, the physical file is removed and the inode released for use by another file. If the file protection is such that you are not allowed to delete the file (do not have the appropriate write permission), but do have write permission to the directory that contains the file, you will see the following:

```
$ rm /a/file/to/DELETE↵
rm: override protection 644 for /a/file/to/DELETE? y↵
$
```

A response of Y will override the protection that prevents deletion. A response of N will not delete the file. Either way, if the deletion is successful, no message will be produced. Only if there is an error will any message appear. If you are not permitted to delete the file due to permissions and do not have write access to the directory that contains the file, you will still get the override prompt, but it will not work:

```
$ rm /a/file/to/DELETE↵
rm: override protection 644 for /a/file/to/DELETE? y↵
rm: /a/file/to/DELETE not removed.
Permission denied
$
```

If you attempt to delete a file that does not exist, you will receive the message:

```
rm: /a/file/to/DELETE: No such file or directory
```

You cannot delete a directory file:

```
$ rm /a/file/to ↵
rm: /a/file/to directory
$
```

To remove the entire contents of a subdirectory, equivalent to deleting a Partitioned Dataset on the mainframe, the `-r` (recursive deletion) is used:

```
$ rm -r /u/dhorvath/cobol/proj_2↵
$
```

This will delete all the files contained in the directory /u/dhorvath/cobol/proj_2 and will get rid of the directory proj_2. The result is that all of the COBOL code for proj_2 is thrown away, just as if I had deleted the PDS 'DHORVATH.COBOL.PROJ2'. Be very careful with this command option. If there were any directories under /u/dhorvath/cobol/proj_2, their contents would be deleted and then the directories themselves would be deleted. A strong note of caution—do not ever enter the following:

```
$ rm -r /↵                          Do not do! Ever!
$
```

Or while in the directory / enter the following `rm` command:

```
$ pwd↵
/
$ rm -r *↵                          Do not do! Ever!
$
```

Either command will attempt to delete every file in the root file system (including the bootable image of the UNIX operating system) and then delete every file that you are allowed (based on file and directory permissions). On one project, a consultant accidentally did just as shown in the second example. She thought she was in one of her subdirectories that she did not need anymore. Fortunately, we had a backup and she did not have root permissions (system administrator permissions), or the entire system would have disappeared! It was truly an accident and we all joked about it, but you cannot expect your co-workers to be so forgiving. The system administrator even made a sign up and posted it in her cubical: "No, No, Nanette, No more `rm -r *`"

Another simple mistake while using the rm command is to enter it as follows:

```
$ rm * .txt↵                        # *, a space, .txt - do not do this!
$
```

Because there is a space between the asterisk <*> and .txt, the shell interprets it to mean: delete everything and then delete the file with the name .txt. The user probably wanted to delete everything with a suffix of .txt (*.txt without a space). Be careful what you type—if the shell can interpret it, it will.

The other function that IEFBR14 is used for is to create empty files being used in other processing. ISPF Dataset Utility also allows the allocation of a file. There are two ways to create a file with UNIX commands. The first is:

```
$ touch /a/file/to/CREATE↵
$
```

This command was mentioned in the problem determination to determine permissions. It works by attempting to open the specified file and then closing it. If the file already exists, the date and time reported by the `ls` command will be updated. An empty file is created if the named file does not already exist. If you do not have write permission on an existing file or the directory that contains it, you will get one of the following messages:

```
touch: cannot change times on /a/file/to/CREATE
```

If you do not have write permission to the directory, you will get the following message if the file does not exist:

```
touch: /a/file/to/CREATE cannot create
```

You will also get that message if the directory does not exist. The other way to create an empty file is as follows:

```
$ > /a/file/to/CREATE↵
$
```

which will force the creation of an empty file. If you get the message:

```
ksh: /a/file/to/CREATE: file already exists
```

the option `noclobber` is enabled, which prevents you from truncating (clobber) an existing file by accident. You can either turn noclobber off with the following command:

```
$ set +o noclobber↵
$
```

or you can retain the protection the noclobber option offers and use a slightly different form of the command:

```
$ >| /a/file/to/CREATE↵
$
```

which forces the creation of an empty file or truncation of an existing file to length zero. If I know the file already exists, I will delete it first and then touch to create an empty version. Doing it this way provides a definite trail of actions performed.

If you do not have write permission to an existing file, to the directory to create a new file, or attempt to create a file in a nonexistent directory, you will get the following message:

```
ksh: /a/file/to/CREATE cannot create
```

CREATE, DELETE, AND RENAME DIRECTORY COMMANDS (mkdir, rmdir, AND mv)

Directories and subdirectories are manipulated with different commands. A mainframe PDS can easily be replaced with a subdirectory under UNIX. The PDS contains members, a subdirectory contains other files. The PDS typically groups things together like COBOL code, whereas a subdirectory can be set up for the same function. They both hold collections of things: The mainframe calls them members, UNIX calls them files. To create a subdirectory, you enter the following:

```
$ mkdir /a/file/to↵
$
```

The parent directories (/a/file) of the new subdirectory (to) must already exist or you will get the following messages:

```
mkdir: cannot access Directory /a.
/a: No such file or directory
```

There is a flag for `mkdir` that will create any or all of the directories in the specified path (`-p`):

```
$ mkdir -p /a/file/to↵
$
```

will create /a, /a/file, and finally /a/file/to directories if they do not exist. If you attempt to create a directory that already exists, you will get the message:

```
mkdir: cannot make directory /a/file/to
```

If you do not have write permission to the directory where your new directory will be created, you will be told:

```
mkdir: cannot access /a/file.
```

Getting rid of a directory is easy:

```
$ rmdir /a/file/to↵
$
```

However, it must be empty. If the directory contains files, rmdir will display an error message to inform you that the directory is not empty. You must empty out the directory (delete the files) first or you can use the recursive (`-r`) option for `rm` as shown above to delete the contents and then the directory.

To rename a directory, you can use the `mv` command. Some versions of UNIX also have a `mvdir` command that performs the same function:

```
$ mv /a/file/to /a/file/new_name↵          On all versions
$ mvdir /a/file/to /a/file/new_name↵       On some versions
$
```

Note that all versions of UNIX support the `mv` command to rename directories and some versions support mvdir. With either command, you can only change the last part of the pathname. For instance, the following command probably will not work:

```
$ mv /a/file/to /a/big_file/new_name↵          Not likely
$
```

If you want to rename multiple parts of a pathname, that is, you want to rename multiple directories, you need to use multiple commands:

```
$ mv /a/file/to /a/file/new_name↵                    Step 1
$ mv /a/file /a/big_file↵                            Step 2
$
```

You do not have to rename the lowest level first, it just tends to be easier. Compare the following two commands to the ones above:

```
$ mv /a/file /a/big_file↵                            Step 1
$ mv /a/big_file/to /a/big_file/new_name↵            Step 2
$
```

If you get the following message, you attempted to rename a directory between two filesystems:

```
mv: cannot mv directories across file systems
```

You will have to create the directory in the new location, move all the files (using wildcards) to the new location, and then delete the old one. Or you could create a symbolic link connecting the original directory to its new location.

ISPF Dataset List Utility Replacement

The ISPF Dataset List Utility screen, accessed through menu choice 3.4 on the mainframe, is a menu and an information source. It allows you to enter commands to perform actions on the files listed. It also gives you information about the files. You can Browse, Edit, Delete, Rename, get Long Information, get Short Information, Catalog, Uncatalog, Print, Print the Displayed index, Display Member List for a PDS, Compress, Free Unused Space, or enter any TSO command to act on the dataset shown. There are four different display modes for the information/menu: Volume displays the volume a dataset is stored on; Space shows how much space is allocated and used; Attrib displays the record and file structure information; and Total shows all of this and more. The mainframe <right> or <pf11> key allows you to cycle through those screens.

The ISPF Dataset List Utility screens follow with discussion of UNIX replacements. Screen 3.13 shows the input screen, although most people using this screen leave the option field blank for the dataset list.

After entering the information shown and pressing <enter>, you are presented with the first Data Set List Utility screen, Screen 3.14.

Under native UNIX, the information from Screen 3.14 can be obtained through the `df` command, which is covered in Problem Determination—Available Space. Both Screen 3.14 and the `df` command shows which volumes (filesystems) a file is stored on.

More information is available from this utility on the mainframe. After pressing <right> or <pf11> on the mainframe, the information about the datasets changes as shown on Screen 3.15.

Under native UNIX, the information from Screen 3.15 can be obtained through the use of `ls -l` to get the actual space used in bytes and the `du` command to determine the number of blocks used. If you need to know the percentage of space used, apply the formula:

percent-used = space-from-ls / (blocks-from-du * 512) * 100.

Screen 3.13 - ISPF Dataset List Utility

```
---------------------------- DATA SET LIST UTILITY ----------------------------
OPTION ===>

 blank  - Display data set list *          P - Print data set list
 V      - Display VTOC information only    PV - Print VTOC information only

Enter one or both of the parameters below:
 DNAME LEVEL ===> TOP.NXT.GROUP.PMA1.LOC*
  VOLUME     ===>

INITIAL DISPLAY VIEW    ===> VOLUME  (VOLUME,SPACE,ATTRIB,TOTAL)
  CONFIRM DELETE REQUEST ===>  YES     (YES or NO)

* The following line commands will be available when the list is displayed:

B - Browse data set        C - Catalog data set        F - Free unused space
E - Edit data set          U - Uncatalog data set      = - Repeat last command
D - Delete data set        P - Print data set
R - Rename data set        X - Print index listing
I - Data set information   M - Display member list
S - Information (short)    Z - Compress data set TSO cmd, CLIST or REXX exec
```

Screen 3.14 - ISPF Dataset List Utility - <enter>

```
DSLIST - DATA SETS BEGINNING WITH TOP.NXT.GROUP.PMA1.LOC* ------  ROW 1 OF 17
  COMMAND ===>

COMMAND     NAME                                        MESSAGE      VOLUME
------------------------------------------------------------------------------
            TOP.NXT.GROUP.PMA1.LOCLIN                                ??????
            TOP.NXT.GROUP.PMA1.LOCLIN.BKUP                           ??????
            TOP.NXT.GROUP.PMA1.LOCLIN.BKUP.G0031V00                  160224
            TOP.NXT.GROUP.PMA1.LOCLIN.BKUP.G0032V00                  162574
            TOP.NXT.GROUP.PMA1.LOCLIN.BKUP.G0033V00                  164832
            TOP.NXT.GROUP.PMA1.LOCLIN.BKUP.G0034V00                  169969
            TOP.NXT.GROUP.PMA1.LOCLIN.BKUP.G0035V00                  168521
            TOP.NXT.GROUP.PMA1.LOCLIN.G0045V00                       900736
            TOP.NXT.GROUP.PMA1.LOCLIN.G0046V00                       900736
            TOP.NXT.GROUP.PMA1.LOCLIN.G0047V00                       900737
            TOP.NXT.GROUP.PMA1.LOCLIN.G0048V00                       900802
            TOP.NXT.GROUP.PMA1.LOCLIN.G0049V00                       900735
            TOP.NXT.GROUP.PMA1.LOCLIN.G0104                          MIGRAT
            TOP.NXT.GROUP.PMA1.LOCLIN.G0105                          MIGRAT
            TOP.NXT.GROUP.PMA1.LOCLIN.G0106                          MIGRAT
            TOP.NXT.GROUP.PMA1.LOCLIN.G0107                          MIGRAT
            TOP.NXT.GROUP.PMA1.LOCLIN.ZIP                            MIGRAT
******************************END OF DATA SET LIST********************
```

Screen 3.15 ISPF Dataset List Utility - <right> or <pf11>

```
DSLIST - DATA SETS BEGINNING WITH TOP.NXT.GROUP.PMA1.LOC* ------ ROW 1 OF 17
  COMMAND ===>                                                   SCROLL ===> CSR

COMMAND     NAME                                      TRACKS %USED  XT  DEVICE
--------------------------------------------------------------------------------
            TOP.NXT.GROUP.PMA1.LOCLIN
            TOP.NXT.GROUP.PMA1.LOCLIN.BKUP
            TOP.NXT.GROUP.PMA1.LOCLIN.BKUP.G0031V00
            TOP.NXT.GROUP.PMA1.LOCLIN.BKUP.G0032V00
            TOP.NXT.GROUP.PMA1.LOCLIN.BKUP.G0033V00
            TOP.NXT.GROUP.PMA1.LOCLIN.BKUP.G0034V00
            TOP.NXT.GROUP.PMA1.LOCLIN.BKUP.G0035V00
            TOP.NXT.GROUP.PMA1.LOCLIN.G0045V00             1   100   1   3380
            TOP.NXT.GROUP.PMA1.LOCLIN.G0046V00             1   100   1   3380
            TOP.NXT.GROUP.PMA1.LOCLIN.G0047V00             1   100   1   3380
            TOP.NXT.GROUP.PMA1.LOCLIN.G0048V00             1   100   1   3390
            TOP.NXT.GROUP.PMA1.LOCLIN.G0049V00             1   100   1   3380
            TOP.NXT.GROUP.PMA1.LOCLIN.G0104
            TOP.NXT.GROUP.PMA1.LOCLIN.G0105
            TOP.NXT.GROUP.PMA1.LOCLIN.G0106
            TOP.NXT.GROUP.PMA1.LOCLIN.G0107
            TOP.NXT.GROUP.PMA1.LOCLIN.ZIP
***************************** END OF DATA SET LIST**************************
```

The mainframe utility will provide more information. After pressing <right> or <pf11> again on the mainframe, the information about the datasets changes as shown on Screen 3.16.

Since UNIX does not track any information about the internal structure of a file, the information provided on Screen 3.15—DSORG (Dataset organization), RECFM (Record format), LRECL (Logical record length), and BLKSIZ (Physical block size) is not available. After pressing <right> or <pf11> one final time on the mainframe, the information about the datasets changes as shown on Screen 3.17.

The information on Screen 3.17 is a combination of Screens 3.14, 3.15, and 3.16 as well as the addition of the creation, expiration, and last access date for the dataset. On the mainframe, a dataset can be set to expire on a certain date. That is, it is automatically deleted on the specified date. UNIX does not have such a mechanism, although it would be fairly easy to implement using shell scripts. If your application requires this functionality, again, discuss it with your system administrator.

The transitional editors provide some features similar to the ISPF Dataset List Utility. SPF/UX has the Library Utilities (menu option 3.1), which provides a means to Rename, Delete, Select a subdirectory, Edit, and Browse files. After the directory to work with is entered, SPF/UX presents a simple list of the files contained therein. It does not provide any other information about the files (like the ISPF Dataset List Utility does). The SPF/UX screens are not shown due to their simplicity.

uni-SPF has the Directory Utility (menu option 3.1), which provides a means to Browse, Copy, Delete, Edit, Print, and Rename files. It also can Make Directories and support navigation by

Screen 3.16 - ISPF Dataset List Utility - <right> or <pf11> again

```
DSLIST - DATA SETS BEGINNING WITH TOP.NXT.GROUP.PMA1.LOC* ------ ROW 1 OF 17
  COMMAND ===>                                                  SCROLL ===> CSR

COMMAND  NAME                                      DSORG RECFM    LRECL  BLKSZ
-------------------------------------------------------------------------------
         TOP.NXT.GROUP.PMA1.LOCLIN
         TOP.NXT.GROUP.PMA1.LOCLIN.BKUP
         TOP.NXT.GROUP.PMA1.LOCLIN.BKUP.G0031V00
         TOP.NXT.GROUP.PMA1.LOCLIN.BKUP.G0032V00
         TOP.NXT.GROUP.PMA1.LOCLIN.BKUP.G0033V00
         TOP.NXT.GROUP.PMA1.LOCLIN.BKUP.G0034V00
         TOP.NXT.GROUP.PMA1.LOCLIN.BKUP.G0035V00
         TOP.NXT.GROUP.PMA1.LOCLIN.G0045V00          PS    FB          80  3120
         TOP.NXT.GROUP.PMA1.LOCLIN.G0046V00          PS    FB          80  3120
         TOP.NXT.GROUP.PMA1.LOCLIN.G0047V00          PS    FB          80  3120
         TOP.NXT.GROUP.PMA1.LOCLIN.G0048V00          PS    FB          80  3120
         TOP.NXT.GROUP.PMA1.LOCLIN.G0049V00          PS    FB          80  3120
         TOP.NXT.GROUP.PMA1.LOCLIN.G0104
         TOP.NXT.GROUP.PMA1.LOCLIN.G0105
         TOP.NXT.GROUP.PMA1.LOCLIN.G0106
         TOP.NXT.GROUP.PMA1.LOCLIN.G0107
         TOP.NXT.GROUP.PMA1.LOCLIN.ZIP
******************************END OF DATA SET LIST***************************
```

Screen 3.17 - ISPF Dataset List Utility - <right> or <pf11> third time

```
COMMAND NAME                                         MESSAGE            VOLUME
   TRACKS % XT DEVICE  DSORG RECFM LRECL BLKSZ  CREATED    EXPIRES REFERRED
-------------------------------------------------------------------------------

       TOP.NEXT.GROUP.PMA1.LOCLIN                                       ??????

-------------------------------------------------------------------------------

       TOP.NEXT.GROUP.PMA1.LOCLIN.BKUP                                  ??????

-------------------------------------------------------------------------------

       TOP.NEXT.GROUP.PMA1.LOCLIN.BKUP.G0031V00                         160224

-------------------------------------------------------------------------------

       TOP.NEXT.GROUP.PMA1.LOCLIN.BKUP.G0032V00                         162574

-------------------------------------------------------------------------------

       TOP.NEXT.GROUP.PMA1.LOCLIN.BKUP.G0033V00                         164832

-------------------------------------------------------------------------------

       TOP.NEXT.GROUP.PMA1.LOCLIN.BKUP.G0034V00                         169969

-------------------------------------------------------------------------------
```

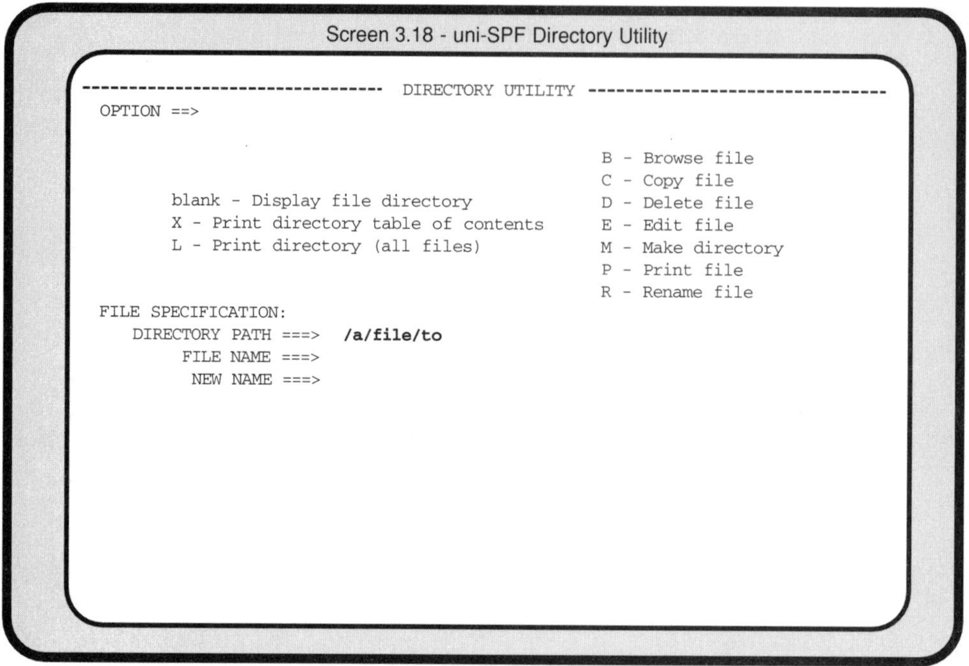

Screen 3.18 - uni-SPF Directory Utility

Selecting Subdirectories. After the directory to work with is entered, uni-SPF presents a detailed list of the files contained therein. Screen 3.18 shows the initial entry screen.

After selecting the directory to work with and pressing <enter>, you are presented with the menu and information screen shown in Screen 3.19.

Screen 3.19 displays a number of columns that are similar to those shown in Screens 3.14 through 3.17: a column for file operation, the filename, the owner, file size, file type, permissions, and when the file was last modified. This is the same information produced by the ls -al command. The filenames can be in upper or lower case, or any combination. There are several files that look like mainframe Generation Data Groups (GDG), which are not part of native UNIX; they were created and are used by a series of shell scripts in Appendix B (Hints and Techniques). The owner is important for file processing because there are different permissions for a file owner, members of a group, and then the rest of the world. It is also useful to determine the purpose of a file (so you know whom to ask). File size is the space used by that file. File type will be blank for most files, if there are any files that are not ordinary UNIX files, the appropriate flag will be shown. In this case, there are two directories shown:

.	Current Directory
..	Parent Directory

The permissions help you determine if you can even access the file shown and the date modified shows how old the file is. When a file is created, the modification date is when the file was completed (a close executed).

Screen 3.19 - uni-SPF Directory Utility - <enter>

```
DIRECTORY /a/file/to --------------------------------------- ROW 000001 OF 000030
  COMMAND==>                                                   SCROLL ==> PAGE

 X:  B-Browse, C-Copy, D-Delete, E-Edit, P-Print, R-Rename, S-Select directory.

  X NAME                     OWNER           SIZE TYP PERM'S      MODIFIED
    .                        your_id         2260  d  rwxr-x--- Nov 14 10:15
    ..                       your_id         1536  d  rwxr-x--- Nov  2  7:05
    CREATE                   your_id            7     rw-r----- Nov 14  4:29
    DELETE                   your_id            7     rw-r----- Nov 14  4:29
    FILE                     your_id     85033472     rw-r----- Nov 12  1:35
    a.dummy.name             your_id            0     rw-r----- Nov 13  0:43
    A.RATHER_LARGE_FILE      your_id     61975552     rw-r----- Nov 14  2:08
    ANOTHER_FILE           . dhorvath           7     rw-r----- Nov 14  2:37
    MORE.DATA                dhorvath     3205632     rw-r----- Nov 14  4:12
    MY_SMALL_FILE            dhorvath           7     rw-r----- Nov 14  4:29
    GDG.EXAMPLE.G0001V00     dhorvath      136704     rw-r----- Nov 12  1:36
    GDG.EXAMPLE.G0002V00     dhorvath      136704     rw-r----- Nov 13  0:44
    GDG.EXAMPLE.G0003V00     your_id       136704     rw-r----- Nov 14  2:09
    GDG.EXAMPLE.gdgbase      another            7     rw-rw-rw- Nov 14  2:09
    ANOTHER.GDG.gdgbase      another            7     rw-r----- Nov 13 23:10
    YET_ANOTHER_GDG.gdgbase  another            7     rw-r----- Nov 13 23:10
    A_SMALL_FILE             another           17     rw-r----- Nov 14  4:29
```

This screen also allows navigation through the directory structure. To move up one level, simply select the .. directory. To move into the save subdirectory, simply select it. One warning about using uni-SPF: the file size may not be accurate. A fixed column width is used and if the file size has too many digits (larger than 99,999,999 bytes), the highest characters will be omitted. This is not a serious problem, but can be a bit disconcerting if you expect a file to be a certain size and it looks much smaller in the display.

find COMMAND

Most native UNIX commands do not provide menus. UNIX is known as a command line-oriented operating system, so, with the exception of the transitional tools detailed previously, there really is no equivalent to the ISPF Dataset List Utility Screen. There are, however, a number of tools to take its place. The ls command provides essentially the same information as the Dataset List and supports a variety of wildcards. Another thing that the ISPF Dataset List Utility Screen is used for is to locate datasets when you are not sure of the name or location. UNIX provides a robust replacement for this function through:

```
$ pwd↵                                    To show where we are
/a/file/to
$ find . -name "*FILE*" -ls↵              Find file starting in current directory
666589 61975 -rw-r----- 1 yourid users   61975552 Nov 14  2:08 ./A.RATHER_LARGE_FILE
666123     1 -rw-r----- 1 dhorvath users        7 Nov 14  4:29 ./MY_SMALL_FILE
123333     1 -rw-r----- 1 another  users       17 Nov 14  4:29 ./A_SMALL_FILE
$
```

This command will search for any file with a name containing FILE starting with the current directory and searching all subdirectories. If it finds any, it will produce a listing similar to the `ls -l` command. Column headings are not printed, but the columns are inode number, size in kilobytes, file permissions, number of links, owner, group, size in bytes, modification date, and, finally, the path and filename. Notice that the columns do not line up. That is because the first file is so large, the normal field used to show the size in kilobytes is too small; rather than lose information, the column size is expanded. The format of the path may look a little odd, but, in fact, it is consistent with what has been covered so far. ./Filename is a way of showing that the file is stored in this directory. Remember that a directory of . is the current directory and the slash is required to separate directory from filename.

The first parameter of the `find` command is where to start the search. The first option is `-name` followed by the filename you are searching for; the normal wildcard rules apply. The last option tells find to produce a listing similar to `ls`. Another option will just show the directory and filename:

```
$ pwd↵                                 To show where we are
/a/file/to
$ find . -name "*FILE*" -print↵        Find file starting in current directory
./A.RATHER_LARGE_FILE
./MY_SMALL_FILE
./A_SMALL_FILE
$
```

If I have no idea where a file might be or I am searching for a version from a particular date or revision (the earliest I can find, for instance) that could be in any one of many places, so I will use a find command to search the entire directory structure. Starting at the root directory, this will search every subdirectory and report on any files that match the criteria.

```
        $ find / -name "*stuff*" -ls↵         Find file anywhere
        find: cannot read dir /etc/fixes: Permission denied
664433  1 -rw-r-----  1 another  users   123 Sep 02  1:11 /u/another/sub/big_stuff
        $
```

You can expect to see many repetitions of the error message that `find` is unable to read a directory. Every directory that you do not have execute permissions to (required to determine the contents of the directory), will cause this message. Unless your system administrator is sloppy (or you are the system administrator), you will not be allowed to look at many directories. Although not shown in this example, you may see many entries for files that the `find` command locates.

In addition to just reporting about the files that are found, `find` can be directed to execute a command on each of the files it finds. When a program abends, it creates a file in the current directory named core. Many system administrators execute the following command on a periodic basis to clean up these junk files:

```
$ find / -name "core" -exec rm {} \;↵
$
```

The `-exec` flag tells the find command to pass everything that follows until the semicolon <;> to the command processor as a subprocess. find will substitute the filename for the paired curly brace characters <{> and <}>. The semicolon has a backslash <\> before it so that the command shell does not process it as a command separator. The semicolon has special meaning to the shell (putting multiple commands on the same line) that we do not want here. In fact, the processes with the backslash is known as escaping a character because it prevents the special meaning. Any character being used for a special purpose is referred to as a meta-character. There is more information about meta-characters in Chapter 4.

Another application is to perform a function on a specific file stored in different subdirectories. If each subdirectory is a different production job within a particular day (/960101/job_5, /960102/job_5, etc.), and the log files are stored in a compressed format, the following command will uncompress them all:

```
$ find /the_day -name "job_log.Z" -exec uncompress {} \;↵
$
```

We could process them further with another `find -exec` command using `grep` to search the contents or `ls` to determine the size, or even `vi` to edit them. When done, the following `find` command would reverse the process:

```
$ find /the_day -name "job_log" -exec compress {} \;↵
$
```

The compress command compresses a file and saves it under the original name with a .Z suffix. Uncompress takes a file with a .Z suffix, uncompresses it, and saves it under the original name without the suffix. This is known as compressing or uncompressing in place, although it is not a good idea to have a file in the same subdirectory with and without the suffix at the same time (file and file.Z) because a compress would replace file.Z and an uncompress would replace file.

PIPES AND REDIRECTION AND THE more COMMAND

When searching the entire directory structure for a file with wildcards, there may be many files that meet the criteria. It can find so many files so fast that the information scrolls off the screen before you can even notice it. The same can happen with the ls command on large directories. The solution is to direct the output of the command into another command that will pause the screen. One such command is more and is used as follows:

```
$ find / -name "*" -print | more↵        Find every file everywhere
find: cannot read dir /etc/fixes: Permission denied
/
/bin
/bin/sh
/bin/cpio
/bin/echo
/bin/mv
/bin/cp
```

```
         and many more until the screen is full
-More-
```

Pressing the <enter> key will show one line at a time, pressing the <space> bar will result in another screen full. Pressing <q> or <Q> will end the process and return you to the shell prompt.

The character between the `find` command and the `more` command is the vertical bar character and is known in UNIX terminology as the pipe character (|). The output from the first command is piped to the second command as input. The commands run in parallel, that is, more does not wait until find has printed all files. As `find` produces a record, more can display it. Sometimes, the first command creates output so slowly that it looks like more is waiting for a full screen before doing anything, but that is not the case.

The pipe character redirects the stdout file of the first command from the screen to the second command. At the same time, the stdin file of the second command is redirected from the keyboard to the stdout of the first command. In this way, the connection between the two commands acts as a one-way pipe. Pipes can be used with multiple programs in series. For instance, if I wanted to see all files in the system in a sorted order, I can send the output of find to the `sort` command and then send the output of the sort to more so data is not lost:

```
$ find / -name "*" -print | sort | more↵
find: cannot read dir /etc/fixes: Permission denied
/
/.history
/.phdir
/.profile
/Clipboard
/Filecabinet
         and many more until the screen is full
-More-
```

Notice how the order is different than the example without the sort.

Output can be redirected through a pipe to another program. It can also be redirected to a file:

```
$ find / -name "*" -print > ~/big_find↵
find: cannot read dir /etc/fixes: Permission denied
$ ls -al ~/big_find↵                        Look at file
-rw-r-r-  1 dhorvath users    36623 Feb 10 14:03 /u/dhorvath/big_find
$ more ~/big_find↵                          Look at contents of file
/
/bin
/bin/sh
/bin/cpio
/bin/echo
/bin/mv
         and many more until the screen is full
-More-(0%)
```

The file /u/dhorvath/big_find was created (or replaced if it already existed) with the output of the find command. It occupies a total of 36,623 bytes, and when looking at the contents with the more command, it contains the same data as the original find | more example. The prompt from the more command is now a little different in that it shows the percentage of the output shown. After one screen worth, 0 percent of the file has been shown. What that really means is that 1 percent of the file has not been reached yet.

Some versions of `more` support a neat trick. By pressing <v> or <V> at the prompt, they will allow full screen manipulation of the file by passing control to the `vi` editor in read-only mode (actually the `view` command). Where available, you end up at exactly the same place in the file even if you have scrolled through many screens using more. More information about vi and view is available in Chapter 6 (Editors).

The advantages of redirection to a file over redirection through a pipe are twofold: The output can be manipulated many different ways when stored in a file, and the stdout and stderr outputs do not mix together. The error messages produced by find go to the screen with file or pipe redirection. If you pipe stdout through the more command, any error (stderr) and normal (stdout) output will get intertwined. This can be visually confusing.

One solution is to redirect stderr to a file, just like what is done with stdout. There are two common uses for this feature: to throw away error messages or to save them for later processing. The following example throws away the errors:

```
$ find / -name "*" -print 2>/dev/null | more↵
/
/bin
/bin/sh
/bin/cpio
/bin/echo
/bin/mv
/bin/cp
          and many more until the screen is full
—More—
```

The error messages displayed to the file stderr were redirected to /dev/null, which is the bit-bucket. We can also send them to a real file for further processing:

```
$ find / -name "*" -print 2>~/find_errors | more↵
/
/bin
/bin/sh
/bin/cpio
/bin/echo
/bin/mv
/bin/cp
          and many more until the screen is full
—More— Q                                No need to press the <enter> key
```

```
$ more ~/find_errors↵                       Look at file contents
find: cannot read dir /etc/fixes: Permission denied
find: cannot read dir /lost+found: Permission denied
find: cannot read dir /home/lost+found: Permission denied
find: cannot read dir /home/an_user/mail: Permission denied
find: cannot read dir /home/an_user/.MCOM-cache: Permission denied
find: cannot read dir /home/an_user2/Mail/inbox: Permission denied
find: cannot read dir /home/an_user2/Mail/draft: Permission denied
      and many more until the screen is full
—More—(49%)
```

In this case, all we did was look at the errors at another time. We could have searched, sorted, edited, or even printed the error messages. To redirect the normal output to one file and the errors to another is easy, just use both forms of output redirection:

```
$ find / -name "*" -print > ~/big_find 2>~/find_errors ↵
$
```

To redirect both stdout and stderr to the same file, the forms are:

```
$ find / -name "*" -print > ~/big_find 2>&1↵
$ find / -name "*" -print 2>~/big_find 1>&2↵
$
```

These two commands perform exactly the same redirection. Only the terminology is a little different. The first command redirects stdout to a file and then redirects stderr to that same file. The second command redirects stderr to a file and then redirects stdout to that same file. The resulting output file will contain exactly the same data in the same sequence. The order of the redirection operators is important, because the physical file being redirected to must be specified before using the symbolic form of the redirection (&1 or &2).

So far, output redirection has been shown through the use of the redirection and pipe operators. Input redirection has been shown through the use of the pipe operator. There is also an input redirection operator that redirects stdin from the keyboard to accept input from a file. This is the same as changing a mainframe SYSIN DD * to SYSIN DD DSN=A.FILE,DISP=SHR.

If the `more` command is used without a filename on the command line, it expects to read input from stdin. Using the pipe operator changes stdin by connecting it to stdout of another command. To redirect the stdin of the more command to use an existing file:

```
$ more < ~/find_errors↵                     Look at file contents
find: cannot read dir /etc/fixes: Permission denied
find: cannot read dir /lost+found: Permission denied
find: cannot read dir /home/lost+found: Permission denied
find: cannot read dir /home/an_user/mail: Permission denied
find: cannot read dir /home/an_user/.MCOM-cache: Permission denied
find: cannot read dir /home/an_user2/Mail/inbox: Permission denied
find: cannot read dir /home/an_user2/Mail/draft: Permission denied
```

Screen 3.20 - TSO HELP

```
READY
HELP.↵
 LANGUAGE PROCESSING COMMANDS:

  ASM         INVOKE ASSEMBLER PROMPTER AND ASSEMBLER F COMPILER.
  CALC        INVOKE ITF:PL/1 PROCESSOR FOR DESK CALCULATOR MODE.
  COBOL       INVOKE COBOL PROMPTER AND ANS COBOL COMPILER.
  FORT        INVOKE FORTRAN PROMPTER AND FORTRAN IV G1 COMPILER.

  PROGRAM CONTROL COMMANDS:

  CALL        LOAD AND EXECUTE THE SPECIFIED LOAD MODULE.
  LINK        INVOKE LINK PROMPTER AND LINKAGE EDITOR.
  LOADGO      LOAD AND EXECUTE PROGRAM.
  RUN         COMPILE, LOAD, AND EXECUTE PROGRAM.
  TEST        TEST USER PROGRAM.
  TESTAUTH    TEST APF AUTHORIZED PROGRAMS.

  DATA MANAGEMENT COMMANDS:

  ALLOCATE    ALLOCATE A DATA SET WITH OR WITHOUT AN ATTRIBUTE
              LIST OF DCB PARAMETERS.
  ALTLIB      DEFINE OPTIONAL, USER-LEVEL, OR APPLICATION-LEVEL SETS OF
  ***
```

and many more until the screen is full

```
—More—
```

Although this example is actually silly, it illustrates the point. It is very easy to change the input source for a program from the keyboard to a file. This feature makes it easy to convert interactive programs to run in a batch mode by providing the input from a file. There is one big difference between this example using the ~/find_errors file and the prior one, however. More does not report the percentage of file displayed on its prompt line. The command shell performs all redirection, which means that the command is opening stdin, not the file ~/find_errors. Therefore, the command has no way of determining the file size and cannot determine how much has been shown.

HOW TO GET HELP

When learning a new operating system, you are constantly thinking about how to do something. When learning to use a new command or on one that is infrequently used, the same occurs. The command that will do what you want, the options the command requires, and what the error messages mean are all important to figuring out how to do something.

The mainframe provides a simple help facility under TSO. It is invoked through the TSO HELP command. Screen 3.20 shows the first screen of output. The command presents a list of commands that have help available along with a short one-line description of their function. To get help for any of the listed commands, the command name is used as the parameter to the TSO HELP command.

Screen 3.21 - TSO HELP LISTALC

```
READY
HELP LISTALC↵

  FUNCTION -
    THE LISTALC COMMAND IS USED TO DISPLAY THE NAMES OF CURRENTLY
    ALLOCATED DATA SETS.

  SYNTAX -
              LISTALC STATUS  HISTORY  MEMBERS  SYSNAMES
       REQUIRED - NONE
       DEFAULTS - NONE

  OPERANDS -
       STATUS    - DDNAME AND DATA SET DISPOSITION ARE DISPLAYED.
       HISTORY   - CREATION AND EXPIRATION DATES, DATA SET ORGANIZATION AND
                   SECURITY STATUS ARE DISPLAYED.
       MEMBERS   - MEMBER AND ALIAS NAMES OF PARTITIONED DATA SETS ARE
                   DISPLAYED.
       SYSNAMES - SYSTEM ASSIGNED NAMES ARE DISPLAYED.
   READY
```

Screen 3.21 shows the result of the TSO HELP LISTALC. LISTALC is the TSO command that displays allocated datasets.

LISTALC is a rather simple TSO command, taking only one screen to display the help information. For many of the other commands, the help requires many screens to display all the options and operands available.

The difficulty with TSO HELP is that you must know the command to request help about. You could search the list produced by HELP with no parameters, but if the short description does not answer your question, you will have a difficult time finding the correct command to get help about.

Most UNIX systems do not have a `help` command. Those that do, contain very limited information with some commonly used commands and directing you to a manual or another person.

```
$ help↵
Look in a printed manual for general help if you can.  You should
have someone show you some things and then read the manual.

The commands:
  man -k keyword     lists commands relevant to a keyword
  man command        prints out the manual pages for a command
are helpful; other basic commands are:
  cat                - concatenates files (and displays)
```

```
  finger          - user information lookup program
  ls              - lists contents of directory
  mail            - sends and receives mail
  msgs            - system messages and junk mail
  passwd          - changes login password
  who             - who is on the system
  write           - writes to another user
You could find programs about mail by the command:    man -k mail
and display the documentation via:      man mail
You can log out by typing "exit".

$
```

Or more commonly, you will get the following response:

```
$ help↵
ksh: help:  not found
$
```

Because there is no such command. Fortunately, UNIX does have a help-like facility under a different name.

HELP UNDER UNIX—man, apropos, AND whatis COMMANDS

To get help under UNIX, you read the manual. Not a paper manual, although there are plenty of those, but instead, you read the on-line manual:

```
$ man cp↵                          get information about the copy command
                  The contents of the manual entry for the copy command show here
$
```

Because each vendor has a copyright on their manual pages and their contents differ slightly, the real manual page for the cp command was not shown. The following example with a fictitious manual entry shows the major sections:

```
$ man special_command↵          get information about the special_command
special_command(1)


Name
  special_command - do something very special

Synopsis
  special_command [flags] [ source ] remotedest
  Options:
    [-a -b -c]
```

```
Description
  special_command is used to do something so very special that
  it would take many pages to tell you about it.

  This part of the manual provides information about features
  and functions that this command performs.  It may also note
  some commands that you may want to use with this one.

Parameters
  source       - This is where something comes from
  remotedest   - This is where something is going to

Flags

  -a   This flag causes the command to do something really
       special.
  -b   This is the default and causes the command to do the
       normal thing it is supposed to do.
  -c   Does something really bizarre that you could do.
Exit Status

  This command returns the following exit values:

  0   Successful completion.

  >0  An error occurred.

Examples

  1.   To do the normal thing with this command:

  special_command file_in file_out

See Also
  another_command(5), super_command(1C), cp(1)

Bugs
  If you combine the -a and -b switches on the same command, the
  file may grow by about 35%.  Using -b and -c will reverse this
  process.  Using -a and -c will not cause the problem.
$
```

The manual entry is known as the *manual page* or *man page*. For long manual pages, the more command is automatically used to scroll one screen at a time. When commands are referenced in the manual, the name or number of the reference manual section is shown in parentheses. For instance, the `cp` command is shown as cp(1) because the documentation appears in Section One. Depending

Figure 3.3
UNIX Reference Manual Sections

Numbered Section	Named Section	Type of Information
1	C	Generally used commands - available to any user. Includes:
1C		Communications with other systems
1G		Graphics and CAD
1L		Local commands or third-party tools added to system
1M	ADM	Commands generally used by the System Administrator. Most of these commands are not available to the general user
2	S	Software Development - System Calls and Error Numbers
3	S	Software Development - Subroutines and Libraries. Includes:
3C		Standard C Library
3M		Math Library
3S		Standard C I/O Library
3X		Specialized Libraries
4	F	File Formats used by standard UNIX utilities
5	M	Miscellaneous information not found elsewhere
6		Game Documentation. Also known as System Demonstrations. Usually omitted
7	F	Special Files - descriptions of devices and peripherals

on the version of UNIX, the sections of the reference manual are numbered 1 through 7 plus 1M or named ADM, C, F, M, and S. Figure 3.3 shows the types of information in each of the sections.

Each section in the manual begins with an introduction providing an overview of the section. The introduction provides general information about the remainder of the section and useful summaries. The commands are organized alphabetically in the printed documentation. Since there is more than one introduction, the way to read the manual page on-line for a specific section is:

```
$ man -s 2 intro↵          get information about the section 2 introduction
        The contents of the manual entry for the section 2 introduction shown here.
$
```

The `-s` flag allows you to specify which section of the manual to get the page. Most of the commands in this book come from section one of the reference manual.

As mentioned, the specific information in each vendor's manual pages may differ, but they essentially contain the same information. *Name* is the name of the command and a short description of what it does; some commands are grouped together; for instance, there is one manual page for `cp`, `mv`, and `ln` because they are functionally similar. *Synopsis*, sometimes known as *Syntax*, is a short description of the command, its options and parameters. *Description* is a much longer discussion of the command covering the features and functions of the command as well as any related commands that may be used in conjunction with the current command. *Parameters* describe the command line parameters that the command expects, some of which may be optional. *Flags* are the options that change the behavior of the command; this section describes them and which flags may be used with others and which must be used alone. Every command returns a value or *Exit Status* to the operating system when it ends (equivalent to the mainframe Condition Code or Return Code), the possible values and their meanings are described. *Examples* are provided because commands can be so complex that just reading about them is not much help. *See Also* is helpful because it shows commands that are related to the current one; it may even show commands that perform opposite functions. The final section, *Bugs*, does not appear for all commands; a better title would be *Warnings* because the problems described are not necessarily programming errors—they are just unexpected results.

If you request a manual page that does not exist, you will see one of the following messages:

```
$ man nosuch↵                    get information about the nosuch command
man: nosuch: entry not found
man: nosuch: no match found in database
$
```

The manual pages and TSO HELP are very similar except that UNIX provides enhanced searching for information and much more information is included. One way to search for information is to manually perform hypertextish searches using the See Also section, which is of limited use. Another way uses the man command automated search techniques. The man command will perform a keyword search:

```
$ man -k transfer↵               keyword is transfer
ftp         ftp (1)    - file transfer program
ftpd        ftpd (1m)  - file transfer protocol server
tftp        tftp (1)   - trivial file transfer program
tftpd       tftpd (1m) - Internet Trivial File Transfer Protocol server
ypxfr       ypxfr (1m) - transfer NIS map from a NIS server to host
$
```

Any manual entry with the word transfer in the *Description* will be shown. From this list you may find the command you are looking for. Another command that performs the same function is:

```
$ apropos transfer↵              keyword is transfer
ftp         ftp (1)    - file transfer program
ftpd        ftpd (1m)  - file transfer protocol server
tftp        tftp (1)   - trivial file transfer program
tftpd       tftpd (1m) - Internet Trivial File Transfer Protocol server
ypxfr       ypxfr (1m) - transfer NIS map from a NIS server to host
$
```

Some systems also have a command that searches the short description (*Name*) section for a keyword:

```
$ whatis man↵
man         man (1)     - find and display reference manual pages
man         man (5)     - macros to format Reference Manual pages
$
```

The primary differences between `man -k/apropos` and `whatis` are that `man -k/apropos` search for a full word in the *Description* and whatis searches for any match in the short description (*Name*). All of the searches are case insensitive with lower and upper case characters being treated as the same. By default, a request for a manual page will return the first one found. Requesting the manual page for the man command will get the one from section one. To get the other one, the `-s` (section) flag is required:

```
$ man -s 5 man↵                    get information about the macros
                     The contents of the manual entry for the man macros show here.
$
```

It is possible save the output of a manual page through redirection. To save the information for the cp(1) command in a file, the following command is used:

```
$ man cp > manual_page_for_cp↵          save information about the cp command
$
```

The help facilities under TSO have expanded recently with the addition of the IBM BookManager software. BookManager provides the text of the system manuals with extensive search facilities. Some versions of UNIX provide similar facilities with hypertext links between topics (the IBM InfoExplorer under AIX is one). Learn to use the manual pages even if your current system has a more advanced tool since not every version has one. Your installation could bring in a machine from another vendor using UNIX and, suddenly, the advanced tool is gone and you are back to the normal manual facilities.

*PRINTING AND REPLACING ISPF HARDCOPY UTILITY AND /*ROUTE PRINT*

On the mainframe, printing is accomplished by directing output to a specific SYSOUT queue which ends up being directed to a printer. The printer could be local to the mainframe in the computer room or a remote printer on the other side of the country. UNIX printing is accomplished by directing the output to a specific printer queue. The printer queue may feed one or many printers which might be local or remote. Printing can also be accomplished by directing output (writing) to the printer devices defined (/dev/lp for example).

Printing an existing dataset on the mainframe is accomplished using IEBGENER to the SYSOUT, IEBPTPCH to the SYSOUT, or using ISPF Hardcopy Utility. The IEBGENER looks like:

```
//GENER     EXEC PGM=IEBGENER
//SYSUT1    DD DSN=THE.INPUT.FILE,DISP=OLD
//SYSUT2    DD SYSOUT=C,DCB=(LRECL=133,BLKSIZE=133,RECFM=FBA)
//SYSPRINT DD SYSOUT=*
```

```
//SYSOUT   DD SYSOUT=*
//SYSIN    DD DUMMY
/*
```

which works fine if the dataset contains ANSI printer control with a record length of 133. The IEBPTPCH utility is useful for datasets that do not meet this criteria:

```
//PRINTI   EXEC PGM=IEBPTPCH
//SYSUT1   DD DSN=THE.INPUT.FILE,DISP=OLD
//SYSUT2   DD SYSOUT=C,DCB=LRECL=80
//SYSPRINT DD SYSOUT=*
//SYSOUT   DD SYSOUT=*
//SYSIN    DD *
PUNCH
/*
```

The PUNCH statement is used instead of PRINT because PUNCH outputs the characters as they are stored in the file while PRINT outputs them in groups of eight characters with each group separated by two blanks with a blank line between each printed line. The only drawback to PUNCH is that it only prints 80 characters at a time.

The ISPF Hardcopy Utility provides a convenient way to print existing datasets to a printer. The printer can be local to or remote from the mainframe. To print to most printers, a batch job is submitted that copies the dataset to the print queue. An example of the ISPF Hardcopy Utility is shown in Screen 3.22.

The /*ROUTE PRINT JES2 command determines the remote system and/or printer that output goes to by default. No matter which tool you use, what you are doing is sending your output to a SYSOUT, to a print queue class.

UNIX PRINT COMMANDS (lp AND lpr)

UNIX has commands that direct output to the printer. The most commonly used one is lp (short for line printer):

```
$ lp -dprinter file_to_print↵          send file to printer named printer
$
```

Your system administrator should have defined a default printer device which is where your printed output will go if you do not specify a destination with the `-d` flag. The destination can be a specific printer or a queue that feeds multiple printers. Destination names will vary by installation because they are set up by the system administrator.

One big difference between mainframe and UNIX queue behavior is that the mainframe makes a copy of the file being printed and stores it in the JES spool; UNIX uses the original file. If you change the file between the time you issue the lp command and the time it actually prints, the changed file will print. Three other commonly used flags for `lp` are `-c`, `-n`, and `-w`. `-c` forces the `lp` command to make a copy of the file before printing it (more like mainframe queue

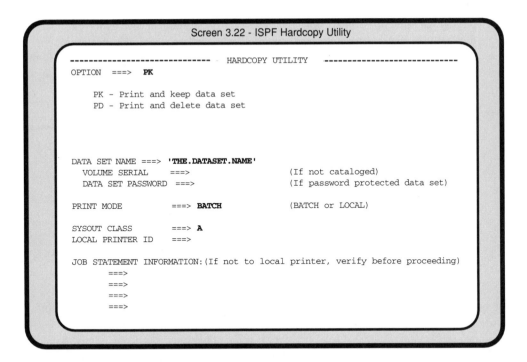

Screen 3.22 - ISPF Hardcopy Utility

```
------------------------------  HARDCOPY UTILITY  ----------------------------
OPTION  ===>  PK

    PK - Print and keep data set
    PD - Print and delete data set



DATA SET NAME ===> 'THE.DATASET.NAME'
  VOLUME SERIAL     ===>                  (If not cataloged)
  DATA SET PASSWORD  ===>                 (If password protected data set)

PRINT MODE          ===> BATCH            (BATCH or LOCAL)

SYSOUT CLASS        ===> A
LOCAL PRINTER ID    ===>

JOB STATEMENT INFORMATION:(If not to local printer, verify before proceeding)
       ===>
       ===>
       ===>
       ===>
```

behavior), -n is used to specify the number of copies printed, and -w will write a message on your screen when the file has printed; if that screen has signed off, mail will be sent instead. You can combine all the options:

```
$ lp -dmy_lan_ptr -c -w -n3 file_to_print↵     send file to my_lan_ptr
$
```

This lp command will send the output to a printer on the local area network named my_lan_ptr, copy the file to the queue before printing, print 3 copies, and write a message to my screen when done. The -m option will always send mail when the printing is done while -w will attempt to write to the screen and send mail if it cannot. Banner page printing (header or trailer) depends on how the individual printer is configured. On some versions of UNIX, there is another command to spool files to the printer, lpr. The command syntax is slightly different, but the result is the same. To send a file to the printer:

```
$ lpr -P printer -s file_to_print↵     send file to printer named printer
$
```

By default, lpr copies files to the queue before printing. To prevent it, -s is used. There is no -w flag, but there is a -m that sends mail when the printing is done. The number of copies is specified with -# instead of -n:

```
$ lpr -P my_lan_ptr -m -#3 file_to_print↵     send file to my_lan_ptr
$
```

By specifying the printer or printer queue (`lp -d` or `lpr -P` commands), you have routed the output to them. The physical printers may be local or remote; the systems administrator defines them to your system and UNIX takes care of the physical data transport. By specifying the printer, you are performing the same function as the JES2 /*ROUTE PRINT command.

UNIX PRINT STATUS COMMANDS (lpstat AND lpq)

Each print job is assigned a job number. That job number can be used to cancel a print job. To determine printer status and print job number, the `lpstat` command is used:

```
$ lpstat↵
Queue       Dev    Status    Job    Files User     PP  %     Blks Cp Rnk
-----       ---    ------    ---    ---   ----     -   -     --   -  -
printer     lp0    RUNNING          123   yourid   2   5     20   1  1
printer     lp0    WAITING          125   yourid   0   0     20   3  2
my_lan_ptr:        RUNNING          124   yourid   1   3     20   1  1
my_lan_ptr:        WAITING          126   yourid   0   0     20   3  2
$
```

The queue *printer* is assigned to /dev/lp0 and has two jobs: one active and one waiting to print, numbered 123 and 125 respectively. Both were printed by you. The first has printed 2 pages and is 5% complete, it occupies 20 disk blocks, one copy is being printed, and it is first in line. The second has not started printing, is also 20 disk blocks, three copies will be printed and it is next in line. The files that we printed to the queue *my_lan_ptr* are the same as those sent to *printer*, except that job 124 has not printed as much as job 123 (probably because the request was issued later).

On some versions of UNIX, there is another command to check the status of print jobs: `lpq`. The `lpq` command reports on any jobs in the default printer queue unless you specify the queue with the -P flag. To get the same information from `lpq` as we got from `lpstat`, the following commands are needed:

```
$ lpq -P printer↵
Queue       Dev    Status    Job Files User      PP %   Blks  Cp  Rnk
-----       ---    ------    ---   ---    ----   - -    --    -   -
printer     lp0    RUNNING   123        yourid   2 5    20    1   1
printer     lp0    WAITING   125        yourid   0 0    20    3   2
$ lpq -P my_lan_printer↵
Queue       Dev    Status    Job Files User      PP %   Blks  Cp  Rnk
-----       ---    ------    ---   ---    ----   - -    --    -   -
my_lan_ptr:        RUNNING   124        yourid   1 3    20    1   1
my_lan_ptr:        WAITING   126        yourid   0 0    20    3   2
$
```

CANCELING UNIX PRINT JOBS (cancel AND lprm COMMANDS)

To cancel a print job, you can use the following command:

```
$ cancel 123↵
$
```

Some versions use the `lprm` command to cancel print jobs:

```
$ lprm 123↵
$
```

The `lprm` command can be used to cancel all jobs by a particular user on a printer. To cancel all the jobs on the system printer:

```
$ lprm -P printer -↵
$
```

The minus sign alone is used to mean the current user.

PRINTING FROM PROGRAMS AND COMMANDS (REDIRECTION TO PRINTER)

The `lp` and `lpr` commands can accept the data to print from stdin—through redirection or via a pipe. This function is commonly used to print the output of a program. In the following examples, `lp` will be used; `lpr` is also valid if that is the command available to you. Instead of sending a manual page to the screen or to a file, we can print it:

```
$ man lp | lp              Print manual page for the lp command on the printer
$
```

Will print the manual page for the `lp` command on the default printer. I can replace the more at the end of the multiple-command pipe example from the section on redirection:

```
$ find / -name "*" -print | sort | lp -d my_lan_ptr↵
$
```

Instead of the sorted output of find coming to the screen, it goes to the printer. The output from stdout can also be sent to a printer through redirection:

```
$ find / -name "*" -print > /dev/lp0↵
$
```

stdout will now go to the printer connected as the device /dev/lp0. In reality, it will go through a queue connected to that device so that a single process does not tie up the device during long wait or processing portions of the program.

Printing a file that contains mainframe (ASA) printer control characters in the first character position is a problem under UNIX because the operating system does not interpret them for the printer. Appendix B (Hints and Techniques) contains the program filter_asa.c, written in the C programming language, that will convert from ASA to ASCII printer control. The program can handle flat sequential (no record separators) and line sequential files by detecting the name by which it is executed. It can be used as a filter or will operate on an existing file if specified on the command line.

```
$ filter_asa asa_print_file | lp↵                    filter file & print
$
```

Will convert a sequential file with ASA control characters to ANSI printer control and send the result to the default printer. The converted report can be stored in a file for review or printing at a later time:

```
$ filter_asa asa_print_file > /a/new/file/CVTED↵
$
```

IDCAMS REPLACEMENT

The mainframe IDCAMS utility is part of AMS (the Access Method Services) and is used to create and delete Generation Data Groups and VSAM datasets. Since those types of files are foreign to UNIX, there is no direct replacement for the utility. This example shows many of the functions that IDCAMS is used for:

```
//IDCAMS    EXEC PGM=IDCAMS
//SYSOUT    DD SYSOUT=*
//SYSPRINT DD SYSOUT=*
//SYSIN     DD *
 DEF GDG (NAME(A.GDG.NAME) LIM(3))
 LISTCAT -
    ENTRIES(FILES.TO.LIST) ALL
 DELETE    A.GDG.SPECIFIC.GENERATION.G0001V00 PURGE
 DELETE    THE.ENTIRE.GDG.INCLUDING.BASE
     GENERATIONDATAGROUP PURGE
/*
```

CREATING AND DELETING GENERATION DATA GROUPS

Since Generation Data Groups are so important to the behavior of many applications, Appendix B (Hints and Techniques) has three KornShell scripts that implement them. Those files are:

gdg_idcm.ksh — Used to create a Generation Data Group (the GDG base file). Corresponds to IDCAMS DEFINE GDG.

gdg_use.ksh — Used to determine specific filename based on bias (0, +1, -1), name with specific generation attached (G1234V00), or name without bias or generation (GDG group - concatenate all generations together). Corresponds to JCL GDG processing.

gdg_del.ksh — Used to delete specific file name based on bias (0, -1, etc.), name with specific generation attached (G1234V00), or name without bias or generation (all generations). To remove the Generation Data Group itself, the rm command is used to remove the GDG base file. Corresponds to IDCAMS DELETE.

To create a GDG with the name /appdata/payroll/employee/PAY, the following command is executed:

```
$ cd /appdata/payroll/employee↵                Go to proper directory
$ gdg_idcm.ksh PAY 3 ↵                         Create GDG group
$ ls -al PAY*↵                                 Look at directory
-rw-r--r--   1 dhorvath users                  13 Feb 11 18:21 PAY.gdgbase
$ more PAY*↵                                   Look at contents of GDG control file
3 0000 0000
$
```

The first command creates the base to control the GDG files once they are created. The file contains thirteen bytes (as shown by the `ls -al` command), which consists of three fields. The first field is the number of generations allowed, the second is the highest generation in existence, and the last field is the lowest generation. The last field is used for information only and is not important to the processing of the other scripts. To create the next GDG file, the gdg_use.ksh script is used with the parameter of the file and bias:

```
$ gdg_use.ksh PAY +1 ↵                         Create next generation
$ ls -al PAY*↵                                 Look at directory
-rw-r--r--   1 dhorvath users                   0 Feb 11 18:23 PAY.G0001V00
-rw-r--r--   1 dhorvath users                  13 Feb 11 18:23 PAY.gdgbase
$ more PAY*↵                                   Look at contents of control file
3 0001 0000
$
```

The first generation of the GDG was created with a length of zero bytes and the control file (base) was updated to show the highest generation of one. You may wonder how your program will know to use the file PAY.G0001V00; this will be covered in chapter 4 (JCL, PROCs, and CLIST's become Shell Scripts). Essentially, there is a way to replace mainframe DD statements and when doing so, the gdg_use.ksh command will be used to create and report the proper file name. Notice that a bias of +1 was used to create the next generation, the script will accept biases of 0 for latest version, -1 for previous version, -2 for prior to previous version, etc.

The last script will delete generations:

```
$ gdg_del.ksh PAY 0 ↵                          Delete latest generation
$ ls -al PAY*↵                                 Look at directory
-rw-r--r--   1 dhorvath users                  13 Feb 11 18:25 PAY.gdgbase
$ more PAY*↵                                   Look at contents of control file
3 0000 0000
$
```

The gdg_del.ksh script deleted the latest version of the GDG. To delete all generations, the bias (0) would be left off. It takes one more command to actually delete the entire GDG:

```
$ rm PAY.gdgbase↵                              Delete the GDG base
$ ls -al PAY*↵                                 Look at directory
PAY*: No such file or directory
$
```

Creating and Deleting VSAM Datasets

Many tools have replacements for VSAM datasets. ISAM and relative record (direct access) files are common among the COBOL languages available for UNIX. Sequential files are part of native UNIX. The most common uses of IDCAMS with VSAM files is the allocation of empty space and deletion of files no longer needed.

Typically, after running the IDCAMS utility to allocate or create a VSAM dataset, a program (usually written in COBOL) is run to load the data into the new dataset. Under UNIX, the program that was written to load the VSAM dataset can be converted to load an ISAM file; the disk space is automatically allocated by the operating system as needed. For VSAM Relative Record datasets, a direct access file is created and space is automatically allocated as needed as data is loaded into the file.

When creating an ISAM file, the tools typically create two files, the data file and the index file. If the name of the data file is /appdata/payroll/employee/ADDRESSES or /appdata/payroll/employee/ADDRESSES.dat, the index will be stored in /appdata/payroll/employee/ADDRESSES.idx. Direct access files do not have any special naming conventions.

To delete an ISAM file, it is important to delete both the data and the index portions. Wildcards can be used or you can specify the individual files; I prefer to specify them since it is safer. Deleting ADDRESSES* is fine so long as there is not a file ADDRESSES_WORK. The commands to delete the ADDRESSES ISAM file are:

```
$ pwd ↵                                    Determine current directory
/appdata/payroll/employee
$ rm ADDRESSES↵                            Delete ISAM data
$ rm ADDRESSES.dat↵                        Delete ISAM data—some tools
$ rm ADDRESSES.idx↵                        Delete ISAM index
$ ls -al ADDRESSES*↵                       Look at directory
ADDRESSES*: No such file or directory
$
```

Some of the tools have utilities to load data from sequential files into ISAM or create empty ISAM files if the application has a requirement. In Microfocus COBOL, the utilities are fhutil and fhcreate respectively.

ISPF SDSF or IOF Replacement

There are two applications that run under ISPF that are used to show the status of jobs in the input queue, executing, and in the output queue. These applications may also provide information about CPU usage and access to the system console log.

For SDSF, the first screen encountered is the Primary Option Menu shown in Screen 3.23.

UNIX provides equivalents to the DA option (display active users), I (jobs in input queue), and O (jobs in output queue). It has nothing close to the H option (held output jobs) because files are not held in the queue or spool—they are stored as disk files. The DA option is shown in Screen 3.24.

Screen 3.23 - ISPF SDSF Primary Option Menu

```
VIRSM2 ---------------------- SDSF PRIMARY OPTION MENU --------------------------

COMMAND INPUT  ===>                                        SCROLL  ===>  CSA

    TYPE AN OPTION OR COMMAND AND PRESS ENTER.


    DA              - Display active users of the system
    I               - Display jobs in the JES2 input queue
    O               - Display jobs in the JES2 output queue
    H               - Display jobs in the JES2 held output queue
    ST              - Display status of jobs in the JES2 queue

    TUTOR           - Short course on SDSF (ISPF only)
    END             - Exit SDSF

                            Use help key for more information.

           5665-488 (C) COPYRIGHT IBM CORP. 1981, 1991. ALL RIGHTS RESERVED
```

Screen 3.24 - ISPF SDSF Display Active

```
SDSF DA SYSC PAGING   51.62 SIO 1263.58 CPU  77.50%      LINE 1-1 (1)

 COMMAND INPUT ===>                                        SCROLL ===> CSR

 NP JOBNAME STEPNAME PROCSTEP TYPE JNUM  OWNER  C POS DP PGN REAL PAGING SI
    DBHDBH   TESTDB2  WTBN     TSU  6824 DBHDBH    IN 8F 65  188   0.00  0.
```

Scrolling the screen right will provide the following statistics:

```
NP JOBNAME PGN PAGING   SIO   CPU%  ASID ASIDX EXCP-CNT   CPU-TIME  SR DMN
   DBHDBH  65   0.00   0.00  0.18    85  0055    7,518      16.24        2
```

ps COMMAND

The closest UNIX equivalent to SDSF is the `ps` command which reports process status. To determine which processes you are running, issue the following command:

```
$ ps↵                                   Default process status
   PID TTY     TIME COMMAND
 17937 pts/4   0:00 ps
 17857 pts/4   0:08 -ksh
$
```

It does not look like I am doing very much at the moment. I have two processes running with process id (used to uniquely identify every process in the system) numbers of 17937 and 17857, both attached to the same terminal (pts/4). The `ps` command did not use very much CPU time (reported as 0 minutes, 0 seconds). The process known as ksh has used a total of eight seconds since it started. To get more information, use the `-f` (for full listing) option:

```
$ ps -f↵                               Full process status
UID       PID    PPID    C    STIME       TTY    TIME  COMMAND
dhorvath  17938  17857   22   19:36:43    pts/4  0:00  ps
dhorvath  17857  1       4    09:17:20    pts/4  0:08  -ksh
$
```

The full process status shows the same information as the default plus the userid, process id of the parent, processor utilization for scheduling, and start time. The parent process is the process that owns the current process. The `ps` command, process 17938 is owned by process 17857 which happens to be the shell processing commands that I type in. That parent of that process is process 1—the operating system. The lower the processor utilization number, the lower the amount of CPU the process is attempting to use. The `ps` command is using more CPU because it is active, `ksh` is using less because it is inactive waiting for the `ps` command to complete before it accepts more input.

By default, the `ps` command will only show your current process and any subprocesses that it owns. If you are using multiple terminals, have a terminal emulator running multiple sessions, or are running background processes, it will not show the other processes. Some versions of UNIX support a `-u` flag followed by the userid you want to see. Another approach is to request information about every process (`-e` flag) and use another command to strip off the users you want to see:

```
$ ps -u dhorvath -f↵                  Full process status, all my processes
     UID   PID  PPID  C    STIME TTY     TIME COMMAND
dhorvath 17983     1 81 21:03:04 pts/6   0:04 -ksh
dhorvath 17987 17857 47 21:03:19 pts/4   0:01 ps
dhorvath 17857     1  4 09:17:20 pts/4   0:08 -ksh
$
```

```
$ ps -e -f | grep dhorvath↵           Full process status, all processes
dhorvath 17983     1 81 21:03:04 pts/6   0:04 -ksh
```

```
dhorvath 18000 17857 46 21:05:34 pts/4  0:01 ps
dhorvath 18001 17857  4 21:05:34 pts/4  0:00 grep dhorvath
dhorvath 17857     1  4 09:17:20 pts/4  0:08 -ksh
$
```

Both commands produce the same result: showing all current processes owned by dhorvath. The second form pipes the output of `ps` into `grep` which is used for simple searches (more about `grep` later in this chapter). grep displays every line that contains the characters dhorvath. When using the `-f` option, you may see portions of the command line in the Command column.

At some installations, the SDSF DA screen allows you to view the active jobs of other users. The PREFIX command determines which active jobs are shown by searching for the specified characters in the beginning of the job name. The UNIX `ps` command can mimic SDSF DA PREFIX with the `-u` or `-e` flags. The `-u` flag will display processes owned by specified users and will accept a list of users separated by commas; it does not allow the use of wildcards. The `-e` flag will show all processes owned by all users and you can filter the users or processes through grep.

With either of these commands, it is possible to determine what someone else is doing by substituting their userid for dhorvath. This is one way to determine if a coworker is busy before you go over to chat about the game last night. It can also be used by the system administrator or a manager to ensure that the system is being used for productive work and not games or surfing the net.

There is one more option for `ps` that you may want to know, and that is the `-l` (long display):

Long process status

```
$ ps -l↵
  F S   UID   PID  PPID  C PRI NI ADR SZ:RSZ   WCHAN TTY    TIME COMD
  1 R   102 18004 17857 48  72 20  60  7: 10         pts/4  0:01 ps
  1 S   102 17857     1  3  40 20  f3 28:  6   4b7dc pts/4  0:10 -ksh
$
```

The columns that you have not already seen are F (Flags), S (process State), UID (user id number for process), PRI (process priority, lower numbers mean higher priority), NI (Nice value, default priority), ADR (Memory address of the process), SZ (size in blocks of memory image of process), RSZ (size in blocks of real memory used), WCHAN (wait channel—the event on which the process is waiting or sleeping), and the rest are the same for the `-f` (full) flag. You can combine `-l` and `-f`, either with `-u` or `-e`.

The values in the F (flags) are in octal and are additive (can be added together to create the resulting flag) with the following values:

01	In memory
02	System Process
04	Locked in memory (usually for a physical I/O)
10	Being swapped out of memory
20	Being traced by another process
40	Another flag used in tracing

The values in the S (process State) are mutually exclusive and can have the following values:

I	Intermediate (switching between modes)
O	Nonexistent process
R	Running (active)
S	Sleeping (waiting for an event)
T	Stopped
W	Waiting (waiting for I/O)
X	Growing (waiting for more memory)
Z	Terminated (shutting down)

Based on these flags and states, the command shell is in memory and sleeping (waiting for the ps command to complete); the ps command is in memory and actively running. There can be many processes in a Run state; most will be in Sleep or Wait state.

Because a user can have multiple shells running at any one time, on many systems the `ps` command will flag the login shell with a minus sign prefix. The command `-ksh` is a login shell; running a command procedure may invoke `ksh` or another shell as a sub-shell which would be shown as just ksh.

Missing from the output of the `ps` command is an indication of how busy the computer happens to be. That information is available through the `uptime` or `w -u` commands:

```
$ uptime↵
  08:36AM  up 13 days,   1:08,  5 users,  load average: 0.96, 1.12, 1.08
$ w -u↵
  08:36AM  up 13 days,   1:08,  5 users,  load average: 0.96, 1.12, 1.08
```

Both of these commands produce the same output. The first column is the current time; time since last system reboot follows in days, hours, and minutes; the number of users is reported and then the number of processes running. The load average is the average number of processes waiting to run over the last 1, 5, and 15 minutes.

The SDSF output queue functions, shown in Screen 3.25, can be replaced with the lpstat command. The purpose of both is to show jobs printing or waiting to print. Although the amount of information displayed differs between the two systems, the functions performed are essentially equivalent.

The following example of the `lpstat` command was run on a different system than the examples in the UNIX Print Status Commands (`lpstat` and `lpq`) section above. The information shown is the same but the queues are different:

```
$ lpstat↵
Queue     Dev    Status     Job    Files       User      PP  %  Blks Cp Rnk
-----     ---    ------     ---    -----       ----      -   -  ---   -  -
hppcl     lp0    RUNNING    435    .profile    dhorvath  2  59   3    1  1
bsh       bshde  READY
lands     lp0    READY
hpps      lp0    READY
techser   lpeps  READY
techser   techs  READY
```

Screen 3.25 - ISPF SDSF Display Output Jobs

```
SDSF OUPUT ALL CLASSES  ALL FORMS    LINES 1      LINE 0-0 (1)
 COMMAND INPUT ===>                                      SCROLL ===> CSR
 NP JOBNAME    PRT-REC  TOT-PAGE  PRT-PAGE DEVICE    STATUS    SECLABEL SYSID
     ABCDEF     1,000         15        20   PRT3     ACTIVE                CPU3
```

Scrolling the screen right will provide the following statistics:

```
SDSF OUPUT ALL CLASSES  ALL FORMS    LINES 1      LINE 0-0 (1)
COMMAND INPUT ===>                                      SCROLL ===> CSR
NP JOBNAME    RMT  NODE O-GRP-N  OGID1 OGID2 JP UCS  WTR  FLASH BURST PRMODE
    ABCDEF                                                  N     N
```

Scrolling the screen right will provide the following statistics:

```
SDSF OUPUT ALL CLASSES  ALL FORMS    LINES 1      LINE 0-0 (1)
COMMAND INPUT ===>                                      SCROLL ===> CSR
NP JOBNAME  T PRMODE   ODISP CRDATE   OHR OUTPUT-HOLD-TEXT
   ABCDEF
```

```
datactr    eps31 READY
datactr_prt: no entries
cobol      cob1  READY
cobol      cob2  READY
cobol      cob3  READY
cobol      cob4  READY
cobol      cob5  READY
cobol      cob6  READY
cobol      cob7  READY
cobol      cob8  READY
$
```

On some systems, batch processing or resource queues are implemented the same way as print queues and appear in the lpstat output. On a system with a limited number of licenses for the COBOL compiler, access can be restricted to the license limits through the use of queues. Since the compilation is a small part of the time involved in developing a program, it makes sense to set up queues that will feed resources. Twenty programmers could be coding and when they compile, they share one of the eight licenses; if there are more than eight compile requests submitted, only eight will run at any one time; as resources are freed, other requests will be processed.

The other alternative is for each programmer to sign out or reserve a license, compile their program, then sign in (unreserve) the license. But because the compile time is short compared to the rest of the work involved, the licenses will be tied up unnecessarily, possibly resulting in the work of other programmers being delayed. Some vendors have implemented such a system with a license manager that prevents more than the licensed number of users from accessing a tool.

In the lpstat example above, there is one queue cobol and eight resources that it feeds: cob1 through cob8. The programmer submits a compile request to cobol and it is dispatched to one of the resources.

who, finger, AND *w* COMMANDS

There are three commands that are useful in determining who is on the system (interactive users): who, finger, and w. who is available on all versions of UNIX, finger is part of the TCP/IP suite of tools, and w is available on most versions of UNIX. Without options, the who command will show the userid, terminal, date, and time of signon and where the connection came from:

```
$ who↵
dhorvath   pts/4        Feb 11 09:17     (TS9.SERVR.EDU)
dhorvath   pts/6        Feb 11 21:03     (TS9.SERVR.EDU)
$
```

Since it is Sunday evening, I am the only one on the system. Adding the flag -u will show the process id and time since last activity:

```
$ who -u↵
dhorvath   pts/4        Feb 11 09:17   .     17857       (TS9.SERVR.EDU)
dhorvath   pts/6        Feb 11 21:03  0:17   17983       (TS9.SERVR.EDU)
$
```

The first session is active—I just entered the who -u command, the second has been sitting idle for 17 minutes. The process ids correspond to those from the ps command examples above. There is a special form of the who command:

```
$ who am i↵                            Not a song ...
dhorvath   pts/4        Feb 11 09:17   .     17857       (TS9.SERVR.EDU)
$
```

Which is useful if you come upon a logged in terminal with no one around or if you have several userids and are not sure which one is logged in on a particular session.

The who command has several other options that are very useful in determining system status:

```
$ who -b↵
     .        system boot  Nov 14 20:33
$ who -t↵
     .        old time     Feb  4 03:04
     .        new time     Feb  4 03:04
$
```

The -b flag shows when the system was last rebooted and the -t flag shows the last time the system clock was changed.

The default `finger` command displays information similar to the `who -u` command:

```
$ finger↵
Login        Name                 TTY        Idle    When      Where
dhorvath David . Horvath          pts/4             Sun 09:17  TS9.SERVR.EDU
dhorvath David . Horvath          pts/6      0:17   Sun 21:03  TS9.SERVR.EDU
$
```

The `w` command provides a summary of current system activity. The `w` command with the `-u` option was used above to show system uptime. The default operation of the command is probably the most useful:

```
$ w↵
  08:36AM  up 13 days,   1:08,  5 users,  load average: 0.96, 1.12, 1.08
User      tty     login@     idle     JCPU    PCPU    what
another   pts/0   11:23PM    6:07     0       0       ksh
thisuser  pts/1   30Jan96    3days    875:59  1       -ksh
dhorvath  pts/2   08:50AM    0        23      0       w
yourid    pts/6   08:44AM    2:40     1:17    0       -ksh
another   pts/8   09:02AM    1        23      0       vi
$
```

The heading line is the same as the output of the `uptime` or `w -u` commands. The remainder of the summary is one line per user (if a signon has multiple sessions, they are effectively different users) consisting of the user name, the terminal they are using, the date or time they logged in, the length of time the terminal has been idle (thisuser signed on January 30 and has not done anything for three days), the total amount of CPU time used by all processes connected to the terminal (JCPU), the CPU time used by the current process (PCPU), and finally the current command. A user sitting at the command prompt will show their default shell (-ksh for the user thisuser and you); a user executing a subshell may show that subshell or a process that the subshell has invoked (ksh being run by user another).

ISPF FOREGROUND PROCESSES AND COMMAND REPLACEMENTS

The ISPF Foreground Processes menu presents you with a series of functions that you can execute interactively. Most installations allow compilations, DB2, and other special commands to run at the same priority as the user's TSO/ISPF session. Screen 3.26 shows a typical ISPF Foreground Processes menu. The contents of the menu on your system may vary as installations differ in what they allow to be run in the foreground; the system programmer can configure the menu as desired.

The transitional editors uni-SPF and SPF/UX provide similar screens. uni-SPF provides for system administrator defined menu selections (common tasks) as well as selections you define (private tasks). SPF/UX implements two levels of menus where the system administrator defines the selections available at the top level and you can define a set of UNIX commands to execute. The uni-SPF screen is shown in Screen 3.27 because it is simpler; the SPF/UX screen is visually different but functionally similar.

Screen 3.26 - ISPF Foreground Commands

```
--------------------------  FOREGROUND SELECTION MENU  ---------------------------

OPTION  ===>

Userid        - DBHDBH      Date - 95/02/13  (95.044)  Version  - ISPF 3.5
Procedure     - PROCISPF    Time - 07:31               System   - CPU4

1A ASSEMBLER PANELS
2A COBOL VS & COBOL II PANELS
1  ASSEMBLE AND LINK
2  COBOL VS (R2.4) COMPILE AND LINK
3  LINKAGE EDITOR
4  FORTRAN H COMPILE AND LNK
5  SPUFI
6  IMS MAPS - PSB/DBD MAPPING
7  LISTVTOC PACK OR DATSETS (IEHLIST)
9  C LANGUAGE  COMPILE AND LINK
Z  EASYTRIEVE
```

Screen 3.27 - uni-SPF Foreground Commands

```
----------------------------------  FOREGROUND  ----------------------------------
OPTION  ===>
  PARM  ===> /u/dhorvath                          E TO EDIT A TASK
COMMON TASKS                                   PRIVATE TASKS
  1 ===> Build Release                         21 ===> ls
  2 ===> Start Database                        22 ===> ps -f
  3 ===> Stop Database                         23 ===> cc
  4 ===> C SQL Precompiler                     24 ===> cob
  5 ===> COBOL SQL Precompiler                 25 ===> who -u
  6 ===> FORTRAN                               26 ===> w
  7 ===> FORTRAN SQL Precompiler               27 ===>
  8 ===> SQL Query                             28 ===>
  9 ===> Database Administrator Tool           29 ===>
 10 ===>                                       30 ===>
 11 ===>                                       31 ===>
 12 ===>                                       32 ===>
 13 ===>                                       33 ===>
 14 ===>                                       34 ===>
 15 ===>                                       35 ===>
 16 ===>                                       36 ===>
 17 ===>                                       37 ===>
 18 ===>                                       38 ===>
 19 ===>                                       39 ===>
```

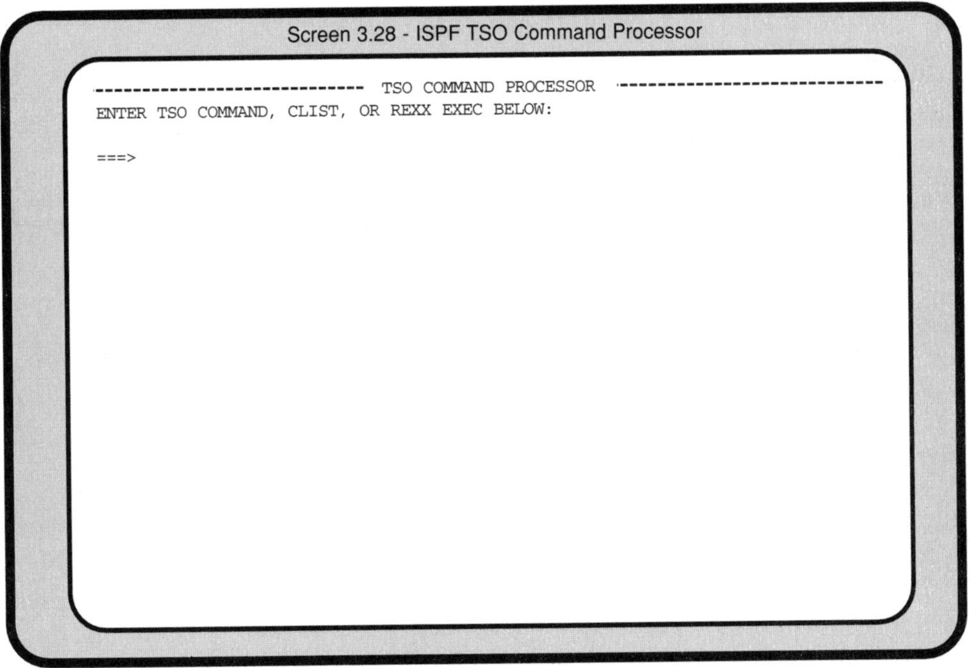

Screen 3.28 - ISPF TSO Command Processor

Most of the time however, UNIX commands are entered at the command line (as shown in the examples earlier in this chapter). The command line is available outside of the transitional editors. The ISPF Command Screen looks almost exactly like the Command screens in uni-SPF and SPF/UX. The screen allows input of a command (TSO for ISPF, UNIX for the transitional editors) and the command output will appear on the screen. The ISPF Command Screen is shown in Screen 3.28.

Any valid UNIX command can be entered at the prompt. While playing around, I went to uni-SPF screen 6, typed in spfux, went to screen 6, typed in unispf, went to screen 6, and typed in ps. I had several copies of SPF/UX and uni-SPF running. Most of the commands shown in this book can also be entered on the command screen.

In addition, the transitional editors allow the use of the exclamation point <!> to issue a UNIX command. At any of the command prompts like the following:

```
-------------- uni-SPF MAIN MENU ---------------
 COMMAND ==> ! ls↵
```

Or:

```
SPF/UX --------------- PRIMARY OPTION MENU ------------- VER 02.05
 OPTION ===> ! ls↵
```

Gives You:

```
bin      c_stuff cobol_stuff

HIT ENTER KEY TO CONTINUE
```

Pressing the <enter> key at this point will return you to the prompt where you entered the command. You can also get a sub-shell which will allow you to enter multiple commands:

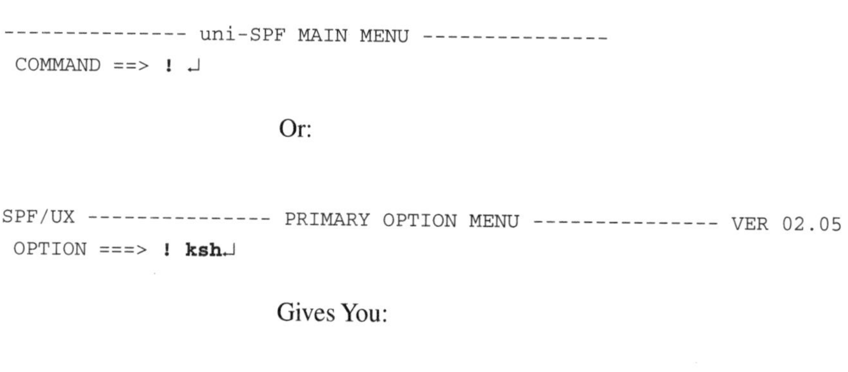

```
--------------- uni-SPF MAIN MENU ---------------
 COMMAND ==> ! ↵
```

Or:

```
SPF/UX --------------- PRIMARY OPTION MENU --------------- VER 02.05
 OPTION ===> ! ksh↵
```

Gives You:

```
$
$ exit↵
```

Leave sub-shell and return to original prompt

Either way, a sub-shell is invoked which allows you to enter any command—including starting up another copy of the transitional editor! Be careful not to sub-shell too much until you are comfortable with the idea; I have seen even experienced UNIX professionals get confused whether they had left the original editor or they were in a sub-shell. The `exit` command leaves a shell—it does not care if it is a sub-shell or the original login shell. So you could accidentally logout without expecting to.

ISPF Background Processes and Batch Submit Replacements

The ISPF Background Processes menu presents you with a series of functions that you can execute in background or batch mode. Most installations prefer that compilations and long DB2 queries run as a batch job which typically run at a lower priority than the user TSO/ISPF session. The system can also limit the number of batch jobs running simultaneously while being largely unable to do so with interactive processes. The ISPF Edit and Browse screens allow you to submit the dataset in the current session to run as a batch job. Screen 3.29 shows a typical ISPF Background Processes menu. The contents of the menu on your system may vary as installations differ in what they allow to be run in the foreground; the system programmer can configure the menu as desired.

The transitional editor uni-SPF provides a similar screen. uni-SPF provides for system administrator-defined menu selections (common tasks) as well as selections you define (private tasks). The uni-SPF screen is not shown since it looks exactly like the Foreground Processes screen shown in Screen 3.27.

Screen 3.29 - ISPF Background Commands

```
-----------------------  BACKGROUND JOB SELECTION MENU  -----------------------
OPTION ===>

Userid       - DBHDBH     Date - 95/02/13  (95.044)    Version  - ISPF 3.5
Procedure    - PROCISPF    Time - 07:31                 System   - CPU4

1A ASSEMBLER PANELS                        8  MAP GENERATION
2A COBOL VS & COBOL II PANELS              9  C LANGUAGE COMPILE AND LINK
1  ASSEMBLE AND LINK                       A  TURNOVER OF FINAL COMPILE/ASSEMBLY
2  COBOL VS(R2.4) COMPILE AND LINK         C  COMPARE SOURCE OR PDS DATASET
3  LINKAGE EDITOR                          D  REQUEST DISK SPACE / TAPE GDG'S
4  ABC GENS AND/OR MOVES                   E  DMAINT FAS COPY MODULE UTILITY
5  DEF - DIF/DOF/MID/MOD/GENERATION        F  FORTRAN H COMPILE AND LINK
6  IMS MAPS - PSB/DBD MAPPING
7  LISTVTOC PACK OR DATSETS (IEHLIST)

   JOB CARDS:
   ==> //JOBNAME JOB (ACCOUNT INFORMATION)
   ==> //*
   ==>
```

UNIX provides facilities to run jobs in the background in a batch mode. While the typical UNIX installation does not have the extensive range of queues and batch processing that a mainframe does, it does have facilities that are quite sufficient and in some ways better.

To run a command or command procedure in the background from your terminal, you enter:

```
$ pwd↵                                        Where are we?
/u/yourid                                     In your home directory
$ find / -name "*" -ls > find.out &↵
[1]     28
$ ↵
[1] +  Done          find . -name "*" -ls > find.out &
```

Since find takes a long time to run when checking the entire system, this example runs it in the background using the ampersand character <&>. The message after the find shows that this is our first background job by the [1] and it has process id 28. The process id shows up on displays from the ps command. Then the prompt appears. Eventually, the job will complete and the final message will appear the next time the enter key is pressed. If there was an error, the code would be shown in parentheses after the Done message. The command is repeated so you can determine which job completed. Generally, you redirect the output of commands to a file so the output does not appear on your screen intermixed with your interactive output.

You can have many jobs running in the background at one time. On most systems, the bgnice option is enabled, which causes background jobs to run nice. Nice is not a synonym for good or well in this context, it is a command that changes the priority of processes. Except for super-users, the nice command can only be used to lower the priority that a process runs at. The find command in the previous example may run longer because it gets less of the CPU, but it will also impact co-workers less.

You can disable `bgnice` with the following command:

```
$ set +o bgnice↵
$
```

To re-enable it, enter the following command:

```
$ set -o bgnice↵
$
```

Multiple commands can be piped together in a background job and other redirection can be used:

```
$ find / -name "*" -ls 2> /dev/null | sort | lp &↵
[1]     30
$ ↵
[1] +  Done          find / -name "*" -ls 2> /dev/null | sort &
```

I do not want to see all the messages about all the directories I am not allowed to see so I send them to the bit-bucket. The found files are sorted and then printed.

Job Control

When you start using background jobs regularly, you will want to know what jobs you have running. There are two ways: using the `ps` command and with:

```
$ jobs↵
[1] +  Running                find / -name "*" -ls > find.out &
$
```

jobs will show any jobs that are running in the background. You can move a background job back into the foreground (and raise its priority) by typing:

```
$ fg %1↵
find . -name "*" -ls 2> /dev/null | sort | lp
$
```

The original command will be echoed. When the command is done, it will return you to the original prompt. You can return a job to the background by suspending it by pressing the suspend key, usually <^Z> to halt the process and then using the `bg` command:

```
$ find / -name "*" -print >xxxyyy 2>/dev/null ↵
^Z                                                   Suspend process
[1] + Stopped (user)          find / -name "*" -print >xxxyyy 2>/dev/null
$ bg↵                                                Make a background job
[1]     find / -name "*" -print >xxxyyy 2>/dev/null&
$ jobs↵                                              Show background jobs
[1] +  Running                find / -name "*" -print >xxxyyy 2>/dev/null
$ ↵
[1] +  Done          find . -name "*" -print > xxxyy 2> /dev/null | sort &
```

The `find` command will run for a while. After entering it, I realized that I forgot to run it in the background and suspended it by pressing <^Z>. The `bg` command started the suspended job in the background and the jobs command verified that it was running. Eventually it will complete and the Done message appears.

If you are not getting the messages (stopped, running, done), the `monitor` option is probably turned off. To enable it, use the following command:

```
$ set -o monitor↵
$
```

Background Job Modifiers (nohup, nice, time, and timex Commands)

When you signoff a UNIX computer, any processes or background jobs are sent a signal known as HUP, which is a mnemonic for hangup. In most cases, this causes the processes to end. Having your long-running background jobs fail because your terminal emulator crashed or the network went down is annoying to say the least. Another command used with background jobs prevents them from detecting the HUP condition; in typical UNIX form, it is known as `nohup`. Some versions of `nohup` also automatically redirect stdout and stderr to a file that defaults to the name nohup.out in your current directory. The command:

```
$ nohup find / -name "*" -ls 2> /dev/null | sort > find.log &↵
[1]     35
$ ↵
[1] +  Done       nohup find . -name "*" -ls 2> /dev/null | sort > find.log &
```

Will run the find command, discard error messages, pipe stdout into sort and then into lp with any output messages stored in find.log. All this occurs in the background, and the processes are immune to the HUP signal. You can still cancel the background using the `kill` command described below.

To determine how long a background process takes, you have several choices. The `time` and `timex` commands are the most common. In their simplest forms, without any options, they produce the same information in slightly different forms:

```
$ time ls > /dev/null↵

real    0m0.07s
user    0m0.01s
sys     0m0.05s
$ timex ls > /dev/null↵

real        0.07
user        0.02
sys         0.04

$
```

Both `ls` commands send their output to the bit-bucket since it is not important to the example here. `time` breaks the time reports into minutes and seconds, `timex` reports seconds only. `real` is another term for elapsed or wall time, or how long the process took to complete. `user` is the amount of CPU time spent in user mode, that is, running your command or code. `sys` is the amount of CPU time spent in system mode that is used for performing all I/O operations. The total CPU time used is determined by adding the user and sys time; resulting in 0.06 seconds in this example.

There may be slight differences between the CPU time distribution between the time and timex commands, but this should not be of any concern. There will be some variance, especially with short-running commands because the numbers are so small. Use whichever one on your system and you will get consistent results. If both are available, choose one and use it consistently. On multiprocessor systems, it is possible for user and sys times to total higher than the real time because there can be more than one CPU working on the problem.

The `nice` command can be used with interactive and batch (foreground and background) processes. It is used to lower the priority of a particular command or shell script that may hog system resources. As the name implies, you use it to be `nice` to other system users.

```
$ nice ls > /dev/null↵
$
```

The command being run under `nice` may take more elapsed time to run. By default, `nice` uses the increment of 10. You can specify an increment of 1 to 19, the higher the value, the lower the priority:

```
$ nice -19 ls > /dev/null↵
$
```

will run the slowest. The `nohup`, `nice`, `time`, and `timex` commands can all be combined together.

Canceling Background Jobs and Commands

The `kill` command allows you to cancel background jobs and executing commands. To end a background job or command, you can use the job number as follows:

```
$ nohup find / -name "*" -ls 2> /dev/null | sort > find.log &↵
[1]     42
$ kill %1↵
[1] +  Terminated   nohup find / -name "*" -ls 2> /dev/null | sort > find.log &
$
```

The job number is specified with a percent sign <%> as a prefix for this form of the `kill` command. There are other uses for the `kill` command in Chapter 5 (Advanced Shell Script and Commands).

The job number is prefixed with a percent sign <%>. You can also use the process id reported when the job was started or is shown by the `ps` command. The following example shows the `kill` command with the process id:

```
$ nohup find / -name "*" -ls 2> /dev/null > find.log &↵
[1]     5835
$ jobs↵
[1] +  Running    nohup find / -name "*" -ls 2> /dev/null > find.log &
$ ps↵
   PID     TTY   TIME CMD
  5835   pts/0   0:00 find / -name * -ls
 26054   pts/0   0:00 -ksh
 60766   pts/0   0:00 ps
$ kill 5835↵
$ ps↵
   PID     TTY   TIME CMD
 26054   pts/0   0:00 -ksh
 30574   pts/0   0:00 ps
[1] + 5835  Done(1)  nohup find / -name "*" -ls 2> /dev/null > find.log &
$
```

The process id is reported when the job is started in the background and can be located through the `ps` command.

By default, the `kill` command sends the SIGTERM (terminate signal) to the specified process. This should cause the process to begin a normal shutdown (end transactions, close files, and perform an orderly exit). However, SIGTERM can be ignored. If a process does not exit after using the default kill command, you can force a process to shutdown through the use of SIGKILL (value 9).

You can even end your current session by killing your shell. However, the shell is smart enough to ignore a signal to terminate, so to really end it, you have to send the SIGKILL signal. The following example shows ksh ignoring SIGTERM and the different ways you can specify the signal to use:

```
$ ps↵                                    Display current processes
   PID    TTY   TIME CMD
  7716  pts/0   0:00 ps
 26054  pts/0   0:00 -ksh
$ kill 26054↵                            Kill (SIGTERM) my login - ignored!
$ kill -15 26054↵                        Kill (SIGTERM) my login - ignored!
$ kill -TERM 26054↵                      Kill (SIGTERM) my login - ignored!
$ kill -9 26054↵                         Kill (SIGKILL) my login
```

Notice that there is no prompt after the final `kill` command: ksh did not ignore SIGKILL and exited, which ended the session. Warning: This is not a good way to log out! It could cause any subprocesses to exit immediately without cleaning up after themselves. The `trap` command in Korn shell can be used to catch (trap) signals from the `kill` command.

JOB SCHEDULING—crontab AND at COMMANDS AND THE cron DAEMON

UNIX provides facilities for job scheduling. Jobs can be scheduled to run once at a specified time or repeatedly on a periodic basis (specific dates and time or a combination of hourly, daily, monthly, and annually). This facility is provided by the cron daemon (cron is short for Chronos, the Greek god of time). A daemon is a system-related background process that runs with the permissions of root and services requests from other processes. The mainframe VTAM (the Virtual Terminal Access Method, which controls connected terminals) would be considered a daemon under UNIX. Daemons are typically started when the system is booted, although they can be shutdown and restarted by the system administrator as needed.

The cron daemon schedules events for `crontab`, `at`, and `sync`. The `crontab` command is used to edit, submit, review, and cancel schedules submitted to cron. Not all versions of UNIX have the `crontab` command; in those cases, the table of schedules for cron is maintained in a text editor, usually by the system administrator. The format of the table does not change whether `crontab` is used or not. The `at` command is used to submit, review, and cancel scheduled jobs. It is used when the job will run one-time only or on an intermittent basis that precludes regular scheduling. The `sync` command is run by cron approximately once a minute to ensure the integrity of the filesystems. The operating system buffers output to the disk in memory and `sync` flushes those buffers to the disk. To improve performance, frequently used directories and the inode tables are buffered in memory, and as files are created, extended, or removed, the buffers change, but only in memory. User files are also buffered in memory and written out to disk when the buffers are full or flushed. By flushing the buffers to disk periodically, the possibility of damage to the filesystem and user files due to a system crash is minimized.

One of the last things the system administrator (or more likely, a shell script) does before a system is rebooted or the power turned off is to execute the `sync` command. It is so important that the sync command is typically run three times in succession, although there is no guarantee that the buffers are actually written to the disk when the `sync` command completes due to system scheduling. Running the command three times ensures that the physical writes are complete.

cron table Format

The format of a cron or `crontab` file is a series of entries that consist of a line with six fields separated by spaces or tabs that contain, in order:

minute to start (0 to 59)
hour to start (0 to 23)
day of month (1 through 31 depending on month)
month of year (1 through 12)
day of week (0 for Sunday through 6 for Saturday)
shell command to execute

The scheduling fields (time and date) can contain one of the following:

a number in the range shown
two numbers separated by a hyphen for an inclusive range
a series of numbers separated by commas
an asterisk <*> to denote all possible values.

The jobs are scheduled for a particular day based on these rules:

when the month, day, and day of week all contain an asterisk, the command executes every day
when the day and day of week are both specified, the command executes when they match
when the month and day are both specified, the command executes when they match
when the day of week is specified, the command executes on those days
when the month, day, and day of week are all specified, the command executes when they match

The command specified in the sixth field is run at the selected date and time. To include both command and stdin input, place the percent sign <%> between the command and the input. Blank lines and lines with the pound sign <#> as the first non-blank character will be ignored.

Multiple commands can be executed at the same time through use of the semicolon command separator <;>, the pipe character <|> or by executing a command procedure that contains multiple commands.

When the cron daemon runs a job, it runs as a subshell in the home directory of the submitter. If you are not logged on, any settings in your .profile file will not take effect. If you have any settings in your .profile that your job needs, you must run .profile in a command procedure with the command you are running. The .profile file is executed when you login to configure your account (similar to the MS/PC-DOS AUTOEXEC.BAT). There is more information about this file in Chapter 7 (Account Configuration).

The cron table entry to run a command at 3:30 AM every day would be:

```
30 03 * * * find / -name "*" -ls | sort
```

The cron table entry to tell you the weekend begins at 4:45 PM every Friday would be:

```
45 16 * * 5 echo The Weekend Begins NOW!  > 'tty'
```

The cron table entry to welcome you to work every workday at 9:30 AM would be:

```
30 9 * * 1-5 echo Good Morning!  > 'tty'
```

The cron table entry to determine who is signed on every Monday and Friday in June and September at 8:30 AM would be:

```
30 8 * 6,9 1,5 who -u
```

The cron table entry to send a message to everyone signed on at 4:00 PM on every Friday in December between the tenth and thirty-first would be:

```
0 16 10-31 12 5 /usr/sbin/wall%Happy Holidays!%Be Happy and Safe.
```

defines stdin to the wall command as:

```
Happy Holidays!
```

and

```
Be Happy and Safe.
```

crontab Command

The `crontab` command is used to manipulate cron tables. If your installation does not have this command, the system administrator will manually maintain the table for cron for all users.

To determine the last time you updated your cron table, use the following command:

```
$ crontab -v↵
crontab file: dhorvath  submission time: Tue Feb 13 14:22:02 1996
$
```

If you do not have a cron table, you will get the following two messages:

```
Can't open yourfile in /usr/spool/cron/crontabs directory.
No such file or directory
```

You will not have a cron table if you never created one or you removed it. To look at the contents of your cron table:

```
$ crontab -l↵
30 03 * * * find / -name "*" -ls | sort
01 10 13 02 * echo "tested" | mail dhorvath
$
```

To remove (delete) your cron table, use the following command.

```
$ crontab -r↵
$
```

Use this command with caution as you will lose all entries. There are three ways to create or modify a cron table using the `crontab` command. One is to enter the `crontab` command alone and then enter the parameters:

```
$ crontab ↵
30 03 * * * find / -name "*" -ls | sort ↵
01 10 13 02 * echo "tested" | mail dhorvath ↵
^D                                                    end of file key
$
```

If you are not careful with this form of the `crontab` command, you can lose all entries as follows:

```
$ crontab ↵
^D                                                    end of file key
$
```

will result in a cron table with no entries. If you accidentally enter the `crontab` command and want to quit without affecting your cron table, use the interrupt key (usually <^C>).

Another way to modify your cron table is to create a file with the cron table entries and feed it to crontab. Assuming a file with the name cron.table:

```
$ crontab cron.table↵
$
```

The final way to maintain your cron table is to invoke `crontab` with the `-e` option as shown in Screen 3.30. This option causes crontab to invoke the editor allowing you to work with the file:

```
$ crontab -e↵
```

Press **<ESC>** followed by **:q!**↵ to exit the editor without saving the changes.

```
$
```

Usage of the visual editor is described in Chapter 6 (Editors). Review that section before using `crontab` with the `-e` option.

at Command

The `at` command is used to submit one-time or infrequently run jobs. cron runs jobs submitted by the `at` command. If your installation does not have this command, the system administrator can manually add the job to the cron table and remove it when done.

To submit a command procedure to `at` is simple, a single command is a little more complicated. The most complicated or confusing part of using the `at` command is specifying when to run. The at command accepts start time in several formats: using the `-t` flag, time, day, or increment.

When using the `-t` flag, the date variable is in the following format with values within [ ] being optional:

[[[[CC]YY]MM]DD]hhmm[.SS]
CC is the two digit century value
YY is the two-digit year value

Screen 3.30 - crontab -e Edit Screen (vi)

```
30 03 * * * find/ -name "*" -is | sort
01 10 13 02 * echo "tested" | mail dhorvath
~
~
~
~
~
~
~
~
~
~
~
~
~
~
~
~
~
~
~
~
"/tmp/crontab8s4DFW" 2 lines, 104 characters
```

MM is the two-digit month with the values 01 through 12
DD is the two-digit day of the month with the values 01 through 31 depending on month
hh is the two-digit hour within the day with the values 00 through 23
mm is the two-digit minute within the hour with the values 00 through 59
.SS is the two-digit second within the minute with the values .00 through .59

If the century and year are omitted, the current year is assumed. If the century is omitted and the year specified, the century will be set to 19 if the year is between 70 and 99 (1970–1999) and 20 if the year is between 00 and 37 (2000–2037). The default value for seconds is .00.

When using the time parameter, you specify the hour of the day or, using the colon <:> as a separator, hours:minutes. The suffixes am, pm, and zulu (Greenwich Mean Time or Coordinated Universal Time) can be applied to the value, otherwise the at command interprets the time provided using a 24-hour clock (hours 00 through 11 are AM, 12 through 23 are PM). You can also use noon, midnight, and now as times. A can be used for AM, P for PM, N for noon, and M for midnight.

The day parameter is optional and is specified as the month, name, and day number with an optional comma <,> followed by the year. It can also be specified as a day of week. The month name can be spelled out or abbreviated to three characters. The day of week can be spelled out or abbreviated to two characters. If you do not specify the day parameter, it will default to today if the time is later than the current time and to tomorrow if the time is earlier. If the month and day number are specified with the year omitted and are less than today, it will be treated as being next year.

The increment parameter involves the time now with an offset. After the word now, a plus sign <+> or the word next is used followed by a number and the units for that number. The units can be minute or minutes, hour or hours, day or days, week or weeks, month or months, and year or years.

To submit a command procedure to execute in 5 minutes:

```
$ at now +5 minutes command_procedure↵
job dhorvath.824244537.a will be run at Tue Feb 13 15:48:57 1996
$
```

To submit a command procedure that will execute on my wife's birthday:

```
$ at 10:00 Aug 12 command_procedure↵
job dhorvath.824244540.a will be run at Mon Aug 12 10:00:00 1996
$
```

To view jobs submitted with the `at` command that are pending, use the following command:

```
$ at -l↵
dhorvath.824244537.a        Tue Feb 13 15:48:57 1996
dhorvath.824244540.a        Mon Aug 12 10:00:00 1996
$
```

You will not see any indication that the job ran on your screen unless you program something in the command procedure itself. When execution is done, the output of all jobs run by cron (submitted by `crontab` or `at`) is mailed back to you. You can also request `at` to send you a mail message that it is complete (in addition to job output):

```
$ at -m now +1 minutes command_procedure↵
job dhorvath.824244677.a will be run at Tue Feb 13 15:55:22 1996
$
```

In the mail will appear:

```
From dhorvath Tue Feb 13 15:57:02 1996
Date: Tue, 13 Feb 1996 15:57:01 -0500
From: dhorvath (David Horvath)
To: dhorvath

cron: Job dhorvath.824244677.a was run.
```

From the `-m` option. With a command procedure that runs the fortune cookie (saying generator) in /usr/games/fortune, the following mail would be received from cron:

```
From daemon Tue Feb 13 15:57:02 1996
Date: Tue, 13 Feb 1996 15:57:02 -0500
From: daemon
To: dhorvath
```

```
A computer, to print out a fact,
Will divide, multiply, and subtract.
        But this output can be
        No more than debris,
If the input was short of exact.
               - Gigo

*************************************************
Cron: The previous message is the standard output
      and standard error of one of your cron commands.
```

This mail message, always generated when cron runs a job, contains the output of the command.

Using the `at` command with another command is slightly more complicated. You cannot put the name of a command in place of the command_procedure in these examples. To use a command with `at`, you must pipe the name of the command into at as shown in this example:

```
$ echo "ls" | at now +1 minutes↵
job dhorvath.824242377.a will be run at Tue Feb 13 16:03:22 1996
$
```

The `ls` command will be executed in a minute. Some versions of at do not accept a command procedure on the command line as shown in the examples above. The hint that you have a problem is:

```
$ at now +1 minutes command_procedure↵
at: bad date specification
$
```

After verifying that the date or time format is correct, then you know your version of at will not accept anything on the command line. All your at commands should then be in the form:

```
$ echo "command_procedure" | at now +1 minutes↵
job dhorvath.824242378.a will be run at Tue Feb 13 16:05:02 1996
$
```

The `at` command will also accept one command from stdin if the neither the pipe nor command line are used to specify a command:

```
$ at now +1 day↵
ls -al↵                                command to run
^D                                     end of file key
job dhorvath.824242382.a will be run at Tue Feb 14 16:65:00 1996
$
```

To cancel a job submitted with at (before it begins executing):

```
$ at -l ↵                              See what is waiting to run
job dhorvath.824242378.a will be run at Tue Feb 13 16:05:02 1996
$ at -r dhorvath.824242378.a↵          Remove that job
```

```
at file: dhorvath.824242378.a deleted
$ at -l ↵                                See what is waiting to run now
$ at -r dhorvath.824242378.a↵            Remove that job again
at: dhorvath.824242378.a does not exist
```

After verifying that the job had not yet run, that `at -r` (remove) command was used with the job number to cancel the job. Another listing of pending at jobs was empty. Attempting to remove the job already canceled or any other job that does not exist will result in the error message.

*JES2 /*ROUTE XEQ AND /*XEQ REPLACEMENT*

In addition to scheduling jobs and running them in a batch mode, jobs can be routed to other systems. Instead of using /*ROUTE XEQ nodename or /*XEQ nodename to submit mainframe jobs to other machines, you can use `rsh`, `remsh`, `rexec`, or `rcmd` under UNIX.

For all of these commands, you must have the proper permissions on the remote system. These permissions are set up in the $HOME/.rhosts and /etc/hosts.equiv files. Contact your systems administrator before using these commands to verify local standards.

rsh and remsh Commands

Depending on which system you are using, you may have `rsh` or `remsh` commands (`rsh` was the original name for the restricted version of the Bourne shell). Some systems change the command for the restricted shell to `Rsh` with `rsh` becoming the remote shell, others kept the original restricted shell name and have remsh instead. The `rsh` and `remsh` remote shell commands behave exactly the same way, only the name may be different. Check the documentation for your system.

These commands execute the specified command or shell script on a remote host. The effect is the same as if you logged in, typed the command, and then logged out when it completed.

Using `rsh` or `remsh` to execute the `ls` command on another system, you would do the following:

```
$ rsh host2 -l dhorvath ls↵
change.log
sz
szc
szjob.log
$
```

The `-l` option allows you to specify the username on the remote system, if you omit it, your username is assumed. You can issue any valid command or execute a shell script.

If there is an error in the `rsh` or `remsh` command itself (options or parameters) or it is unable to login to the remote system, it will return a non-zero status. If command passed to the remote system fails (resulting in a non-zero return code), it is not returned to your local system and `rsh/remsh` returns a successful status. When executing a shell script on the remote system, the last thing it should do is echo a success or failure message (usually a status code) to stdout. If you use the command with the following format, then that value is stored in the environmental variable results:

```
$ RESULTS='rsh host2 my_shell_script'↵
$ echo $RESULTS↵
whatever my_shell_script echoed will appear
$
```

rexec Command

The `rexec` command performs the same function as the `rsh` or `remsh` commands except that it will prompt for a username and password if there is no equivalent on the remote system. The `rsh/remsh` rules apply for return codes.

The following example matches the `rsh` example on a different host:

```
$ rexec hostz ls↵
Name (hostz:dbh): dhorvath↵
Password (hostz:dhorvath): my_passwd↵          Not echoed
change.log
sz
szc
szjob.log
$
```

ISPF SUPER-COMPARE REPLACEMENTS

The ISPF Super-Compare is a utility that will compare two datasets or PDS members and report the differences in five different formats. The possible formats are OVSUM, DELTA, CHNG, LONG, and NOLIST. A listing type of OVSUM shows only the overall summary of the comparison: number of line matches, number of insertions and deletions between the files, number of the insertions and deletions that are paired, and the number of non-paired insertions and deletions. Except for NOLIST, all reports include the OVSUM report. Paired insertions and deletions imply that the number of lines were the same but specific lines changed. Comparing the output of a report program run with the same data at different times (which are included in the heading) would produce a paired insertion and deletion for each time shown since the lines would be different).

The DELTA listing shows the differences between the datasets and the OVSUM results; the differences are flagged to the left of each output line. The CHNG listing type is similar to the DELTA type with the addition of up to ten matching output lines above and below the differences (to aid in finding the changed areas). A LONG listing shows the entire new dataset with the records deleted from the old dataset included. The inserted and deleted data is flagged and the DELTA format is used. With NOLIST, no difference listing is produced; a message is produced on the screen reporting whether the datasets were different or not. NOLIST is useful when you do not care what the differences are, just if there are any.

The Super-Compare utility requires two screens, the new and old dataset entries. Along with the new dataset is the selection for Foreground/Background and Mixed Mode processing. The type of listing to produce, where to store it, and how to handle line numbers join the old dataset entry on the second screen. Screen 3.31 shows the first, new dataset entry screen, and Screen 3.32 shows the second, old dataset entry screen for Super-Compare.

Screen 3.31 - Super-Compare Utility "New" Screen

```
----------------------------------  SUPERC UTILITY  ----------------------------------
COMMAND ===>

SPECIFY "NEW" DATA SET TO BE COMPARED, THEN PRESS THE ENTER KEY.

   PROJECT ===>
   GROUP   ===>            ===>           ===>          ===>
   TYPE    ===>
   MEMBER  ===>                    (Blank or pattern for member selection list
                                    '*' for all members)

"NEW" OTHER PARTITIONED OR SEQUENTIAL DATA SET:
       DATA SET NAME    ===>
       VOLUME SERIAL    ===>          (If not cataloged)

    DATA SET PASSWORD   ===>          (If password protected)

    PROFILE DSN         ===>

    MODE                ===> F        (F - foreground, B - batch)
    MIXED MODE          ===> NO       (Yes or No)
```

Screen 3.32 - Super-Compare Utility "Old" Screen

```
COMPARE -- 'NEW.DATASET.NAME' ---------------------------------------------
  COMMAND ===>

  SPECIFY "OLD" DATA SET TO BE COMPARED, THEN PRESS THE ENTER KEY.

      PROJECT ===>
      GROUP   ===>           ===>            ===>             ===>
      TYPE    ===>
      MEMBER  ===>

  "OLD" OTHER PARTITIONED OR SEQUENTIAL DATA SET:
      DATA SET NAME   ===>
      VOLUME SERIAL   ===>                (If not cataloged)

  DATA SET PASSWORD   ===>                (If password protected)

  LISTING TYPE        ===> DELTA          (DELTA/CHNG/LONG/OVSUM/NOLIST)
  LISTING DS NAME     ===> SUPERC.LIST
  SEQUENCE NUMBERS    ===>                (blank/SEQ/NOSEQ/COBOL)
```

UNIX provides a number of commands to perform similar functions. However, the file must be line sequential with a record separator of line-feed at the end of each record. If the records are not terminated properly, the comparisons may run but the results will be unpredictable and unreliable. C language source code for a simple comparison program for sequential records and those that contain binary data is contained in Appendix B (Hints and Techniques): compare_data.c. Creating a more robust comparison program is relatively easy as the algorithms and code samples have been widely published.

FILE COMPARISON COMMANDS

For text data, UNIX has three basic comparison utilities: `diff`, `cmp`, and `comm`. The `diff` command shows differences in a form very much like the ISPF Super Compare CHNG or DELTA forms without the OVSUM summary. By default, the `cmp` command reports on the first byte that differs between two files and returns a non-zero status, behavior that is similar to ISPF Super Compare NOLIST. The `comm` command shows three columns from the input files. The first column is lines only in the first file, column two contains lines only in the second file, and column three shows lines common to both files. The input files must be in sorted order.

There are a few other comparison utilities: `bdiff`, `diff3`, and `sdiff`. `bdiff` is used on files that are too large for `diff` to process so it splits the two input files into smaller pieces and feeds them to the `diff` command. `diff3` performs a comparison just like the `diff` command but on three files instead of two. `diff3` is useful when you need to compare a baseline and two divergent modifications of that file (such as occurs when multiple programmers are changing the same program at the same time). `sdiff` produces a side-by-side difference listing.

Like the mainframe utility, the UNIX commands use a sophisticated matching algorithm that allows them to resynchronize after a difference. A simple matching algorithm compares two lines and reports any differences. If there is an additional line in one file but all other lines are the same, the simple algorithm will report that all lines after the difference are not the same since it does not attempt to resynchronize or determine where the files do match. The sophisticated matching algorithms are not perfect, but they do prevent an extra line from cascading into many reported differences.

With the following two files:

first	**second**
aaaaaa	aaaaaa
bbbbbb	bbbbbb
cccccc	dddddd
dddddd	cccccc
eeeeee	eeeeee
ffffff	ffffff
gggggg	gggggg
hhhhhh	hhhhhh

diff, cmp, and comm Commands

The `diff` command, which reports on differences between files, behaves as follows:

```
$ diff first second↵
3d2
< cccccc
4a4
> cccccc
$ echo $?↵
1
$
```

The `diff` command reports the changes and sets a return code. The return code is stored in the environment variable question mark <?> that is accessed by prefixing it with a dollar sign <$>. The `echo` command is used to display the value of the return code. Just about every command sets return codes. In most cases, a value of zero means the command executed successfully, a non-zero value means there was an error. When we got the error messages when using `cp` earlier, the return code was also set and could have been checked. The `diff` command will return the value zero if the files are the same, one if they differ, and another value if there is an execution problem. The `cmp` and `sdiff` commands use the same return codes. The comm command only returns a status code if there is an execution error.

The differences themselves are shown by line number and action letter, which are similar in format to the commands for the `ed` editor. The number before the action is the line number for the first file, the number after for the second. After the action line, the command displays all affected lines from the first file prefixed with the less than sign <<>, then a row of three dashes <->, then all affected lines from the second file prefixed with the greater than sign <>>. When there are only affected lines in one file, only the affected lines from that file are displayed, not the dashes or lines from the other file.

The three actions are a, d, and c. The 4a4 in the output above is showing that line 4 in the first file would have to be added after line 4 in the second file to make them the same. The 3d2 shows that line 3 in the first file would have to be deleted (would have occupied the line after 2 in the second file) to make the files the same. The c, or change, action is shown when a line exists in both files but is different. When there are a block of differences, the lines are displayed together.

If the files are the same, `diff` will not output any message and the return value will be zero:

```
$ diff first first↵
$ echo $?↵
0
$
```

The output from `diff` is similar to the command syntax used by the editor ed, but not an exact match. The option `-e` will cause `diff` to output actual `ed` commands to convert the first file to the second. Typically, the output is `diff -e` is redirected to a file for further manipulation of the commands or piped into ed for processing. The following commands show the commands from stdout:

```
$ diff -e first second↵                        Not the same
4a
cccccc
.
3d
$ echo $?↵
1
$ diff -e first first↵                         Are the same
$ echo $?↵
0
$
```

The diff command returns the appropriate status code no matter which option is used. It is possible to maintain multiple versions of a file using the original file and the differences in the form of the output of diff -e. The contents of all the files are combined and fed into the ed editor and saved. This is one method for multiple programmers to work on the same program. At some point the versions are combined to update the base file. An example of this technique is shown in the diff manual page.

The diff command with the -c option will produce a comparison showing lines of context (lines around the change). The output begins with the files identified with their creation dates. Each difference is separated by a line of asterisks. Each line removed from the first file is shown with a minus sign, each one added to the second file are marked with a plus sign, and any that changed are marked with an exclamation point <!>. The following example shows the contexts:

```
$ diff -c first second↵
*** first       Sat Mar 30 15:06:02 1996
-- second      Sat Mar 30 15:06:16 1996
***************
*** 1,5
  aaaaaa
  bbbbbb
- cccccc
  dddddd
  eeeeee

-- 1,5 ----
  aaaaaa
  bbbbbb
  dddddd
  cccccc
  eeeeee
***************
```

```
*** 2,5
  bbbbbb
  cccccc
  dddddd
  eeeeee

-- 1,5 ----
  aaaaaa
  bbbbbb
  dddddd
+ cccccc
  eeeeee

$ echo $?↵
1
$ diff -c first first↵
No differences encountered
$ echo $?↵
0
$
```

The diff command has several other useful options including: -i, -b, and -w. The -i option is used to ignore the case of alphabetic characters during comparisons, -b is used to ignore leading spaces and tabs (to the left of the record) during comparisons, and -w is used to ignore spaces and tabs anywhere in the record during comparisons. As with other commands, the options can be combined except for -b and -w.

The cmp command behaves as follows:

```
$ cmp first second↵
first second differ: byte 15, line 3
$ echo $?↵
1
$
```

The first difference is reported and the return code set when there is a difference. The cmp command supports two options: -s (silent) and -l (display byte number in decimal and the different bytes in octal for all differences). cmp -s is equivalent to ISPF Super-Compare NOLIST:

```
$ cmp -s first second↵                Not the same
$ echo $?↵
1
$ cmp -s first first↵                 Are the same
$ echo $?↵
0
$
```

Notice that cmp sets the return code either way. The cmp -l command shows the byte number in decimal and the bytes that differ in octal:

```
$ cmp -l first second↵                         Not the same
    15 143 144
    16 143 144
    17 143 144
    18 143 144
    19 143 144
    20 143 144
    22 144 143
    23 144 143
    24 144 143
    25 144 143
    26 144 143
    27 144 143
$ echo $?↵
1
$ cmp -l first first↵                          Are the same
$ echo $?↵
0
$
```

Bytes 17 through 27 are different. In the first file, there is a row of the lowercase letter c, in the second a row of the lowercase letter d. The next line, the values between the files are swapped. A lowercase c is octal value 143, a lowercase d is octal 144. Byte position 21 is not different. Why? Because that is where the new-line character is stored and since the lines are the same size, the new-line character occupies the same position in both files.

The comm command behaves as follows:

```
$ comm first second↵
                aaaaaa
                bbbbbb
cccccc
                dddddd
        cccccc
                eeeeee
                ffffff
                gggggg
                hhhhhh
$ echo $?↵
0
$
```

The first column contains records unique to the first file, the second column contains records that are unique to the second file, the final column shows records common to both files. The comm command does not set a return code if there are any differences. If the files are the same, only the third column will contain any data:

```
$ comm first first ↵
                aaaaaa
                bbbbbb
                cccccc
                dddddd
                eeeeee
                ffffff
                gggggg
                hhhhhh
$
```

The comm command supports three options: -1, -2, and -3. Each switch will suppress the printing of its column, and if all three are used, then there will be no output. To see only the common lines, use -1 and -2, to see only the lines that are not in common, use -3:

```
$ comm -1 -2 -3 first second↵
$ comm -1 -2 first second↵
aaaaaa
bbbbbb
dddddd
eeeeee
ffffff
gggggg
hhhhhh
$ comm -3 first second↵
cccccc
        cccccc
$
```

Using the three switches, -1, -2, and -3 together produces no output and, although correct syntax for the command, it is silly to do since it produces no useful information.

bdiff, sdiff, and diff3 Commands

The bdiff command is used when the files to be compared are too large for the diff command to process them. All bdiff does is split the files into smaller sections of a specified number of records and pass the smaller files to the diff command. The following examples show the bdiff command performing comparisons splitting the files and passing two records at a time to the diff command:

```
$ bdiff first second 2↵                  Not the same
3d2
< cccccc
4a4
> cccccc
```

```
$ echo $?↵
0
$ bdiff first first 2↵                    Are the same
$ echo $?↵
0
$
```

The syntax of the difference reporting is the same as that produce by the `diff` command. Because `bdiff`, not `diff`, is the command in use, the return code processing available from `diff` is not available. The default number of records is 3,500, which can be lowered by putting the desired number of records on the command line as the third parameter.

The `sdiff` command produces a side-by-side difference list. The first input file is shown on the left and the second is shown on the right. If the files are the same, the return code is zero; if different, the value is one. The less than sign <<> is used to show records in the first file but not in the second; the greater than sign <>> is used to show records in the second but not the first. The vertical bar <|> is used to show records that differ.

The following example shows the differences between the sample files:

```
$ sdiff first second↵
aaaaaa                                          aaaaaa
bbbbbb                                          bbbbbb
cccccc                                       <
dddddd                                          dddddd
                                             >  cccccc
eeeeee                                          eeeeee
ffffff                                          ffffff
gggggg                                          gggggg
hhhhhh                                          hhhhhh
$ echo $?↵
1
$
```

Comparing two identical files with the `sdiff` command results in:

```
$ sdiff first first↵
aaaaaa                                          aaaaaa
bbbbbb                                          bbbbbb
cccccc                                          cccccc
dddddd                                          dddddd
eeeeee                                          eeeeee
ffffff                                          ffffff
gggggg                                          gggggg
hhhhhh                                          hhhhhh
$ echo $?↵
0
$
```

The `sdiff` command supports two options: `-l` and `-s`. The `-l` option shows the records in the first file on the left and any differences with the second file on the right. The `-s` option only shows the differences. The `-l` option of `sdiff` produces the following:

```
$ sdiff -l first second↵
aaaaaa
bbbbbb
cccccc                                                     <
dddddd
                                                           >    cccccc
eeeeee
ffffff
gggggg
hhhhhh
$ echo $?↵
1
$
```

The `-s` option of sdiff produces the following:

```
$ sdiff -s first second↵
cccccc                                                     <
                                                           >    cccccc
$ echo $?↵
1
$
```

The `diff3` command produces a difference list similar to that produced by the `diff` command but for three files. It does not set a return code if there are any differences. Each set of differences are separated by a line of equal signs <=>. If all three files differ, the line is `====`. If the first file differs where the second and third match, the line is `====1`. If the second file differs where the first and third match, the line is `====2`. and if the third differs from the first and second, the line is `====3`. The changes needed to convert the given file to match the others is provided with either of two codes: `a` for text to be added and `c` for text that needs to be changed. The format of these changes are:

File_number:line_number1 a
File_number:line_number1,line_number2 c

If line_number1 is the same as line_number2 (only one line is changed), the comma and line_number2 will be omitted.

The following example shows the differences between the two sample files (the second file is used as file2 and file3 parameters to `diff3`):

```
$ diff3 first second second↵
====1
1:3c
```

```
  cccccc
2:2a
3:2a
====1
1:4a
2:4c
3:4c
  cccccc
$
```

Line 3 in file 1 is different from that line in the other files. To make the files the same, it would have to be added to files 2 and 3. Line 4 in files 2 and 3 differs from line 1, that line would have to be added to file 1 to make them the same. A comparison with `diff3` of file without any differences will not produce any output.

The `diff3` command supports the `-e` option to format its output as commands for the `ed` editor to apply all changes between files 2 and 3 into file1. Those are the changes flagged ==== and ====3. The -x option produces edit commands to incorporate only changes between all three files (flagged ====). An example of `diff3` with the `-e` option:

```
$ diff3 -e first first second↵
4a
cccccc
.
3c
.
w
q
$
```

The output is slightly different from the `diff` command with the `-e` option—it is designed to be a complete set of commands for the `ed` editor. The script produced by `diff` is designed to be combined with other ones to create the final product. The one produced by `diff3` is designed to stand alone.

The choice of comparison command depends on the kind of comparison desired. Most of the time I just use the `diff` command itself. Your choice will depend on your needs.

ISPF Search-For Replacement

The ISPF Search-For is a utility that searches datasets for single or multiple strings. Within a PDS, individual members or the entire PDS can be searched for the string. The search can take place in the foreground (interactive) or background (batch). When done searching, the utility reports the record number and shows the record contents with the match. At the end of the report, a summary is produced showing the number of records searched, number of hits, and the strings searched for.

Any search string that contains blanks or special characters should be enclosed in single quotes <'>. The search strings can be modified with WORD, SUFFIX, or PREFIX entered

Screen 3.33 - Search-For Utility Initial Screen

```
------------------------------  SEARCH-FOR UTILITY  ------------------------------
COMMAND ===>

SEARCH STRING      ===> STRING1

MULTIPLE STRINGS ===> YES    (Yes to specify additional search strings)

ISPF LIBRARY:
   PROJECT ===>
   GROUP   ===>           ===>          ===>          ===>
   TYPE    ===>
   MEMBER  ===>                   (Blank or pattern for member selection list,
                                   '*' for all members)
OTHER PARTITIONED OR SEQUENTIAL DATA SET:
    DATA SET NAME    ===> 'DBHDBH.PDS.COBOL(XLATECDE)'
    VOLUME SERIAL    ===>           (If not cataloged)

  DATA SET PASSWORD ===>            (If password protected)

  LISTING DSNAME     ===> SRCHFOR.LIST.JCL
  MODE               ===> F           (F - foreground, B - batch)
  MIXED MODE         ===> NO          (Yes or No)
```

after the search string. By default, if the search string is found anywhere in the record, it will be reported. With the WORD modifier, the string must exist as a separate word (not part of another string) for a hit to occur. With SUFFIX and PREFIX, the search string must exist at the end or beginning of a word, respectively, for a hit to occur. A word is defined as any string of alphanumeric characters delimited (preceded and succeeded) by one or more non-alphanumeric characters.

The Search-For utility requires entries to one or two screens depending on the number of search strings. For one search string, only the first screen is required. With multiple search strings, the second is required for entry of the additional strings. When background mode is selected, an additional screen is presented for the entry of JOB card information and creation of JCL. Screen 3.33 shows the first, single-string search and dataset entry screen, while Screen 3.34 shows the second, multiple-string entry screen for Search-For. The JCL creation screen is not shown.

If any of the strings are found, the record is reported as a hit. Logically, this is an or condition between the search strings. There is no way to only select records that have a match on two or more of the strings (an and condition).

UNIX provides several commands that perform similar functions as Search-For. However, the file must be line sequential with a record separator of line-feed at the end of each record. If the records are not terminated properly, the search will not perform properly and if there is a match found, multiple records would be shown since they appear as one record. Creating a search program to work with sequential files is fairly simple and is left as an exercise for the reader.

Screen 3.34 - Search-For Utility Multiple Strings

```
SEARCH --- 'DBHDBH.PDS.COBOL(XLATECDE)' -------------------------------
COMMAND ===>

Specify 1 or more SEARCH STRINGS below:

  ===> STRING1
  ===> STRING2
  ===> 'A B C D E F G'
  ===>
  ===>
  ===>
  ===>
  ===>
  ===>
  ===>

Press ENTER to start search or END command to exit.
```

grep COMMAND

The `grep` command searches files for a specified pattern of characters. Like the mainframe Search-For utility, it is very useful in finding occurrences of reports, sections or portions of reports, variables, sections of code, and words in documents. The name `grep` comes from g/re/p, which is a command within the `ed` editor used to search for regular expressions (re). The `grep` program was originally created by surgery on the `ed` editor, removing all the other things the editor did in favor of the search mechanism.

The `grep` command can be used on files or with a pipe to search the output of another program. When searching files, a single name or wildcards can be specified. For instance:

```
$ grep "An Important String" program1.cbl
$ grep "another string" *.cbl
$ grep "yet another string" proga.cbl progb.cbl progc.cbl
```

If a file is not specified, `grep` takes its input from stdin. If you forget the filename or search string, `grep` will read from the keyboard until you press the end-of-file or interrupt key. Piping the input from another command is a common way of using grep as shown in the example with the `ps` command:

```
$ ps -e -f | grep dhorvath↵                  Full process status, all processes
dhorvath 17983     1 81 21:03:04 pts/6  0:04 -ksh
dhorvath 18000 17857 46 21:05:34 pts/4  0:01 ps
```

```
dhorvath 18001 17857  4 21:05:34 pts/4  0:00 grep dhorvath
dhorvath 17857     1  4 09:17:20 pts/4  0:08 -ksh
$
```

The output of the ps command was filtered through the grep command only finding those entries that contained the specified string.

Using the program xlatecde.cbl in Appendix C (Data Conversion, ASCII and EBCDIC Charts) as the input, a simple search for the word input produces:

```
$ grep input xlatecde.cbl↵
     *                   ASCII.  The input buffer is unchanged.       *
     *                   must be at least as large as input.          *
     *                   character in the input buffer is used to     *
     *                   support it, the input and output buffers     *
$ echo $?↵                                  Check return status
0
$
```

The grep command returns a zero status code if any match to the string is found. If no matches are found, the return code is one.

The example showed four lines with the word input, but that is not all occurrences of the word input, only those sets of characters that match. The word is used in many places dealing with the input buffer, but using uppercase characters. By default, the grep command matches characters exactly. To find the records with the word INPUT:

```
$ grep INPUT xlatecde.cbl↵
       01  XC-INPUT-BUFFER              PIC X(4096).
                                 XC-INPUT-BUFFER,
           MOVE ZERO TO INPUT-WORD.
           MOVE XC-INPUT-BUFFER (BUFFER-INDEX : 1) TO INPUT-CHAR.
           ADD 1 TO INPUT-WORD.
           MOVE EBCDIC-ASCII-XLATE (INPUT-WORD) TO OUTPUT-CHAR.
           MOVE ZERO TO INPUT-WORD.
           MOVE XC-INPUT-BUFFER (BUFFER-INDEX : 1) TO INPUT-CHAR.
           ADD 1 TO INPUT-WORD.
           MOVE ASCII-EBCDIC-XLATE (INPUT-WORD) TO OUTPUT-CHAR.
$ echo $?↵                                  Check return status
0
$
```

If the word input was used with the first character in uppercase (Input) or in a strange pattern (InPuT), it would not be found in the file. It turns out that there are no cases of Input or InPuT in the file as shown by the following examples, so note the return code of one.

```
$ grep Input xlatecde.cbl↵
$ echo $?↵
```

```
1
$ grep InPuT xlatecde.cbl↵
$ echo $?↵
1
$
```

When searching for a particular word, it may be in upper or lower case. You can change the behavior of the `grep` command, making it case insensitive, by using the `-i` option as shown in the following command:

```
$ grep -i input xlatecde.cbl↵
      *                    ASCII.  The input buffer is unchanged.      *
      *                    must be at least as large as input.         *
      *                    character in the input buffer is used to    *
      *                    support it, the input and output buffers    *
       01  XC-INPUT-BUFFER              PIC X(4096).
                                 XC-INPUT-BUFFER,
           MOVE ZERO TO INPUT-WORD.
           MOVE XC-INPUT-BUFFER (BUFFER-INDEX : 1) TO INPUT-CHAR.
           ADD 1 TO INPUT-WORD.
           MOVE EBCDIC-ASCII-XLATE (INPUT-WORD) TO OUTPUT-CHAR.
           MOVE ZERO TO INPUT-WORD.
           MOVE XC-INPUT-BUFFER (BUFFER-INDEX : 1) TO INPUT-CHAR.
           ADD 1 TO INPUT-WORD.
           MOVE ASCII-EBCDIC-XLATE (INPUT-WORD) TO OUTPUT-CHAR.
$
```

All occurrences of the word input were found because the search did not pay attention to the case of the characters. When searching multiple files, the grep command will report the filename along with the matching record:

```
$ grep input xlate*.cbl↵
xlatecde.cbl:     *          ASCII.  The input buffer is unchanged.    *
xlatecde.cbl:     *          must be at least as large as input.       *
xlatecde.cbl:     *          character in the input buffer is used to  *
xlatecde.cbl:     *          support it, the input and output buffers  *
xlateuse.cbl:     * record layout for input (unconverted) and          *
$
```

You can suppress printing of filenames when using the wildcard or specifying multiple names with the `-h` option:

```
$ grep -h input xlate*.cbl↵
      *                    ASCII.  The input buffer is unchanged.      *
      *                    must be at least as large as input.         *
      *                    character in the input buffer is used to    *
      *                    support it, the input and output buffers    *
      *  record layout for input (unconverted) and               *
$
```

You can suppress the printing of the records that match the search string with the `-l` option. It only prints the names of files with matching records once per file:

```
$ grep -l input xlate*.cbl↵
xlatecde.cbl
xlateuse.cbl
$
```

The `-q` (quiet) does not show what the matches were, just that there was a match through the return code mechanism. If a match is found, return code is one, if no match, then zero as shown in the examples below:

```
$ grep -q input xlate*.cbl↵          String does exist
$ echo $?↵
0
$ grep -q Input xlate*.cbl↵          String does not exist
$ echo $?↵
1
$
```

xlatecde.cbl and xlateuse.cbl are both in Appendix C (Data Conversion, ASCII and EBCDIC Charts). Using the wildcard causes `grep` to search every file that begins with xlate and ends in .cbl. The `grep` command will also report the line number for any matches:

```
$ grep -n input xlatecde.cbl↵
4:      *                ASCII.  The input buffer is unchanged.          *
8:      *                must be at least as large as input.             *
14:     *                character in the input buffer is used to        *
23:     *                support it, the input and output buffers        *
$
```

Compare the `grep` command with the `-n` option with the output of the mainframe search for shown in Screen 3.35. The results are similar except `grep` does not produce the summary section.

Another useful option for `grep` is `-v`, which reverses the test. Instead of searching for the string, grep searches for records that do not contain the string. This is very useful for exception searching. To find out who is signed on the system from prior days, the `who` command is piped into the `grep` command with the `-v` option:

```
$ who | grep -v "Jan 02"↵
an_user      pts/5      Jan 01 12:11      (their desk)
not_there    pts/10     Dec 30 09:23      (nowhere around)
$
```

The `grep -v` can be used with files also. The `-h`, `-i`, `-l`, `-n`, `-q`, and `-v` options can be combined (although some combinations are clearly silly).

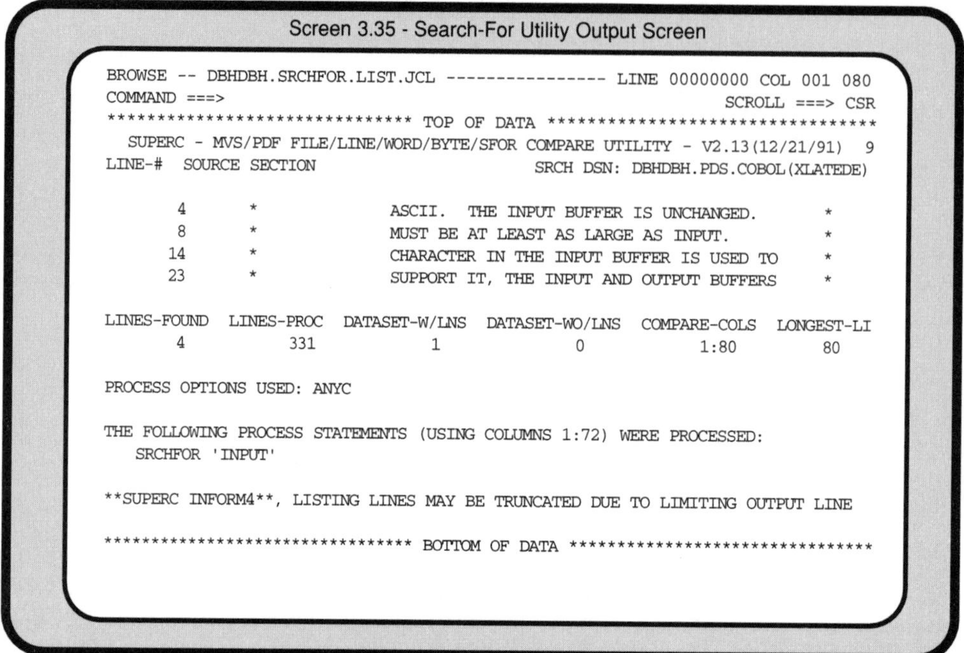

Screen 3.35 - Search-For Utility Output Screen

```
BROWSE -- DBHDBH.SRCHFOR.LIST.JCL ---------------- LINE 00000000 COL 001 080
COMMAND ===>                                                  SCROLL ===> CSR
****************************** TOP OF DATA *********************************
  SUPERC - MVS/PDF FILE/LINE/WORD/BYTE/SFOR COMPARE UTILITY - V2.13(12/21/91)  9
LINE-#  SOURCE SECTION                        SRCH DSN: DBHDBH.PDS.COBOL(XLATEDE)

      4      *                 ASCII.  THE INPUT BUFFER IS UNCHANGED.        *
      8      *                 MUST BE AT LEAST AS LARGE AS INPUT.           *
     14      *                 CHARACTER IN THE INPUT BUFFER IS USED TO      *
     23      *                 SUPPORT IT, THE INPUT AND OUTPUT BUFFERS      *

LINES-FOUND  LINES-PROC  DATASET-W/LNS  DATASET-WO/LNS  COMPARE-COLS  LONGEST-LI
      4          331           1              0             1:80           80

PROCESS OPTIONS USED: ANYC

THE FOLLOWING PROCESS STATEMENTS (USING COLUMNS 1:72) WERE PROCESSED:
   SRCHFOR 'INPUT'

**SUPERC INFORM4**, LISTING LINES MAY BE TRUNCATED DUE TO LIMITING OUTPUT LINE

******************************** BOTTOM OF DATA ********************************
```

In the examples of `grep` so far, simple strings have been shown. The `grep` command can actually search for much more complicated patterns as it interprets commands (expressions) in a simple language used to describe strings. The patterns are a simplified version of what are known as regular expressions. Certain characters have special meaning and are known as meta-characters because they are not the characters they look like—they translate into other characters.

Regular Expressions for grep and egrep

The asterisk <*> is a meta-character to the shell since it is used as a wildcard character in filenames. That is why Figure 2.2 shows the asterisk in a filename as being a bad idea. It is possible to create a file with an asterisk in the name, but it is difficult to use. If you specify the filename with an asterisk, the shell translates it into the filenames of any files that match. There are more meta-characters, and the shell and grep apply different meanings to some of them.

There are two commands in addition to grep that are used to search for strings: egrep and fgrep. grep, the oldest of the three, interprets limited regular expressions in its language; egrep interprets full regular expressions adding the or operator and the ability to group expressions with parentheses; fgrep is a much more efficient version of grep for searching fixed strings but does not interpret regular expressions.

Figure 3.4 shows the regular expressions used by the grep and egrep commands.

The dollar sign <$> is used to search at the end of the record. To search for a word at the end of a record, the dollar sign is used as a suffix to the word as shown:

Figure 3.4
Regular Expressions
for grep and egrep

C	Any regular character C matches itself
\C	Escape any character C turning off any special meaning
^	Match at the beginning of a line
$	Match from the end of the line
.	Match any single character (single character wildcard)
[ ]	Match any one of the characters in the brackets. Ranges are legal [0-9], [a-z], [A-Z], etc.
[^]	Match any one character not in the brackets. Ranges are legal
\n	Match the same thing the nth tagged regular expression matched (grep only)
e*	Match zero or more occurrences of the expression
e+	Match one or more occurrences of the expression (egrep only)
e?	Match zero or one occurrences of the expression (egrep only)
e1e2	Match when expression1 is matched followed by match of expression2
e1|e2	Match when expression1 is matched **or** expression2 is matched (egrep only)
\(e\)	Tagged regular expression, can be nested (grep only)
(e)	Regular expression, can be nested (egrep only)

There is no way to match a new-line character as it is used by the grep family to separate records.

```
$ grep "ZERO$" xlate*.cbl↵
xlatecde.cbl:           IF XC-BUFFER-LENGTH NOT GREATER THAN ZERO
xlateuse.cbl:               IF XLATE-RETURN-CODE NOT EQUAL ZERO
$
```

More complicated search strings are placed within double quotes, especially if they contain special characters or blanks. The circumflex or up-caret <^> is used to search at the beginning of the record. It is used as a prefix to the search string. To find all of the top-level IF statements (not indented), the following command would be used:

```
$ grep "^           IF" xlate*.cbl↵          eleven spaces before IF
xlatecde.cbl:           IF XC-BUFFER-LENGTH NOT GREATER THAN ZERO
xlatecde.cbl:           IF XC-FLAG EQUALS 1
xlateuse.cbl:           IF END-OF-FILE-IND = 'N'
$
```

Remember that code in COBOL programs start in position 12. To determine the records that end in an O (capital letter O) or 6, the following command would be used:

```
$ grep "[O6]$" xlate*.cbl↵
xlatecde.cbl:           IF XC-BUFFER-LENGTH NOT GREATER THAN ZERO
xlatecde.cbl:           ELSE IF XC-BUFFER-LENGTH GREATER THAN 4096
xlateuse.cbl:               IF XLATE-RETURN-CODE NOT EQUAL ZERO
$
```

Any record that contains either O or 6 will match if that single character is at the end of the record. A range can be specified inside the brackets instead of specifying each character:

```
$ grep "[A-D]$" xlate*.cbl↵
xlateuse.cbl:           RECORDING MODE F LABEL RECORDS STANDARD
xlateuse.cbl:           RECORDING MODE F LABEL RECORDS STANDARD
xlateuse.cbl:           PERFORM 1000-PROCESS-EACH-RECORD
xlateuse.cbl:           READ FILEIN INTO EBCDIC-RECORD
xlateuse.cbl:                                   EBCDIC-RECORD
xlateuse.cbl:                                   ASCII-RECORD
$
```

The command `grep "[ABCD]$" xlate*.cbl` would produce the same results.

egrep and fgrep Commands

To locate the records that end with a vowel (A, E, I, O, or U), use the following command:

```
$ egrep "[A]$|[E]$|[I]$|[O]$|[U]$" xlate*.cbl↵
xlatecde.cbl:          IF XC-BUFFER-LENGTH NOT GREATER THAN ZERO
xlatecde.cbl:             MOVE 1 TO XC-RETURN-CODE
xlatecde.cbl:             MOVE 2 TO XC-RETURN-CODE
xlatecde.cbl:          ELSE
xlateuse.cbl:             CALL 'XLATECDE'  USING     XLATE-RETURN-CODE
xlateuse.cbl:             IF XLATE-RETURN-CODE NOT EQUAL ZERO
xlateuse.cbl:             DISPLAY 'TRANSLATION ERROR NUMBER ' XLATE-RETURN-
CODE
xlateuse.cbl:             ELSE
$
```

This demonstrates the use of the or operator that only `egrep` supports. If either A or E or I or O or U appears at the end of a record, then there is a match. The `grep` command supports the ability to tag an expression, which allows it to be referenced further on in the search string with the \n (number) expression. To search for all occurrences of DIVISION, where the capital letter I is used before and after the letter V:

```
$ grep "\(D\)\(I\)\(V\)\2" xlate*.cbl↵
xlatecde.cbl:        IDENTIFICATION DIVISION.
xlatecde.cbl:        DATA DIVISION.
xlatecde.cbl:        PROCEDURE DIVISION USING XC-FLAG,
xlateuse.cbl:        IDENTIFICATION DIVISION.
xlateuse.cbl:        ENVIRONMENT DIVISION.
xlateuse.cbl:        DATA DIVISION.
xlateuse.cbl:        PROCEDURE DIVISION.
$
```

The \2 references the second tagged expression which is the capital letter I. The command `grep "\(D\)\(I\)\(V\)\2\(S\)\2" xlate*.cbl` would also match since the capital letter I is also used after the letter S.

The `fgrep` command is very good at searching large amounts of data for strings, but it does not support expressions, only simple strings:

```
$ fgrep "\(D\)\(I\)\(V\)\2\(S\)\2" xlate*.cbl↵
$ echo $?↵
1
$ fgrep DIVISION xlate*.cbl↵
xlatecde.cbl:       IDENTIFICATION DIVISION.
xlatecde.cbl:       DATA DIVISION.
xlatecde.cbl:       PROCEDURE DIVISION USING XC-FLAG,
xlateuse.cbl:       IDENTIFICATION DIVISION.
xlateuse.cbl:       ENVIRONMENT DIVISION.
xlateuse.cbl:       DATA DIVISION.
xlateuse.cbl:       PROCEDURE DIVISION.
$ echo $?↵
0
$
```

Because no match was found to the string "\(D\)\(I\)\(V\)\2\(S\)\2", `fgrep` set the return code to the value of one. Searching for the simple string "DIVISION" was successful as the output shows and the return code was set to zero.

MIMICKING SEARCH-FOR WORD, SUFFIX, AND PREFIX OPTIONS

One useful option for `grep`, `egrep`, and `fgrep` is the `-w` (word). It behaves the same way as the mainframe Search-For word option in that the string must be alone in a word. The first option searches for the word TO anywhere in the record and is followed by the same command plus the `-w` option. Notice that the first match is different:

```
$ grep "TO" xlate*.cbl↵
xlatecde.cbl:       WORKING-STORAGE SECTION.
xlatecde.cbl:           MOVE ZERO TO XC-RETURN-CODE.
xlatecde.cbl:               MOVE 1 TO XC-RETURN-CODE
xlatecde.cbl:               GO TO XLATE-MAIN-EXIT
```

more matches omitted

```
$ grep -w "TO" xlate*.cbl↵
xlatecde.cbl:           MOVE ZERO TO XC-RETURN-CODE.
xlatecde.cbl:               MOVE 1 TO XC-RETURN-CODE
xlatecde.cbl:               GO TO XLATE-MAIN-EXIT
xlatecde.cbl:               MOVE 2 TO XC-RETURN-CODE
```

more matches omitted

```
$
```

To mimic the PREFIX mainframe option, simply enclose a space within square brackets and use it as a prefix to the string being searched for. Searching for lines that have the word RECORD at the beginning of a word is searched with:

```
$ grep "[ ]RECORD" xlate*.cbl↵
xlateuse.cbl:           RECORDING MODE F LABEL RECORDS STANDARD
```

```
xlateuse.cbl:           RECORD CONTAINS 513 CHARACTERS
xlateuse.cbl:           DATA RECORD IS FILEIN-RECORD.
xlateuse.cbl:           RECORDING MODE F LABEL RECORDS STANDARD
xlateuse.cbl:           RECORD CONTAINS 513 CHARACTERS
xlateuse.cbl:           DATA RECORD IS FILEOUT-RECORD.
xlateuse.cbl:           03  RECORD-LTH                PIC 9(09) COMP-X.
xlateuse.cbl:           DISPLAY 'TOTAL RECORDS PROCESSED = ' REC-COUNT
xlateuse.cbl:           MOVE 513 TO RECORD-LTH.
xlateuse.cbl:      * CONVERT EACH RECORD                          *
xlateuse.cbl:                                         RECORD-LTH
$
```

The xlateuse.cbl program uses the variable names FILEIN-RECORD and FILEOUT-RECORD, although they only appear on lines that have the word RECO as a prefix. To mimic the SUFFIX mainframe option, simply enclose a space and any other appropriate characters (like the period <.> for the end of a statement) as a suffix to the string you are searching for. Searching for lines that have the word RECORD at the end of a word is searched with:

```
$ grep "RECORD[ .]" xlate*.cbl↵
xlateuse.cbl:           RECORD CONTAINS 513 CHARACTERS
xlateuse.cbl:           DATA RECORD IS FILEIN-RECORD.
xlateuse.cbl:       01  FILEIN-RECORD  PIC X(513).
xlateuse.cbl:           RECORD CONTAINS 513 CHARACTERS
xlateuse.cbl:           DATA RECORD IS FILEOUT-RECORD.
xlateuse.cbl:       01  FILEOUT-RECORD  PIC X(513).
xlateuse.cbl:       01  EBCDIC-RECORD.
xlateuse.cbl:       01  ASCII-RECORD.
xlateuse.cbl:      * CONVERT EACH RECORD         *
xlateuse.cbl:       1000-PROCESS-EACH-RECORD.
xlateuse.cbl:                  WRITE FILEOUT-RECORD FROM ASCII-RECORD
$
```

All the instances where the word RECORD appears at the end of a group of characters are shown. In this example, FILEIN-RECORD, FILEOUT-RECORD, and other variables with RECORD in the name are shown because the word appears at the end. These techniques will work with the grep and egrep commands, but not with fgrep since it only accepts simple strings130.

Here is a neat trick combining the `grep` command with the spell command files, which can help you do crossword puzzles. The master dictionary is usually stored as /usr/share/lib/dict/words or /usr/dict/words. To search for words that begin with the letter t, end with e, and are four letters long (typical crossword problem), use the following command:

```
$ grep -i "^t..e$" /usr/dict/words↵
take
tale
tame
tape
```

```
tate
tete
thee
tide
tile
time
tine
tire
tome
tone
tore
tote
tree
true
tube
tune
type
$
```

It is then up to you to figure out which word is the correct one based on the crossword question. The regular expression used (^t..e$) tells the grep command to search for a word that begins (^) with the letter t, can have any other two characters, and the letter e at the end of the record ($). In the master dictionary, each word has its own line. The expression can be expanded for more complicated words or where you know more letters in the word.

SUMMARY

At this point, you should have a basic understanding of the UNIX replacements for the most frequently used mainframe utilities, ISPF menu options, and commands. One popular program run in batch jobs for special processing has been omitted and that is IKJEFT01, also known as TSO. The replacement of IKJEFT01 is unnecessary to a large extent because there is not a separate batch and interactive command language under UNIX like there is on the mainframe.

This chapter is a good reference when you need to replace something you have done on the mainframe with something you have to do under UNIX. The next chapter shows you how to replace jobs.

CHAPTER 4

JCL, PROCs, AND CLISTs BECOME SHELL SCRIPTS

ON THE MAINFRAME, BATCH JOBS ARE WRITTEN IN A LANGUAGE KNOWN AS JCL, supplemented with JES2 or JES3 (Job Entry Subsystem Version 2 or 3) commands. JCL essentially consists of three statements: JOB to identify the unit of work, EXEC to identify steps within the job and to run programs or procedures (PROCs), and DD to identify datasets (Data Definition). There are other JCL statements used to identify procedures, end embedded input, and end a job, but those are supplemental to the big three. JES2 and JES3 commands are used to route job output, identify execution and output limits, and route the job to the proper system or CPU for processing. This chapter is dedicated to providing replacements for JCL and PROCs.

UNIX has what are known as shells. A shell is the program that processes user input: interprets the line, expands substitutions, and then decides what to do with the command entered. A command can be built into the shell, an alias for another command, a binary executable, or a shell script. The `ulimit` command is built into the shell, so you should not be able to find a manual page for it. The shell itself controls or limits the resources you can access. Aliases are ways to give a new name to a command or change its behavior. If you always use `ls -al` to view a directory, you could create an alias with the name `ll`, and every time you type `ll`, the shell expands it to `ls -al` and the processes the command. Binary executables are compiled programs. Shell scripts are files that contain shell and other commands. The language for a script is the same as for interactive access.

On the mainframe, there is a different command language for interactive and batch processing. In batch, JCL is used, under TSO CLIST or REXX are used. Under UNIX, the languages are the same: Korn shell can be interactive or a command procedure. The languages are the same but there are several different ones, so just as CLIST and REXX command procedures can run under TSO, UNIX has multiple shells available. The three most common are Bourne, Korn, and C shells. Bourne Shell, written by Steve Bourne, is the original shell available under UNIX. Korn Shell, written by David Korn, is more recent than Bourne Shell and is backward compatible with it. The C Shell was originally developed at Berkeley and is based, as the name implies, on the C language for its programming structures.

Your system may have one or all of these shells. Because Bourne shell scripts will run under Korn shell and Korn has more functions, people are moving away from Bourne in favor of Korn. Versions of UNIX that are based on BSD UNIX usually have the C shell. Which shell to use is generally a choice based on personal preferences. I prefer Korn over Bourne because of its richness. I prefer Korn over C because I learned Korn first and did not see a substantial benefit to making the transition. The choice may have been already made for you so that there may be a formal or informal standard at your installation.

The system administrator assigns a default shell to your account so when you signon, that is the shell that processes your command input. All three shells have very sophisticated features allowing you to change your environment, create command procedures, and improve the usability of UNIX. The shell is the interface you see with every command you type going through a shell program. Not only does the shell process your input, it also has a full-fledged programming language that can be used in procedures or interactively. The title of the book that describes one of the shells, The Korn Shell Command and Programming Language, written by Morris I. Bolsky and David G. Korn, underscores the point that shells are command and programming languages.

The UNIX operating system is so flexible in part due to its layered design. The hardware is the core, and the kernel surrounds and controls the hardware. The kernel itself is surrounded by programs that are external commands, sometimes known as utilities. You have seen some of these commands in Chapter 3 (Utilities and Commands): `cp`, `ls`, and `ps` for example. Surrounding the utilities is the outer layer or shell. The shell makes the commands easier to use by performing substitution, handling redirection, expanding wildcards into multiple filenames, and in other ways. The shell itself is not part of the operating system and is, in reality, just another program.

Invoking and Exiting Shells

Because the shell is not part of the operating system, you can select the shell that you use. If you want to use a shell other than the default shell assigned by the system administrator, you have two choices: You can request that it be changed or you can invoke the other shell. After all, shells are just programs that can be invoked as commands. To go from Korn to Bourne shells:

```
$ sh↵
$
```

Or:

```
$ bsh↵
$
```

Some systems support the commands sh and bsh; in most cases, there is one file with two links and the Bourne shell is run either way. The default prompts are the same between Bourne and Korn shells. To see what is happening:

```
$ ps -f -u dhorvath↵
    USER       PID  PPID   C    STIME    TTY  TIME CMD
  dhorvath 20511 25621   0 14:11:15  pts/5  0:00 sh
  dhorvath 25621 64515   0 14:11:09  pts/5  0:00 -ksh
  dhorvath 70361 20511   6 14:12:03  pts/5  0:00 ps -f -u dhorvath
$
```

The Korn shell is my login shell (shown by the minus sign prefix to ksh), Bourne shell is handling my input. To go from Korn or Bourne shells to the C shell:

```
$ csh↵
% ps -f -u dhorvath↵
    USER       PID  PPID   C    STIME    TTY  TIME CMD
  dhorvath 16117 20511   0 14:15:17  pts/5  0:00 csh
  dhorvath 20511 25621   0 14:11:15  pts/5  0:00 sh
  dhorvath 25621 64515   0 14:11:09  pts/5  0:00 -ksh
  dhorvath 70390 16117   4 14:15:23  pts/5  0:00 ps -f -u dhorvath
%
```

The C shell shows up as csh. In some cases, it will show as -sh because it is usually used as a replacement for the Bourne shell. The default prompt for the C shell is the percent sign <%>. To leave the extra shells invoked in the two examples above, either the end-of-file key <^D> or the exit command is used:

```
% exit↵
$ exit↵
$ ps -f -u dhorvath↵
     USER       PID  PPID   C     STIME    TTY   TIME CMD
   dhorvath 20597 25621   6 14:20:27  pts/5   0:00 ps -f -u dhorvath
   dhorvath 25621 64515   1 14:11:09  pts/5   0:00 -ksh
$
```

The other shells are gone and all that is left is our default login shell of Korn. Every command that I type will be interpreted by the Korn shell and then processed. If I run a command procedure, by default, it will be interpreted by the same shell.

Creating a Simple Command Procedure

Command procedures can be simple or complicated. If I want to clear my screen and then issue the `who -u` command, I could do it at least three different ways. I could type the commands one after another, I could type them on a single line with a semicolon between them, or I could create a command procedure.

The first two methods look like this:

```
$ clear↵
$ who -u↵
```

Or:

```
$ clear; who -u↵
```

A way to create simple files is through the use of the `cat` command. The `cat` command copies files or stdin of no file is specified to stdout. Often, stdout is redirected to another file causing the `cat` command to behave like the `cp` command. By leaving off the name of the input file, cat will take its input from stdin and process it as if it had come from a file as shown:

```
$ cat > my_who↵
clear↵
who -u↵
^D
$ ls -al my_who↵
-rw-r--r--   1 dhorvath staff         13 Feb 20 14:27 my_who
$ cat my_who↵
clear
who -u
$
```

Personally, I use the `more` command to view the contents of files, because when using the `cat` command, files that are longer than a single screen will not pause and the contents will go flying by. When using the more command with files that are shorter than a single screen, it behaves just like the `cat` command. To run a command procedure, the name is typed:

```
$ my_who↵
ksh: my_who: permission denied
$
```

You created this file but you are not allowed to use it. The `ls -al` command in the prior example gives a clue: The owner has read and write permissions when the rest of the group can only read the file. None of the execute bits are set.

You have several choices at this point. You can invoke the shell with my_who as a parameter, you can invoke the shell with my_who through redirected stdin, you can execute my_who a series of commands to your current shell, or you can convert my_who into a command.

```
$ ksh my_who↵
```

Or:

```
$ ksh < my_who↵
```

Or:

```
$ . my_who↵
```

In the first two cases, a subshell is invoked (just like when Bourne and C shells were invoked from the command line), the commands in the file my_who are executed, and then the subshell exits. When it exits, it returns control to the parent shell, which is your login. In the third case, the commands in my_who are read by the current shell as if they were typed at the command line. The third case is faster because a subshell is not invoked, but if the commands change the current environment, those changes will remain in effect—the current shell reads the commands from the file my_who. The differences between these three examples seem inconsequential, but any environmental changes made by a subshell generally apply only to that subshell and not to the parent.

The other way to execute my_who is to make it executable. To add execute permissions, the `chmod` (Change permission Mode) command is used. The following command will give everyone execute permission to the file:

```
$ chmod +x my_who↵
$ ls -al my_who↵
-rwxr-xr-x   1 dhorvath staff          13 Feb 20 14:27 my_who
$
```

Now the execute permissions are set. More information is provided about the chmod command and setting permissions in Chapter 5 (Advanced Shell Script and Commands). To execute my_who now, the name of the command is entered:

```
$ my_who↵
```

which will clear the screen, display the current system users, and return the prompt. It also invokes a subshell, which protects the current (parent shell) environment from changes made by the subshell. The commands in my_who are executed by the default shell (Korn in this case). Once the execute permissions are set, there is no apparent difference between a binary executable program and a command procedure.

By creating a command procedure, you type one command that executes the two commands you had to type before. More complicated command procedures are usually created using an editor, detailed in Chapter 6 (Editors).

Command procedures are known as shell scripts under UNIX and can be written in any of the shells. Because the default shell for a user may be different than the shell used to create the script and the shells have different programming syntax, there is a way to identify which shell should run a particular script. By including the following line at the beginning of a shell script, the script will be executed by the proper shell:

```
#! /bin/ksh
```
For Korn Shell, or:
```
#! /bin/csh
```
For C Shell, or:
```
#! /bin/sh
```
For Bourne Shell, or:
```
#! /bin/bsh
```
Also for Bourne Shell.

will invoke the proper shell program as a subshell, and any environmental changes made by the subshell will not affect the parent shell. Running the command using the . command of the Bourne and Korn shells will override the first line and force the commands in the script to be executed by the current shell. In this case, any changes made to the environment by the script will remain with the login shell. Parent shells can change the environment that the child receives, but the child cannot change the parent. The same applies to processes as they are invoked within UNIX.

To create a shell script that will show full process status of all my processes (even if logged on multiple times), enter the following:

```
$ cat > psme↵
#! /bin/csh↵
ps -f -u dhorvath↵
^D
$ chmod +x psme↵
$ psme↵
      USER   PID  PPID   C    STIME    TTY  TIME CMD
  dhorvath 18584 78999   6 15:07:15  pts/5  0:00 ps -f -u dhorvath
  dhorvath 25621 64515   0 14:11:09  pts/5  0:00 -ksh
  dhorvath 78999 25621   5 15:07:15  pts/5  0:00 csh ./my_who
$
```

Because the first statement in the shell script is #! /bin/csh, the C shell is invoked as a subshell to run the command procedure. In this example, it does not matter which shell executed the script because it is so simple, but if it were written using C shell syntax and did not have that line, it would not run properly for me since my default shell is Korn. By including the proper syntax at the top of the shell script, the proper shell is invoked no matter which language was used in the script.

Under TSO, CLIST and REXX behave in a similar manner. With the proper comment as the first line, the command intpreter can determine whether the command procedure is written in CLIST or REXX command languages and execute accordingly. Unfortunately, batch processing does not show the same flexibility on the mainframe. Batch command procedures are written using JCL and only JCL.

IKJEFT01 (TSO IN BATCH) REPLACEMENT

Because a TSO session (user) is really a job running on the mainframe through JCL, it is possible to execute TSO commands and tools by invoking TSO within your own batch job. Some tools like the on-line query used with the DB2 relational database are much easier to run under TSO than an equivalent under batch TSO. The easy solution is to execute TSO as a step within the batch job.

In the following example, the DB2 query is run under TSO within a job (using JCL). This is necessary because the mainframe is batch-oriented and an interactive session using TSO runs as a batch job. The command languages for batch jobs (JCL) is different from that used under TSO. For instance, datasets are allocated using different commands.

```
//BATCHTSO  EXEC PGM=IKJEFT01,REGION=8M
//STEPLIB   DD DSN=SOFT.DB2.P.DSNLOAD,DISP=SHR
//SYSTSPRT  DD SYSOUT=*
//SYSTSOUT  DD SYSOUT=*
//SYSPRINT  DD SYSOUT=*
//SYSUDUMP  DD SYSOUT=*
//SYSOUT    DD SYSOUT=*
//SYSTSIN   DD *
DSN SYSTEM (DB2P)  RETRY(5)
RUN PROGRAM(DSNTEP2)  PLAN(DSNTEP2) -
    LIB('SOFT.DB2.P.DSNLOAD')
END
/*
//SYSIN     DD *
  SELECT *
     FROM TABLE_NAME
     WHERE TABLE_FIELD > 123
     ORDER BY OTHER_FIELD
     GROUP BY OTHER_FIELD
;
/*
//*   THIS EXAMPLE USES DB2 IN PRODUCTION
```

Any work that is easier to perform under TSO than in batch is a good candidate for this method. In addition to running DB2 queries, I have also seen this method used to send a message to a signed-on user when a job step completes or abends. There is no way to perform this at the step level within JCL

There is no direct replacement for IKJEFT01 under UNIX because the interactive and batch languages are the same. So long as a shell script is coded properly, it does not matter which shell was active when the command was entered.

What to Do with Batch JCL

Some of the applications that I have worked with have more JCL modules than program source code modules. They have had more lines of code in the production programs than in JCL, but in raw number of members, JCL won out. When moving an application from the mainframe to UNIX, the original JCL cannot be run in the new environment.

The decision regarding what to do with the mainframe JCL when moving to UNIX is a difficult one. If the application is being rewritten during the move, JCL is much less of an issue since many of the original modules are no longer of use. If the application is just moved with a plan of minimal changes, then the JCL becomes much more important. The JCL can be replaced (rewritten) from scratch or translated. Depending on the number of modules involved, rewriting may not be an alternative due to the level of effort involved. Translation can be done in one of four ways: manually, with an internally developed tool, by an external organization (consulting firm), or with a purchased software tool.

Manual translation may be the most time-consuming, but provides excellent examples for learning how to program in shell script. Creating an internal tool to perform the translation may require less elapsed time but requires a high level of UNIX and mainframe expertise. Having a consulting firm translate your JCL has advantages and disadvantages—it can be done in the shortest elapsed time but can be expensive and allows a third party to view your code. Purchased software tools can be expensive but allow the work to be performed internally with a reduced elapsed time.

I have seen one of the purchased software tools in action, and it did a decent job of translating JCL to shell script; JOB, EXEC, and DD statements were replaced with shell scripts. It had significant problems with replacing multiple substitution variables when they were placed next to each other like PARM="&VAR1&VAR2&VAR3". The tool did not recognize the second or third substitutions. The vendor-supplied shell script did not correctly support GDG groups, DISP=NEW, condition code checking (flushing the job), concatenating datasets, or overriding DD statements or PROC substitutions when a job called a PROC.

Although the tool could create and use GDG files, it could not handle a GDG group (concatenating all generations of a GDG for input). Deleting generations from a GDG also experienced problems with unpredictable results at times. DISP=NEW worked in that the tool did not check to verify the file existed, but if the program did not open (create) the file, then there would be no file. Depending on input data, an output file might not be opened, then the output file would not be created; so on the mainframe an empty dataset would exist. Without the empty file, other jobs could not find a file resulting in an error. Condition code checking was not entirely effective—

downstream steps would execute even if prior ones abended—they were not flushed. When concatenating datasets, the tool would copy the first file to a temporary file, then copy that temporary file together with the second file to a new temporary file. The process was repeated for each file in the concatenation, resulting in wasted time and storage space. When using PROCs, using override DD statements in the job or overriding substitutions in the PROC did not work. The override DD statements were ignored and the substitutions were assigned different internal names so they, too, were effectively ignored.

As a group we made extensive modifications to the vendor's script and had to make many changes to the converted JCL. Ignoring the problems that were eventually corrected, the tool did get us to the point of running jobs quicker than if we had to translate by hand.

If you are purchasing a vendor's tool or using a consulting firm to perform the translations, evaluate them very carefully. In my opinion, the best way is to get the vendor or consulting firm to translate a few of your more complex sets of JCL, including jobs, PROCs, and overrides. Then get a mainframe and UNIX expert together to evaluate the results. The UNIX expert can evaluate the shell code and the mainframe expert can help explain what the script is supposed to do. Even better would be one person with strong experience in both environments who can understand JCL and shell script well.

Replacing Jobs in JCL with Shell Scripts

When replacing jobs in JCL with shell scripts, there are a number of important areas that need to be covered. The big three areas are substitutes for the JOB, DD, and EXEC statements. This section covers those and other important topics including return code processing, JOBLIB/STEPLIB/ system libraries, temporary files, DD statements with referbacks, temporary files, symbolics, and comments. Replacement of the EXEC PGM= statement will be covered in the this section, EXEC PROC= in the next. The next section also includes concatenating files, DD DUMMY a.k.a. DD DSN=NULLFILE, symbolics, overrides, and return code processing by a job.

Each of the lines in the following simple job are numbered. Each of the lines will be explained. The job consists of three steps, the third runs only if the first was successful and the second failed.

Line Korn Shell statement

```
1       #! /bin/ksh
2       #
3       #
4       #     Job setup
5       set -o xtrace
6       export JOBNAME="The_Job_Name"
7       export SAVE_PATH=$PATH
8       export JOBLIB="/search/me/first:/search/me/next:/search/me/then:"
9       HLQ=/u/dhorvath/cob_stuff
10      SYSOUT_DIRECTORY="/u/dhorvath/cob_stuff"
11      SYSOUT=${SYSOUT_DIRECTORY}/RUN.LOG
12       > $SYSOUT                              # create sysout file
```

```
SYSERR=${SYSOUT_DIRECTORY}/RUN.LOG
 > $SYSERR                                  # create syserr file
MAX_RC=0
print "$JOBNAME STARTED `date`  " >> $SYSOUT 2>> $SYSERR
#    Step 10
#                 Use STEPLIB and JOBLIB for program
STEPLIB="/search/me/override/one:/search/me/override/two:"
PATH=${STEPLIB}${JOBLIB}${SAVE_PATH}
dd_FILEIN=${HLQ}/FILE.IN    # DISP=(OLD,KEEP,KEEP)
dd_FILEOUT=${HLQ}/FILE.OUT; touch $dd_FILEOUT   # DISP=(NEW,KEEP,DELETE)
dd_ERRORS=${HLQ}/ERROR.FILE; touch $dd_ERRORS  # DISP=(NEW,DELETE,KEEP)
dd_TEMP1=/tmp/$$.'date +"%y%m%d.%H%M%S"'
dd_TEMPN=/tmp/tempn.$$.'date +"%y%m%d.%H%M%S"'
PARM="input parameters"
program_to_run "$PARM" >> $SYSOUT 2>> $SYSERR
step010_rc=$?
print "$JOBNAME STEP010 ENDED `date` RC=${step010_rc} " >> $SYSOUT 2>> $SYSERR
if [ $step010_rc = 0 ]
then
   rm $dd_ERRORS        # DISP=(NEW,DELETE,KEEP)
else
   rm $dd_FILEOUT       # DISP=(NEW,KEEP,DELETE)
fi
if [[ $step010_rc > $MAX_RC ]]
then
   MAX_RC=$step010_rc
fi
#    Step 20    run only if step010 is OK.
#               Use JOBLIB for program
STEPLIB=":"
PATH=${STEPLIB}${JOBLIB}${SAVE_PATH}
if [ $step010_rc = 0 ]
then
   dd_INFILE=${HLQ}/THIS.FILE    # DISP=(OLD,KEEP,KEEP)
   dd_OUTFILE=${HLQ}/THAT.FILE; touch $dd_OUTFILE # DISP=(NEW,KEEP,KEEP)
   dd_REFERBK=${dd_FILEOUT}      # referback to step010 DD
   PARM="other input parameters"
   program2 "$PARM" >> $SYSOUT 2>> $SYSERR
   step020_rc=$?
   print "$JOBNAME STEP020 ENDED `date` RC=${step020_rc} " >> $SYSOUT 2>> $SYSERR
   if [ $step020_rc = 0 ]
   then
      :       # no action
   else
      :       # no action
   fi
```

```
59            if [[ $step020_rc > $MAX_RC ]]
60            then
61               MAX_RC=$step020_rc
62            fi
63         else
64            print "$JOBNAME STEP020 BYPASSED `date` " >> $SYSOUT 2>> $SYSERR
65         fi
66         #
67         #    Step 30     run only if step010 is OK and step020 is bad.
68         #                Use system default for program (PATH)
69         PATH=${SAVE_PATH}
70         if [[ $step010_rc = 0  &&  $step020_rc != 0 ]]
71         then
72            report_error "INPUT parameters" >> $SYSOUT 2>> $SYSERR
73            step030_rc=$?
74            print "$JOBNAME STEP030 ENDED `date` RC=${step030_rc} " >> $SYSOUT 2>> $SYSERR
75            if [ $step030_rc = 0 ]
76            then
77               :        # no action
78            else
79               :        # no action
80            fi
81            if [[ $step030_rc > $MAX_RC ]]
82            then
83               MAX_RC=$step030_rc
84            fi
85         else
86            print "$JOBNAME STEP030 BYPASSED `date` " >> $SYSOUT 2>> $SYSERR
87         fi
88         # Post job processing
89         print "$JOBNAME ENDED `date` MAXIMUM RC=${MAX_RC} " >> $SYSOUT 2>> $SYSERR
90         exit ${MAX_RC}
```

Lines 1 through 16 are setup and initialization. Lines 17 through 39 are for step010, lines 40 through 66 are for step020, and lines 67 through 87 are for step030. The remaining lines, 88 through 90, are for reporting the status of the job.

The first line forces the use of the Korn shell with this script as discussed previously. The next three lines, each beginning with the pound sign character <#>, are comments. Any text that appears after the pound sign on a line are comments that replaces the //* card and putting comments on other cards after a blank space tells the command processor that the command has ended.

Line 5 enables (set -o) the xtrace function within the shell, showing the commands as they are interpreted and executed. This is close to the JOB card MSGLEVEL=(1,0). Without this statement or with it disabled (set +o), it is equivalent to JOB MSGLEVEL=(0,0). There is no way to get the dataset allocation messages provided by JOB MSGLEVEL=(1,1).

The Korn shell parameter noexec allows a job to execute in a manner similar to the mainframe JOB TYPRUN=SCAN. To read commands without executing them:

```
$ set -o noexec
```

To enable the execution of commands:

```
$ set +o noexec
```

For obvious reasons, this command is better used within a script. Most versions of the Korn shell will ignore this option from an interactive shell.

Lines 6, 7, and 8 create environmental variables that subshells will have access to (by use of the export statement). JOBNAME is used to produce output messages, SAVE_PATH is used to save the system-level library location information, and JOBLIB is a replacement for the JOBLIB DD statement. Instead of separate JOBLIB and STEPLIB, there is just PATH. PATH can be changed as needed by the user or a shell script. Because the job example changes the search locations based on the step, the PATH will be changed multiple times.

Where UNIX Looks for Programs and Scripts (the UNIX Path)

UNIX locates executable programs and shell scripts through the environmental variable PATH. When you provide the name of a program (by entering a command), the shell searches for something to run, the PATH tells it where to look and in what order. The PATH is equivalent to the system library, JOBLIB, and STEPLIB all rolled up into one. Each user has his or her own PATH variable that is initialized at login to a standard set of locations by the /etc/environment file. The user can change the PATH in his or her $HOME/.profile file. The /etc/environment file may also set the environment variable $HOME, which points to the login directory of the user.

When the command is entered, the shell searches for that name in the first location specified by the path, then it searches the next, and the next. This continues until there are no more places to search in the path and then the error message `ksh: command_name: not found` is produced. The Korn shell actually searches for commands in other places (aliases and others), which is covered in Chapter 5 (Advanced Shell Script and Commands).

On the mainframe, DD statements in a JOBLIB or STEPLIB can be concatenated. Under UNIX, the subdirectories in the PATH are also concatenated; instead of occupying separate lines, it is one big line with each subdirectory separated by a colon <:> from the others. To specify the current directory as a search location (usually a good idea), the period <.> is used just like another directory.

COBOL programs may be executed by issuing the cobrun command with the program name as a parameter followed by any parameters for the COBOL program itself. The cobrun command loads a run-time library into memory that then executes the COBOL program. The program itself may be in machine language without its called functions (binary code but not link-edited) or in an intermediate code format. The binary code needs the functions contained in the run-time library to run. Intermediate code is a portable format that is interpreted by the run-time library (converted to binary code as executed). The location of those files is determined by the environment variable COBPATH. The cobrun command and setting of the COBPATH environment variable is not necessary if the programs are made into executables (compiled and link-edited).

Environmental Variables and Substitution

The PATH is an environmental variable that can be viewed through use of the echo or print commands:

```
$ echo $PATH↵
```

Or:

```
$ print $PATH↵
.:/application_1/prod/scripts:/application_2/prod/cobol:/usr/ibs/ksh:/usr/tool/bin:/usr2/other_tool/bin:/usr2/spfux/aixbin:/usr2/unispf:/usr2/unispf/twglm:/application_1/tools:/usr/bin:/etc:/usr/sbin:/usr/ucb:/usr/bin/X11:/sbin:.:
$
```

Although it takes multiple lines on the screen, it is all one statement. Environmental variables are stored within the shell and are used to modify actions. PATH is a special environmental variable because the shell uses it to search for commands to execute. COBPATH is a special environmental variable because the cobrun command uses it to search for COBOL programs to execute. TERM is another special environmental variable because the shell and other commands use it to determine the type of terminal you are using.

Within your .profile file, there is a line that looks something like the following:

```
PATH=/application_1/prod/scripts:/application_2/prod/cobol:/usr/ibs/ksh:/usr/tool/bin:/usr2/other_tool/bin:/usr2/spfux/aixbin:/usr2/unispf:/usr2/unispf/twglm:/application_1/tools:/usr/bin:/etc:/usr/sbin:/usr/ucb:/usr/bin/X11:/sbin:.:
```

Or:

```
PATH=$PATH:/u/dhorvath/bin
```

Any time you prefix an environmental variable with a dollar sign <$>, the shell performs substitution (like the ampersand <&> in mainframe JCL). The second PATH example takes the original value of the path, plugs it into the statement with :/u/dhorvath/bin appended to it, and stores the result in PATH, replacing the original value of the path.

There may not be an export statement in your .profile because the shell effectively exports environmental variables in the .profile. In other cases, any environmental variable that must be available to subshells of the current must be exported. There are several ways to export an environmental variable:

```
$ MYVAR="abc"↵
$ export MYVAR↵
```

Or:

```
$ MYVAR="abc"; export MYVAR↵
```

Or:

```
$ export MYVAR="abc"↵
```

The result is the same, all that changes is the coded form. The first example is two commands occupying two lines; the second is two commands on the same line. The final example is one command that combines the export with initialization of the environmental variable.

Remember that the dollar sign <$> is required to work with the value in the variable. The variable name alone will be treated as a string of characters. Another way of performing the substitution is with ${variable_name}—using curly braces <{> and <}> around the variable name. The two forms can be used interchangeably, but the second form must be used if there is no way for the shell to tell where the variable name ends and other text begins.

The following examples (using environmental variables TEST1 through TEST6) illustrate the use of the variables and substitutions. The first example initializes TEST1 with the letters ABCDEF and verifies that they are stored:

```
$ export TEST1="ABCDEF"↵
$ echo TEST1↵
TEST1
$ echo $TEST1↵
ABCDEF
```

The first echo did not have a dollar sign prefix on the variable so it is treated as text. The second echo allowed substitution to occur and showed the value stored in TEST1. In the second example, TEST2 is assigned the value in TEST1 and echoed to confirm this:

```
$ export TEST2=$TEST1↵
$ echo $TEST2↵
ABCDEF
```

TEST2 now contains the same thing as TEST1. The third test shows that the ${} syntax works the same as the dollar sign prefix on a variable:

```
$ export TEST3=${TEST1}↵
$ echo $TEST3↵
ABCDEF
```

Looking at the prior two examples, the question that immediately comes to mind is why use the second syntax? After all, it is more typing, more chances to hit the wrong character, and in some ways uglier looking. But if you are trying to do something that prevents the shell from being able to determine the variable name, then it is necessary. If you want to append the text GHIJKL to the text in TEST1 and store it in another variable (TEST4 or TEST5):

```
$ export TEST4=$TEST1GHIJKL↵
$ echo $TEST4↵

$ export TEST5=${TEST1}GHIJKL↵
$ echo $TEST5↵
ABCDEFGHIJKL
```

TEST4 is empty or a null string. The shell was unable to find a variable with the name TEST1GHIJKL. Any variable that the shell cannot find is treated as being empty or null. In order to build the concatenated string, the second form of substitution syntax is used to create TEST5. The curly braces tells the shell where the variable begins and ends. The substitution can then take place and the entire string is stored in TEST5.

The first example showed what happened if you attempted to view a variable without the $ or ${} prefix, the final example shows what happens if you use the variable in something other than an echo. Unless a substitution prefix is used, the characters to the right of the equal sign are treated as text.

```
$ export TEST6=TEST1↵
$ echo $TEST6↵
TEST1
$
```

Using environmental variables is a much larger topic and this introduction will be expanded further on in this book. The handling of environmental variables is similar to the SET feature available in versions of MVS newer than 4.0, which has the form:

```
// SET ENAME='SOME-VALUE'
```

Replacing Jobs in JCL with Shell Scripts—Lines 9 through 90

Lines 9 and 10 create environmental variables that only this copy of the shell can access. They are local variables while the ones on lines 6, 7, and 8 are global. HLQ is the high-level qualifier for all files. SYSOUT_DIRECTORY is where all system output is directed.

Lines 11 and 12, 13 and 14 are used to define the locations for normal and error messages respectively. Each command will have stdout redirected to $SYSOUT and stderr redirected to $STDERR. First the environmental variable is defined and then the storage file is created empty. Since the commands will append their output to the end of the storage file, it is important to make it empty at the start (or output from previous runs will remain).

Line 15 initializes the variable MAX_RC to zero. MAX_RC will contain the highest return code from any command in the job and is used for reporting at job completion.

Line 16 displays a message showing when the job began. The date command displays the current date and time. It is enclosed in backquotes <`> to force the shell to execute date as a command and treat the output as a string. That string is displayed by the print command. This technique can also be used to store the output of a command in an environmental variable. The following example gets the current terminal of the user and then displays it:

```
$ curr_tty=`tty`↵
$ echo Terminal is ${curr_tty}↵
Terminal is /dev/pts/1
$
```

The first step of the job, step010, occupies lines 17 through 39. Lines 17 and 18 are comments describing the step.

Line 19 defines the libraries (subdirectories) to search for this step. Line 20 creates a new PATH by combining the STEPLIB, JOBLIB, and SAVE_PATH variables in that order. The STEPLIB overrides the JOBLIB, which overrides the default search path.

Lines 21 through 25 are data file definitions for the program being run on line 27. The environmental variable names must begin with a prefix of dd_ before the name used in the program. In a COBOL program, the uppercase portion of the variable is the same as the ASSIGN TO value without any of the modifiers like UT-S- or UT-R- that are commentary in nature. Instead of having the code the high-level qualifier on each data definition, it was defined on line 9, which makes the job easier to change if the file locations move.

For the existing file on line 21 (DISP=OLD), nothing else is necessary. When the program opens the file, it will fail and produce a return code to for further processing. If you wanted the script to handle the condition, you could code the following between lines 21 and 22:

```
if [[ ! -f $dd_FILEIN || ! -r $dd_FILEIN ]]
then
    print "$JOBNAME STEP010 FAILED ${dd_FILEIN} NOT FOUND `date` " >> $SYSOUT 2>>
$SYSERR
     exit 99
fi
```

The `-f` flag checks to see if the file exists and is a regular file (not a directory, pipe, link, or device). The exclamation point <!> is the not operator changing the test to: If the file does not exist or, it exists and is not a regular file, then the condition is true. With the `-r` flag, if the file exists and is readable, the expression is true. The condition is true if the file does not exist or it exists and is not readable. If either of the conditions is true, the entire condition is true because the vertical pipes together <||> is the or operator.

To check a file that will be written to (replaced or updated), use the `-w` flag instead of the `-r`. The `-w` flag checks to see if the file exists and you have write permission to it.

The files in lines 22 and 23 will be created (DISP=NEW). To ensure their existence even if the program does not create them, the touch command is used. The greater than operator could also be used, which would ensure the file was created and was empty.

Lines 24 and 25 are used for temporary files. Temporary files are typically placed in the directory /tmp unless the system administrator creates a special temporary area for your application. The dollar sign <$> is a special variable; it contains the current process id. To access the value, the substitution character is used (also the dollar sign) as <$$>. Line 24 creates a temporary file without a name, equivalent to a DD without a DSN—only the process id, a period, the date in the format YYMMDD.HHmmSS. So long as you do not create unnamed temporary files one right after the other, you will get a unique name, even if multiple copies of the job are running at the same time. Line 25 creates a temporary file equivalent to a DD DSN=&&TEMPN with the name tempn, followed by a period, the process id, a period, and the date in the format YYMMDD.HHmmSS.

Line 26 defines the variable PARM to simulate the PARM= parameter on the EXEC statement. The values it contains are substituted when the variable is used on line 27.

Line 27 executes the program (like the EXEC PGM= statement in JCL). Normal output (stdout) is redirected and appended to the SYSOUT file; error output (stderr) is redirected and appended to the SYSERR file. The output of program_to_run is appended to the output files with the >> (redirect and append stdout) and 2>> (redirect and append stderr) instead of the > and 2> redirection. Redirection with single greater than signs creates a new file for output. We want the stdout and stderr from each program in this job to go into the same file.

The question mark <?> on line 28 is a special variable because it contains the return code from the last command. To access the value, the substitution character is used as <$?>. The value is saved in the variable step010_rc because the return code is set after every command. By saving the value, it can be checked in a later step.

Line 29 reports when the step ended and whether it was successful or not (by printing the return code).

Lines 30 through 35 are part of an if statement structure. Line 30 is the test and 31 specifies the code to execute if the comparison is true. If the return code from step010 is zero, then the code for successful completion is executed. In this case, line 32 deletes the error file that is the disposition from DISP=(NEW,DELETE,KEEP)—keep only if there is a failure.

Line 33 begins the else portion of the if test. If the return code from step010 is not zero, then the code for failure is executed. In this case, line 34 deletes the output file that is equivalent to DISP=(NEW,KEEP,DELETE).

Line 35 ends the if structure begun on line 30.

Lines 36 through 39 are another if statement structure. If the return code from step010 is higher than the current highest return code, it should replace the old value. This code appears after each step so that the highest return code can be reported at the end of the job. The structure of the if statement is a little different, in that tests within a single set of square brackets are the old Bourne format with limited functionality, tests within double set of square brackets are Korn format that provide additional features (such as greater than comparisons).

The second step of the job, step020, occupies lines 40 through 65. Lines 40 and 41 are comments describing the step.

Because there is not a special STEPLIB for this step, lines 42 and 43 change the PATH to include an empty STEPLIB, the JOBLIB, and the original search path SAVE_PATH.

The rest of the step, lines 44 through 65, are contained within an if statement structure. This is equivalent to COND=(0,LT,STEP010) on the EXEC PGM= statement. Lines 44 and 45 cause the step to be executed if step010 is successful. Versions 4.0 and newer of MVS support an if-then/else/endif structure (the else or false portion of the structure is optional) in the general form:

```
// IF (STEP010.RC GE 6 AND STEP010.RC LE 12) THEN
    JCL to execute if the return code from STEP010 is between 6 and 12
// ELSE
    JCL to execute if the return code from STEP010 is not between 6 and 12
// ENDIF
```

Lines 46 and 47 are similar to the data definitions in step010.

Line 48 is an example of a data definition that refers back to a prior one. The filename stored in dd_FILEOUT will be stored in dd_REFERBK. This is equivalent to a DD DSN=*.STEP010.FILEOUT.

Lines 49 and 50 define parameters for the program in this step and then run program2. Lines 51 and 52 save the return code and print the step completion message.

Lines 53 through 58 are part of an if statement structure. If the return code from step020 is zero, then the code for successful completion is executed. In this case, line 55 does nothing, since the successful dispositions were all KEEP. The colon character <:> is used whenever a statement is required but none is used (NO-OP). There must be a statement between then/else and else/fi or then/fi; if there is no statement that should be executed, then the colon character fills the need. Another name for the colon character when used this way is the Null Statement.

Line 56 begins the else portion of the if test. If the return code from step020 is not zero, then the code for failure is executed. In this case, line 57 also does nothing since the failure dispositions were all KEEP.

Line 58 ends the if structure begun on line 53. This code is included to standardize the structure of each step and provide for future changes. The processing overhead that this puts on the CPU is minimal.

Lines 59 through 62 are another if statement structure performing the same function as the code in step010: change the highest return code if the one from this step is higher.

Line 63 is the else condition to the else that began on line 44. If step010 failed, this step is not executed and a message to that effect is printed out. Line 65 ends the if condition begun on line 44 and the step, step020.

The final job step, step030, occupies lines 66 through 88. Lines 66, 67, and 68 are comments describing the step.

This step decides to use only the original search path SAVE_PATH, completely ignoring the JOBLIB and not providing any STEPLIB. This is something that mainframe JCL does not support.

The rest of the steps, lines 70 through 87, are contained within an if statement structure. This is equivalent to COND=((0,NE,STEP010),(0,EQ,STEP020) on the EXEC PGM= statement. Lines 70 and 71 cause the step to be executed only if step010 is successful and step020 was not.

Lines 46 and 47 are similar to the data definitions in step010.

There is no data or PARM definitions for this step.

Line 72 runs report_error. Lines 73 and 74 save the return code and print the step completion message.

Lines 75 through 80 are part of an if statement structure. If the return code from step030 is zero, then the code for successful completion is executed. Like lines 55 and 57, nothing is done here because there were no data definitions or dispositions to clean up. Like step020, this code is included to standardize the structure of each step and provide for future changes, with minimal processing overhead.

Lines 81 through 84 are another if statement structure performing the same function as the code in step010 and step020: change the highest return code if the one from this step is higher.

Line 85 is the else condition to the else that began on line 70. If step010 failed or step020 was successful, this step is not executed and a message to that effect is printed out. Line 87 ends the if condition begun on line 70 and the step step030.

The remaining lines, 88, 89, and 90, are post-processing for the job. A message is printed with the maximum return code within the job. That return code is then returned to the operating system through the exit statement so it can be checked by the process that ran the job. The job may have been run by scheduling software, a user, another job, or cron. No matter how the job was run, when it completes, the return code in the parent process (<$>) will contain the maximum return code that this job produced.

Replacing Jobs and PROCs in JCL with Shell Scripts

This section covers the EXEC PROC= statement and how jobs and PROCs interact. It also includes information on concatenating files, DD DUMMY a.k.a. DD DSN=NULLFILE, symbolics, overrides, and return code processing by a job. The differences between jobs alone and jobs with PROCs are highlighted.

Each of the lines in the following job are numbered. Each of the lines will be explained. The job consists of one step that runs a PROC with three steps. The PROC is similar to the simple job in the prior section.

Line Korn shell statement

```
1       #! /bin/ksh
2       #
3       #
4       #      Job setup
5       set -o xtrace
6       export JOBNAME="The_Job_Name"
7       export SAVE_PATH=$PATH
8       export JOBLIB="/search/me/first:/search/me/next:/search/me/then:"
9       HLQ=/u/dhorvath/cob_stuff
10      SYSOUT_DIRECTORY="/u/dhorvath/cob_stuff"
11      SYSOUT=${SYSOUT_DIRECTORY}/RUN.LOG
```

```
12        > $SYSOUT                              # create sysout file
13       SYSERR=${SYSOUT_DIRECTORY}/RUN.LOG
14        > $SYSERR                              # create syserr file
15       MAX_RC=0
16       print "$JOBNAME STARTED `date`  " >> $SYSOUT 2>> $SYSERR
17       #    Step 10
18       #               Use STEPLIB and JOBLIB for program
19       STEPLIB="/search/me/override/one:/search/me/override/two:"
20       PATH=${STEPLIB}${JOBLIB}${SAVE_PATH}
21       jobs_proc ${HLQ} ${SYSOUT} ${SYSERR} '' other
22       step010_rc=$?
23       print "$JOBNAME STEP010 ENDED `date` RC=${step010_rc} " >> $SYSOUT 2>> $SYSERR
24       if [ $step010_rc = 0 ]
25       then
26          :
27       else
28          :
29       fi
30       if [[ $step010_rc > $MAX_RC ]]
31       then
32          MAX_RC=$step010_rc
33       fi
34       # Post job processing
35       print "$JOBNAME ENDED `date` MAXIMUM RC=${MAX_RC} " >> $SYSOUT 2>> $SYSERR
36       exit ${MAX_RC}
```

Lines 1 through 16 are setup and initialization. Lines 17 through 33 are for step010. The remaining lines, 34 through 36, are for reporting the status of the job.

The setup and initialization lines are the same between simple job and job with PROCs examples.

Lines 17 and 18 are comments for step010. Lines 19 and 20 define the path that is searched for the file jobs_proc. As far as the shell is concerned, jobs_proc is just another program, utility, command, or script. The special meaning is assigned by us.

Line 21 executes the PROC. Instead of being able to override default parameters in the PROC with EXEC PROC=procname,SYMBOLIC='NEW-VALUES', positional parameters are used. In this case, the first is the high-level qualifier for filenames, the second is the SYSOUT file, the third is the SYSERR file, the fourth is empty (a pair of single quotes <‘>), and the final parameter is the word other. Within the PROC, those values will be assigned to the variables $1, $2, $3, $4, and $5 (see the explanation on line 7 of the PROC).

Lines 22 and 23 save the return code and print the step completion message.

Lines 24 through 29 are part of an if statement structure. If the return code from step010 is zero, then the code for successful completion is executed. In this case, line 26 does nothing, since there is nothing special required, no disposition processing. Line 27 begins the else portion of the if test. If the return code from step010 is not zero, then the code for failure is executed. In this case, line 28 also does nothing since there is nothing to do on failure.

Line 29 ends the if structure begun on line 24. This code is included to standardize the structure of each step and provide for future changes. The processing overhead that this puts on the CPU is minimal.

Lines 30 through 33 are another if statement structure used to change the highest return code if the one from this step is higher. Again, this if statement is unnecessary since there is only one step in the job, but it is standardized and causes minimal processor overhead. Since there is only one step, it could be replaced with line 32 alone:

```
MAX_RC=$step010_rc
```

The remaining lines, 34, 35, and 36, are post-processing for the job. A message is printed with the maximum return code within the job. That return code is then returned to the operating system through the exit statement so it can be checked by the process that ran the job.

Each of the lines in the following PROC are numbered. Each of the lines will be explained. The PROC consists of three steps, the third runs only if the first was successful and the second failed. It is very similar to the simple job in the prior section.

Line Korn shell statement

```
1    #! /bin/ksh
2    #
3    #
4    #     Proc setup
5    set -o xtrace
6    MAX_RC=0
7    HLQ=${1:-"/u/dhorvath"}
8    SYSOUT=${2:-"default_sysout.log"}
9    SYSERR=${3:-"default_syserr.log"}
10   print "$JOBNAME $0 STARTED `date`  " >> $SYSOUT 2>> $SYSERR
11   #    Step 10
12   #              Use STEPLIB and JOBLIB for program
13   STEPLIB=${5:-"/search/me/override/one:/search/me/override/two:"}
14   PATH=${STEPLIB}${JOBLIB}${SAVE_PATH}
15   dd_FILEIN=${HLQ}/FILE.IN    # DISP=(OLD,KEEP,KEEP)
16   dd_FILEOUT=${HLQ}/FILE.OUT; touch $dd_FILEOUT   # DISP=(NEW,KEEP,DELETE)
17   dd_ERRORS=${HLQ}/ERROR.FILE; touch $dd_ERRORS   # DISP=(NEW,DELETE,KEEP)
18   dd_MAYNEED=${4:-"/dev/null"}                    # DD DUMMY/override
19   dd_TEMP1=/tmp/$$.'date +"%y%m%d.%H%M%S"'
20   dd_TEMPN=/tmp/tempn.$$.'date +"%y%m%d.%H%M%S"'
21   PARM="input parameters"
22   program_to_run "$PARM" >> $SYSOUT 2>> $SYSERR
23   step010_rc=$?
```

```
print "$JOBNAME $0 STEP010 ENDED `date` RC=${step010_rc} " >> $SYSOUT 2>> $SYSERR
if [ $step010_rc = 0 ]
then
   rm $dd_ERRORS        # DISP=(NEW,DELETE,KEEP)
else
   rm $dd_FILEOUT       # DISP=(NEW,KEEP,DELETE)
fi
if [[ $step010_rc > $MAX_RC ]]
then
   MAX_RC=$step010_rc
fi
#    Step 20     run only if step010 is OK.
#                Use JOBLIB only for program
STEPLIB=":"
PATH=${STEPLIB}${JOBLIB}${SAVE_PATH}
if [ $step010_rc = 0 ]
then
   dd_INFILE=${HLQ}/THIS.FILE    # DISP=(OLD,KEEP,KEEP)
   dd_OUTFILE=${HLQ}/THAT.FILE; touch $dd_OUTFILE # DISP=(NEW,KEEP,KEEP)
   dd_REFERBK=$dd_FILEOUT        # refer back to prior DD example
   PARM="other input parameters"
   program2 "$PARM" >> $SYSOUT 2>> $SYSERR
   step020_rc=$?
   print "$JOBNAME $0 STEP020 ENDED `date` RC=${step020_rc} " >> $SYSOUT 2>> $SYSERR
   if [ $step020_rc = 0 ]
   then
      :        # no action
   else
      :        # no action
   fi
   if [[ $step020_rc > $MAX_RC ]]
   then
      MAX_RC=$step020_rc
   fi
else
   print "$JOBNAME $0 STEP020 BYPASSED `date` " >> $SYSOUT 2>> $SYSERR
fi
#
#    Step 30     run only if step010 is OK and step020 is bad.
#                Use system default libraries (PATH)
PATH=${SAVE_PATH}
if [[ $step010_rc = 0  &&  $step020_rc != 0 ]]
then
   report_error "INPUT parameters" >> $SYSOUT 2>> $SYSERR
   step030_rc=$?
   print "$JOBNAME $0 STEP030 ENDED `date` RC=${step030_rc} ">>$SYSOUT 2>> $SYSERR
```

```
70         if [ $step030_rc = 0 ]
71         then
72            :        # no action
73         else
74            :        # no action
75         fi
76         if [[ $step030_rc > $MAX_RC ]]
77         then
78            MAX_RC=$step030_rc
79         fi
80      else
81         print "$JOBNAME $0 STEP030 BYPASSED `date` " >> $SYSOUT 2>> $SYSERR
82      fi
83      # Post job processing
84      print "$JOBNAME $0 ENDED `date` MAXIMUM RC=${MAX_RC} " >> $SYSOUT 2>> $SYSERR
85      exit $MAX_RC
```

Lines 1 through 10 are setup and initialization. Lines 11 through 34 are for step010, 35 through 60 for step020, and 61 through 82 for step030. The remaining lines, 83 through 85, are for reporting the status of the PROC.

Lines 1 through 6 are similar to the jobs: specifying the shell, comments about the file, MSGCLASS=(1,0), and initializing the maximum return code variable.

Line 7 is different from any of the substitutions shown so far. The high-level qualifier is set to the first parameter on the line with the command job_procs on it (line 21 in the job). If that parameter is missing or empty (known as a null parameter), the value /u/dhorvath is used. In this example, the actual value will be /u/dhorvath/cob_stuff because the default value is overridden in the job.

Lines 8 and 9 define the files for the SYSOUT (stdout) and SYSERR (stderr). It is assumed that the driver JCL job has already created the files. If no parameter is passed in $2 or $3, then the default will be used, just like parameters in a mainframe PROC statement.

Line 10 prints a message that the PROC has begun. The job and PROC names are shown. Because JOBNAME is exported by the driver job, the PROC can access it—the parent has set up the environment for the child. The filename of the PROC is stored in $0, the filename of a shell script is always stored in $0 so it is available for processing within the script. All of the print statements in the PROC include the variables $JOBNAME and $0 to identify them as coming from this PROC.

Step 10 occupies lines 11 through 34. The first seven lines are the same in the PROC and the simple job with the exception of the STEPLIB. The STEPLIB on line 13 is set to the fifth positional parameter on the command line (line 21 in the job) or, if no value is provided, set to /search/me/override/one: /search/me/override/two:.

Line 18 is new. It demonstrates how to have a DD DUMMY a.k.a. DD DSN=NULLFILE and override it if necessary. Any DD that is DUMMY or DSN=NULLFILE will immediately return an end-of-file condition if read from and will absorb any data written to it (dumping it in the bit-bucket). If no parameter is specified in position 4 of job line 21, then the default of /dev/null is used. In this example, positional parameter 4 is '' or an empty string, and the default is used. If a value had been specified, then it would have been used.

Lines 19 through 30 are the same as the simple job example. Two temporary files are created, parameters for the program defined, the program executed (program_to_run), the return code saved, a message generated showing the step was finished, and the return code processed. A successful step010 gets rid of the error file and a failed step deletes the output file mimicking mainframe disposition processing.

Lines 31 through 34 perform return code checking. If the return code of the current step is higher than the maximum return code, then it replaces the maximum.

Step 20 occupies lines 35 through 60. With the exception of the PROC name in the print statements, this step is the same as the step020 in the simple job.

Step 30, occupying lines 61 through 82, is also the same as step030 in the simple job with the exception of the print statements.

Lines 83 through 85 are post processing for the PROC. A message is printed with the maximum return code within the PROC. That return code is then returned to the job through the exit statement so it can be checked. The only difference in the code between the PROC and the job is the print statement that contains the PROC name.

In reality, the only difference between a job and a PROC in shell scripts is a conceptual one. It is the belief that a job will call or execute a PROC, that a PROC cannot be executed directly from the command line, and that the job must set up certain variables for the PROC to run correctly.

Prior to Version 4.0 of MVS, only a job could execute a PROC. A PROC could only execute programs, not other PROCs. After that release, PROCs could be nested—one PROC can execute another. The Korn shell supports this capability because shell scripts behave like any other command, there is no distinction between the two like there is on the mainframe.

The INCLUDE JCL statement was also added with that release of MVS, the ability to insert pieces of JCL from another PDS within a job or PROC during execution. Although the Korn shell does not have an include command, the functionality can be mimicked by executing statements within the current shell process. As mentioned previously, the dot command causes the commands in the specified file to be executed in the current shell, the same as including them into the current file for execution. The format would be:

```
. included_file_name
```

Running Jobs

As shown earlier in this chapter, there are several ways to run jobs interactively under UNIX. They can be executed as part of the current shell or as part of a subshell; they can be executed in the foreground (interactive) or in the background (batch); they can be submitted from the terminal or scheduled via cron. Each of the JCL-in-script examples were executed twice, once with step020 succeeding and once with it failing.

Each of the jobs was executed with the following command:

```
$ nohup time jobs_1 > JCL.LOG &↵
$
```

All stdout and stderr that are not redirected will go into the file JCL.LOG in the current directory. Each of the steps sends its stdout and stderr into another file (RUN.LOG). The stdout and stderr from the nohup command should not be sent to the file as the redirection on the individual steps in that job. Because of the way the processes are created and the resulting output files are shared, the redirected step output would be lost.

Sample Output—Job, Step, and Program Output —Simple Job Run Successfully

The first sample run involves the simple job with successful completion. The command was submitted using nohup, redirecting the stdout and stderr for the entire job to the file JCL.LOG, and running it in the background. The job was submitted interactively, but could just as readily been run through cron.

All program_to_run and program2 do is output its name followed by any input parameters from the command line.

```
$ nohup time jobs_1 > JCL.LOG &↵
[1]     5461
$ ↵                              (After waiting a few moments)
[1] + 5461       Done                  nohup time jobs_1 > JCL.LOG &
$ cat RUN.LOG↵
The_Job_Name STARTED Tue Feb 20 10:03:59 EST 1995
program to run input parameters
The_Job_Name STEP010 ENDED Tue Feb 20 10:03:59 EST 1995 RC=0
program 2 other input parameters
The_Job_Name STEP020 ENDED Tue Feb 20 10:04:00 EST 1995 RC=0
The_Job_Name STEP030 BYPASSED Tue Feb 20 10:04:00 EST 1995
The_Job_Name ENDED Tue Feb 20 10:04:00 EST 1995 MAXIMUM RC=0
$ echo $?↵
0
$
```

The job started at 10:03:59 on February 20, 1995. Step 10 ended with a return code of zero within the same second; its command line parameters were "input parameters." Step 20 ended with a return code of zero at 10:04:00; its command line parameters were "other input parameters." Step 30 was bypassed since its conditions were not met, and the job ended. The maximum return code during job execution was zero as reflected in the last message and proven by displaying the return code of the job itself.

The file, JCL.LOG, contains output similar to the JCL listing from a mainframe job. With the proper settings, you will see all of the executable lines as they are executed (with substitutions). Line 5 in both jobs consists of the statement set -o xtrace. To turn the trace off, use set +o xtrace. The line number on the left of the execution example below was created by the following command:

```
$ export PS4='[$0+$LINENO]'↵
$
```

Which sets the prompt for xtraces to a square bracket, the name of the script being run (job or PROC), the plus sign, the line number being executed in the current file, and, finally, another square bracket. The contents of JCL.LOG follow:

```
[./jobs_1+6]export JOBNAME=The_Job_Name
[./jobs_1+7]export SAVE_PATH=.:/application_1/prod/scripts:/application_2/prod/
cobol:/usr/ibs/ksh:/usr/tool/bin:/usr2/other_tool/bin:/usr2/spfux/aixbin:/usr2/
unispf:/usr2/unispf/twglm:/application_1/tools:/usr/bin:/etc:/usr/sbin:/usr/ucb:/
usr/bin/X11:/sbin:.:
[./jobs_1+8]export JOBLIB=/search/me/first:/search/me/next:/search/me/then:
[./jobs_1+9]HLQ=/u/dhorvath/cob_stuff
[./jobs_1+10]SYSOUT_DIRECTORY=/u/dhorvath/cob_stuff
[./jobs_1+11]SYSOUT=/u/dhorvath/cob_stuff/RUN.LOG
[./jobs_1+13]1> /u/dhorvath/cob_stuff/RUN.LOG
[./jobs_1+13]SYSERR=/u/dhorvath/cob_stuff/RUN.LOG
[./jobs_1+15]1> /u/dhorvath/cob_stuff/RUN.LOG
[./jobs_1+15]MAX_RC=0
[./jobs_1+16]date
[./jobs_1+16]print The_Job_Name STARTED Tue Feb 20 10:03:59 EST 1996
[./jobs_1+16]1>> /u/dhorvath/cob_stuff/RUN.LOG 2>> /u/dhorvath/cob_stuff/RUN.LOG
[./jobs_1+19]STEPLIB=/search/me/override/one:/search/me/override/two:
[./jobs_1+20]PATH=/search/me/override/one:/search/me/override/two:/search/me/
first:/search/me/next:/search/me/then:.:/application_1/prod/scripts:/applica-
tion_2/prod/cobol:/usr/ibs/ksh:/usr/tool/bin:/usr2/other_tool/bin:/usr2/spfux/
aixbin:/usr2/unispf:/usr2/unispf/twglm:/application_1/tools:/usr/bin:/etc:/usr/
sbin:/usr/ucb:/usr/bin/X11:/sbin:.:
[./jobs_1+21]dd_FILEIN=/u/dhorvath/cob_stuff/FILE.IN
[./jobs_1+22]dd_FILEOUT=/u/dhorvath/cob_stuff/FILE.OUT
[./jobs_1+22]touch /u/dhorvath/cob_stuff/FILE.OUT
[./jobs_1+23]dd_ERRORS=/u/dhorvath/cob_stuff/ERROR.FILE
[./jobs_1+23]touch /u/dhorvath/cob_stuff/ERROR.FILE
[./jobs_1+24][./jobs_1+24]date +%y%m%d.%H%M%S
dd_TEMP1=/tmp/18549.960220.100359
[./jobs_1+25][./jobs_1+25]date +%y%m%d.%H%M%S
dd_TEMPN=/tmp/tempn.18549.960220.100359
[./jobs_1+26]PARM=input parameters
[./jobs_1+27]program_to_run input parameters
[./jobs_1+27]1>> /u/dhorvath/cob_stuff/RUN.LOG 2>> /u/dhorvath/cob_stuff/RUN.LOG
[./jobs_1+28]step010_rc=0
[./jobs_1+29]date
[./jobs_1+29]print The_Job_Name STEP010 ENDED Tue Feb 20 10:03:59 EST 1996 RC=0
[./jobs_1+29]1>> /u/dhorvath/cob_stuff/RUN.LOG 2>> /u/dhorvath/cob_stuff/RUN.LOG
[./jobs_1+30][ 0 = 0 ]
[./jobs_1+32]rm /u/dhorvath/cob_stuff/FILE.OUT
```

```
[./jobs_1+36][[ 0 > 0 ]]
[./jobs_1+42]STEPLIB=:
[./jobs_1+43]PATH=:/search/me/first:/search/me/next:/search/me/then:.:/application_1/prod/scripts:/application_2/prod/cobol:/usr/ibs/ksh:/usr/tool/bin:/usr2/other_tool/bin:/usr2/spfux/aixbin:/usr2/unispf:/usr2/unispf/twglm:/application_1/tools:/usr/bin:/etc:/usr/sbin:/usr/ucb:/usr/bin/X11:/sbin:.:
[./jobs_1+44][ 0 = 0 ]
[./jobs_1+46]dd_INFILE=/u/dhorvath/cob_stuff/THIS.FILE
[./jobs_1+47]dd_OUTFILE=/u/dhorvath/cob_stuff/THAT.FILE
[./jobs_1+47]touch /u/dhorvath/cob_stuff/THAT.FILE
[./jobs_1+48]dd_REFERBK=/u/dhorvath/cob_stuff/FILE.OUT
[./jobs_1+49]PARM=other input parameters
[./jobs_1+50]program2 other input parameters
[./jobs_1+50]1>> /u/dhorvath/cob_stuff/RUN.LOG 2>> /u/dhorvath/cob_stuff/RUN.LOG
[./jobs_1+51]step020_rc=0
[./jobs_1+52]date
[./jobs_1+52]print The_Job_Name STEP020 ENDED Tue Feb 20 10:04:00 EST 1996 RC=0
[./jobs_1+52]1>> /u/dhorvath/cob_stuff/RUN.LOG 2>> /u/dhorvath/cob_stuff/RUN.LOG
[./jobs_1+53][ 0 = 0 ]
[./jobs_1+55]:
[./jobs_1+55][[ 0 > 0 ]]
[./jobs_1+69]PATH=.:/application_1/prod/scripts:/application_2/prod/cobol:/usr/ibs/ksh:/usr/tool/bin:/usr2/other_tool/bin:/usr2/spfux/aixbin:/usr2/unispf:/usr2/unispf/twglm:/application_1/tools:/usr/bin:/etc:/usr/sbin:/usr/ucb:/usr/bin/X11:/sbin:.:
[./jobs_1+70][[ 0 = 0 ]]
[./jobs_1+70][[ 0 != 0 ]]
[./jobs_1+86]date
[./jobs_1+86]print The_Job_Name STEP030 BYPASSED Tue Feb 20 10:04:00 EST 1996
[./jobs_1+86]1>> /u/dhorvath/cob_stuff/RUN.LOG 2>> /u/dhorvath/cob_stuff/RUN.LOG
[./jobs_1+89]date
[./jobs_1+89]print The_Job_Name ENDED Tue Feb 20 10:04:00 EST 1996 MAXIMUM RC=0
[./jobs_1+89]1>> /u/dhorvath/cob_stuff/RUN.LOG 2>> /u/dhorvath/cob_stuff/RUN.LOG
[./jobs_1+90]exit 0

real    0.9
user    0.1
sys     0.2
```

The last three lines are the output from the time command when the job was executed. This job took less than 1 second of elapsed time to run and consumed a total of 0.3 CPU seconds.

Sample Output—Job, Step, and Program Output—Simple Job Run Failed

The second sample run involves the simple job with a step that failed. The command was submitted using nohup, redirecting the stdout and stderr for the entire job to the file JCL.LOG, and running it in the background. The job was submitted interactively, but could just as readily been run through cron.

The first step runs program_to_run, which merely outputs its name followed by any input parameters from the command line. The second step runs program2, which performs the same function and returns an error (program failure or abend). The third step now has its input conditions met and executes.

```
$ nohup time jobs_1 > JCL.LOG &↵
[1]     5463
$ ↵                              (After waiting a few moments)
[1] + 5463       Done                 nohup time jobs_1 > JCL.LOG &
$ cat RUN.LOG↵
The_Job_Name STARTED Tue Feb 20 10:03:15 EST 1995
program to run input parameters
The_Job_Name STEP010 ENDED Tue Feb 20 10:03:15 EST 1995 RC=0
program 2 other input parameters
The_Job_Name STEP020 ENDED Tue Feb 20 10:03:15 EST 1995 RC=27
report errors INPUT parameters
The_Job_Name STEP030 ENDED Tue Feb 20 10:03:15 EST 1995 RC=0
The_Job_Name ENDED Tue Feb 20 10:03:15 EST 1995 MAXIMUM RC=27
$ echo $?↵
27
$
```

The job started at 10:03:15 on February 20, 1995. Step 10 ended with a return code of zero within the same second its command line parameters were "input parameters." Step 20 ended with a return code of 27 (some error) the same second; its command line parameters were "other input parameters." Step 30 was executed since its conditions were met, it ended with a return code of zero the same second. The job then ended with the maximum return code displayed in the message. The echo as the next command verified the return code of the job itself.

Sample Output—Job, Step, and Program Output—Job/PROC Run Successful

The third sample run involves the job with a PROC that ran successfully. The command was submitted using nohup, redirecting the stdout and stderr for the entire job to the file JCL.LOG, and running it in the background. The job was submitted interactively, but could just as readily been run through cron.

The first (and only step) in the job runs the PROC. The first two steps in the PROC run program_to_run and program2, which merely outputs their name followed by any input parameters from the command line. The third step does not have its input conditions met and does not execute.

```
$ nohup time jobs_p > JCL.LOG &↵
[1]     5465
$ ↵                              (After waiting a few moments)
[1] + 5465       Done                 nohup time jobs_p > JCL.LOG &
$ cat RUN.LOG↵
The_Job_Name STARTED Tue Feb 20 10:04:20 EST 1995
The_Job_Name ./jobs_proc STARTED Tue Feb 20 10:04:20 EST 1995
program to run input parameters
```

```
The_Job_Name ./jobs_proc STEP010 ENDED Tue Feb 20 10:04:20 EST 1995 RC=0
program 2 other input parameters
The_Job_Name ./jobs_proc STEP020 ENDED Tue Feb 20 10:04:20 EST 1995 RC=0
The_Job_Name ./jobs_proc STEP030 BYPASSED Tue Feb 20 10:04:20 EST 1995
The_Job_Name ./jobs_proc ENDED Tue Feb 20 10:04:20 EST 1995 MAXIMUM RC=0
The_Job_Name STEP010 ENDED Tue Feb 20 10:04:20 EST 1995 RC=0
The_Job_Name ENDED Tue Feb 20 10:04:20 EST 1995 MAXIMUM RC=0
$ echo $?↵
0
$
```

The job started at 10:04:20 on February 20, 1995. The PROC jobs_proc began during the same second. Step 10 ended with a return code of zero within the same second, its command line parameters were "input parameters." Step 20 ended with a return code of zero within the same second; its command line parameters were "other input parameters." Step 30 was bypassed since its conditions were not met, and the PROC ended. The maximum return code from the PROC was returned to the job and job step 10 ended successfully (because the PROC ended successfully). The job ended with a maximum return code of zero as reflected in the last message and proven by displaying the return code of the job itself.

The file, JCL.LOG, contains output similar to the JCL listing from a mainframe job. Only those lines relevant to the differences between simple jobs and jobs with PROCs will be shown. In the following example, line 21 of the job runs the PROC and the lines that follow coming from the PROC:

```
[./jobs_p+21]jobs_proc /u/dhorvath/cob_stuff /u/dhorvath/cob_stuff/RUN.LOG /u/
dhorvath/cob_stuff/RUN.LOG  other
[./jobs_proc+6]MAX_RC=0
[./jobs_proc+7]HLQ=/u/dhorvath/cob_stuff
[./jobs_proc+8]SYSOUT=/u/dhorvath/cob_stuff/RUN.LOG
[./jobs_proc+9]SYSERR=/u/dhorvath/cob_stuff/RUN.LOG
```

The parameters are expanded on the command line and lines 7, 8, and 9. Because no parameter was specified for position 4, line 18 in the PROC defaulted to the value in the PROC as shown:

```
[./jobs_proc+18]dd_MAYNEED=/dev/null
```

The PROC runs steps 10 and 20. Step 30 is bypassed. When the PROC ends, it prints the message and returns the maximum return code to the calling program (line 85). The job saves the return code for future processing (line 22) as shown below:

```
[./jobs_proc+84]print The_Job_Name ./jobs_proc ENDED Tue Feb 20 10:04:20 EST 1996
MAXIMUM RC=0
[./jobs_proc+84]1>> /u/dhorvath/cob_stuff/RUN.LOG 2>> /u/dhorvath/cob_stuff/RUN.LOG
[./jobs_proc+85]exit 0
[./jobs_p+22]step010_rc=0
```

The return code processing at the end of a PROC closely mimics the return code processing at the end of a job. The only difference is that after the PROC ends, the job saves the return code, after a job ends, the return code is not. The final three lines are the output from the time command when the job was executed. This job took less than 1 second of elapsed time to run and consumed a total of 0.5 CPU seconds:

```
real   0.9
user   0.2
sys    0.3
```

Using a PROC required slightly more CPU time because more statements were executed, but the difference really is not significant when performing large amounts of processing. The elapsed time remained the same.

Sample Output—Job, Step, and Program Output—Job/PROC Run Failed

The final sample run involves the job with a PROC that has a step that failed. The command was submitted using nohup, redirecting the stdout and stderr for the entire job to the file JCL.LOG, and running it in the background. The job was submitted interactively, but could just as readily been run through cron.

The first step in the PROC runs program_to_run, which merely outputs its name followed by any input parameters from the command line. The second PROC step runs program2, which performs the same function and returns an error (program failure or abend). The third PROC step now has its input conditions met and executes.

```
$ nohup time jobs_p > JCL.LOG &↵
[1]     5469
$ ↵                                  (After waiting a few moments)
[1] + 5469        Done                    nohup time jobs_p > JCL.LOG &
$ cat RUN.LOG↵
The_Job_Name STARTED Tue Feb 20 10:03:39 EST 1995
The_Job_Name ./jobs_proc STARTED Tue Feb 20 10:03:39 EST 1995
program to run input parameters
The_Job_Name ./jobs_proc STEP010 ENDED Tue Feb 20 10:03:40 EST 1995 RC=0
program 2 other input parameters
The_Job_Name ./jobs_proc STEP020 ENDED Tue Feb 20 10:03:40 EST 1995 RC=27
report errors INPUT parameters
The_Job_Name ./jobs_proc STEP030 ENDED Tue Feb 20 10:03:40 EST 1995 RC=0
The_Job_Name ./jobs_proc ENDED Tue Feb 20 10:03:40 EST 1995 MAXIMUM RC=27
The_Job_Name STEP010 ENDED Tue Feb 20 10:03:40 EST 1995 RC=27
The_Job_Name ENDED Tue Feb 20 10:03:40 EST 1995 MAXIMUM RC=27
$ echo $?↵
27
$
```

The job started at 10:03:39 on February 20, 1995. The PROC jobs_proc began during the same second. Step 10 ended with a return code of zero at 10:03:40; its command line parameters were "input parameters." Step 20 failed, ending with a return code of 27 within the same second; its command line parameters were "other input parameters." Step 30 was executed since its conditions were met, and then the PROC ended. The maximum return code from the PROC (27) was returned to the job and job step 10 failed (because the PROC failed). The job ended with a maximum return code of 27 as reflected in the last message and proven by displaying the return code of the job itself.

CONCATENATING FILES

When multiple DD statements are associated with a single DD name, the operating system treats all the datasets specified as a single dataset for the program. When the end of the first dataset is reached, it is closed and the next opened. This is repeated without program intervention until the end of the last dataset is reached and the program is informed of the end-of-file condition. UNIX does not provide the ability to concatenate files on the fly like the mainframe, but it does provide facilities to concatenate files.

There are two ways to replace mainframe dataset concatenation under UNIX: temporary files and pipes. To the program being executed, there is one file, just like on the mainframe. The difference is the complexity of the script code and disk space required. With temporary files, the members of the concatenated dataset are copied into a single temporary file that the program reads as the original name. With pipes, a named pipe is created and the multiple files are copied through the pipe into the program as the program is executing. The two sides of the pipe (writer and reader) run a the same time, the writer being a subprocess of the job or PROC running.

Concatenated Datasets Through Temporary Files

The simplest way to replace concatenated datasets is to create a temporary file that the program then reads. Temporary space is used, and there can be a performance issue if there is a large volume of data. In addition, there must be enough temporary space to handle the combined files. Remember the 2 GB file size limit within many versions of UNIX—the combined files must not exceed this limit. If you expect to concatenate large volumes of data (over 100 MB), use named pipes for those files instead.

The following segment of a script concatenates five files into a temporary file that is assigned the DD name of the original concatenated DD:

```
#   Concatenate the files belonging to INFILE
dd_INFILE=/tmp/$$.'date +"%y%m%d.%H%M%S"'
dd_CONC1=${HLQ}/FILE.IN.1                        # DISP=(OLD,KEEP,KEEP)
dd_CONC2=${HLQ}/FILE.IN.NEXT                     # DISP=(OLD,KEEP,KEEP)
dd_CONC3=${HLQ}/FILE.IN.THIRD                    # DISP=(OLD,KEEP,KEEP)
dd_CONC4=${HLQ}/FILE.IN.FOURTH                   # DISP=(OLD,KEEP,KEEP)
dd_CONC5=${HLQ}/FILE.IN.LAST                     # DISP=(OLD,KEEP,KEEP)
cat $dd_CONC1 $dd_CONC2 $dd_CONC3 $dd_CONC4 $dd_CONC5 > $dd_INFILE
step123a_rc=$?
#
#   STEP 123
if [step123a_rc != 0]
```

```
then
   dd_OUTFILE=${HLQ}/THE.OUTPUT.FILE; touch $dd_OUTFILE #DISP=(NEW,KEEP,DELETE)
   PARM="Program Parameters"
   the_program $PARM >> $SYSOUT 2>> $SYSERR
   step123_rc=$?
#   The rest of the step...
   rm $dd_INFILE                               # clean up when done
#   The rest of the job...
```

If the `cat` command fails, it will return a non-zero status and the rest of the job can be bypassed. An if statement can be added after each DD for the concatenated files to verify it exists and is readable.

Concatenated Datasets Through Named Pipes

The other way to replace concatenated datasets is to create a named pipe and have the writer feed data to the program as it reads the data. Practically zero space is used in the temporary area and there is no need to worry about running out of temporary space or reaching the UNIX 2 GB file size limit. The script, however, is more complex.

The following segment of a script concatenates five files through a pipe that is assigned the DD name of the original concatenated DD:

```
#   Concatenate the files through a pipe that runs
#   as a subprocess.
dd_INFILE=/tmp/$$.'date +"%y%m%d.%H%M%S"'
mknod $dd_INFILE p
step123a_rc=$?
dd_CONC1=${HLQ}/FILE.IN.1                    # DISP=(OLD,KEEP,KEEP)
dd_CONC2=${HLQ}/FILE.IN.NEXT                 # DISP=(OLD,KEEP,KEEP)
dd_CONC3=${HLQ}/FILE.IN.THIRD                # DISP=(OLD,KEEP,KEEP)
dd_CONC4=${HLQ}/FILE.IN.FOURTH               # DISP=(OLD,KEEP,KEEP)
dd_CONC5=${HLQ}/FILE.IN.LAST                 # DISP=(OLD,KEEP,KEEP)
#
#   STEP 123
if [step123a_rc != 0]
then
   cat $dd_CONC1 $dd_CONC2 $dd_CONC3 $dd_CONC4 $dd_CONC5 > $dd_INFILE &
   dd_OUTFILE=${HLQ}/THE.OUTPUT.FILE; touch $dd_OUTFILE
                                          # DISP=(NEW,KEEP,DELETE)
   PARM="Program Parameters"
   the_program $PARM >> $SYSOUT 2>> $SYSERR
   step123_rc=$?
#   The rest of the step...
#   after completion of step:
   rm $dd_INFILE
#   the rest of the job...
```

If the mknod command fails, it will return a non-zero status and the rest of the job can be bypassed. An if statement can be added after each DD for the concatenated files to verify it exists and is readable. The `cat` command is a subprocess that runs at the same time as the_program; as the `cat` command writes data to the pipe, the_program reads it from the pipe. As far as the_program is concerned, there is one very large file.

The `mknod` command is used to make special files: pipes or devices. When creating a named pipe, the first parameter is the filename to use and the second is the letter p (for pipe). If mknod is unable to create a pipe with the name specified (because of permissions, an invalid path name, or because a file or pipe already exists with that name), it prints a message and sets the return code to non-zero. On some systems, you must use the `mkfifo` command to create a named pipe. Another name for a named pipe is a fifo (first in, first out). The syntax for the command is:

```
mkfifo pipe_name
```

At first glance, the concept of a named pipe moving data from one program (the `cat` command) running in the background to the current job into another program (the_program) may be difficult to comprehend. Think of the pipes between your faucet and the water company. The pumps put water in the pipe at the same time you are turning on the faucet to fill your glass. When you are not filling your glass, no water flows (at least through that faucet if the washers are in good shape). If the water company had a problem and water pressure was very low, you would have to wait for your glass to fill—a little would splash out, a little wait, and then more water splashing into your glass. If the `cat` command can keep up with the_program, it just keeps pumping data through. If the_program can consume data faster than the `cat` command can send it through, then the_program will wait.

It is important to remove the named pipe when done with them, which is why there is an `rm` command after step123 runs. Otherwise there will be a bunch of these files using up directory entries in the /tmp directory.

Instream Proc Replacement

The PROCs shown with jobs so far are known as cataloged procedures because they are stored in a cataloged dataset somewhere. The PROCs are written, stored in a PDS, and used as needed. Another form of PROC is the instream PROC, so named because it is stored with the job that drives it. An instream PROC is frequently used to test the JCL within a PROC; when complete, it is moved into its own member of a PDS. Instream PROCs can be mimicked with script files of their own (cataloged procedure) or with functions within a script. The function is defined at the top of the script and used at the bottom, like an instream PROC.

A simple function that runs one step is shown below:

Line **Korn shell statement**

```
#! /bin/ksh
#
#
# Instream PROC replacement with a function:
#
```

```
function instream_proc # ${HLQ} ${SYSOUT} ${SYSERR}
{
   MAX_RC=0
   HLQ=${1:-"/u/dhorvath"}
   SYSOUT=${2:-"default_sysout.log"}
   SYSERR=${3:-"default_syserr.log"}
   print "$JOBNAME $0 STARTED `date`  " >> $SYSOUT 2>> $SYSERR
#       Step 10
#               Use STEPLIB and JOBLIB for program
   PATH=${JOBLIB}${SAVE_PATH}
   dd_FILEIN=${HLQ}/FILE.IN   # DISP=(OLD,KEEP,KEEP)
  dd_FILEOUT=${HLQ}/FILE.OUT; touch $dd_FILEOUT  # DISP=(new,keep,KEEP)
   PARM="input parameters"
   program_to_run "$PARM" >> $SYSOUT 2>> $SYSERR
   step010_rc=$?
  print "$JOBNAME $0 STEP010 ENDED `date` RC=${step010_rc} " >> $SYSOUT 2>> $SYSERR
   if [ $step010_rc = 0 ]
   then
      :        # No action to perform
   else
      :        # No action to perform
   fi
   if [[ $step010_rc > $MAX_RC ]]
   then
      MAX_RC=$step010_rc
   fi
   return ${MAX_RC}
}
#     Job setup
set -o xtrace
export JOBNAME="The_Job_Name"
export SAVE_PATH=$PATH
export JOBLIB="/search/me/first:/search/me/next:/search/me/then:"
HLQ=/u/dhorvath/cob_stuff
SYSOUT_DIRECTORY="/u/dhorvath/cob_stuff"
SYSOUT=${SYSOUT_DIRECTORY}/RUN.LOG
 > $SYSOUT                                # create sysout file
SYSERR=${SYSOUT_DIRECTORY}/RUN.LOG
 > $SYSERR                                # create syserr file
MAX_RC=0
print "$JOBNAME STARTED `date`  " >> $SYSOUT 2>> $SYSERR
#    Step 10
#               Use STEPLIB and JOBLIB for program
STEPLIB="/search/me/override/one:/search/me/override/two:"
PATH=${STEPLIB}${JOBLIB}${SAVE_PATH}
instream_proc ${HLQ} ${SYSOUT} ${SYSERR}
```

```
52      step010_rc=$?
53      print "$JOBNAME STEP010 ENDED `date` RC=${step010_rc} " >> $SYSOUT 2>> $SYSERR
54      if [ $step010_rc = 0 ]
55      then
56         :
57      else
58         :
59      fi
60      if [[ $step010_rc > $MAX_RC ]]
61      then
62         MAX_RC=$step010_rc
63      fi
64      # Post job processing
65      print "$JOBNAME ENDED `date` MAXIMUM RC=${MAX_RC} " >> $SYSOUT 2>> $SYSERR
66      exit ${MAX_RC}
```

Lines 4 through 33 are the function instream_proc. Line 6 defines the function itself. The environmental variables after the pound sign <#> on the line are comments of the positional parameters the PROC (function) expects to receive.

The contents of the function are defined within a pair of curly braces <{ }> and occupies lines 7 through 33.

Lines 8 through 31 are the same for cataloged procedures (scripts) and instream PROCs (functions). Line 32 is the primary difference between the two types of code structures. When a function ends, the return code is passed by using the return statement. The return statement replaces the exit statement used in scripts. If the return statement is used outside of a function, it behaves just like the exit statement; an exit statement within a function will cause the script to end.

Lines 34 through 66 contain the script equivalent to driver JCL that sets up, runs, and then cleans up after the procedure/function is complete.

Additional Information on Redirection

Several forms of redirection have been covered: the pipe character <|>, redirection of output creating a new file >, and redirection of output appending to an existing file >>. We can redirect stdout and stderr as well as force them to be redirected to the same output file. There are additional forms of redirection for handling of input.

Programs normally accept input from stdin (standard input); Korn allows this to be changed to a file or the lines that follow in a script. Instead of providing input from the keyboard, using the < stdin redirection operator with a file converts an interactive program to batch (so long as you know the flow).

Figure 4.1 provides a summary of the redirection operators available with the Korn shell. Because it is obsolete, it is recommended that you do not use <^> as the pipe character, but you may come across it in older shell scripts.

Figure 4.1
Korn Shell Redirection

Symbol	Meaning
> file	Sends stdout (standard output) to the named file
>> file	Appends stdout to the named file
>| file	Sends stdout to the named file even if noclobber is enabled (force truncation)
pr1|pr2	Sends output of process 1 to stdin (standard input) of process 2
pr1^pr2	Obsolete pipe character (old equivalent for |)
2> file	Sends stderr (standard error) output to named file
2>> file	Appends stderr to the named file
2>&1	Sends stderr (2) and stdout (&1) together as merged output
1>&2	Sends stdout (1) and stderr (&2) together as merged output (equivalent to 2>&1)
< file	Accepts stdin (standard input) from the named file
<< END	Accepts stdin from the current file until END occurs at the beginning of a line Will perform substitution. Known as "here document"
<<\END	Accepts stdin from the current file until END with no substitution
<< 'END'	Accepts stdin from the current file until END with no substitution

When using a pipe between two commands, it can be useful to save the output of the first command to a file as well as pass it to the next command. The `tee` command performs this function (tee is the plumbing name for the pipe fitting used when one pipe feeds two others) by writing to the file named on the command line and passing the stdin to stdout for piping into the next command.

The typical usage of the `tee` command is as follows:

```
$ ps -ef | tee processes | grep dhorvath↵
dhorvath   94     1  3  Feb 21  000   0:07 ksh
dhorvath  503    94 50 20:50:48 000   0:01 ps
dhorvath  504    94  5 20:50:48 000   0:00 tee
dhorvath  505    94  6 20:50:48 000   0:00 grep
$ more processes↵
     UID   PID  PPID  C   STIME   TTY  TIME COMMAND
    root     0     0  0  Feb 21     ? 1549:24 swapper
    root     1     0  3  Feb 21     ?  0:02 init
    root     2     0  0  Feb 21     ?  0:01 pagedaemon
    root     3     0  0  Feb 21     ?  0:01 windaemon
    root    77     1  3  Feb 21    w1  0:01 getty
    root    78     1  3  Feb 21     ?  0:00 getty
dhorvath    94     1  3  Feb 21   000  0:07 ksh
    root    73     1  3  Feb 21    w3  2:15 smgr
      lp    64     1  3  Feb 21     ?  0:00 lpsched
dhorvath   503    94 50 20:50:48 000  0:01 ps
```

```
dhorvath   504    94  5 20:50:48 000   0:00 tee
dhorvath   505    94  6 20:50:48 000   0:00 grep
$
```

The `grep` command reduced the number of lines shown; all lines were written to the file processes for further action.

Embedded SYSIN in Korn Shell

Another way of redirecting stdin is with <<. This operator will redirect the input from the current shell script as stdin to the program. The input ends when the end of file is reached or the specified string ("END" in figure 4.1) is found at the beginning of a line.

Both < and << are means of redirecting stdin, which is equivalent to SYSIN on the mainframe. The regular stdin redirection < is equivalent to the following SYSIN:

```
//STEPN EXEC PGM=RUNME
//SYSIN DD DSN=A.FILE.NAME,DISP=SHR
```

Is equivalent to:

```
runme < /a/file/NAME
```

Under UNIX.

The "here document" redirection operator, <<, is equivalent to a SYSIN DD * with an explicit delimiter or SYSIN DD DATA. SYSIN DD * with a delimiter is used to specify a delimiter other than the default end-of-data statement, /*, in JCL like the following example:

```
//STEPN EXEC PGM=RUNME
//SYSIN DD *,DLM='EOJ'
          data
/*        more data
EOJ
```

Is equivalent to:

```
runme << EOJ
          data
/*        more data
EOJ
```

The SYSIN ends with "EOJ." Another form is used when the data contains records that begin with two slashes, //, which MVS interprets as JCL. An example of SYSIN DD DATA looks like:

```
//STEPN EXEC PGM=RUNME
//SYSIN DD DATA
          data
//        more data with // at the beginning (i.e., JCL)
/*
```

And a regular SYSIN DD * is:

```
//STEPN EXEC PGM=RUNME
//SYSIN DD *
        data
/*
```

Both are equivalent to:

```
runme << '/*'
        data
//      more data with // at the beginning (i.e., JCL)
/*      more data
```

because records beginning with // or /* have no special meaning to the Korn shell. This is the form used to replace a SYSIN with embedded data. On the mainframe, PROCs cannot contain embedded data, but the shell imposes no such restrictions on scripts.

The following example uses the cat command with the here document redirection operator:

```
$ cat << EOD > testfile↵
> line1↵
> line2↵
> this is a line that is a little long↵
> this line has EOD but not at beginning↵
> this is the last line↵
> EOD↵
$ cat testfile↵
line1
line2
this is a line that is a little long
this line has EOD but not at beginning
this is the last line
$
```

Every line up to but not including the line that began with EOD was stored in the file testfile. This was proven by looking at the contents of testfile with another cat command.

To demonstrate the use of the here document (embedded SYSIN) feature within a command procedure requires a little more work on your part. If you create a command procedure like the following (using cat or an editor) with the name temp_ksh:

```
$ cat > temp_ksh↵
#! /bin/ksh↵
cat << ABC↵
asdf↵
asdfasdfasdfasdf↵
asdfasdfadsfasdfasdf↵
```

```
asdfasdfasdfasdfasdfasdf↵
ABC↵
ps -ef | grep dhorvath↵
^d
$
```

You can run it and see the results. First it has to be changed to an executable (execute permissions set) and then executed as a command:

```
$ chmod +x temp_ksh↵
$ temp_ksh↵
asdf
asdfasdfasdfasdf
asdfasdfadsfasdfasdf
asdfasdfasdfasdfasdfasdf
   dhorvath 31916 82341   4 19:30:18  pts/3  0:00 ps -ef
   dhorvath 53004  9452   0 18:00:59  pts/3  0:00 -ksh
   dhorvath 59053 82341   1 19:30:18  pts/3  0:00 grep dhorvath
   dhorvath 82341 53004   4 19:30:17  pts/3  0:00 ksh ./temp_ksh
$
```

The `cat` command copied the text from the command procedure to stdout until it reached the characters ABC at the beginning of a line. Then `cat` exited and the next command (`ps -ef | grep dhorvath`) was executed. The same approach can be used on programs that use the COBOL accept verb or otherwise look for input from stdin.

ISPF Retrieve or Command History

There are two more Korn shell environmental variables that control the ability to retrieve previously entered commands. The text of the last series of commands that are entered from the terminal are saved in a history file. By default, 128 commands are saved; this can be changed by placing the following command in the $HOME/.profile file:

```
set HISTSIZE=256
```

The history file defaults to $HOME/.history unless the HISTFILE environmental variable is set as follows:

```
set HISTFILE=$HOME/other_history
```

Your best bet is to leave HISTFILE alone. You may want to increase the number of saved commands if you are particularly busy (I set HISTSIZE to 256).

The saved commands can be retrieved using the `fc` command. Most systems have the name `history` aliased to be `fc -l`. Either way, they will show somewhere around the previous 16 commands entered. The following shows the typical output:

```
$ fc -l↵
46      vi .profile
```

```
47      ls
48      ls -a
49      ls -al | more
50      rm .kshistory
51      echo $FCEDIT
52      alia
53      alias
54      history
55      whence fc
56      which fc
57      alias | grep fc
58      echo $- &
59      history
60      history 10
61      fc -l
$
```

A range can be specified:

```
$ fc -l 10 20↵
10      ( echo $-; ) &
11      ( echo $-; )
12      set +o xtrace
13      ls
14      more xxx
15      more ttt
16      vi lineno
17      chmod +x lineno
18      lineno
19      echo $OLDPWD
20      cd bin
$
```

To retrieve a specific command, the `fc -e -` command is used. Most systems have the name `r` aliased to be `fc -e -`. Either way, the command retrieves the specified command and then executes it. Either the number of the saved command or the beginning of the command executed.

The command number 47 is a `ls` command (see above), the `fc` command to re-execute it is:

```
$ fc -e - 47↵
ls
c_stuff    cob_stuff    COMB_HAIR    first    function_test
Mail       bin          mbox         my_who    paren.exam
second     temp_ksh
$
```

To retrieve the last echo command in <()>, you would use the following command:

```
$ fc -e - "( echo"↵
( echo  $-; )
sih
$
```

The `fc` command also allows a limited ability to edit the command being processed. By entering one string to replace another, the command can be modified:

```
$ fc -e - '$-'='$RANDOM' "( echo"↵
5758
$
```

The general syntax for the substitution is old=new. The echo command is retrieved and then the substitution takes place. In this example, the $- (show shell flags) is replaced with $RANDOM (retrieve random number) and then executed. If you do not do a substitution, the command is echoed before being executed; if you perform a substitution, it is not. Unless there is an error in the fc command entry, it will not show up in the command history while the retrieved command will.

Another way of accessing commands in the history file is through command line editing (vi, emacs, or gmacs). These allow expanded search and command modification.

VI COMMAND LINE EDITING MODES

The vi command line editing mode is enabled with the `set -o vi` command. It has two modes: input and edit (or control) modes. When you are first entering a command (at the prompt), you are in input mode and none of the vi edit commands work. To enter edit mode, the escape key is pressed (<ESC> or <ESCAPE> on the keyboard). Then the vi commands are used to find a prior command and perform any changes needed.

Many commands will accept a numeric count before the command letter. Avoid using arrow keys on your keyboard when using vi line editing mode because those keys generate sequence of characters that include the <ESCAPE> key, which the shell can interpret as vi commands.

To find commands saved in the history file, you can use the commands shown in Figure 4.2.

To edit your input, use the commands shown in Figure 4.3.

To move around the command line, you use the motion edit commands shown in Figure 4.4.

To modify the current line, use the commands shown in Figure 4.5.

To retrieve the command you entered two commands ago, enter the following:

```
$ <ESC>kk
```

The line will be replaced with the command you entered with the cursor at the beginning of the command (shown by the underscore):

```
$ ( echo $RANDOM; )
```

Figure 4.2
vi Command History Search Commands

Key	Purpose
count k	Get prior command. Each time k is pressed, another command is retrieved
count -	<minus> equivalent to k
count j	Get next command. Each time j is pressed, the next command is retrieved
count +	<plus> equivalent to j
count G	Get the command numbered count. G alone gets the oldest command
/String	Search backward through the history for a command that contains String
?String	Search forward through command history for a match on String
n	Search for next match of the most recent / or ? commands
N	Reverse search for next match of the most recent / or ? commands
/	Search for next match of the most recent / command
?	Search for next match of the most recent ? command

Figure 4.3
vi Input Edit Commands

Key	Purpose
erase	User-defined erase key - delete previous character
^W	Delete previous word (separated by blanks)
^V	Erase next character
\	Discard special meaning of next erase or kill character

Figure 4.4
vi Motion Commands

Key	Purpose
count l	Move cursor one character to the right
count<space>	Equivalent to count l
count w	Move cursor one word to the right
count W	Move cursor to character after next space (space delimited word)
count e	Move cursor to end of word to the right
count E	Move cursor to character before next right (end of space delimited word)
count h	Move character one character to the left
count b	Move cursor one word to the left
count B	Move cursor left of first character after next space (start of space delimited word)
count f char	Find the next char to the right on the current line
count F char	Find the next char to the left on the current line
count t char	Equivalent to f char followed by h
count T char	Equivalent to F char followed by l
;	Repeats most recent f, F, t, or T (last single character find command)
,	Reverses most recent f, F, t, or T
0	Move cursor to beginning of line
^	Move cursor to first non-blank character (at or near beginning of line)
$	Move cursor to end of line

Figure 4.5
vi Text Modification Commands

Key	Purpose
a	Enter input mode to enter text after current character
A	Enter input mode to enter text at end of line
D	Delete to the end-of-line starting with the current character
dd	Delete the entire line
count dw	Delete the current word
i	Enter input mode to enter text before current character
I	Enter input mode to enter text at the start of line
#	Enter the comment character at start of line (save line in history, do not execute)
R	Enter input mode to replace characters including the current one
r char	Replace the current character with char
count x	Delete current character
count X	Delete character to left of cursor
~	Change the current character from lower to upper or upper to lowercase
u	Undo the last modification command
U	Undo all text modifications of this command
v	Enter the visual editor with the current command
<^L>	Reprint current command (must not be in input or replace mode)
<^R>	Equivalent to <^L> on some systems
<^J>	Execute current command (independent of mode)
<^M>	<enter> - Execute current command (independent of mode)

To move the cursor to the word RANDOM, you would press <w><w><w> or <3w> to move right three words. You could also press the <space> bar or <l> key eight times or use <8<space>> or <8l> resulting in:

```
$ ( echo $RANDOM; )
```

To change the word RANDOM to SECONDS, you can use <dw> to delete the word resulting in:

```
$ ( echo $; )
```

The <i> followed by the word SECONDS to insert the replacement text:

```
$ ( echo $SECONDS; )
```

To execute the command, press the <enter> key. If you want to make more changes to the line, press the <escape> key to exit input (replace) mode and perform the other steps you want.

If you are ever unsure what mode you are in, press the <escape> key to revert to edit mode. There are more commands that the vi command line editing supports that are not used frequently so were omitted. There are many ways to do the same thing, each perfectly correct, but too much choice can be confusing. If the vi editor supports the command, there is a high probability that the command line editing will support it.

Because I generally use the vi editor, I use vi command line editing mode. The emacs editor is not available on all systems although your installation may standardize on it, which makes learning the emacs command line editing mode useful.

emacs AND *gmacs* COMMAND LINE EDITING MODES

The emacs and gmacs command line editing modes are enabled with the `set -o emacs` and `set -o gmacs` commands respectively. It has only one mode—input. Commands are entered using control characters and in combination with the Meta key. On most keyboards, the Meta key is the same as the escape <ESC> or <ESCAPE> key. In the figures below, a combination of keys that uses the Meta key are shown as M-f (press the <ESCAPE> key, release it, then press the lowercase <f> key). You do not enter the minus sign <->, it is only there to separate the Meta key from the <f> key. You can edit the current line or locate a prior command and perform any changes needed.

Many commands will accept a numeric count before the command itself. For commands that use the Meta key, the sequence is Meta, count, and the command character. For commands that do not require the Meta key, to enter a count, you must prefix the command character with Meta and then the count.

The emacs editor was created at MIT during the late 1970s. The gmacs editor is a version of emacs supported by the Free Software Foundation under its GNU (GNU is Not UNIX) program.

To find commands saved in the history file, you can use the commands shown in Figure 4.6.

To edit your input, use the commands shown in Figure 4.7.

To move around the command line, you use the motion edit commands shown in Figure 4.8.

To retrieve the command you entered two commands ago, enter the following:

```
$ ^P^P
```

The line will be replaced with the command you entered with the cursor at the end of the command (shown by the underscore):

```
$ ( echo $RANDOM; )_
```

To move the cursor to the word RANDOM, you would press <M-b> to move left one word. You could also press the <^B> key nine times or use <M-9-^B> resulting in:

```
$ ( echo $RANDOM; )
```

To change the word RANDOM to SECONDS, you can use <M-d> to delete the word resulting in:

```
$ ( echo $; )
```

Then type the word SECONDS to insert the replacement text:

```
$ ( echo $SECONDS; )xc
```

To execute the command, press the <enter> key.

There are more commands that the emacs and gmacs command line editing supports that are not used frequently so were omitted. There are many ways to do the same thing, each perfectly

Figure 4.6
emacs Command History Search Commands

Key	Purpose
M-<	Get the oldest command from history
M->	Get the most recent (last entered) command in history
^N	Get the next command from history
^P	Get the prior command in history
^RString	Search backward through the history for a command that contains String
^R	Search for next match of String

Figure 4.7
emacs Edit Commands

Key	Purpose
erase	User-defined erase key - delete previous character
^D	Delete current character
M-d	Delete current word
M-^H	Delete previous word
M-h	Delete previous word
M-^?	Delete previous word. If interrupt character is <DEL>, this will not work
^T	Swap current character with next character **(emacs)**
^T	Swap two previous characters **(gmacs)**
^C	Capitalize current character
M-C	Capitalize current word
^K	Erase from current position to end of line
kill	User-defined kill key - delete entire current line
\	Escape next character - removing special meaning from next character

Figure 4.8
emacs Motion Commands

Key	Purpose
^F	Move cursor one character to right
M-f	Move cursor one word to right
^B	Move cursor one character to the left
M-b	Move cursor one word to left
^A	Move cursor to beginning of line
^E	Move cursor to end of line
^] char	Move cursor to char on current line (to right of current position)
<^L>	Reprint current command (must not be in input or replace mode)
<^J>	Execute current command (independent of mode)
<^M>	<enter> - Execute current command (independent of mode)

correct, but too much choice can be confusing. If the emacs or gmacs editor supports the command, there is a high probability that the command line editing will support it too.

SUMMARY

You have reached the end of the shell programming chapter. With what you know now, you can do the same things under UNIX that you are used to using JCL, PROCs, and the interactive mainframe command procedure languages like CLIST, REXX, and others. The common command languages under UNIX are Bourne, Korn, and C shell; there are other, non-commercial shells that most business installations will not use because there is no vendor to support them. You should learn one of the common shells even though there have been religious wars over which one is better, but you need to know at least one. There is also a version REXX available for UNIX, MS/PC-DOS, and other operating systems. Although it may be very useful, it is not yet considered by most UNIX professionals to be a UNIX tool. There is another command procedure language known as `perl` (Practical Extraction and Report Language) that is becoming very popular because it includes the functionality of various shells, `awk`, `sed`, and other UNIX commands. The `perl` language can also handle binary data and fixed length sequential files, which the other tools cannot, but it is not a commercial product.

CHAPTER 5

ADVANCED SHELL SCRIPTS AND COMMANDS

This chapter contains advanced topics on shell scripting that are expansions of the concepts shown in Chapters 3 and 4. Because of their nature, inclusion in the earlier chapters would have added to the complexity of the material and made it more difficult to understand. This information covers those areas where shell programming languages supersede mainframe JCL.

In addition, this chapter contains information on UNIX commands that may not have mainframe equivalents but can be very useful as you become more familiar with UNIX. With the distributed nature of UNIX installations, you may find yourself performing such tasks as mounting tapes, backing up and restoring files, and administering security for your files and programs.

KORN SHELL META-CHARACTERS

In the section on Replacing Jobs in JCL With Shell Scripts: Environmental Variables and Substitutions, the dollar sign character is used to get the value of an environmental variable (instead of the variable name being used as text). The dollar sign was assigned special meaning. To review, when any character is being used for a special purpose, it is known as a meta-character. In database terminology, the information (data) about the data in the database is known as meta-data. The data may be employee information, accounts payable, or anything else. The information about data—format, names (files, records, or tables), and fields (fields in a record or columns in a table)—are all meta-data.

The redirection operators shown in Figure 4.1 are meta-characters. The characters have special meaning to the shell that produces specific behavior instead of just being the characters themselves.

Figure 5.1 shows additional meta-characters. Many of these characters have already been described, such as the wildcard characters <*> and <?>, command separator <;>, background execution <&>, and variable substitution <$> and <${ }>.

When used in a regular expression, [chars] can be used to match any single character. The chars can be a single character, multiple characters, or even a range. To locate all the files that begin with the lowercase letter <c>:

```
$ ls -d [c]*↵
c_stuff             cob_stuff
$
```

The `-d` option was used on the `ls` command so that the name of subdirectories would be shown and not their contents. There are two files that begin the lowercase letter <c>, both happen to be directories. To see all the files that begin with the uppercase letter <C>:

```
$ ls -d [C]*↵
```

Figure 5.1
Korn Shell Meta-characters

<table>
<tr><th>Symbol</th><th>Meaning</th></tr>
<tr><td>*</td><td>In filenames, match any string zero or more characters in length</td></tr>
<tr><td>?</td><td>In filenames, match any single character</td></tr>
<tr><td>[chars]</td><td>In filenames, match any single character; can be range like [a-z], [A-Z], or [0-9]</td></tr>
<tr><td>proc1;proc2</td><td>Command separator or terminator; executes proc1 and then proc2</td></tr>
<tr><td>proc1&</td><td>Execute command in background</td></tr>
<tr><td>`proc`</td><td>Execute command proc and replace string with stdout from the command</td></tr>
<tr><td>(proc)</td><td>Execute command or commands in a subshell</td></tr>
<tr><td>{proc}</td><td>Execute command or commands in current shell (rare)</td></tr>
<tr><td>\</td><td>Alone on line used to continue long commands</td></tr>
<tr><td>\char</td><td>Discard special meaning for character char; pass char as char, not function</td></tr>
<tr><td>'stuff'</td><td>Use literal meaning of stuff - do not perform substitution</td></tr>
<tr><td>"stuff"</td><td>Use literal meaning of stuff after performing $, 'proc' and \char substitutions</td></tr>
<tr><td>#</td><td>Begin comment. If at start of line, entire line is comment</td></tr>
<tr><td>var=avalue</td><td>Assign avalue to the environmental variable var</td></tr>
<tr><td>proc1 && proc2</td><td>Run the first command, and, if successful, run the second</td></tr>
<tr><td>proc1 || proc2</td><td>Run the first command, and, if not successful, run the second</td></tr>
<tr><td>$0, $1, etc</td><td>$0 is the name of a shell script; $1 - $9 are positional parameters</td></tr>
<tr><td>$var</td><td>Substitute the value of the shell variable</td></tr>
<tr><td>${var}</td><td>Substitute the value of the shell variable (useful when concatenating strings)</td></tr>
<tr><td>${var:-value}</td><td>Substitute the value of the shell variable if set, use value otherwise</td></tr>
<tr><td>${var:=value}</td><td>Substitute the value of the shell variable if set, set it to and use value otherwise</td></tr>
<tr><td>${var:?error}</td><td>Substitute the value of the shell variable if set, display error message otherwise</td></tr>
<tr><td>${var:+value}</td><td>Substitute the value of the shell variable if set, otherwise nothing</td></tr>
</table>

Redirection operators omitted. See Figure 4.1

```
COMB_HAIR
$
```

There is only one file that begins the uppercase letter <C>. To see all the files that begin with the letter <c> in upper or lowercase:

```
$ ls -d [cC]*↵
COMB_HAIR          c_stuff             cob_stuff
$
```

There are three files that begin with the letter <c> in upper or lowercase. This is useful if you want to see all the files that begin with the letter <c> and do not care (or do not remember) what the case should be.

In each of the three examples above, the regular expression compares the first character of the filename with the value in the <[]> and then matches the rest of the filename with the wildcard <*> (match any zero to many characters). A single character, multiple characters, a range of characters, or even multiple ranges can be specified, but remember, they only match against a single character in a filename.

To specify a range, a minus sign or hyphen <-> is used to show the range. To find all the files that begin with the lowercase characters <a>, <b>, or <c>:

```
$ ls -d [a-c]*↵
bin                 c_stuff             cob_stuff
$
```

As with the single and multiple character examples of the <[]>, the `-d` option was used on the `ls` command so that the name of subdirectories would be shown and not their contents. There are three files that begin with the lowercase letters <a>, <b>, or <c>, all of which are directories. To see all the files that begin with the uppercase letters <A>, <B>, or <C>:

```
$ ls -d [A-C]*↵
COMB_HAIR
$
```

There is only one file that begins the uppercase letters <A>, <B>, or <C>. To see all the files that begin with the letters <a>, <b>, or <c> in upper or lowercase:

```
$ ls -d [a-cA-C]*↵
COMB_HAIR           bin                 c_stuff
cob_stuff
$
```

There are four files that begin with the letters <a>, <b>, or <c> in upper or lowercase. This is useful if you want to see all the files that begin with those letters and do not care (or do not remember) what the case should be.

Multiple matches can be combined to search for specific groups of filenames. To find all the files that begin with upper or lowercase letters <a>, <b>, or <c> with the next character being an upper or lowercase letter <o>, you would use the following syntax:

```
$ ls -d [a-cA-C][oO]*↵
COMB_HAIR  cob_stuff
$
```

Now there are only two files that match the criteria, a regular file (COMB_HAIR) and a subdirectory (cob_stuff).

If you want to run a command or series of commands in a subshell so that their output is combined, the <()> are used as follows:

```
$ (echo "this is a heading";ps -ef | grep dhorvath) | more↵
this is a heading
   dhorvath 32426 56620   1 11:40:31  pts/3  0:00 more
   dhorvath 52137 60584   6 11:40:31  pts/3  0:00 ps -ef
   dhorvath 56620 30251   1 09:13:52  pts/3  0:00 -ksh
   dhorvath 60584 56620   1 11:40:31  pts/3  0:00 grep dhorvath
$
```

The output from the echo command ("this is a heading") and the output of the ps and grep piped combination will be processed by the more command as if they were one command piping output into it. This is very useful when you have the output of multiple commands that you want to go to the same place. This example, because there was not much output, did not really require the more command, but if there was, it would be very useful. The redirection through a pipe into the more command could be replaced with redirection to a file and then the file viewed:

```
$ (echo "this is a heading";ps -ef | grep dhorvath) > paren.exam↵
$ more paren.exam↵
this is a heading
   dhorvath 56620 30251   0 09:13:52  pts/3  0:00 -ksh
   dhorvath 58034 56620   1 11:43:41  pts/3  0:00 grep dhorvath
   dhorvath 60595 58034   7 11:43:41  pts/3  0:00 ps -ef
$
```

Now we can have a nice report in a single step. The command line shown above could be placed in a shell script to run when needed.

It is also possible to run a series of commands in the current shell through the use of the curly braces <{ }>; <()> runs them in a subshell. The disadvantage in running in the current shell is that any changes made to the environment by the commands will remain in effect when done. Any environmental variables changed within the command will affect the current session long after the commands were executed. There are effectively no differences between what you can do with <{ }> and <()>. However, there must be a semicolon character <;> after each command including the last one when using <{ }>. The following example is similar to the <()> example:

```
$ { echo "heading"; ps -ef | grep dhorvath ; } > braces.exam↵
$ more braces.exam↵
heading
   dhorvath 20322 35384   7 12:42:17  pts/3  0:00 ps -ef
   dhorvath 20579 35384   1 12:42:17  pts/3  0:00 grep dhorvath
   dhorvath 35384 24375   1 12:41:40  pts/3  0:00 -ksh
$
```

Note that the ps and grep commands are both owned by process id 35384, the login Korn shell. If we could see the echo command, it too would have the same owner process id. In the example with the <()>, this is not the case.

When working with long lines, the command line may scroll left and right automatically or you can enter the command on multiple lines. The backslash character <\> (used by MS/PC-DOS as the directory separator character) followed by the <enter> key can be used to create a command that crosses multiple lines. The following example shows a long command within parentheses, this will work with commands without the <()> and <{ }>:

```
$ (echo "this is a very very very very very long heading";\↵
> ps -ef | grep dhorvath) > paren.exam↵
$ more paren.exam↵
this is a very very very very very long heading
```

```
    dhorvath 20325 35384   0 12:53:34  pts/3  0:00 grep dhorvath
    dhorvath 30310 20325   7 12:53:34  pts/3  0:00 ps -ef
    dhorvath 35384 24375   1 12:41:40  pts/3  0:00 -ksh
$
```

The greater than sign <>> on the second line is known as the more input system prompt. It is displayed when more input is expected for the current command. The same will occur if you do not complete a structure that has an open and a close. The <()> and <{ }> meta-characters have two parts: the open or begin <(> and <{> and the close or end <)> and <}>. If there is an open without the close, you will be prompted to complete the command as follows:

```
$ ( echo "abc";↵
> echo "def" )↵
abc
def
$
```

The same will occur with the double quotes <"> around a string:

```
$ echo "abc↵
> def"↵
abc
def
$
```

However, the enter key (new line) will be considered part of the string and the output will be on two lines. Using the backslash character will allow you to continue on a new line while the output remains on one:

```
$ echo "abc\↵
> def"↵
abcdef
$
```

The behavior with the single quotes <'> is a little different. When used without the continuation character, the behavior is the same: two lines of output are produced. When used with the continuation character, two lines of output still are produced and include the continuation character. The example shows these results:

```
$ echo 'abc↵
> def'↵
abc
def
$ echo 'abc\↵
> def'↵
abc\
def
$
```

This happens because no substitution occurs within any string identified with single quotes <'>. The backquote <`> will follow the same rules as the double quote, but the results may not be what you expect because the shell believes that one command ends when you press <enter> and expects that another command will follow on the next line. The following `ls -al` command is split into two lines, with the shell seeing two commands: `ls` and `-al`. It cannot find any command known as -al:

```
$ lab=`ls↵
>  -al`↵
ksh[2]: -al:  not found
$ echo $lab↵
c_stuff cob_stuff COMB_HAIR first function_test Mail bin
mbox my_who paren.exam second temp_ksh
$
```

Note that the `ls` command executed and the output is stored in the environmental variable lab. If you use the backslash character to split the command over multiple lines, it will work as expected (the shell would see `ls -al` as one command). You will get the results you expect if different commands appear on the continued line as shown:

```
$ lab=`ls↵
> ps`↵
$ echo $lab↵
c_stuff cob_stuff COMB_HAIR first function_test Mail bin
mbox my_who paren.exam second temp_ksh PID TTY TIME CMD
6675 pts/3 0:00 ps 35384 pts/3 0:00 -ksh
$
```

The shell saw two different commands and was able to find the two commands (`ls` and `ps`) to execute.

The pipe redirection operator can also be used to split long commands over multiple lines so long as the split occurs between the pipe character <|> and the command the output is being piped into. The following example shows two commands split between two lines using the pipe redirection operator. Note that more commands and lines could have been used:

```
$ ps -ef |↵
> grep dhorvath↵
   dhorvath 27197 35384   7 13:31:29  pts/3  0:00 ps -ef
   dhorvath 35384 24375   0 12:41:40  pts/3  0:00 -ksh
   dhorvath 44094 35384   0 13:31:29  pts/3  0:00 grep dhorvath
$
```

The && and || operators (described below) behave the same as the pipe redirection operator.

Multiple means command continuation can be used together in just about any combination, but be careful because once you start splitting commands across multiple lines, it becomes difficult to determine what characters are needed to end the command.

The examples of line continuation shown have been from the command line (interactive shell), the same can be applied within shell scripts. The difference is that when creating a shell script, the more input system prompt (usually the greater than sign <>>) will not be shown. The following example creates a shell script using the cat command, makes it executable, and then runs it:

```
$ cat > split.ksh↵
#! /bin/ksh↵
ls -al |↵
grep "c_stuff"↵
^d
$ chmod +x split.ksh↵
$ split.ksh↵
drwxrwsr-x   3 dhorvath    staff        2048 Feb 12 08:08 c_stuff
$
```

As far as the shell is concerned, the `ls` and `grep` commands are joined by the pipe and it does not matter which line they are on. It is perfectly legal to use the continuation character <\> with meta-characters that would otherwise continue the line. In other words, you would put a backslash after the pipe character in the shell script split.ksh and it would not affect its behavior.

The backslash <\> character has another function: the literal meaning operator. When used with another character, that character is used, not any special meaning attached to it. In order to print a vertical bar <|>, its special meaning (pipe redirection operator) must be discarded. In order to print a dollar sign <$>, its special meaning (substitute value of variable) must be discarded. The backslash character will do this as shown:

```
$ abc=an_env_var↵            Create an environmental variable
$ echo def$abc↵
defan_env_var                Substitution occurred
$ echo def\$abc↵
def$abc                      $ character shown
$
$ echo abc|def↵
ksh: def:  not found         "abc" piped into command def
$ echo abc\|def↵
abc|def                      | character shown
$
```

In the first `echo` command, the value of the environmental variable abc is substituted (the dollar sign is the substitution operator) and appended to the string def. In the second `echo` command, there is no substitution because the special meaning is discarded. The third `echo` is interpreted by the shell as echoing the characters abc into the command def that the shell is unable to find, the vertical bar is the pipe operator. In the final echo, the vertical bar is treated as a simple character because the special meaning was discarded.

You can also use the backslash character with the grep command. To grep, a period matches any single character; to search for the dot character, you must discard the special meaning. To find any processes that have a period in the command or command parameters, the following is required:

```
$ ps -ef | grep "\."↵
dhorvath 42694 35378    0 13:57:40  pts/3   0:00 grep \.
    root 15283  3284    0    Feb 03       -   0:00 /usr/etc/rpc.mountd
    root 15541  3284    0    Feb 03       -   0:00 /usr/etc/rpc.statd
    root 15800  3284    0    Feb 03       - 16:42 /usr/etc/rpc.lockd
$
```

There are several commands running that have a period in their name and the grep command I am executing has a period as a parameter (what I am searching for). The same technique can be used with files or any other place you use grep to search for something.

The && and || operators are conditional execution operators. Depending on the result of the command on the left side of the operator, the command on the right may or may not be executed. This allows you to execute multiple commands depending on the results of predecessors. The && operator is used as

command1 && command2

The first command, command1, will always execute. If it is successful, the second command will run. This technique is useful when the second command performs operations on data produced by the first and should not run if the first fails. The || operator is used as

command1 || command2

The first command, command 1, will always execute. If it is not successful, the second command will run. This technique is useful to perform cleanup if the first command fails.

Any command, including shell scripts and the <()> operators can be used with the && and || operators.

In the following example of the && operator, the file .profile exists and abc does not:

```
$ ls .profile && ps↵
.profile
   PID     TTY  TIME CMD
 35378  pts/3  0:00 -ksh
 51381  pts/3  0:00 ps
$ ls abc && ps↵
abc not found
$
```

Because the `ls` command succeeds in the first case, the `ps` command is executed. Because the `ls` command fails in the second case, the `ps` command is not executed.

In the following example of the || operator, the file .profile exists and abc does not:

```
$ ls .profile || ps↵
.profile
$ ls abc || ps↵
abc not found
   PID    TTY  TIME CMD
 35378  pts/3  0:00 -ksh
 37265  pts/3  0:00 ps
$
```

Because the `ls` command succeeds in the first case, the `ps` command is not executed. Because the `ls` command fails in the second case, the `ps` command is then executed.

In the following example, using multiple || operators, the files abc and def do not exist:

```
$ ls abc || ls def || ps↵
abc not found
def not found
   PID    TTY  TIME CMD
 35378  pts/3  0:00 -ksh
 37373  pts/3  0:00 ps
$
```

The first `ls` command fails, so the second is executed. The second `ls` command fails, so the `ps` command is executed. The following example shows the || operator used with multiple commands:

```
$ ls abc || (ps; ls)↵
abc not found
   PID    TTY  TIME CMD
 35378  pts/3  0:00 -ksh
 37373  pts/3  0:00 ps
c_stuff cob_stuff COMB_HAIR first function_test Mail bin
mbox my_who paren.exam second temp_ksh
$
```

Since the file abc is not found, the `ls` command fails causing the commands in the parentheses (`ps` and `ls`) to be executed. The best way to learn about these operators is to try them and try them with other operators like the pipe and other redirection operators.

SPECIAL SHELL VARIABLES

The Korn shell has a number of variables that it sets automatically for you when you invoke a shell script. As shown in the section on Replacing Jobs in JCL with Shell Scripts: Environmental Variables and Substitutions, there are a series of variables, $1 through $9, that contain any

Figure 5.2
Korn Shell Special Parameters and Variables

Special Parameters	Purpose
$0	Path and file name of shell script being executed
$1 ... $9	First through Ninth positional argument from command line
$#	Number of arguments on command line
$-	Option flags - set by shell or explicitly by script
$?	Return code from previous command or process
$$	Process ID of current shell
$!	Process ID of most recently started background process
$_	Temporary variable (usually last argument to previous command)
$@	All positional arguments from command line - split into individual pieces in loop
$*	All positional arguments from command line - as one field

Special Variables	Purpose
$ERRNO	Error code of last error
$LINENO	Number of current line executed in script - [line] in JCL replacement examples
$OLDPWD	Previous working directory (used by cd - command)
$PPID	Process ID of parent shell
$PWD	Present working directory
$RANDOM	Random number between 0 and 32767. Can be initialized
$REPLY	Used by read command to store user input from stdin
$SECONDS	Elapsed time of current shell process

arguments from the command line. $0 is a special parameter because it contains the path and filename of the command being executed so it can know its name.

Figure 5.2 shows the important special parameters and variables with the Korn shell along with their purposes.

When there are more than nine arguments on the command line, there are a number of ways to process them. The $# environmental variable allows the script to know how many arguments are on the command line. Looping through the contents of $@ (positional arguments from command line) is one way. Another is to save the values in $1 through $9 and use the shift command to replace the current values in $1 through $9 with the next set of command line arguments. If there are more than 18 arguments, this process can be repeated as many times as needed.

Special parameters are single characters like <1> and <#>; variables have recognizable names like REPLY and PWD. To check the values of the special parameters and variables, it is necessary to create a shell script. The following will create the script posit.ksh using the cat command (you can use cat or an editor if you want to try it). Enter only the characters in bold—the characters to the left (s1 to s36, s for script) are for referencing the source line in descriptions:

```
      $ cat > posit.ksh↵
s1    #! /bin/ksh↵
s2    echo "\$@ " $@↵
```

```
s3   for i in "$@"↵
s4   do print "$i" -↵
s5   done↵
s6   ↵
s7   echo "\$* " $*↵
s8   for j in "$*"↵
s9   do print "$j" -↵
s10  done↵
s11  ↵
s12  echo "\$# " $#↵
s13  echo "\$- " $-↵
s14  echo "\$? " $?↵
s15  echo "\$\$ " $$↵
s16  ↵
s17  ps -ef > /dev/null &↵
s18  echo "\$! " $!↵
s19  echo "\$_" $_↵
s20  echo " 0 " $0 " 1 " $1 " 2 " $2 " 3 " $3↵
s21  echo " 4 " $4 " 5 " $5 " 6 " $6 " 7 " $7↵
s22  echo " 8 " $8 " 9 " $9 " 10 " $10 " 11 " $11↵
s23  shift 9↵
s24  echo " shifted 9"↵
s25  echo " 0 " $0 " 1 " $1 " 2 " $2 " 3 " $3↵
s26  echo " 4 " $4 " 5 " $5 " 6 " $6 " 7 " $7↵
s27  echo " 8 " $8 " 9 " $9 " 10 " $10 " 11 " $11↵
s28  ↵
s29  echo "ERRNO " $ERRNO↵
s30  echo "LINENO " $LINENO↵
s31  echo "OLDPWD " $OLDPWD↵
s32  echo "PPID " $PPID↵
s33  echo "PWD " $PWD↵
s34  echo "RANDOM " $RANDOM↵
s35  echo "REPLY " $REPLY↵
s36  echo "SECONDS " $SECONDS↵
     ^d
```

The blank lines are for readability, no other purpose. If you get an error regarding lines s23 and s28 once you run this script, remove references to $10 and $11, as these are not valid command line arguments and may not be handled properly on your system. The minus sign <-> on lines s4 and s9 are to show where the string ends in the output and have no special meaning to the command. Notice that <\$> is used inside the double quotes for each of the echo commands that show the special parameters to prevent the creation of a substitution (like <$#>) instead of showing the string $#.

After the file is saved, the script must be made executable and then run with a series of arguments. Arguments within single <'> and double <"> quotes are treated as one argument even if they contain spaces, but they behave differently: No substitution occurs within the single quotes <'>, but can occur within double quotes <">. This example does use any environmental variables in the command line. The output will not have the characters to the left (o1 to o42, o for output), which are for referencing the specific lines in descriptions:

```
        $ chmod +x posit.ksh↵
        $ posit.ksh a b c d e f abc g h i j k l m n "abc def" 'ghi jkl'↵
o1      $@  a b c d e f abc g h i j k l m n abc def ghi jkl
o2      a -
o3      b -
o4      c -
o5      d -
o6      e -
o7      f -
o8      abc -
o9      g -
o10     h -
o11     i -
o12     j -
o13     k -
o14     l -
o15     m -
o16     n -
o17     abc def -
o18     ghi jkl -
o19     $*  a b c d e f abc g h i j k l m n abc def ghi jkl
o20     a b c d e f abc g h i j k l m n abc def ghi jkl -
o21     $#  17
o22     $-  sm
o23     $?  0
o24     $$  30262
o25     $!  24448
o26     $_ 684
o27      0  ./posit.ksh  1  a  2  b  3  c
o28      4  d  5  e  6  f  7  abc
o29      8  g  9  h  10  a0  11  a1
o30      shifted 9
o31      0  ./posit.ksh  1  i  2  j  3  k
o32      4  l  5  m  6  n  7  abc def
o33      8  ghi jkl  9   10  i0  11  i1
o34     ERRNO  25
o35     LINENO  30
o36     OLDPWD  /u/dhorvath/bin
o37     PPID  54325
o38     PWD  /u/dhorvath
o40     RANDOM  27133
```

```
o41     REPLY
o42     SECONDS  708
        $
```

Line s2 produced o1, all of the command line arguments as one string. Lines s3 through s5 contain an example of a loop in the Korn shell that produces lines o2 through o18, the individual command line arguments. Lines o17 and o18 are the arguments that were contained in double <"> and single <'> quotes on the command line. They contain spaces and may contain other special characters, but the delimiters are not shown. All of these come from the variable $@.

Line s7 produced o19, all of the command line arguments as one string. When used this way, $* and $@ are exactly the same. Lines s8 through s10 loop through $* produced line o20, substantially different from the output using $@ in the loop in lines s3 through s5.

Line s12 shows the number of arguments on the command line, as shown on line o21, is 17 in this example. Line s13 shows the option flags set by the shell or the script itself, o22 shows the flags to be ism. Shell input from stdin and output to stderr, and background jobs run as separate process. See the Korn shell Flags section later on in this chapter for more information on shell flags.

Line s14 shows the return code from the previous command; as line o23 shows, the previous echo command was successful. Line s15 shows the current process id, shown on line o24 as 30262. Line s17 starts a ps command in the background with output directed to the bit-bucket. Line s18 shows the process id of the most recently started background job (the ps command), shown as 24448 on line o25. Line s19 shows the temporary variable that currently has the value 684 on line o26. The temporary value is typically the last argument of the prior command but is used by many functions within the shell and could have any value.

Lines s20 through s22 produce output shown as lines o27 through o29. These are the environmental variables $0, $1, through $9. An attempt is made to show variables $10 and $11. The result on line o29 is a0 and a1 respectively: $1 is shown with the string 0 or 1 appended to it. On some systems, the shell may detect and report these two as errors since there are no positional parameters known as $10 and $11. Because posit.ksh was executed from the current directory, it is shown as ./posit.ksh.

Since there are only nine command line argument environmental variables, the shift command, shown on line s23, is used to discard the original values in $1 through $9. In this case, the value of the shift is 9, replace all the current variables. Line s24 produces o30 to report that a shift has occurred.

Lines s25 through s27 produce the output shown on lines o31 through o33. $0 does not change after a shift. Since there were a total of 17 arguments (as shown on the command line and $#), $9 is now empty as there is no value to store in it. The behavior of $10 and $11 has not changed, just the value in $1 has changed from the letter a to i.

The Korn shell sets a series of variables automatically. Lines s29 through s36 produces lines o34 through o42 showing the values contained. Line s29/o34 is the last error code produced; it is not set back to zero when there is no error. Line s30/o35 shows the current line number within the script being executed. Line s31/o36 shows the prior working directory and is used by the `cd -`

command to return. Line s32/o37 shows the process id of the process that executed this shell (the parent shell). Line s33/o38 shows the current working directory.

Line s34/o40 is a random number between 0 and 32767 that changes each time it is referenced. By assigning a numeric value to RANDOM, you can initialize the sequence of random numbers. One good way that provides a semblance of random starting point is to initialize RANDOM to the current process id as follows:

```
RANDOM=$$
```

Line s35/o41 shows the value returned by the read command. The read command is another way, besides command line arguments, to get information into a shell script. Generally, a prompt is displayed for the user, the read command issued, and then the value in REPLY is used as follows:

```
echo "Enter the value for something"
read
something=$REPLY
```

It is necessary to save the value of REPLY because the next read command will change it.

The final line, s36/o42, shows the number of seconds of elapsed time since the current shell was invoked. The system automatically updates this value every second. You can also set the variable SECONDS to a particular value and the system will update it from that point forward.

Additional Environmental Variable Substitution (Using Meta-characters)

Several of the environmental variable substitution forms were discussed in the JCL replacement sections, so some of this section will be repetitive. But this is important enough of a subject to repeat to make sure it is understood and expand on the areas not yet covered. The different forms of substitution are shown in Figure 5.1.

In general, an environmental variable is defined by setting it to a value via the equal sign:

```
$ env_var="abc"↵
$
```

The string abc is stored in the environmental variable env_var. In this form, the variable is local to this shell, that is, a subshell will not receive the value. To make the variable available to a child (subshell), it must be exported. No matter what the subshell does, it cannot create or change an environmental variable used by the parent. It is strictly a one-way passing of variables.

In the following examples, the `echo` command is used to show what the final substitution is:

```
1     $ echo env_var↵
      env_var
2     $ echo $env_var↵
      abc
3     $ echo ${env_var}↵
      abc
      $
```

Using the first echo command, the string env_var is displayed because no substitution was requested. The second and third echo commands display the contents of the environmental variable env_var, which is abc. The first form is easier to type while the second behaves better when concatenating strings together as shown in the following:

```
4       $ echo $env_varABC↵

5       $ echo ${env_var}ABC↵
        abcABC
        $
```

The fourth echo command displayed nothing—the shell searched for an environmental variable with the name env_varABC and could find nothing, so no substitution took place. The fifth echo command produced the desired results: the contents of env_var concatenated with ABC to produce abcABC.

The next form of substitution with the :- operator, substitutes the value from the environmental variable if it is set and substitutes the value to the right of the :- if it is not:

```
6       $ echo ${env_var:-you}↵
        abc
        $ no_env_var=↵
7       $ echo ${no_env_var:-you}↵
        you
8       $ echo ${no_env_var}↵

        $
```

The sixth echo shows the value of env_var (abc) since it is defined. To make sure it was not defined, no_env_var was set to nothing. When the seventh echo is executed, the value you is displayed since there is no value in no_env_var. Just to be sure, the eighth echo displays nothing since there is no_env_var is not defined.

The next form of substitution, with the :? operator, substitutes the value from the environmental variable if it is set and displays the error message right of the :- if it is not:

```
9       $ echo ${env_var:?No Such value}↵
        abc
10      $ echo ${no_env_var:?No Such value}↵
        ksh: no_env_var: No Such value
11      $ echo $?↵
        1
12      $ echo ${no_env_var}↵

        $
```

The ninth echo shows the value of env_var (abc) since it is defined. When the tenth echo is executed, the error message is displayed since there is no value in no_env_var. The eleventh echo shows the return code from the tenth echo. It is non-zero since an error occurred, this condition can be tested for to enable a shell script to exit if it happens. Just to be sure, the twelfth echo displays nothing since no_env_var is not defined.

The next form of substitution, with the := operator, substitutes the value from the environmental variable if it is set, substituting the value to the right of the :- if it is not and setting the environmental variable to that value:

```
13      $ echo ${env_var} " - " ${env_var:=you} " " ${env_var}↵
        abc - abc   abc
14      $ echo ${no_env_var} " - "${no_env_var:=you} " " ${no_env_var}↵
         - you   you
        $
```

The thirteenth echo shows the value of env_var before, with, and after the := operator, displaying the same value (abc) each time since it is defined. When the fourteenth echo is executed, no value is displayed before the := operator (no_env_var is undefined), with the := operator, the value you is shown, and afterward, the value you is displayed again since no_env_var is now defined with the value you.

The final form of substitution, with the :+ operator, substitutes the value to the right of the operator if the environmental variable is set and does nothing if it is not. It does not change the environmental variable to the new value:

```
15      $ echo ${env_var} " - "${env_var:+you} " " ${env_var}↵
        abc  - you   abc
        $ no_env_var=↵
16      $ echo ${no_env_var} " - "${no_env_var:+you} " " ${no_env_var}↵
         -
        $
```

The fifteenth echo shows the value of env_var before and after using the :+ operator (abc) as well as with it—since env_var is defined, the operator substitutes you. To make sure no_env_var is not defined, it is set to nothing. When the sixteenth and final echo is executed, no values are displayed since there is no value in no_env_var.

The form of substitution that you choose as a programmer all depends on what you are trying to accomplish. If all you need to do is simple substitution—move the value of a variable around, then the simple forms are fine. If you need to have a default value, then the :- is the operator to use. If you want an error message produced for the user, there is the :? operator. If you want to have a default value and set the environmental variable to that value in addition to returning it, then use :=. I personally have never found a use for the final operator, :+, which returns a default value if the variable is set and does nothing if it is not. That does not mean there is no use, just that I have not figured it out.

KORN SHELL FLAGS

The Korn shell supports a number of flags that can be set on the command line when the shell is invoked or set via the set command from within a shell script. The flags can also be set on the

Figure 5.3
Korn Shell Flags

Flag	Purpose	
a	All parameters are automatically exported	
e	If the shell is not interactive and it fails, report error and exit	
f	Do not expand pathnames	
h	Each command becomes a tracked alias when first encountered Default for non-interactive shells	
i	Interactive shell - input and output through terminal	
k	Provided for compatibility with Bourne Shell, use not recommended Allows assignment of environmental variables on command line	
m	Background jobs run as a separate process and a line will print when done	
n	Read commands but do not execute them	
o	Accepts an option as follows:	
	allexport	same as **a**
	bgnice	execute background jobs at lower priority
	emacs	enables emacs style line editing
	errexit	same as **e**
	gmacs	enables gmacs (gnu emacs) style line editing
	ignoreeof	prevent shell from exiting on end-of-file (must use the exit command)
	keyboard	same as **k**
	markdirs	append a trailing </> to directory names
	monitor	same as **m**
	noblob	same as **f**
	noclobber	prevents overwriting of an existing file
	noexec	same as **n**
	nolog	do not store definitions of functions in history file
	nounset	same as **u**
	trackall	same as **h**
	verbose	same as **v**
	vi	enables vi style line editing
	xtrace	same as **x**
r	Restricted shell, only certain commands allowed	
s	Commands are read from standard input, shell output (ksh: ... messages) written to stderr	
s	In the set command, the -s flag causes the command line arguments to be sorted	
t	Execute one command without substitution	
u	Report an error when an unset environmental variable is encountered	
v	Print the commands without substitution	
x	Print commands and their arguments as they are executed	

Use a minus sign <-> before the flag to turn it on and the plus sign <+> to turn it off.

interactive command line with the set command since there is really no distinction between a script and an interactive session to the shell.

Figure 5.3 shows the valid flags. Some of the flags have different meanings depending on where they are used. The s flag on the ksh command line means that the commands are read from standard input and shell output is written to stderr. If it is used in a set command, it causes the command line arguments to be sorted in ascending sequence.

There are several ways to turn on printing of the commands as they are executed:

```
#! /bin/ksh -x
#! /bin/ksh -o xtrace
set -x
set -o xtrace
```

The x flag and the option xtrace (set with the o flag) perform the same function. The x flag syntax is included for compatibility purposes from the Bourne shell.

You have already seen the bgnice, monitor, noexec, and xtrace options in examples in earlier sections and chapters. To be honest, these are almost the only ones of which I have had any use. The one other option I use on a regular basis is vi. The vi option enables command line editing using the same commands as the vi editor. There are emacs and gmacs line editing modes that perform similar functions with different keys.

Restricted or Trusted Shells

Restricted shells are used to setup users and execution environments with fewer capabilities, lower privileges, and less access than the standard shells. The Bourne shell can be invoked in a restricted form as `rsh`, `Rsh`, or `sh -r`. Because `rsh` is a command that is part of TCP/IP (remote shell), the original command for the restricted shell, `rsh`, has been renamed on many systems. The Korn shell supports a restricted shell by invoking it as `ksh -r` or as `rksh` on some systems.

The system administrator can force a user into one of the restricted shells by setting it up as his or her default shell in the /etc/passwd file. A shell script can force itself to run using the restricted shell by specifying it on the first line (#! /bin/Rsh). A user can also invoke the restricted shell interactively.

`Rsh` prevents the user from changing directories (using the `cd` command), changing the value of the environmental variable $PATH, specifying an explicit path or putting a </> in a command name, and redirecting output. The use also may be limited to certain commands. These restrictions take effect after the .profile is executed after login.

If the user invokes a shell script as a command, `Rsh` invokes `sh` to execute it. Through this mechanism, it is possible to create scripts for the user that have access to all the features of the shell while limiting him or her to a menu of commands. This prevents the user from doing anything that the system administrator does not want him or her to do. The .profile has complete control over user actions by performing setup and putting the user in the proper directory with its limited commands and procedures.

Often, the system administrator will create a directory of commands (in /usr/rbin) that are safe for users under the restricted shell to execute. There is also a restricted version of the ed editor called red that prevents the user from doing such things as invoking a subshell. The restricted Korn shell enforces the same restrictions as the restricted Bourne shell. There is no facility for a restricted access C shell. The typical software developer will not run under a restricted shell. It is just for users whose access needs to be limited.

LOOPING AND CONDITIONALS

In real programs, it is very rare that the code is executed in a straight line. Commands are repeated for a number of data items and code is executed if certain conditions are met. Depending on the value in an environmental variable, the flow must change or commands repeated to process the contents.

The Korn and Bourne shells support three looping structures: for, while, and until with two commands to prematurely exit the loop: break and continue. The shells also support conditional structures using if - then - elif - else - fi and case. The Korn shell also supports the select statement, which quickly creates menus. All of these commands support testing expressions, which are comparisons of two variables and special conditions for files.

Testing expressions are enclosed in a set of square brackets <[]> for Bourne shell and a double set of brackets <[[]]>for Korn shell. With few exceptions, the Bourne constructs can be used in a Korn shell script with single or double sets of square brackets (Korn supports either); the exceptions will work within a single set of square brackets.

for Loop

The simplest looping structure is the for loop. The loop repeats one or more commands contained within the loop structure (between the commands do and done). The for loop in Korn and Bourne shells are different from the looping structure in most languages. In other words, it does not simply increment through a series of values until a limit is reached. Instead, it executes the commands in the loop with the values in the for statement.

The general structure is (keywords in bold print):

> **for** variable **in** value1 value2 ... valuen
> **do**
>   commands
> **done**

An example showing the four seasons:

```
$ for SEASON in winter spring summer fall↵
> do↵
>    echo $SEASON↵
> done↵
winter
spring
summer
fall
$
```

Notice that the for loop takes multiple lines and the shell realizes it, providing automatic continuation. It is traditional to indent the commands between the do and done to make the structure more visible to the eye. If the keywords in or do are part of the values, they should be contained in double quotes <">. In the section on Special Shell Variables, the environmental variable $@

was looped through with a for loop (lines s2 through s5, output lines o2 through o18). These loops can be nested, but different variables should be used for each.

For larger examples, a shell script should be created using an editor or the cat command. The following example creates a shell script to show two nested loops:

```
$ cat > nestfor.ksh↵
for OUTER_LOOP in A B↵
do↵
   for INNER_LOOP in first second third↵
   do↵
      echo $OUTER_LOOP $INNER_LOOP↵
   done↵
done↵
^d
```

After creating the file, it must be made executable and then run:

```
$ chmod +x nestfor.ksh↵
$ nestfor.ksh↵
A first
A second
A third
B first
B second
B third
$
```

The inner loop executes for its data items each time the outer loop executes for one its data items.

Producing a loop through numeric is a little more complicated than in most other programming languages. All the values must be listed as shown in the following example:

```
$ for LOOP_INDEX in 2 3 4 5↵
> do↵
>    echo $LOOP_INDEX↵
> done↵
2
3
4
5
$
```

while Loop

The while loop repeats so long as the expression or command in the structure returns a true (non-zero) value. Any commands in the conditional section are executed at least once, whereas the commands in the body of the loop may not be executed if the conditional is false. Both Korn and Bourne shells support the while loop.

The general structure is (keywords in bold print):

while expression or command
do
        commands
done

Using an expression (more about expressions in Conditionals), the following loop will run until the user enters the word end:

```
while [[ $REPLY != "end" ]]
do
  read
  # do something based on reply
done
```

The following example is a while forever loop—the while command will never end since the result is always true. If the executed command (run_command) fails, then the break command is executed that exits from the loop.

```
while true
do
   run_command
   if [[ $? -ne 0 ]]
   then
      break
   else
      :
   fi
   # do other things
done
```

The single colon <:> is the null statement, equivalent to the COBOL NEXT SENTENCE or the C stand-alone semicolon <;>. It does nothing but take the place where a command is required.

The next example shows the use of the while with a command instead of a comparison:

```
echo "Enter the first file to list"
read
while ls $REPLY
do
   echo "Enter another file to search for"
   read
done
```

So long as the filename exists, the `ls` command returns a good status code (equivalent to true), so the loop continues, and the user is prompted for more files to list. When a filename is entered that does not exist, the `ls` command returns a bad status code (equivalent to false) and the loop ends.

Another use of the while loop and read command combined are to loop through files. The following example reads through a file that has three variables, separated by spaces in each record, which are separated by the new-line character:

```
while read first second third
do
   # process the data...
   echo "first field is $first"
   echo "second field is $second"
   echo "third field is $third"
done < /the/path/and/file_name
```

When the read command encounters end-of-file or another input error, it returns a bad status code (equivalent to false) and the loop ends. Because there are variables on the read command, the input fields are stored in them instead of the special environmental variable $REPLY.

until Loop

The until loop repeats so long as the expression or command in the structure returns a false (zero) value. Any commands in the conditional section are executed at least once. The commands in the body of the loop may not be executed if the conditional is false. Both Korn and Bourne shells support the until loop.

The general structure is (keywords in bold print):

until expression or command
do
        commands
done

Using an expression (more about expressions in Conditionals), the following loop will run until the user enters the word end:

```
until [[ $REPLY = "end" ]]
do
  read
  # do something based on reply
done
```

This is different from the first example under while because the conditional expression has been reversed. The while example used <!=> for not-equal and this until example used <=> for equal-to. So long as the user enters something other than the word end, the loop will continue. When it is entered, the condition becomes true, which causes the loop to exit.

The following example will run until the user enters a valid UNIX command:

```
command=no_such_unix_CoMmAnD
until $command
do
   echo "Invalid command, enter another:"
   read
done
```

Ending Loops Early—Break and Continue

The break and continue commands change the behavior of a loop. The break command ends processing of a loop before the end conditions are met and is a very useful way to bail out of a loop if an error occurs. The continue command skips the remainder of the commands in the do/done area and returns to the test portion of the loop.

The general structure is (keywords in bold print):

break

continue

The break command was shown with the while loop, causing the current loop to end (exit from it). The continue command allows us to skip statements below the continue:

```
$ for loop in 1 2 3↵
> do↵
>    echo "before continue" $loop↵
>    continue↵
>    echo "after continue" $loop↵
> done↵
before continue 1
before continue 2
before continue 3
$
```

Normally, there would be some form of logic around the continue command so it does not skip the remaining code in the loop unconditionally. The best way to understand the difference between continue and break is to see the same example again:

```
$ for loop in 1 2 3↵
> do↵
>    echo "before break" $loop↵
>    break↵
>    echo "after break" $loop↵
> done↵
before break 1
$
```

Testing Expressions

The Korn and Bourne shells support many of the same conditional or testing expressions because the Korn shell is upwardly compatible with the Bourne shell. When using these expressions in a loop or conditional structure, the expression is contained within a pair of square brackets <[]> for Bourne syntax and a double pair of square brackets <[[]]> for Korn. Except for those expressions listed as Bourne only in Figure 5.4, the Bourne constructs can be used in a Korn shell script with single or double sets of square brackets (Korn supports either). The Bourne only expressions will work in Korn shell if you use a single set of square brackets, but there are better syntax forms for those exceptions.

Figure 5.4 shows the Korn and Bourne Shell conditional expressions.

The Bourne shell supports both the single square brackets <[]> and the test command; Korn supports the Bourne syntax and its double square bracket <[[]]> syntax. No matter which syntax is used, the result is available for the conditional and looping structures as well as being stored in the return code variable $?.

To determine if a file exists:

```
$ pwd↵                          Where are we?
/u/dhorvath
$ test -f .profile↵             It was there the last time I checked...
$ echo $?↵                      Check the return code
0
$ [ -f .profile ]↵              Bourne shell syntax
$ echo $?↵
0
$ [[ -f .profile ]]↵            Korn shell syntax (newer)
$ echo $?↵
0
$
```

They all return true (zero) because there is a file with the name .profile in my home directory. Try it with a file that does not exist and see the results:

```
$ ls no_such↵                   Make sure it is not there
no_such not found
$ test -f no_such ↵
$ echo $?↵                      Check the return code
1
$ [ -f no_such ]↵               Bourne shell syntax
$ echo $?↵
1
$ [[ -f no_such ]]↵             Korn shell syntax (newer)
$ echo $?↵
1
$
```

Figure 5.4
Korn and Bourne Shell Testing Expressions

Shell	Expression	Purpose
B	expr1 -a expr2	Evaluates to true if expression1 and expression2 are both true
B	expr1 -o expr2	Evaluates to true if either expression1 or expression2 is true
B K	! expression	Evaluates to true if the expression is false (logical not)
B K	-b file	Evaluates to true if the file exists and is a block special file (device)
B K	-c file	Evaluates to true if the file exists and is a character special file (device)
B K	-d file	Evaluates to true if file exists and is a directory
B K	-f file	Evaluates to true if file exists and is a regular file
B K	-g file	Evaluates to true if file exists and the set-group-id bit is set
B K	-k file	Evaluates to true if file exists and the sticky bit is set
B K	-n file	Evaluates to true if the length of string is not zero
B K	-p file	Evaluates to true if file exists and is a named pipe (fifo)
B K	-r file	Evaluates to true if file exists and is readable
B K	-s file	Evaluates to true if file exists and has a non-zero size
B K	-t descriptor	Evaluates to true if the descriptor is connected to a terminal
B K	-u file	Evaluates to true if file exists and the set-user-id bit is set
B K	-w file	Evaluates to true if file exists and is writable
B K	-x file	Evaluates to true if file exists and is executable
B K	-z str	Evaluates to true if the length of string is zero
B K	\(expression \)	Used to group expressions to override normal order of evaluation
B K	nbr1 -eq nbr2	Evaluates to true if integer nbr1 is the same as integer nbr2
B K	nbr1 -ge nbr2	Evaluates to true if integer nbr1 is not less than integer nbr2
B K	nbr1 -gt nbr2	Evaluates to true if interger nbr1 is greater than interger nbr2
B K	nbr1 -le nbr2	Evaluates to true if integer nbr1 is greater than integer nbr2
B K	nbr1 -lt nbr2	Evaluates to true if integer nbr1 is not greater than integer nbr2
B K	nbr1 -ne nbr2	Evaluates to true if integer nbr1 is less than integer nbr2
B K	str1 != str2	Evaluates to true if string1 is not the same as string2
B K	str1 = strr2	Evaluates to true if string1 is the same as string2
K	-G file	Evaluates to true if file exists and the group id matches the effective group id of the current process
K	-L file	Evaluates to true if file exists and is a symbolic link
K	-O file	Evaluates to true if file exists and the user id matches the effective userid of the current process
K	-o option	Evaluates to true if the option is set
K	~ file	Evaluates to true if file exists and is a socket
K	expr1 && expr2	Evaluates to true if expression1 and expression2 are both true
K	expr1 || expr2	Evaluates to true if either expression1 or expression2 is true
K	file1 -ef file2	Evaluates to true if file exists and is the same as file2 (link)
K	file1 -ot file2	Evaluates to true if file exists and is older than file2
K	file1 -nt file2	Evaluates to true if file exists and is newer than file2
K	str != pattern	Evaluates to true if string does not match pattern
K	str = pattern	Evaluates to true if string matches pattern
K	str1 < str2	Evaluates to true if string1 is less than string2
K	str1 > str2	Evaluates to true if string1 is greater than string2

Where shell is (K)orn or (B)ourne.

Since the file does not exist (confirmed with the ls command, if you try this example and find that you have a file with the name no_such, pick another name and try again), the value one (for false) is returned. Many other languages use zero for false and one (or non-zero) for true. Pay careful attention to your script code until this is second nature. Because

I switch between C and shell script (among other languages) programming, I always have to think about it.

The space between the left square braces and the expression and between the expression and the right square braces is very important—it must be there. Strings and other things can be compared. Environmental variables can be substituted for the filename in the above examples and in the string examples that follow:

```
$ test "abc" = "abc"↵                     Strings should match
$ echo $?↵
0
$ test "abc" != "abc"↵                    Strings do match (false)
$ echo $?↵
1
$ [ "abc" = "abc" ]↵                      Strings should match
$ echo $?↵
0
$ [ "abc" != "abc" ]↵                     Strings do match (false)
$ echo $?↵
1
$ [[ "abc" = "abc" ]]; echo $?↵           Strings should match
0
$ [[ "abc" != "abc" ]]; echo $?↵          Strings do match (false)
1
$
```

The last two examples combined the echo on the same line as the test. This will work with any of the forms since the semicolon <;> is the command separator and is independent of the commands it separates.

Examples for numeric (integer) comparisons follow:

```
$ [ 5 -lt 3 ]; echo $?↵                   Should be false
1
$ [ 5 -gt 3 ]; echo $?↵                   Should be true
0
$ test 5 -lt 3; echo $?↵                  Should be false
1
$ test 5 -gt 3; echo $?↵                  Should be true
0
$ [[ 5 -lt 3 ]]; echo $?↵                 Should be false
1
$ [[ 5 -gt 3 ]]; echo $?↵                 Should be true
0
$
```

If you are using the Bourne shell, you are limited to the Bourne forms. Using the Korn shell provides enhancements.

if/then—else—fi and elif/then Conditional Tests

The basic form of conditional tests is the if - then - else structure. An if/then (and else if necessary) are ended with a fi (if spelled backwards). At least one statement must come after each if/then, else, and elif/then statement.

The general structure is (keywords in bold print):

if command or expression
then
command
fi

if command or expression
then
command
else
other_command
fi

if command or expression
then
command
elif command or expression
then
other_command
else
yet_another_command
fi

You can have one or many commands after an if/then, elif/then, or else. If you want to have a portion of an if but have no commands to execute, then use the null statement, the colon <:>. This is very useful when you have logic that is very straightforward but have nothing to do if it is true, only if it is false (else). To reverse the logic such that what was true is now false and false becomes true, so that you now have code to execute when it is true, can be very complicated and be difficult to read and maintain. An example of this follows:

```
if [[ $str1 > $str2 && $str3 > $str4 ]]
then
        :
else
        do_something_here
fi
```

Reversing the logic would result in an if statement that looks something like:

```
if [[ !( $str1 > $str2 ) || !( $str3 > $str4 ) ]]
```

or slightly simpler but not as readable as the original:

```
if [[ !( $str1 > $str2 && $str3 > $str4 ) ]]
```

There is a trick if you prefer to see the then portion of an if construct on the same line as the if—use the semicolon to separate the commands! The if/then would look like:

```
if [[ -f .profile ]] ; then
```

which may be more legible to you. The shell should not care, the choice is up to you.

A common use of the if/then/elif is for decision trees such as menu processing as shown in the following:

```
echo "A) ls command"
echo "B) ps command"
echo "C) who -u command"
echo "select one:"
read
if [[ $REPLY = "A" ]] ; then
   ls
elif [[ $REPLY = "B" ]] ; then
   ps
elif [[ $REPLY = "C" ]] ; then
   who -u
else
   echo "Invalid Choice"
fi
```

If you select one of the options (A, B, or C), the related command will be executed. If you enter something else, you will get the error message. While this works very well, there are ways that require less code and are more readable, such as the case statement.

case Statement

The case statement is used when there are a series of available options that would otherwise require a large conditional test with multiple if, elif, and else statements. It is especially useful when creating a menu or verifying a series of values. A case statement is ended with esac (case backwards).

The general structure is (keywords in bold print):

case $selection_variable **in**
  pattern|other_pattern) command
    second_command ;;
  yet_another_pattern) another_command ;;
  *) command_if_no_other_matches ;;
esac

A pattern of one or more characters is used to select the command or series of commands to execute when it is matched. Multiple patterns can be used to select a command by separating them with a vertical bar <|>. The selection is completed by a pair of semicolons <;;>. The shell interprets the patterns in the case statement one at a time and when it finds one that matches, executes the related commands, and stops evaluating. The final pattern shown, *), is optional but serves as the default—if nothing else matches, its command will be executed. Without the default, if there is no match, the next statement executed is the one that follows the esac.

Implementing the final if/then/elif example (decision tree) with a case statement would be done as follows:

```
echo "A) ls command"
echo "B) ps command"
echo "C) who -u command"
echo "select one:"
read
case $REPLY in
   A|a) ls ;;
   B|b) ps ;;
   C|c) who -u ;;
   *) echo "Invalid Choice" ;;
esac
```

With the added advantage that upper or lowercase letters can be used to select the option instead of them having to be uppercase or having more complex conditional expressions in the original example.

select Statement

The select is not available in the Bourne shell, it is unique to Korn. It is a way of presenting menus to the user in an easy-to-program form. It reduces the need to manually create the menu for the user.

The general structure is (keywords in bold print):

select $selection_variable in option1 option2 "option 3"
do
        commands
done

Typically, a case or if/then/elif structure is used within the select to perform the proper command. Implementing the final if/then/elif example (decision tree) with a select and case statement would be done as follows:

```
$ select sel in "ls command" "ps command" "who -u command"↵
> do↵
>    case $sel in↵
>       ls*) ls ;;↵
>       ps*) ps ;;↵
>       who*) who -u ;;↵
>       *) echo "oops, try again"↵
```

```
>     esac↵
> done↵
1) ls command
2) ps command
3) who -u command
#? 1↵
c_stuff cob_stuff COMB_HAIR first function_test Mail bin
mbox my_who paren.exam second temp_ksh
#? ↵
1) ls command
2) ps command
3) who -u command
#? today↵
oops, try again
#? ^d
$
```

The way to exit from a select is by pressing end-of-file or have a command that executes a break statement (such as a quit menu option). A quick way of creating a menu for a user to limit the commands he or she can execute is shown in the following example:

```
$ select var in ls ps "who -u" break↵
> do↵
>     $var↵
> done↵
1) ls
2) ps
3) who -u
4) break
#? 1↵
c_stuff cob_stuff COMB_HAIR first function_test Mail bin
mbox my_who paren.exam second temp_ksh
#? 4↵
$
```

In a true menu like this, you would use the exit command instead of break, and have the $HOME/.profile file execute it and assign a restricted shell to the user. The user selects a number and the command is placed in the environmental variable var, which is then executed.

There is one more area in shell scripting that should be covered, arithmetic expressions, which is a fancy term for mathematical operations within the shell.

ARITHMETIC EXPRESSIONS AND RELATED COMMANDS (let, expr)

The Bourne shell does not have any means to perform arithmetic operations directly; you must use the expr command. The Korn shell, however, will let you perform arithmetic with the expr command or the let Korn shell command.

Figure 5.5
Bourne Shell Arithmetic Operators (expr Command)

```
Operator          Operation
expr1 \| expr2    Return expr1 if both are non-zero, return expr2 otherwise
expr1 \& expr2    Return expr1 if both are non-zero, returns zero otherwise

expr1 =expr2      Result of integer or string compare - true if expr1 equals expr2
expr1\>expr2      Result of integer or string compare - true if expr1 is greater than expr2
expr1\>=expr2     Result of integer or string compare - true if expr1 is not less than expr2
expr1\<expr2      Result of integer or string compare - true if expr1 is less than expr2
expr1\<=expr2     Result of integer or string compare - true if expr1 is not greater than expr2
expr1!=expr2      Result of integer or string compare - true if expr1 is not equal to expr2

expr1 + expr2     Returns sum of two integers
expr1 - expr2     Returns result of integers expr1 minus expr2

expr1 \* expr2    Returns result of integers expr1 multiplied by expr2
expr1 / expr2     Returns result of integers expr1 divided by expr2
expr1 % expr2     Returns result of integers expr1 modulo expr2 (remainder of expr1 / expr2)

expr1: expr2      Returns true if expr1 matches regular expression expr2 (pattern matching)
```

Operators that have special meaning to the shell are escaped (<*> for instance).
Operators are shown in order of precedence, grouped operators share same level.
The default precedence can be overridden through the use of the \(and \) operators.

Since Korn will support both methods, we will look at the older (Bourne) method first. Figure 5.5 shows the operators available under Bourne.

Because the asterisk character <*> has special meaning to the shell, it must be escaped through the use of the backslash <\>. The following example multiplies 8 times 2, stores the result in abc, and then shows the result with an echo command:

```
$ abc=`expr 8 \* 2`; echo $abc↵
16
$
```

Pay careful attention to the quote characters around the expr command. They are backquotes <`> that cause the contents to be executed and the result returned. A single expr command can process multiple operations at one time:

```
$ abc=`expr 8 + 2 \* 2`; echo $abc↵
12
$
```

The multiplication occurred first and then the addition according to the rules of precedence. If you want the addition to occur first, you must use parentheses to override the rules as shown:

```
$ abc=`expr \(8 + 2 \) \* 2`; echo $abc↵
20
$
```

The addition takes place and then the multiplication. Because the parentheses characters <(> and <)> have special meaning to the shell, they too must be escaped as shown. These examples have used constants; environmental variables will also work.

Figure 5.6 shows the operators for the Korn shell with the let command.

A simple example multiplies 3 and 2 together:

```
$ let abc=3*2; echo $abc↵
6
$
```

If you put spaces between the 3 and the asterisk or the asterisk and the 2, the command would not produce the expected results:

```
$ let abc=3 * 2; echo $abc↵
ksh: c_stuff: bad number
3
$
```

The shell evaluated this expression to mean: Assign the value 3 to the variable abc, expand the meta-character asterisk <*> (to all the filenames in the current directory), and since it is still part of the `let` command, try to use it as an operator or operand. That is why the bad number message was produced. With other operators, putting spaces in may give you a syntax error as in this example with the plus sign <+>:

```
$ let abc=3 + 5; echo $abc↵
ksh: +: syntax error
3
$
```

Again, the shell tried to evaluate the plus sign as something besides being part of the let statement and produced an error message since it could not figure it out. The value 3 was stored in the environmental variable. The way the statement should be entered (without spaces or with spaces and quoted) is as follows:

```
$ let abc=3+5; echo $abc↵                  No spaces
8
$ let abc="3 + 5"; echo $abc↵              Spaces and double quotes
8
$
```

A single let command can process multiple operations at one time:

```
$ let abc=3+5*2; echo $abc↵
13
$
```

Figure 5.6
Korn Shell Arithmetic Operators (let Command)

<table>
<tr><th>Operator</th><th>Operation</th></tr>
<tr><td>-expr</td><td>Return the negation of expr (unary minus)</td></tr>
<tr><td>!expr</td><td>Return to logical negation of expr (return false for true and true for false)</td></tr>
<tr><td>~expr</td><td>Return the bitwise negation of expr (every bit will be flipped)</td></tr>
<tr><td>expr1 * expr2</td><td>Returns result of integers expr1 multiplied by expr2</td></tr>
<tr><td>expr1 / expr2</td><td>Returns result of integers expr1 divided by expr2</td></tr>
<tr><td>expr1 % expr2</td><td>Returns result of integers expr1 modulo expr2 (remainder of expr1/expr2)</td></tr>
<tr><td>expr1 + expr2</td><td>Returns the sum of two integers</td></tr>
<tr><td>expr1 - expr2</td><td>Returns result of integers expr1 minus expr2</td></tr>
<tr><td>expr1<=expr2</td><td>Returns the result of integer or string compare - true if expr1 is less or equal expr2</td></tr>
<tr><td>expr1>=expr2</td><td>Returns the result of integer or string compare - true if expr1 is not less than expr2</td></tr>
<tr><td>expr1> expr2</td><td>Returns the result of integer or string compare - true if expr1 is greater than expr2</td></tr>
<tr><td>expr1< expr2</td><td>Returns the result of integer or string compare - true if expr1 is less than expr2</td></tr>
<tr><td>expr1==expr2</td><td>Returns the result of integer or string compare - true if expr1 is equals expr2</td></tr>
<tr><td>expr1!=expr2</td><td>Returns the result of integer or string compare - true if expr1 is is not equal to expr2</td></tr>
<tr><td>expr1 & expr2</td><td>Returns the result of integer or string compare - true if expr1 equals expr2</td></tr>
<tr><td>expr1 ^ expr2</td><td>Performs bitwise xor - a bit is one if the bit in either exp1 or expr2 is one</td></tr>
<tr><td>expr1 | expr2</td><td>Performs bitwise or on exp1 and exp2. A bit is one if the bit is one in either</td></tr>
<tr><td>expr1&&expr2</td><td>Return the logical and result - if expr1 is false, expr2 is never evaluated</td></tr>
<tr><td>expr1 || expr2</td><td>Return the logical or result - if expr1 is true, expr2 is never evaluated</td></tr>
</table>

Spaces are not allowed between operators and expressions unless the entire expression is quoted.
Korn shell operators do not require escaping when used with Korn commands (like let).
Operators are shown in order of precedence; grouped operators share same level.
The default precedence can be overridden by using the \(and \) operators.

The multiplication occurred first and then the addition according to the rules of precedence. If you want the addition to occur first, you must use parentheses to override the rules as shown:

```
$ let abc=(3+5)*2; echo $abc↵
ksh: syntax error: '(' unexpected
$ let abc=\(3+5\)*2; echo $abc↵
16
$
```

Remember that the parentheses characters have special meaning to the shell. In this case, the <()> must be escaped or the shell will produce an error message. When coded properly, addition takes place and then the multiplication. These examples have used constants, although environmental variables will also work.

Figure 5.7
Flags to Set Variable Attributes with typeset

Flag	Behavior
-H	Ignored under UNIX. Converts UNIX pathnames to the host operating system format
-i	Variable is forced to be an integer. A string cannot be stored in a variable of this type
-l	Variable is forced to lowercase. Any uppercase characters are automatically converted
-L	Left-justify variable. Strings default to -L
-Lno	Left-justify variable. Field width is set by no. Remove any leading zeroes
-LZ	Left-justify variable. Remove any leading zeroes
-LZno	Left-justify variable, field width is set by no. Remove any leading zeroes
-r	Variable is readonly
-R	Right-justify variable
-Rno	Right-justify variable. Field width is set by no
-RZ	Right-justify variable. Fill field with leading zeroes
-RZno	Right-justify variable, field width is set by no. Fill field with leading zeroes
-t	Variable is tagged. Typeset -t alone will show all tagged variables and value
-u	Variable is forced to uppercase. Any lowercase characters are automatically converted
-x	Variable is automatically exported. Value is available to subshells
-Z	Same as -RZ

Valid forms of typeset command are:

```
typeset flag variable
typeset flag variable=value
typeset flag variable=value variable=value2
```

To turn off flag for a variable, use a plus sign <+> instead of the minus sign <-> before the flag.

VARIABLE ATTRIBUTES

In the Bourne shell, environmental variables are defined by their usage. If the variable contains a string, it is a string variable. If it contains numbers only, it can be treated as a numeric (integer) variable. The Korn shell provides a way to define attributes for a variable. These attributes further define the status or appearance of the variable.

The command to set environmental variable attributes under the Korn shell is typeset. Figure 5.7 shows the flags that are used to set attributes for environmental variables with the typeset command.

The `typeset` command is very useful when you need to specify the size of a field (if you are building a filename that will contain a four-digit number that needs to occupy four digits, even if the value is 3). It is also useful for character case conversions to ensure that input or a variable contains the characters in one case only.

The following example shows a four-digit right-justified, zero-filled environmental variable:

```
$ typeset -RZ4 rzi_var="12"↵
$ echo $rzi_var↵
0012
$ typeset -RZ4 rzi_var2="Ab"↵
$ echo $rzi_var2↵
```

```
Ab
$
```

Notice that this only works on numeric values: It will not zero-fill with a value of Ab. Upper and lowercase conversions are shown in the following:

```
$ typeset -u uc_var="abcdef"↵
$ echo $uc_var↵
ABCDEF
$ typeset -l lc_var="AbCdEfGhIj<>."↵
$ echo $lc_var↵
abcdefghij<>.
$
```

Notice how the original values are converted when they are stored in the environmental variable. With the exception of `typeset -r`, there is no requirement to define the value in the variable on the typeset command itself. Because `typeset -r` sets the variable to read-only, it must have its value defined. The following example shows it in action:

```
$ typeset -r RO_var↵
$ RO_var=a2e3↵
ksh: RO_var: is read only
$ typeset -r RO_var2=b4e5↵
$ echo $RO_var2↵
b4e5
$ RO_var2=asdf↵
ksh: RO_var2: is read only
$
```

Once the variable RO_var is typeset, we cannot assign a value to it. If we want it to have a value, it must be assigned in the typeset command as was done with RO_var2.

The following example shows the `typeset` command with the `-i` (integer) switch and multiple variables in one command:

```
$ typeset -i int_var int_var2↵
$ int_var=abc↵
ksh: abc: bad number
$ int_var=12345↵
$ echo $int_var↵
12345
$
```

Once an environmental variable is defined as an integer, you cannot assign a string to it.

To determine which variables have attributes, you can use the typeset command with no flags or variables to see all the variables and their attributes. The following command will show all variables with attributes and their values:

```
typeset -
```

To get a list of all variables that have attributes but do not want to see the attributes themselves, use the following command:

```
typeset +
```

To see the variables that have a particular attribute (like read-only), you use the typeset command with the flag but no variables or values. The following example shows the variables that are read-only with their values (-r) and without (+r):

```
$ typeset -r↵
RO_var2=b4e5
$ typeset +r↵
RO_var2
$
```

To remove an attribute from an environmental variable, use the flag with a plus sign <+> instead of the minus sign <->. The following example removes the read-only attribute from RO_var2:

```
$ typeset +r RO_var2↵          Remove read-only attribute
$ typeset +r↵                  Show read-only variables (none)
$
```

More About Where UNIX Looks for Programs and Scripts

The information provided in Chapter 4 about the UNIX Path was a simplification. There are other places that UNIX searches in addition to the directories specified in the path. In reality, the Korn shell performs a lot more processing for commands before it ever searches the path. The following occurs, in order, for a command:

- Alias (alias substitution is performed and search resumes)
- Specified pathname (like fully qualifying the `ls` command as /usr/bin/ls)
- Reserved word (like while)
- Built-in command (like echo)
- Function
- Tracked alias (along portions of path)
- Path

Aliases are defined with the `alias` command. A command with the pathname specified tells the shell where the command is through a relative or absolute pathname. The reserved words are statements in the shell like the while loop or an if statement. The built-in commands are part of the shell itself (the echo, alias, and whence commands are often built into the shell as opposed to external commands). Functions are like PROCs for the shell; they are defined once and remain available. Tracked aliases are created with the `alias -t` command or by enabling trackall in the shell, and are frequently used programs that the shell retains the location of so it does not have to search the path for them. Finally, if the shell has not found the desired command, it searches the path. If the command is not in the path, then you get the error message `ksh: command: not found`.

There are two commands to determine what command or script is being executed: which and whence. The alias command is used to create a short-hand name for other commands.

which, where, and alias Commands

To find out where the echo command is stored, try the following command:

```
$ which echo↵
/usr/bin/echo
$
```

If you have multiple versions of an executable or shell script and need to know which version is being executed, use the which command.

The whence command is built into the Korn shell and is used to determine the absolute pathname to a command much like the which command. However, whence knows about Korn shell reserved words, aliases, built-in commands, functions, tracked aliases, and the path.

By default, whence behaves like the which command. With the -v (verbose) option, whence searches the other types of items in the shell. The following example shows whence behavior:

```
$ whence echo↵
/usr/bin/echo
$ whence -v echo↵
echo is a shell builtin
$
```

Because of the way that the Korn shell searches for commands, the built-in echo will be executed. In other shells, the command stored in /usr/bin is available.

Because whence knows about aliases in Korn shell, it will search them too. The following assigns an alias to the echo command:

```
$ alias echo=ls↵
$ whence echo↵
ls
$ whence -v echo↵
echo is an alias for ls
$
```

Because of the way that the Korn shell searches for commands, the alias for echo will cause the ls command to be executed.

The difference between which and whence is shown better in the following example:

```
$ which type↵
no type in .:/application_1/prod/scripts:
/application_2/prod/cobol:usr/ibs/ksh:/usr/tool/bin:
/usr2/other_tool/bin:/usr2/spfux/aixbin:/usr2/unispf:
```

```
/usr2/unispf/twglm:/application_1/tools:/usr/bin:/etc:
/usr/sbin:/usr/ucb:/usr/bin/X11:/sbin:.:
$ whence type↵
whence -v
$ whence -v type↵
type is an exported alias for whence -v
$
```

The `type` command is an alias for the command `whence -v`. The `which` command could not find it since it does not know about Korn shell aliases. The `whence` command shows what is aliased to the command; `whence -v` gives a fuller description.

The `alias` command provides a way of creating abbreviations and pseudonyms for frequently used commands and option combinations. They are often included in the .profile, .login, .kshrc, and .cshrc files to assign them when logging in or starting a subshell.

The name is an abbreviation for the specified command that can have options assigned to it. The following is an alias I use:

```
$ alias ll='ls -al'↵
$
```

Since I use the `ls -al` command almost all the time, I made an abbreviation for it. When I type `ll`, the shell substitutes `ls -al`.

When an alias is defined within single quotes <'>, any environmental variables are resolved when the aliased command is executed. When double quotes <"> are used, the environmental variable substitution occurs immediately.

You can replace commands with an alias, but it is not good practice to export them (using the `-x` option). If you wanted the `ls` command to behave like my `ll` command, you could do the following:

```
$ alias ls='ls -al'↵
$
```

Just do not use `-x` to export it or you could cause scripts to run incorrectly.

The `alias` command with a name only will display the alias defined for that name. An alias command without any name will display all aliases. With the `-x` option, it will display the exported aliases.

ADVANCED COMMANDS

Chapters 3 and 4 showed the UNIX commands to replace what you were familiar doing on the mainframe. More information about the commands listed in Figure 5.8 can be found in the man pages for your system. Although they are less frequently used than most commands, they can be very handy.

Figure 5.8a
Advanced Command Summary - Part 1 of 2

Command	Purpose
compress	Compress data using the modified Lempel-Zev algorithm
	Resulting file will have a .Z suffix; original file is discarded
uncompress	Return a compressed file to normal. Discards compressed file (one with .Z suffix)
zcat	Uncompresses a compressed file to stdout
	Used to uncompress a file while retaining the compressed version
pack	Compress data using Huffman coding
	Resulting file will have a .z suffix; original file is discarded. Use compress instead
unpack	Uncompresses a packed file to normal. Discards the compress file (.z suffix)
pcat	Uncompresses a packed file to stdout
	Used to unpack a file and retain the packed version
passwd	Used to change a user's password. On some systems, it can be used to change other user information in the /etc/password file
su	Used to become another user temporarily (without logging out and back in)
	Stands for super user - the default user for the command
cpio	Copy (cp) files in and out (io) of cpio archive format
	Used to backup data or package files together
tar	Tape archive and restore - used to backup and restore data to tapes or disks
ltail	Display the lines at the end of a file, default is 10 lines
head	Display the lines at the beginning of a file, default is 10 lines
more	Page through data in a file or piped stdout
	Use <space> to get next page or <enter> for next line
pg	Page through data in a file or piped stdout. Use <enter> to get next page
hostname	Display network name of current system. Equivalent to uname -n
uname	Display information about the current system. The -a option will show all information including operation system name and nodename.
finger	Determine who is using a system; when a user is specified, it will display additional information about them including their $HOME/.plan and $HOME/.project files
who	Display information about users of the system
	Use the -u option to see currently logged in users
who am i	Special form of the who command used to determine who is logged onto a particular terminal
id	Display your userid, user name, group id and group name
tty	Display the device name of the terminal
groups	Display groups that you belong to

File Security

In most mainframe installations, file security is centrally administered. In other words, it is handled by specific individuals instead of by the file owner. In some installations, however, individual file owners are allowed to administer their own files, usually through one of the third-party mainframe security packages. Because of the variety of packages available on the mainframe, only the UNIX file security commands are shown.

The `chmod` command changes the access permissions to the file. You must have ownership of the file or the directory that contains it.

Figure 5.8b
Advanced Command Summary - Part 2 of 2

Command	Purpose
mail	Read and send electronic mail
talk	Hold a two way electronic conversation with another user
write	Send a short message to another user's screen
learn	Computer-based training that is distributed with some versions of UNIX
make	Performs compilation and linkediting based on a set of rules stored in a file known as makefile. Dependencies between source and object files (program calls function in other source module or uses header file) are described in these rules to ensure that only the code that changed will be compiled
ld	The ld command is used to build executables from object modules and libraries (archives). Most of the compilers (as, cc, cbl) will execute ld by default or with the proper switch almost eliminating the need for you to ever use this command directly. By default, the executable will be named a.out
ar	Create an archive library (similar to a PDS) for use by ld
fuser	Determines which users have a file open
cal	Displays a calendar for the month and year you specify
bc	Basic programmable algebraic calculator Actually invokes dc to perform operations
dc	RPN (Reverse Polish Notation) based arithmetic calculator
true	This command does nothing, but does it very successfully - returns zero status
false	This command does nothing, but does it unsuccessfully - returns non-zero status
lex	Lexical analyzer that processes a series of regular expressions that describe the way the language syntax works together. Used with yacc
yacc	Yet Another Computer Compiler - converts the syntax of a programming language described in BNF (Bacus Normal Form) into a series of subroutines to parse the language. When lex and yacc generated functions are combined, they provide the parsing and analysis portions of a compiler
sed	Stream editor - used to apply edits to a stream of bytes (i.e., piped data) or to multiple files (global or gang editing)
awk	Named from the initials of the authors - Aho, Weinberger, and Kernighan (of Kernighan & Ritchie, the creators of the C language). A programming language that looks like C but with advanced features
tr	Translates characters in a file based on regular expression rules Can be used to translate from lowercase to uppercase
strings	This command searches a file for strings of four or more printable characters and displays them to stdout. Very useful when searching for text within binary files
file	Used to determine the type of an unknown file. It uses rules that are embedded in the command and contained in the file /etc/magic

The modes (permissions) of a file are determined by numeric or alphanumeric values. When using ls -al, the first fields are the file permissions as shown in the following example:

```
$ ls -al change_me↵
-rw-r--r--   1 dhorvath users          5 Mar 18 19:10 change_me
$
```

In this example, the owner has read and write permissions, members of the group have read, and the rest of the world has read permissions. It was shown as:

```
-rw-  r--  r--
```

This can be expressed numerically as:

```
 6    4    4
```

Normally written as 644. Each combination of permissions has a corresponding value. The values are used in octal and are:

```
---    0
--x    1
-w-    2
-wx    3
r--    4
r-x    5
rw-    6
rwx    7
```

When grouped together as three digits, the owner is the first digit, the group is the second, and the world is the third. To change a file so that it is read-only to the owner and no permissions to anyone else, it would be 400 (`-r--------` in an `ls -al` listing).

There are special flags (that set the S and T flags in `ls -al`) that can be combined with the normal permissions:

4000	Set userid when executed
2000	Set group ID when executed
1000	Enable sticky bit causing executable to be locked in paging file when executed

In the following example, a file with 644 permissions is changed to 400 and then back again with `ls -al` listings to confirm the permissions:

```
$ ls -al change_me↵
-rw-r--r--   1 dhorvath users          5 Mar 18 19:10 change_me
$ chmod 400 change_me↵
$ ls -al change_me↵
-r--------   1 dhorvath users          5 Mar 18 19:10 change_me
$ chmod 644 change_me↵
$ ls -al change_me↵
-rw-r--r--   1 dhorvath users          5 Mar 18 19:10 change_me
$
```

Another way of changing file modes uses flags (alphabetic values) to express the permissions. Most people who are familiar with permissions can use either mode and many like to show off by just using the numeric values and calculating the appropriate values in their minds.

The command consists of three parts: which permission to change, how to change the permission, and what to set them to. Then comes the file to be changed. The which part is:

u	Owner (user) permissions
g	Group permissions
o	Everyone else's (others) permissions
a	All permissions (user, group, and other)

The how part is:

+	Add the permission
-	Remove the permission
=	Set the permission to

The what part is:

r	Read permission
w	Write permission
x	Execute permission
s	User or group set-ID
t	Set the sticky bit
u,g,o	Use the existing permission taken from user, group, or other field

Although this looks very confusing, once you are used to the rules, it is very simple.

Try the following example on your system:

```
$ ls -al change_me↵
-rw-r--r--   1 dhorvath users          5 Mar 18 19:10 change_me
$ chmod u=r,g=,o= change_me↵
$ ls -al change_me↵
-r--------   1 dhorvath users          5 Mar 18 19:10 change_me
$ chmod u=rw,g=r,o=g change_me↵
$ ls -al change_me↵
-rw-r--r--   1 dhorvath users          5 Mar 18 19:10 change_me
$
```

The permissions for the file are shown to confirm an initial value of 644. The permissions are changed to 400 by setting the user permissions to read, the group and other permissions to nothing. After confirming that the permissions had been set to 400, they were changed back to 644 by setting the user permissions to read and write, the group permissions to read, and the other permissions to the same as group. The last `ls -al` command confirmed all this.

Figure 5.9
UNIX File Permissions

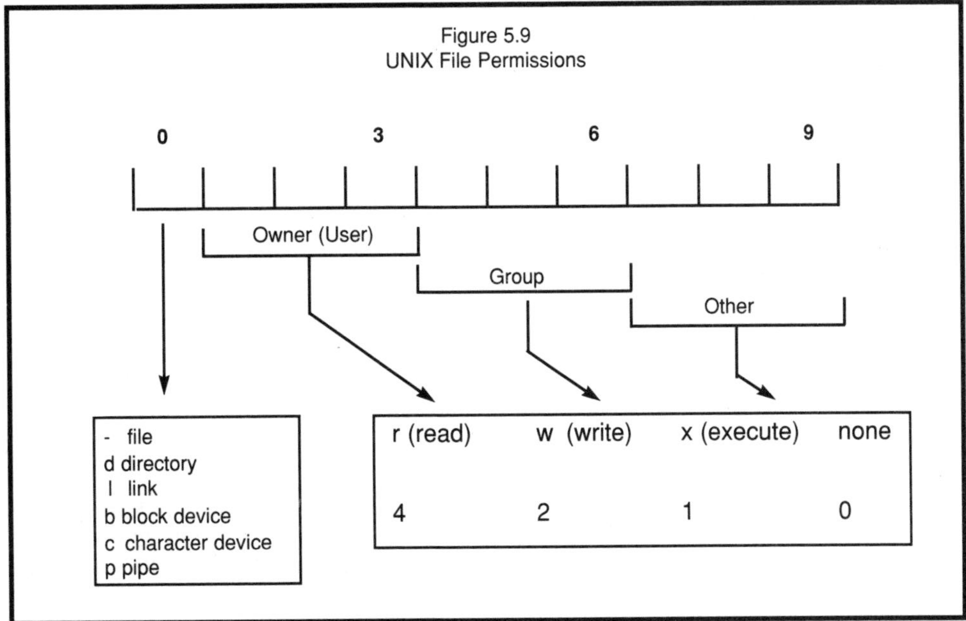

Another way of doing the same thing would be to change the permissions as in the following example:

```
$ chmod u-w,g-rw,o=g change_me↵
$ ls -al change_me↵
-r--------   1 dhorvath users         5 Mar 18 19:10 change_me
$ chmod u+w,g+r,o+r change_me↵
$ ls -al change_me↵
-rw-r--r--   1 dhorvath users         5 Mar 18 19:10 change_me
$
```

The permissions are changed to 400 by removing the write permission from the user, removing read and write permissions from group, and setting the other permissions to group. After confirming that the permissions had been set to 400, they were changed back to 644 by adding write to the user permissions, adding read to the group permissions, and setting the other permissions to the same as group. The last `ls -al` command confirmed all this.

Figure 5.9 is another way of looking at file permissions.

It really is very simple once you have tried it a few times and get used to the table with the numeric values.

The three categories of modes are owner, group, and all others. The system administrator can change the owner of a file with the chown command, just as if the new owner had created the file him or herself. The group ownership of a file can be changed by the file owner causing the group permissions to be applied to a different set of users.

The chgrp command is shown in the following example:

```
$ ls -al change_me↵
-rw-r--r--   1 dhorvath users          5 Mar 18 19:10 change_me
$ chgrp root change_me↵
$ ls -al change_me↵
-rw-r--r--   1 dhorvath root           5 Mar 18 19:10 change_me
$ chgrp users change_me↵
$ ls -al change_me↵
-rw-r--r--   1 dhorvath users          5 Mar 18 19:10 change_me
$
```

The file was originally owned by dhorvath with a group of users. It was changed to the root group, which means that any members of that group would have group permissions to the file. Because I own it, I can change it back to the users group.

In addition to changing the group ownership of a file, you can change the group to which you belong. The newgrp command will change you to a specified group, and you can then access files that belong to that group through their group permissions. Any files you create will belong to the new group.

In the following example, the id command is used to determine the current and available groups while the newgrp command is used to change the current group membership:

```
$ id↵
uid=6061(dhorvath) gid=103(faculty) groups=103(faculty),100(users)
$ newgrp users↵
$ id↵
uid=6061(dhorvath) gid=100(users) groups=103(faculty),100(users)
$
```

If no group is specified, you will be reset to your default group, which is set in the /etc/passwd file. If you are not listed as a member of the group, you will be prompted for the group password. If you are listed as a member of the group in /etc/group, there is no need for a password because you are already authorized.

When you create a file, it is assigned permissions, the default permissions defined by the umask command. The mode is created by subtracting the desired default permissions from 666. To create files with -rw-r--r-- permissions (644) by default, you take 666, subtract the desired permissions of 644, ending up with a result of 022. That is the value you use for mode.

Without a mode, umask will display the current setting as shown below:

```
$ umask↵
022
$
```

You should use this command to determine your current umask and decide if it should be different.

CHAPTER 6

EDITORS

On the mainframe, there are two basic ways of editing files: a line-oriented editor and a full-screen editor. Under TSO, the full-screen editor is part of ISPF; under VM/CMS, it is Xedit. Under UNIX, you can use uni-SPF, uni-Xedit, or SPF/UX to perform full-screen editing with commands that you are used to. But to a large extent, these tools are only transitional. To be considered a true UNIX professional, you need to learn one or more of the native UNIX editors such as `vi` (visual). Because `vi` supports commands from `ex` and `ed`, both line-oriented editors, you will end up learning those editors to a certain extent also.

The transitional tools do have their place, however. You can be productive on a UNIX box very quickly using them because you do not have to learn the command set for a new editor. The uni-SPF editor has a particularly powerful and unique feature—it can edit fixed sequential format files (no record separator), even if they contain binary data. This is done through profiles, which tell the editor the length of records in the file. The only downside is that profiles must be set up for each record length that a file in your application or installation may use and you must manually enter it for each file being edited. The browse command does not support profiles, only edit; but you can always cancel out of edit if all you want to do is look at data. Screen 6.1 shows the option menu (uni-SPF screen 0).

Selecting option 7 will allow you to review, create, or delete options as shown in Screen 6.2.

Selecting the profile lrecl512 (by putting an S beside it or entering S lrecl512 at the COMMAND prompt) will get you Screen 6.3.

The key to this screen is the LENGTH parameter for RECORD FORMAT. This setting causes uni-SPF to treat records as being MAX RECORD LENGTH bytes long, even if they may have internal record separators. The DATA parameter for RECORD FORMAT is the proper selection for line sequential files. With this profile, uni-SPF knows that our records are 512 bytes long and do not have record separators.

Screen 6.4 shows the edit entry screen with the entry for the profile. This only works when the EDITOR is spf. When a file is edited, it will be treated as a collection of fixed length (512 bytes) records in a sequential file. If the format of the file is different (DATA instead of LENGTH or a different MAX RECORD LENGTH), it will not behave properly when edited. If the file looks weird, confirm that the proper profile was used.

The edit and browse entry screens for SPF/UX supports the entry of record lengths as shown on the SPF/UX edit entry screen (Screen 6.5). However, this does not provide the capability to edit fixed length records in sequential file, only line-sequential files.

Screen 6.1 - uni-SPF Options Screen

```
--------------------------- MODIFY SESSION PARAMETERS ---------------------------
COMMAND ==> 7↵

  1 TERMINAL           - Terminal characteristics
  2 LIST/LOG           - Default disposition of log and list files
  3 PF KEYS            - Function key definitions
  7 PROFILE            - Edit profile definitions
  K KEYBOARD MAPPINGS  - Keyboard translations
```

Screen 6.2 - uni-SPF Options - Profile Menu Screen

```
------------------ uni-SPF PROFILE LOCATOR ---------------- ROW 000033 OF 000064
COMMAND ==> S lrec1512↵                                        SCROLL ==> PAGE

  A - Add      S - Select/Edit       D - Edit

S PROFILE NAME
-------------------------------------------------------------------------------
   lrec1150
   lrec1151
   lrec1250
   lrec1250
   lrec1262
   lrec1300
   lrec1304
   lrec1312
   lrec13981
   lrec1435
   lrec1512
   lrec1524
   lrec1535
   lrec1547
   lrec180
   lrec194
```

Screen 6.3 - uni-SPF Options - Profile Editor Screen

```
----------------------------- uni-SPF PROFILE EDITOR ----------------------------
COMMAND ==>

  PROFILE NAME              : lrec1512
    RECORD FORMAT         ==> LENGTH          (DATA or LENGTH)
    MAX RECORD LENGTH     ==> 512             (2-4096)
```

Screen 6.4 - uni-SPF Edit Entry Screen

```
------------------------------- EDIT - ENTRY PANEL ------------------------------
COMMAND ==>

  FILE SPECIFICATION:
       DIRECTORY PATH ===>   /u/dhorvath
            FILE NAME ===>   del_me.ksh       (blank for selection list)

  EDITOR ===> spf                            (SPF, XEDIT, or VI)

  PROFILE ===> lrec1512
```

Screen 6.5 - SPF/UX Edit Entry Screen

```
------------------------------- EDIT - ENTRY PANEL ------------------------------
COMMAND ==>

ISPF LIBRARY:
   PROJECT  ===>
   GROUP    ===>
   TYPE     ===>
   MEMBER   ===>

OTHER DATA SET:
   DATA SET NAME   ===> /u/dhorvath/del_me.ksh

FIXED LENGTH RECORDS ===> YES   RECORD LENGTH  ===> 512   (MAXIMUM 4096)


Press [END] to return.
```

One very nice feature of ISPF is its limited context-sensitive help. If you press <pf1> after an error, ISPF provides you additional information about the error:

```
----------------------  ISPF/PDF PRIMARY OPTION MENU "DOWN     " IS NOT ACTIVE
OPTION  ===> <pf1>
```

Results in:

```
----------------------  ISPF/PDF PRIMARY OPTION MENU "DOWN     " IS NOT ACTIVE
OPTION  ===>
THE COMMAND OR PF KEY ENTERED IS NOT DEFINED.
```

Pressing <pf1> again will either get further expanded help on the error or start the ISPF tutorial. Pressing <pf1> without an error or T (for tutorial) followed by <enter> when in the main menu will also get the tutorial screen shown in Screen 6.6.

The uni-SPF editor provides similar context-sensitive help. For instance, if you enter help after an error, it provides you with additional information about the error:

```
--------------------------- uni-SPF MAIN MENU ----------------INVALID OPTION
COMMAND ==> help↵
```

Screen 6.6 - ISPF Tutorial Screen

```
TUTORIAL -------------------- TABLE OF CONTENTS -------------------- TUTORIAL
OPTION ==>

                 ---------------------------------------------
                 | ISPF PROGRAM DEVELOPMENT FACILITY TUTORIAL |
                 ---------------------------------------------
    The following topics are presented in sequence, or may be selected
    by entering a selection code in the option field:
       G GENERAL      - General information about ISPF
       0 ISPF PARMS   - Specify terminal and user parameters
       1 BROWSE       - Display source data or output listings
       2 EDIT         - Create or change source data
       3 UTILITIES    - Perform utility functions
       4 FOREGROUND   - Invoke language processors in foreground
       5 BATCH        - Submit job for language processing
       6 COMMAND      - Enter TSO command, CLIST, or REXX exec
       7 DIALOG TEST  - Perform dialog testing
       8 LM UTILITY   - Perform library administrator utility functions
       9 IBM PRODUCTS - Use additional IBM program development products
      10 SCLM         - Software Configuration and Library Manager
       X EXIT         - Terminate ISPF using log and list defaults
   The following topics will be presented only if selected by number:
       A APPENDICES   - Dynamic allocation errors and ISPF listing formats
       I INDEX        - Alphabetical index of tutorial topics
```

Resulting in:

```
--------------------------- uni-SPF MAIN MENU ----------------INVALID OPTION
COMMAND ==> help
You have entered an unrecognized command or option in the command field.
```

However, entering help again does not provide you with a tutorial. There is no on-line tutorial provided within the uni-SPF editor, but there is an extensive printed manual that is usually installed on-line.

Pressing <pf1> or help at any point in SPF/UX puts you in the on-line tutorial help as shown in Screen 6.7.

I keep mentioning these two specific products because I have had a chance to use them. I am not expressing an opinion on the quality or suitability for your use. Before purchasing any tool, you should evaluate it very carefully. There may be additional transitional editors on the market by the time you read this, versions and features may have changed, and, because there are so many different UNIX systems, the tool may not be available for your system. In some cases, the tool may be available, but it is an old version. In general, vendors tend to keep their software most up-to-date for the platforms where they have the largest installed base or most sales. They devote less effort to the other platforms because of simple economics—they make less money. The less popular (valuable to the vendor) platforms get updated after the more popular.

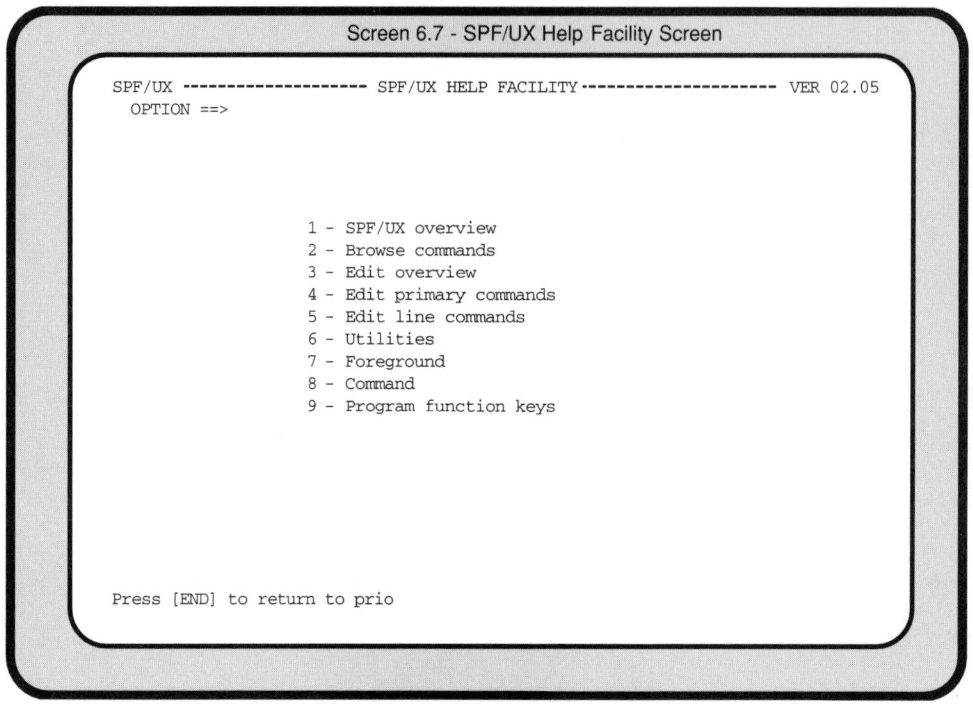
Screen 6.7 - SPF/UX Help Facility Screen

```
SPF/UX -------------------- SPF/UX HELP FACILITY-------------------- VER 02.05
  OPTION ==>



                    1 - SPF/UX overview
                    2 - Browse commands
                    3 - Edit overview
                    4 - Edit primary commands
                    5 - Edit line commands
                    6 - Utilities
                    7 - Foreground
                    8 - Command
                    9 - Program function keys




Press [END] to return to prio
```

Figures 6.1 through 6.4 show the equivalencies between ISPF, the transitional tools, and vi for modes, commands, line commands, and special keys. Some of the information for uni-SPF and SPF/UX has been tested while much of it is based on the documentation only. If you require a feature, test it during evaluation. The `vi` equivalents are from personal experience and have been tested.

Figure 6.1 shows the mode equivalents between ISPF, the transitional tools, and vi.

A special note about the read-only (browse) mode of `vi` and `view`: It is different from ISPF browse in that you can modify the file in the current session, you are just prohibited from saving it under the same name. ISPF browse does not let you change anything on the screen, because it does not allow any command that would. The end result is the same: You can look at the contents of a file but not change that file.

Figure 6.2 shows the command equivalents between ISPF, the transitional tools, and `vi`. The meaning of the `vi` commands will be explained later. Under ISPF, some of these commands are only available under edit mode. With `vi`, they can be used while editing or browsing.

Figure 6.3 shows the line command equivalents between ISPF, the transitional tools, and `vi`. The meaning of the `vi` commands will be explained later. Under ISPF, these commands are only available under edit mode, with `vi`, they can be used while editing or browsing.

Figure 6.4 shows the special key equivalents between ISPF, the transitional tools, and `vi`. Once again, the meaning of the `vi` commands will be explained later. Under ISPF, some of these commands are only available under edit mode, with `vi`, they can be used while editing or browsing.

Figure 6.1
ISPF, Transitional Tools and vi Mode Equivalents

ISPF	uni-SPF	spf/UX	vi equivalent
edit	Y	Y	vi
browse	Y	Y	vi -R or view

Figure 6.2
ISPF, Transitional Tools and vi Command Equivalents

ISPF	uni-SPF	spf/UX	vi equivalent
AUTOSAVE	Y	Y	Must explicitly cancel
BOUNDS	Y	Y	No equivalent
CANCEL	Y	Y	:q or :q! - second form required if file changed
CAPS	Y	Y	use <CAPS LOCK> key on keyboard
CHANGE	Y	Y	:s or :g/re/s
COPY	Y	Y	:lineno :re filename
CREATE	Y	Y	:w newfilename
CUT	Y	Y	yy, Y
DELETE	Y	Y	dd, :lineno d
DOWN	Y	Y	+ ^ f <down-arrow> j ^ d ^ j ^ n
END	Y	Y	:wq, :wq! (if filename changed during session), ZZ, :x
EXCLUDE	Y	Y	No equivalent
FIND	Y	Y	/ or ?
HEX	Y	Y	No equivalent. Use od (object dump) command
LEFT	Y	Y	h or <left arrow> b B
LOCATE	Y	Y	:lineno or lineno G
MOVE	Y	Y	:lineno :re filename :sh↵rm filename↵exit
PASTE	Y	Y	p, P
PROFILE	Y	Y	:set all, .exrc file
RCHANGE	Y	Y	:sr or repeat :s or :g/reg-exp/s
RECOVERY	N	N	(recover after failure or hangup) vi -r
RENUM	N	N	No equivalent
REPLACE	Y	Y	:1,$d :re %
RESET	Y	Y	^L (redraw screen)
RETRIEVE	Y	Y	No equivalent in vi. Line editing and history in shell
RFIND	Y	Y	n or N
RIGHT	Y	Y	`l` or <right arrow> w W e E
SAVE	Y	Y	:w or :w!
SORT	Y	N	No equivalent in vi. Sort command
SPLIT	Y	Y	No direct equivalent in vi. Can have multiple sessions
SUBMIT	N	N	No equivalent. Can use equivalent to TSO instead
SWAP	Y	Y	No equivalent. Can have multiple sessions
TABS	Y	Y	Tabs supported. Can change size of tabstops
TSO	Y	Y	:sh or :! command
UNDO	N	N	u or U
UP	Y	Y	- ^b k <up arrow> ^ u ^ p

Figure 6.3
ISPF, Transitional Tools and vi Line Command Equivalents

ISPF	uni-SPF	spf/UX	vi equivalent
a	Y	Y	(after this line) most commands imply before or after
b	Y	Y	(before this line) most commands imply before or after
c/cc/cN	Y	Y	(copy line) yy p or Y p or y'mark p
d/dd/dN	Y	Y	(delete line) dd or Ndd or d'mark
i/iN	Y	Y	(insert line) o (before line), O (after line)
lc	Y	Y	(lowercase) ~ (switch case)
m/mm/mN	Y	Y	(move line) dd p or Ndd p or d'mark p
o/oo/oN	Y	Y	(overlay line) No equivalent.
r/rr/rN	Y	Y	(replicate line) yy p or Y p or y'mark p
shift left/right data or columns	Y	Y	>><<(shift left / right by tab stops) Can remove or insert columns in shell.
tj	Y	Y	(text join) J
ts	Y	Y	(text split) <move cursor> i ↵
uc	Y	Y	(uppercase) ~ (switch case)
.label	Y	Y	m (mark)

Figure 6.4
ISPF, Transitional Tools and vi Special Key Equivalents

ISPF	uni-SPF	spf/UX	vi equivalent
<eol>	Y	Y	$
<erase eol>	Y	Y	D
start of line	↵	↵	^ or 0 or <enter> for next line
<pa1>	N	N	(cancel input) u or U
<insert>	Y	Y	i (before cursor), a (after cursor), I (begin of line), A (at eol)
<reset>	Y	Y	<esc> - exit from insert, append, or replace modes
overwrite	Y	Y	r (replace single character), R (replace many characters)
<delete>	Y	Y	x (at cursor), X (left of cursor)
<home>	Y	Y	H

The ISPF essentially has one mode: changing the contents on the screen. To enter a line command, you type over the line numbers on the specific line; to enter a command, you go to the command prompt and enter it. By default, when you type in the edit area, you overtype or replace the current contents of that line. By pressing the <insert> key, your terminal will allow you to insert text on the current line. Pressing another key, <reset> on the mainframe, other keys for the transitional editors, will allow you to replace again.

Figure 6.5
vi Modes

Mode Verbose vi	Mode vi	Description
INSERT	INPUT	Allows input. Command is i or I
OPEN	INPUT	Allows input on new line. Command is o or O
REPLACE 1CHAR	REPLACE 1CHAR	Next entry will overtype cursor position. Command is r
REPLACE	REPLACE	Overtype until done. Command is R
APPEND	INPUT	Allows input at end of line. Command is A
APPEND	INPUT	Allows input after cursor. Command is a
CHANGE	INPUT	Replaces text to end of line. Command is C
CHANGE	INPUT	Replaces text to end of object. Command is c
CHANGE	INPUT	Replace text at cursor, then allow input of new. Command is s
INPUT	INPUT	Replace entire line. Command is S
none shown	none shown	Command mode. Allows navigation or entry of other commands

The <escape> key will exit from text entry mode and return you to command mode.

Figure 6.6
Special vi Command Entry Modes

Mode	Description
:	Process ed or ex command
/ or ?	Find next or find previous
:! or :sh	Execute shell command

The `vi` editor has two formal modes: text entry and command entry because there is no reserved area to enter commands like there is under ISPF. A particular key can have multiple meanings. For instance, the letter <k> can be just a letter or it can mean go-up-one-line. Within text entry, there may be up to seven different mode messages displayed on the status line depending on the version of `vi`. Figure 6.5 shows these modes and their equivalents between versions.

When there is no mode message, you are in command entry. Within command entry, there are commands that show up on the status line and behave like special forms of the mode (shown in Figure 6.6).

EDITING WITH vi

Now is a good time to get started with `vi`. Enter the following command to create a new file (if new_file exists in your directory, pick another name):

```
$ vi new_file↵
```

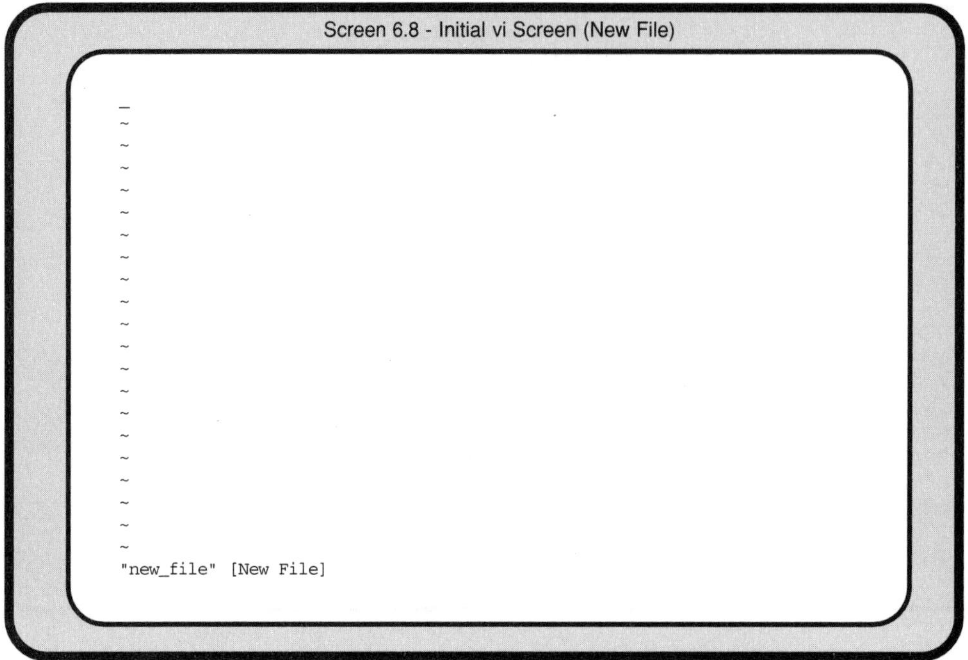

In all the vi examples, the current cursor position will be shown with an underscore. Your screen will clear and you will see the screen shown in Screen 6.8, the initial vi screen (new file).

This is the way a vi session with a new file looks. The filename, status, and size are shown on the bottom line until you perform some action. Since this is a new file, all the lines show the tilde <~> character to show you that the lines on the screen really do not exist. You will also see lines with the tilde character if you scroll to the bottom of the file and the editor needs to show lines on the screen that do not exist yet. If you were to use vi with an existing file (like the .profile file), the message at the bottom of the screen would look like:

```
".profile" 82 lines, 2312 characters
```

Using vi -R or view to browse the same file would get you the following message at the bottom of the screen:

```
".profile" [Read only] 82 lines, 2312 characters
```

The modes in Figure 6.5 are shown on the screen if showmode is enabled within vi. There are a number of options that you can set to modify the behavior of vi and show the modes in Figure 6.5. To see the current value of the options, enter the following from within vi:

```
:set all↵
```

Screen 6.9 shows what happens as you press the keys (not including <enter> (<↵> above)).

Screen 6.9 - vi :set all Entry Screen

```
~
~
~
~
~
~
~
~
~
~
~
~
~
~
~
~
~
~
~
~
:set all_
```

Screen 6.10 - vi :set all Output Screen

```
~
~
~
~
~
:set all
noautoindent          nomodeline                      noslowpen
autoprint             nonumber                        nosourceany
nobeautify            nooptimize                      tabstop=0
closepunct='".,;)]}   paragraphs=IPLPPPQPP LIpplpipbp tags=tags /usr/lib/tags
directory=/var/tmp    partialcharacter=-              term=vt220
noedcompatible        prompt                          noterse
noerrorbells          noreadonly                      timeout
noexrc                redraw                          ttytype=vt220
flash                 remap                           warn
hardtabs=8            report=5                        window=23
noignorecase          scroll=11                       wrapscan
linelimit=1048560     sections=NHSHH HUuhsh+c         wrapmargin=0
nolisp                shell=/bin/ksh                  nowriteany
nolist                shiftwidth=8                    wraptype=word
magic                 noshowmatch
mesg                  noshowmode
 [Hit return to continue]_
```

When you press the <enter> key, the command is executed. You will see something that looks like Screen 6.10.

Your system may have different options or the settings may be different. Pressing <enter> again will get you back to the original screen. The option that shows the `vi` modes at the bottom of the screen is known as showmode. In my `vi` session, it is enabled, but if it is not enabled for you (noshowmode shown on the set all screen), you can use the following command:

```
:set showmode↵
```

To disable the display of modes, you would use the following command:

```
:set noshowmode↵
```

If you do not like the options set when you start `vi`, you can change them with a `:set` command every time you start a new editing session, or you can save the commands in configuration file that `vi` automatically reads when it starts. That file is $HOME/.exrc by default. You should create one; quit from editing new_file with the following `vi` command:

```
:q!↵
$
```

CREATING A vi CONFIGURATION FILE ($HOME/.exrc)

Create .exrc in your default directory with `vi`. First make sure you are in the proper directory and that the file does not already exist. If it does, skip to modifying an existing file. Use the following commands to create .exrc:

`$ pwd ↵`	Should be in home directory
`/u/dhorvath`	
`$ ls -al .exrc ↵`	Make sure there is not one already
`.exrc not found`	
`$ vi .exrc ↵`	Create the configuration file

Again, you will get the initial vi screen for new files as shown in Screen 6.11.

We want showmode enabled, and since it may not be the default, enter the following:

```
:set showmode↵
```

Press the lowercase letter <i> to enter input mode, you will see the words INPUT MODE at the bottom, and will be able to enter text. Type in the following:

```
" These are the settings that I prefer for ex and vi↵
set showmode↵
```

The first line (beginning with a double quote <">) is a comment line. The second line enables the mode message at the bottom of the screen. The screen will look something like what is shown in Screen 6.12.

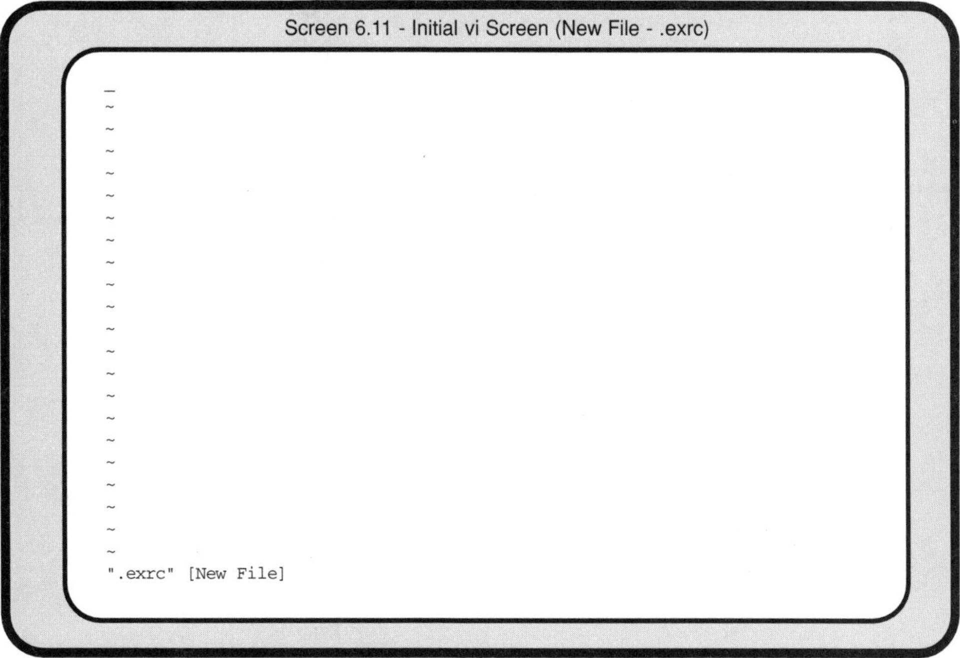
Screen 6.11 - Initial vi Screen (New File - .exrc)
".exrc" [New File]

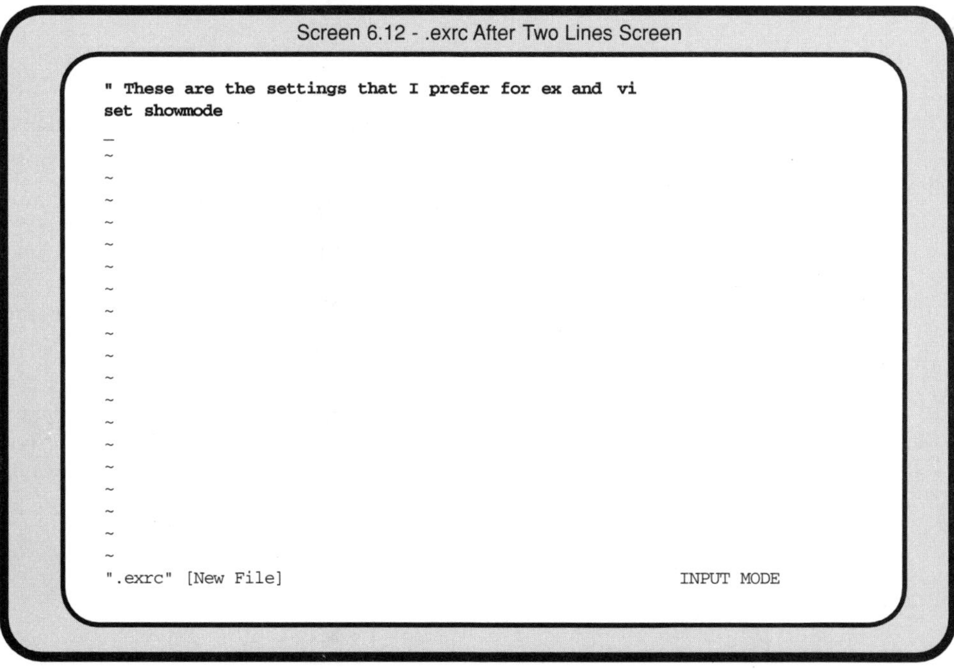
Screen 6.12 - .exrc After Two Lines Screen
" These are the settings that I prefer for ex and vi
set showmode
".exrc" [New File]
INPUT MODE

Screen 6.13 - .exrc Completed Screen

```
" These are the settings that I prefer for ex and vi
set showmode
set number
# Any line after this one will be ignored
_
~
~
~
~
~
~
~
~
~
~
~
~
~
~
~
~
~
".exrc" [New File]
```

If you want to have vi show line numbers on the left side of the screen, you can enter the following:

set number↵

These line numbers will not be stored in the file and I consider them a distraction, but you may like them. Try it out; the examples will not use them for space reasons. You can always change the line to nonumber later or use the following command within a vi session:

:set nonumber↵

There is one more thing to put in the file:

 # Any line after this one will be ignored↵

At some time in the future, you may have a command in your .exrc that you want to disable for a while but do not want to delete. You could insert a double quote <"> at the beginning of the line to make it a comment or you could move it after the line you just entered. The `vi` editor will ignore any lines that appear after the line with a pound sign <#> in it. When you start `vi` with this line in your .exrc file, you may get the following message (which is safe to ignore):

```
[Extra characters at end of "#" command]
```

Press the <escape> key to exit input mode and your screen will look like Screen 6.13.

Notice that the mode area of the status line is blank, because vi is in command mode now. My .exrc looks like this except I am actually using nonumber. To save the file, enter any one of the following lines:

```
ZZ
:wq↵
:x↵
```

Any one of these will save your file if it does not already exist. You will then see the following:

```
".exrc" [New File] 5 lines, 120 characters
$
```

You have created your first file using the `vi` editor!

One warning about using the `ZZ` command to save a file and exit `vi`. Be very careful to press the <shift> key when pressing the uppercase letter Z. If you press the <control> key, you will be entering <^Z>; on some UNIX versions <^Z> will suspend the current process and return you to the shell prompt. The `vi` session remains on hold in the background so you have not lost your editing, but it has not been saved yet and is wasteful of system resources. If this happens to you, use the following command

```
fg↵
```

To unsuspend your vi session. Use the `ZZ` command with the <shift> key at this point.

BROWSING WITH vi

Now is a good time to check out the browse functionality of the `vi` editor. Enter the following command:

```
$ view .exrc↵
```

You will start the `vi` editor to with the existing file .exrc as shown in Screen 6.14. The cursor will be at the very beginning of the file (at the first double quote <">).

Change the file with the following keys to put a new comment at the top of the screen:

```
O" this is the top line <ESC>
```

The uppercase letter <O> opens a new line before the current one and places you in text entry mode with INPUT or INSERT shown as the mode. The command <O> will not show on the screen. Type in the comment and press the <escape> key when done. This will return you to command entry mode of `vi`. Attempt to save the file with one of the following commands:

```
ZZ
:wq↵
:x↵
```

You will get the following message at the bottom:

```
".exrc" File is read only
```

Screen 6.14 - view - vi Browse Screen

```
" These are the settings that I prefer for ex and vi
set showmode
set number
# Any line after this one will be ignored

~
~
~
~
~
~
~
~
~
~
~
~
~
~
~
~
~
".exrc" [Read only] 5 lines, 120 characters
```

To quit, use the following command:

```
:q↵
```

Since you changed the file, you will get the following message:

```
No write since last change (:quit! overrides)
```

Even though you should not be able to save a file while browsing, vi warns you if you are going to throw away any changes. Use the exclamation point <!> to override the warning as shown:

```
:q!↵
$
```

You can change from browse mode (read-only) to edit mode two ways: override read-only on write or change the settings to no read-only. Use this information with caution! The command below overrides the read-only mode for the file:

```
:wq!↵
```

The following command changes the settings to ignore read-only mode:

```
:set noreadonly↵
```

After this command, you can use `ZZ`, `:wq`, or `:x` commands to save the file and exit.

HEAVY-DUTY vi EDITING EXAMPLE

Now for an exercise using many of the `vi` commands. Create a new file with the following command:

```
$ vi text_example↵
```

Press the lowercase letter <i> for insert mode, and type in the text below. There are typing errors in the text on purpose and the layout is not pretty. Yes, you have seen much of this text just a few pages ago. You can use the <backspace> of <^H> key to discard characters to the left of the cursor. They will not be erased until you press <escape> to end input, or you can overtype them. Pressing the <^W> key will erase an entire word, pressing the kill character will erase the input on the current line. Type it in exactly as shown, pay attention to the positions of the <enter> key:

```
I keep mentioning these two products because I have had a chance to use them.  I
 am not expressing an opinion on teh quality or suitability for your use.↵
↵
In some cases,↵
teh tool may be available, but it is an old version.↵
↵
In general, vendors tend to keep their software most up-to-date for the↵
platforms where tehy have the largest installed base or most sales.↵
They devote less effort to the other platforms because of simple economics -↵
they make less money.  The less popular (valuable to the vendor) platforms↵
get updated after the more popular.↵
```

Then press the <escape> key to return to command mode. Your screen should look like the session shown in Screen 6.15.

To save a copy of the file as it exists now, enter the following write command:

```
:w↵
"text_example" [New file] 10 lines, 562 characters
```

The command and the message will appear at the bottom of the screen and then the cursor will return to its original position at the bottom of the text. Do not be concerned if your numbers are slightly different. You may have put one space where I put two or hit <enter> an extra time or two.

Moving around the Screen

There are a number of ways you can move around on the screen. The navigation commands work in `vi` command entry mode (not text entry), if a mode is showing on the screen, these keys will not work. Press <escape> to exit any mode shown on the screen.

If you press <^F>, the screen will scroll down based on the option scroll (11 in this case). Pressing <^B> will scroll the screen back the way it was. Pressing the <^D> key in `vi` will scroll down half a screen, <^U> will scroll up a half screen. The cursor is no longer on the last line; to get there press the uppercase letter <G> to go to the end of file; you will not see the letter on the screen.

Screen 6.15 - Big vi Edit Session Initial Entry Screen

```
I keep mentioning these two prodcts because I have had a chance to use them. I
 am not expressing an opinion on teh quality or suitability for your use.
In some cases,
the tool may be available, but it is an old version.

In general, vendors tend to keep their software most up-to-date for the
platforms where tehy have the largest instralled base or most sales.
They devote less effort to the other platforms because of simple economics -
they make less money.  The less popular (valuable to the vendor) platforms
get updated after the more popular.

_
~
~
~
~
~
~
~
~
~
~
~
~
```

If you pressed <^F> twice with this example file, the terminal will beep the second time, because `vi` is unable to scroll forward any more (the bottom of the file is displayed). The same applies to using the other scroll commands to scroll too far.

To move up a line, you can press the lowercase <k>, minus sign <->, and in some cases, with the <up arrow> key on your keyboard. To move down, you can press the lowercase <j>, plus sign <+>, or maybe the <down arrow> key. To move multiple lines, you can press the key repeatedly or type a number followed by the key.

Press uppercase <G> to go to the end of the file. Press lowercase <k> three times. Type the number <3> and then press the lowercase <k>. The three times you pressed <k> moved you up three lines, the second method moved you up another three lines.

To go to the top of the file, you can use either of the following in command entry mode:

1G	Command not seen on screen
:1↵	Command shows at bottom of screen

Try one or both of them to go to the top of the file. The first line you typed in occupies two lines on the screen because it is very long. When you use any of the up or down navigation keys, the two lines on the screen are treated as one. It is really only one line, but your screen is not wide enough to show it.

To move to the end of the line, press the dollar sign <$> key. To go back to the beginning of the line, press the number zero <0> key. Although you will not see a difference in this example, the up-caret <^> key will take you to the first non-whitespace character on the line. If this line had blanks at the beginning, the <0> and <^> would behave differently. Try these keys out now. The <$> will take you to the end of the second line, <0> or <^> will take you to the beginning of the first.

To move to the very last character of the file, enter the following:

```
G$
```

You can move right one character by pressing the lowercase <l>, the <spacebar>, and, in some cases, the <right-arrow>. You can move left one character by pressing lowercase <h>, the <backspace>, and maybe even the <left-arrow>. Pressing <^H> is another way of entering a <backspace>; the key that has backspace printed on it may actually generate a <del> character. As with the vertical movement keys, these keys will accept a repeat count as a prefix. To move to a particular column in a line, you enter the line number followed by the vertical bar <|>. As with the other command keys, you will not see these keys as you press them. If you do see the keys, you are probably in text entry mode.

Make sure you are at the beginning of the first line. Press the <spacebar> seven times. You should be at the beginning of the word mentioning. Pressing <89|> will get you to the word expressing. Pressing <4h> will move you back four characters to the beginning of the word not.

You can also move backward and forward by words instead of single characters. The lowercase character <w> will move you forward to the beginning of the next word; punctuation characters are considered words. The lowercase character <b> will move you back to the beginning of the word with punctuation counting as words. The lowercase character <e> will take you to the end of the next word with the same punctuation behavior. The uppercase versions of these commands (<W>, <B>, and <E>) move the same way except that punctuation is ignored. All support repeat counts.

Go to the beginning of the first line. Press <3w> and you will be at the beginning of the word these. Press <e> to go to the end of the same word. Press <e> again and you will go to the end of the next word (two). Pressing <b> will take you back to the beginning of the same word (two). Pressing <b> again will take you to the beginning of the prior word (these).

From the beginning of the line, <30w> will take you to the period at the end of the sentence. From the beginning of the line, <31w>, <32w>, <99w> will all take you to the end of the line in most versions of `vi`. In some of the newer versions, it will take you to subsequent lines. Try this out and see how your version behaves.

The <^G> key is handy. It tells you the name of the file, its status (new, read-only, or modified), what line you are on, and how far through the file that position is. Try the following (you will not see the <^G>):

```
^G
"text_example" [Modified] line 8 of 10 --80%--
```

Finding Text in vi (Moving to Specific Text)

To find a string in the file, there are two commands you can use: forward slash </> and question mark <?> followed by the string to find. The difference is that </> searches forward from the cursor and <?> searches backward. To repeat a find in the same direction, use the uppercase <N> key; you can repeat a find in the opposite direction by using the lowercase <n>.

The `find` command can take a simple string, including blanks, or a more complicated pattern using the same rules as the grep expressions. Remember that the `grep` command is a stripped down version of the `ex` editor command.

Go to the beginning of the file. Search for the words less money with the following command:

```
/less money↵
```

You should end up on the third word on the eighth line (less money). Go back to the beginning of the file and search for the word less. You should end up at the third word of the seventh line (less effort). Pressing the lowercase <n> will find the next instance of the same word (at less money). Pressing uppercase <N> will reverse and repeat the search, taking you back to the seventh line (less effort).

Go to the end of the file with the uppercase <G> command. Search for the word the backwards with the following command:

```
?the↵
```

You should end up at the fourth word on the ninth line (the more). Press lowercase <n> to repeat the find in the same direction taking you to line 8 (the vendor). Pressing the uppercase <N> will reverse and repeat the search, taking you back to the ninth line (the more) again.

There is a section later on, Moving from ISPF FIND and RFIND to `vi`, that shows how to express in `vi` many of the find commands you are used to using in ISPF.

You can now move around a file in `vi` and know where you are; we already discussed creating, saving, and inputting data. Here come the commands on how to change the text in your file.

Joining and Splitting Lines

Go to line two of the file (in some cases). This really should be one line. Press the uppercase <J> to join the current line with the next. Screen 6.16 shows the screen after the line join operation:

The line join command always puts a space at the end of the current line before it attaches the next line. If we made a mistake, joining the wrong lines for instance, we can undo the mistake by using the lowercase <u> undo command. Undo the join and the screen should look like Screen 6.15. There is a limited redo command, which will repeat the last change. To rejoin the line and make the file look like what was shown in Screen 6.16, press the period <.> key and the last change (join) will be repeated.

The uppercase <U> will restore the current line, discarding any changes. It is a bigger undo than <u>.

Screen 6.16 - Big vi Edit Session After Join Screen

```
I keep mentioning these two prodcts because I have had a chance to use them. I
 am not expressing an opinion on teh quality or suitability for your use.
In some cases, the tool may be available, but it is an old version.

In general, vendors tend to keep their software most up-to-date for the
platforms where tehy have the largest instralled base or most sales.
They devote less effort to the other platforms because of simple economics -
they make less money.  The less popular (valuable to the vendor) platforms
get updated after the more popular.

~
~
~
~
~
~
~
~
~
~
~
~
```

Although `vi` will save our work in progress so we can recover in the event of a network or system failure, it is a good idea to save what you are doing periodically.

The first line is way too long, so we should shorten it. Go to the uppercase I at the beginning of the second sentence (first line), and enter the following:

```
i↵
<ESC>
```

After you press the <i>, the INPUT or INSERT mode should show. Press <enter> to split the line and then press <escape> to leave input mode. Now the one long line that took two lines on the screen to show is now two separate lines.

Adding and Replacing Text

The lowercase <i> allows you to input before the cursor position. The lowercase <a> allows you to input after the current cursor position. You are in an input mode until you press the <escape> key. Uppercase <I> puts you into input mode at the beginning of the line and uppercase <A> allows you to append to the end of the line. Lowercase <o> opens a new line below the current one and places you in input mode; uppercase <O> does the same above the current line. If you place a repeat count before any of these commands, the text you enter will be repeated that many times.

After reading the first three sentences, I decided that the second and the third should be one sentence joined with a semicolon <;>. There are a couple of changes required. The period <.> at

Screen 6.17 - Big vi Edit Session After Replace Screen

```
I keep mentioning these two prodcts because I have had a chance to use them.
I am not expressing an opinion on teh quality or suitability for your use;
in some cases, the tool may be available, but it is an old version.

In general, vendors tend to keep their software most up-to-date for the
platforms where tehy have the largest instralled base or most sales.
They devote less effort to the other platforms because of simple economics -
they make less money.  The less popular (valuable to the vendor) platforms
get updated after the more popular.

~
~
~
~
~
~
~
~
~
~
~
~
/\.
```

the end of the second sentence needs to be changed and the first word of the third sentence (In) needs to be lowercase.

There are a couple of ways to make these changes. Move the cursor to the period <.> at the end of the second sentence. There are several ways to move there. You could use the end-of-line <$> key or you could find (/) the period. Because the period <.> has special meaning as a pattern (refer back to `grep`), it must be escaped as follows:

```
/\.↵
```

The lowercase <r> will allow you to change the one character at the cursor and then leave the cursor there when done. The uppercase <R> will allow you to change characters to the end of line and then behaves as though it was an append <A> command; this continues until you press <escape>. Use the lowercase <r> to change the period to a semicolon as shown:

```
r;
```

After you press the <r>, the REPLACE 1 CHAR mode should show. Press <;> to replace the period. The REPLACE 1 CHAR mode message will go away and the cursor will be sitting over the <;>.

If you place a repeat count before the <r> or <R> command, the text you enter will be repeated that many times.

To change In to in, press the <enter> key to move to the beginning of the next line and then press the tilde <~> key. It will change uppercase <I> to lowercase <i> and move the cursor to the next character. Pressing tilde repeatedly will convert multiple characters. It converts uppercase characters to lowercase and vice versa. This is one of the few commands that will not accept a repeat count.

Screen 6.17 shows the progress so far. The `find` command still shows at the bottom of the screen because `vi` has not needed to use that line again, so it has not changed.

Marking or Labeling Text

There is another useful set of commands that deals with marks. These are similar to ISPF .labels or the after and before line commands. The delete, yank (pull for copy), and paste (move or copy) commands work with marks to perform block actions. You can also navigate with marks by moving to previously created ones. You can have up to 26 marks in any one file because they are identified with lowercase letters. A mark can be at any position on a line: the beginning, the middle, or at the end. The position is determined by the cursor when the mark command is issued.

Move your cursor to the beginning of the second line. Press the lowercase <m> and select an identifier by pressing lowercase <a>. Press lowercase <w> four times to move to the word an. Put a mark at this position by entering <mb>. Press lowercase <j> three times to move to the beginning of the word tend. Put a mark at this position by entering <mc>. We now have three marks in the file. Go to the end of the file with the uppercase <G> command.

To go to a mark, press the backquote <`> and then the mark you want to see. <`a> will take you to the beginning of the second line, <`b> will go to the word an on the same line, and <`c> will take you to the word tend on line 5. You can also move to the beginning of the line with the mark with the normal quote character <'>. By pressing <'b> you will move to the beginning of line 5.

Using marks with other commands will be described with those commands.

Changing Text

One set of commands that I really never use are the change and substitute commands. Instead, I use replace <r> or <R>. The lowercase <c> takes the next character as the object to change (w for word, l for single character, $ for from cursor to end of line, and c for entire line). When the object has been changed, the command behaves like an insert. The uppercase <C> is equivalent to <c$>. The lowercase <s> replaces the current character with the next character typed and then behaves like an insert. The uppercase <S> replaces the entire line, behaving as though the line was deleted and then the uppercase <O> command used. All of these commands end when the <escape> key is pressed.

The following is an example of the <cw> command used to change a word. Move to the beginning of the word two on the first line, it will be replaced with the word three. The line will look like:

```
I keep mentioning these two products because I have had a chance to use them.
```

Enter the following change command and the screen will change (you will not see the cw):

```
cw
I keep mentioning these tw$ products because I have had a chance to use them.
```

As you type the first three characters of the word three, it will overwrite the word two. The cursor will then be on the space between the old word two (now thr) and the next word, products:

```
I keep mentioning these thr_products because I have had a chance to use them.
```

When you type the remaining two characters in the word three (ee), they will be inserted:

```
I keep mentioning these three_products because I have had a chance to use them.
```

When you press <escape> to exit the change mode, the cursor will move to the last character in the word three.

```
<escape>
I keep mentioning these three products because I have had a chance to use them.
```

When using the <c$> or <C> command, it will replace the characters from the cursor to the end-of-line. When you are done and press <escape>, the rest of the line will be deleted. The <cc> command replaces characters starting at the beginning of the line with the entire line deleted before you start entry.

The following is an example of the <s> command used to change a character and then insert text. Move to the end of the word products on the first line, it will be changed to product as. The line will look like:

```
I keep mentioning these three products because I have had a chance to use them.
```

Enter the following substitute e command and the screen will change (you will not see the s):

```
s
I keep mentioning these three product$ because I have had a chance to use them.
```

As you type the <space>, it will overwrite the s in products. The cursor will then be on the space after the word product:

```
I keep mentioning these three product _because I have had a chance to use them.
```

When you type the new word, as, it will be inserted:

```
I keep mentioning these three product as_because I have had a chance to use them.
```

The line is now too long to fit on the screen and has wrapped again. When you press <escape> to exit the change mode, the cursor will move to the last character in the word as.

```
<escape>
I keep mentioning these three product as because I have had a chance to use them.
```

When using the <S> command, it will delete the line and enter input mode.

Deleting Text

There are several ways to delete things. Lowercase <x> will delete the character under the cursor; uppercase <X> will delete the character to the left of the cursor. The lowercase <d> command will delete objects (w for word, l for current character—equivalent to x, $ for from cursor to end-of-line, and d for entire line). Uppercase <D> is equivalent to <d$>.

The screen is looking a little messy again, so get rid of the new word as from the first line. Move the cursor to the beginning of the word as on the first line:

```
    I keep mentioning these three product as because I have had a chance to use them
.
```

Press the lowercase <x> and the letter a goes away:

```
    I keep mentioning these three product s because I have had a chance to use
them.
```

The uppercase <X> deletes in the other direction. Move the cursor one character to the right and the line will look like:

```
    I keep mentioning these three product s_because I have had a chance to use
them.
```

Now press the uppercase <X> to get rid of the s. The line will look like:

```
    I keep mentioning these three product _because I have had a chance to use
them.
```

If I decide that I no longer like lines 5 and 6, I can get rid of them. To delete a line, move the cursor there and use lowercase <dd> to delete one line. Get rid of line 5 with the <dd> command.

The ex delete command will delete the current line, any single line, or any range of lines that you enter. Since you just deleted line 5, the old line 6 is now line 5. To delete it with the ex delete command, use the following:

```
:d↵
```

There is another really useful form of the delete command <dw>. The w is for word. To get rid of the phrase of simple economics, on what is now line 5, move the cursor to the word of and use the lowercase <dw> command. Since there are four word-like objects (the minus sign counts as a word), a repetition count is useful:

```
:4dw
```

Will delete all the words in the phrase changing the feeling of the sentence a little bit, making it more direct.

To delete a block of text, mark the position of the beginning of the block, mark the end of the block, then use the following commands (assuming <a> marks the beginning and <b> marks the end):

```
`ad`b
```

This is a little different from the behavior of the ISPF block delete commands. ISPF deletions are complete lines while these are just the block itself. To match ISPF block deletes, mark the beginning of the block and the beginning of the line after the block. You can then use the command above or the following:

```
`ad'b
```

which will delete from the beginning of the first mark to the beginning of the next mark (which is on the line after the block end. Use whichever is more comfortable for you.

Multiple lines can be deleted through block deletes, using a repeat count with the delete line (lowercase <dd>) command, or with the ex command:

```
:1,$d↵
```

This reads as follows: starting at line 1, to the end-of-file, delete lines.

Copying and Moving Text

To move text, a delete and then undelete are done. To move the first line to become the third, move the cursor to the beginning of the first line, then press the lowercase keys <dd> to delete the line. Move the cursor down one line and press the lowercase <p> for paste command. The deleted line will be pasted after the current one.

Each time you delete an object (character, word, or line), it is saved in a series of hidden buffers, numbered 1 through 9, that will hold the last nine deletions. The paste will paste the most recent deletion onto the screen. To retrieve from register 3, the command looks like:

```
"3p
```

If you attempt to retrieve something from a register that has not been used yet, you get the following message:

```
Nothing in register 7
```

To copy text, you use the lowercase <y> (for yank) command and then paste the buffer where you want it. The simplest form is <yy> to yank an entire line into the paste buffer. To copy the first two lines after the third line, the yank command is used with a repetition count as follows:

`1G`	Go to beginning of file
`2yy`	Copy the next two lines into paste buffer
`jj`	Move down two lines
`p`	Paste buffer after third line

The first two lines are now also lines 4 and 5. There are up to 26 yank buffers, with the letters a through z that can hold copied text. To specify the buffer, it is noted before the yank command as follows:

`"b3yy`	Copy 3 lines into buffer b.

To paste from one of the named yank buffers, the letter is used on the paste command, which is instead of the number when pasting deletion buffers. This is useful to save multiple pieces of code or text and move it around.

You can take advantage of the ability to undelete characters to correct typographical errors and switch characters around. When I am really typing fast, I often switch the letters e and h in the word the. Go to the top of the file and move to the first occurrence of the word the (use cursor movement or find). Move the cursor over one character so it is over the lowercase letter <e>. Then enter the following:

```
xp
```

The two letters are swapped and the word is now spelled correctly.

Substituting Text

Another way to correct text is through the ex substitution command, the simplest form of which is:

```
:s/from_string/to_string/
```

which will change the first from_string to to_string on the current line. If from_string is not on the current line, you will get an error message. Like the `:D ex` command, the `ex` substitute command can take a line number or range of lines in the following forms:

```
:start,ends/from_string/to_string/
:lines/from_string/to_string/
```

The strings are separated by characters that will not be part of the strings themselves. If you need to change something that contains the forward slash character </>, you can use the semi-colon <;> or double quotes <"> instead. After the last slash (or other character), you can specify the modifiers c for confirm before each change, p to print the change (like the CHNG ==> in the line number under ISPF), and g to change all occurrences on a line. These parameters can be combined to change all occurrences on a line, but confirm first by using gc.

The ex substitute command will accept the same regular expressions that grep does. There are still two places where the word the was misspelled as teh. Move the cursor to the second line and enter the following ex command:

```
:s/teh/the/↵
```

The line will change and the cursor return to the beginning of the line. It does not matter where on the line the cursor was, the ex substitute returns it to the beginning. It now looks like:

```
I am not expressing an opinion on the quality or suitability for your use;
```

To repeat a substitution, you can use the ampersand <&> or the following:

```
:sr↵
```

If you use either method now, you will get the following message:

```
Substitute pattern match failed
```

because there is not another word teh on the same line. If you moved the cursor down to the line with the word tehy (should be they) and pressed ampersand <&>, the line would be changed (wait, do not do it here).

The final form of text substitution involves the ex global search command. As mentioned before, this command is the basis for the grep command because it was shown in manuals as:

```
:g/re/p
```

This command searches for matches to the regular expression inside the forward slashes </> and then prints them (the p option). In the simplest form, it will find and print all occurrences throughout the file. The search can be limited by specifying a line number or range of numbers:

```
:start,endg/search_string/p
:lineg/search_string/p
```

Without the p parameter, the cursor will be placed on the last line with a match. Another option is nu, which will show the line number along with the line that contains the match. As with the ex substitute command, the strings are separated by characters that will not be part of the strings themselves.

Go to the beginning of the file, and we will search for any words that are spelled with teh in them since I constantly make that mistake. Type the following command and you will see the line that matches the pattern:

```
:g/teh/p↵
platforms where tehy have the largest installed base or most sales.
[Hit return to continue] ↵
```

After you press <enter>, the cursor will be at the beginning of the last line that matched the pattern. Go back to the beginning of the file, so we can search for the misspelled word again and get the line numbers:

```
:g/teh/nu↵
     6  platforms where tehy have the largest installed base or most sales.
[Hit return to continue] ↵
```

After you press <enter>, the cursor again will be at the beginning of the last line that matched the pattern.

The ex global search command can be combined with the substitution command as follows:

```
:g/search_string/s//replace_string/
```

Without line numbers, the entire file is searched. With line numbers, only those lines will be searched. The options for the substitute command still apply (p, c, and g). The combined global

Screen 6.18 - Big vi Edit Session Final Screen

```
I am not expressing an opinion on the quality or suitability for your use;
in some cases, the tool may be available, but it is an old version.
I keep mentioning these three product  because I have had a chance to use them.
I am not expressing an opinion on the quality or suitability for your use;
in some cases, the tool may be available, but it is an old version.

They devote less effort to the other platforms because of simple economics -
they make less money.  The less popular (valuable to the vendor) platforms
get updated after the more popular.

~
~
~
~
~
~
~
~
~
~
~
~
```

search and substitute ex commands follow the same rules as the commands individually. The strings are separated by characters that will not be part of the strings themselves.

Since there are still misspelled words, the following example will search the entire file to replace it. Since there could be words that really contain the string, the prompt will be used. Go to the beginning of the file and enter the following ex global search and substitute command:

```
:g/teh/s//the/c↵
platforms where tehy have the largest installed base or most sales.
                ^^^y↵
[Hit return to continue] ↵
```

Since the word is spelled incorrectly, enter <y> and <enter> to make the change. When you press <enter> again, the cursor will be at the beginning of the line with the last change.

You can also combine the global search ex command with other ex commands like delete line. To delete every line that contains a particular string, you would use the form:

```
:g/search_string/d
```

Every line in the file that contained the search string would be deleted.

The screen now looks substantially different. It should look like Screen 6.18.

This is the end of the big vi editing example. There are other commands and actions, but you can be very productive with the ones in this example. The find and change (ex substitute)

Figure 6.7
ISPF Find Command Replacement Under vi

ISPF Command	vi Command	Description
find string all	:1,$g/string/p	Display all lines that contain string
find string next	/string	Find the next occurrence of string starting at cursor
find string prev	?string	Find the previous occurrence of string starting at cursor
rfind	n	Find the next occurrence of string in current direction
rfind (reverse)	N	Find the next occurrence of string in opposite direction
find string prefix	/[^a-zA-Z]string	Find string at the beginning of a word (defined by not having any alpha character before it)
find string suffix	/string[^a-zA-Z]	Find string at the end of a word (defined by not having any alpha character after it)
find string word	/[^a-zA-Z]string[^a-zA-Z]	Find string that is entire word (defined by not having any alpha character around it)
find string first	1G/string	Go to the top of the file and find the next occurrence of string
find string last	G$/string	Go to the end of the last record in the file and find the previous occurrence of string

Remember that there is no need to put quotes or double quotes around the search string even if it contains spaces or special characters. Special characters may have to be escaped though.

The find parameters can be combined (i.e., find first string word).

commands will take some getting used to as you change from ISPF or the transitional editors. The next two sections should help that process.

MOVING FROM ISPF FIND AND RFIND TO vi

Although there are not direct replacements for the `find` command options such as find first or find word, there are ways of replicating the behavior. Figure 6.7 shows the replacement for the different ISPF find command options and parameters in `vi`. You may be able to find other ways of replacing the ISPF find options.

Unfortunately, there is no way to replace the column bounded searches that ISPF supports. There is also no real replacement for ISPF find p. (find based on pattern) when used for binary data. Finding other patterns is easy so long as they fit the grep regular expression rules.

MOVING FROM ISPF CHANGE AND RCHANGE TO vi

Although there are no direct replacements for the change command options such as change first or change word, there are ways of replicating the behavior. Figure 6.8 shows the replacement for

Figure 6.8
ISPF Change Command Replacement Under vi

ISPF Command	vi Command	Description
change all	:g/string/s//new_string/g	Replace every occurrence of every line
change lines	:line,lines/string/new_string/g	Replace every occurrence on specified lines
change lines	:line,lines/string/new_string/	Replace first occurrence on specified lines
rchange	:sr or &	Repeat last substitute command
change next	/string :s/string/new_string/	Find next string and then change it
change prev	?string	Find previous string and then change it
change prefix	:g/[^a-zA-Z]string/s//new_string/	Change the string when found at the beginning of a word (defined by not having any alpha character before it)
change suffix	:g/string[^a-zA-Z]/s//new_string/	Change the string when found at the end of a word (defined by not having any alpha character after it)
change word	:g/[^a-zA-Z]string[^a-zA-Z]/s//new_string/	Change the string when found alone as a word (defined by not having any alpha character around it)

the different ISPF change command options and parameters in `vi`. You may be able to find other ways of replacing the ISPF change options. Unfortunately, there is no way to replace the column bounded changes that ISPF supports.

COMMAND SUMMARIES

The remainder of this chapter consists of command summaries: Important `vi` Settings (`:set` Options), `vi` Command Summary, and `ed/ex` Command Summary.

Important vi Settings (:set Options)

Figure 6.9 shows the important settings under `vi`. The version of `vi` you are using may have different options. You can check the documentation for your version through the `man` command or by checking the paper manual.

You can set these options in your .exrc file or by entering the `set` command while using the editor.

Figure 6.9
Important vi Settings (:set options)

Option	Default	Description
autoindent	noautoindent	When enabled, the text entry modes will start at the same indentation as the previous line
autoprint	autoprint	Print line after changes (substitute, join, and others)
beautify	nobeautify	Discard all control characters in file except for <tab>, <newline>, and <form-feed>
closepunct	"'.,;0)}]	Used by word movement commands (B, E, W)
directory	/tmp	Directory where vi stores buffer files. If this area is full or you do not have permission to write, you will get an error
errorbells	noerrorbells	Suppress beep when an error occurs
hardtabs	8	Hardware tab stop settings
ignorecase	noignorecase	When enabled, upper and lowercase are treated the same in regular expressions (find, :g, and :s)
linelimit	1040560	Maximum number of lines allowed in editing session
lisp	nolisp	Modify behavior to handle lisp program code more easily
list	nolist	Display lines in :list format (show tabs and end-of-line)
magic	magic	Allow full regular expression syntax; nomagic limits the valid characters to ^ and $
mesg	mesg	Allows messages from other users, nomesg disables them
novice	nonovice	Provides additional assistance to novice vi users. Set to novice by vedit
number	nonumber	Print line numbers next to each line on the screen
optimize	optimize	Optimize output to terminals
readonly	noreadonly	Prevent writes to edited file. Set to readonly by vi -R or view
redraw	noredraw	Allows vi to simulate an intelligent terminal on a dumb terminal
report	5	Display feedback from commands after they affect five lines
scroll	Half screen	Number of lines scrolled for ^D command. Usually 11 lines
shell	User's shell	Shell executed with :sh or ! command. Usually same as the user's default shell
showmatch	noshowmatch	Useful with lisp - cause editor to jump to corresponding (or { when) or } is pressed; cursor remains there for 1 second
showmode	noshowmode	Show the vi mode on status line
slowopen	varies	Depends on terminal. Enabled for slow and dumb terminals
tabstop	8	Tabs in input file are expanded to this length
term	$TERM	User's terminal type
terse	noterse	Displays short messages when enabled
ttytype	$TERM	User's terminal type
warn	warn	Prevent :q for files not changed since last save
window	23	Size of text window on screen
wrapmargin	0	Defines margin for automatic line wrapping
wrapscan	wrapscan	:g and :s will scan entire file
writeany	nowriteany	Default prevents saving files as certain (system) names

To enable an option:	:set option
To disable an option:	:set nooption
To set the value of an option:	:set option=value

vi Command Summary

The following figures contain the commands we have reviewed in this chapter; many of the commands were also shown in Figures 4.2 through 4.5, `vi` Command Line Editing Modes. This

Figure 6.10
vi Cursor Movement

<table>
<tr><th>Key</th><th>Description</th></tr>
<tr><td>count |</td><td>Move cursor one character to right</td></tr>
<tr><td>count <space></td><td>Move cursor one character to right</td></tr>
<tr><td>count <→></td><td>Move cursor one character to right (not on all systems)</td></tr>
<tr><td>count h</td><td>Move cursor one character to left</td></tr>
<tr><td>count <^H></td><td>Move cursor one character to left</td></tr>
<tr><td>count <←></td><td>Move cursor one character to left (not on all systems)</td></tr>
<tr><td>count j</td><td>Move cursor down one line</td></tr>
<tr><td>count +</td><td>Move cursor down one line (to beginning of line)</td></tr>
<tr><td>count <^N></td><td>Move cursor down one line</td></tr>
<tr><td>count <↓></td><td>Move cursor down one line (not on all systems)</td></tr>
<tr><td>count <↵></td><td>Move cursor down one line (to beginning of line)</td></tr>
<tr><td>count k</td><td>Move cursor up one line</td></tr>
<tr><td>count -</td><td>Move cursor up one line (to beginning of line)</td></tr>
<tr><td>count <^P></td><td>Move cursor up one line</td></tr>
<tr><td>count <↑></td><td>Move cursor up one line (not on all systems)</td></tr>
<tr><td>count w</td><td>Move cursor one word to the right</td></tr>
<tr><td>count W</td><td>Move cursor to character after next space (space delimited word)</td></tr>
<tr><td>count e</td><td>Move cursor to end of word to the right</td></tr>
<tr><td>count E</td><td>Move cursor to character before next space (end of space delimited word)</td></tr>
<tr><td>count b</td><td>Move cursor to beginning of word to left</td></tr>
<tr><td>count B</td><td>Move cursor left to first character after next space (start of space delimited word)</td></tr>
<tr><td>count f char</td><td>Find the next char (to right) on the current line</td></tr>
<tr><td>count F char</td><td>Find the next char (to left) on the current line</td></tr>
<tr><td>count t char</td><td>Equivalent to f followed by h</td></tr>
<tr><td>count T char</td><td>Equivalent to F followed by l</td></tr>
<tr><td>|</td><td>Repeat the last f, F, t, or T in the same direction</td></tr>
<tr><td>,</td><td>Repeat the last f, F, t, T in the opposite direction</td></tr>
<tr><td>0</td><td>Move cursor to beginning of line</td></tr>
<tr><td>↵</td><td>Move to beginning of next line</td></tr>
<tr><td>^</td><td>Move cursor to first non-blank character (at or near beginning of line)</td></tr>
<tr><td>$</td><td>Move cursor to end of line</td></tr>
<tr><td>H</td><td>Move cursor to top of current screen (not file)</td></tr>
<tr><td>L</td><td>Move cursor to bottom of current screen (not file)</td></tr>
<tr><td>M</td><td>Move cursor to middle of current screen (not file)</td></tr>
<tr><td>m place</td><td>Mark current cursor position with place. Place can be a through z</td></tr>
<tr><td>` place</td><td>Move cursor to mark place</td></tr>
<tr><td>' place</td><td>Move cursor to beginning of line containing place</td></tr>
<tr><td>``</td><td>Move cursor to previous mark or location</td></tr>
<tr><td>''</td><td>Move cursor to beginning of line containing previous mark or location</td></tr>
</table>

Repetition count is optional.

is because the command line `vi` editing mode is based on the original `vi` editor. Figure 6.10 shows cursor movement keys.

Figure 6.11
vi Screen Movement Keys

Key	Description
count <^B>	Scroll screen up
count <^F>	Scroll screen down
count <^D>	Scroll half screen down
count <^U>	Scroll half screen up
line G	Go to line
G	Go to last line in file
z object	Move line at cursor to position When object is <enter> top, <.> middle, <-> bottom

Repetition count is optional.

Figure 6.11 contains basic screen movement keys for vi.

Figure 6.12 summarizes the text modification keys for vi.

Figure 6.13 shows the key combinations to swap different types of text around, such as characters, words, and lines.

Figure 6.14 contains other vi commands.

ex and ed Command Summary

The ed editor is an early line-oriented UNIX editor; the `ex` editor built on ed and retained much of the same syntax. The `ed` and `ex` commands are available from within `vi`. To access them, use the colon <:> to enter a single command, or <Q> to exit visual mode and enter the line mode of `ex`. Figure 6.15 shows the file commands for the `ed` and `ex` editors.

Figure 6.16 shows the movement and modification commands for the `ed` and `ex` editors.

Figure 6.17 shows the configuration commands for the ex and vi Editors (<:> commands and in .exrc).

Figure 6.12
vi Text Modification Keys

Key	Description
a	Enter input mode after current character
A	Enter input mode at end-of-line
i	Enter input mode before current character
I	Enter input mode at start of line
o	Open line after current line - create new line and enter input mode
O	Open line before current line - create new line and enter input mode
r char	Replace the current character with char
R	Enter replace mode to replace characters including current one
J	Join current and next line after inserting space inbetween
.	Repeat last command (including input)
count x	Delete current character
count X	Delete character to left of cursor
count d object	Delete current object. Object is d for line, w for word, $ for to end-of-line
D	Delete to end-of-line (equivalent to d$)
u	Undo the last text modification on this line
U	Undo all changes to current line
count ~	Change the case of the current character
s	Change current character and then enter insert mode
S	Equivalent to ddO - replace current line
c object	Change current object. Object is c for line, w for word, $ for to end-of-line
C	Equivalent to c$
count y object	Yank object into buffer. Object is y for line, w for word, space for character
count Y	Equivalent to yy (yank line)
p	Paste after current position
P	Paste before current position

Buffer for yank and paste commands can be specified by prefixing command characters by "buffer". Buffer can be the letters a through z. Deletions go into buffers 0 through 9, which can be recovered with paste commands.

Repetition count is optional. It can be used on input and replace mode commands causing entered text (up to the <escape> or first <↵>) to be duplicated.

Figure 6.13
Swapping Text in vi

Key	Description
xp	Swap current and next character
dwwjp	Swap current and next word
ddp	Swap current and next line

Figure 6.14
Other vi Commands

Key	Description
Q	Leave visual mode and return to ex command mode
/string	Find string after cursor position (down)
?string	Find string before cursor position (up)
/	Repeat most recent find down
?	Repeat most recent find up
n	Repeat most recent find in same direction
N	Repeat most recent find in opposite direction
\	Discard special meaning of next character
<^G>	Display information about file and current position
<^L>	Reprint current screen
<^R>	Reprint current screen on some systems
<^M>	<enter> - Execute current command or move to new line
<escape>	Return to command mode (from input, replace, or change modes)
:	Allow entry of one ed/ex command
ZZ	Save and quit
<^V>	In input mode, quote next character (escape any special meaning)
<^W>	In input mode, erase to beginning of current word

Figure 6.15
ed and ex Editor File Commands

Key	Description
q	Quit if the file has not changed or has been saved since last change
q!	Quit even if file changed and not saved
m,n w	Write (save) file
m,n w file	Write current file to new file
m,n w >> file	Append current file to new file
m,n wq	Write file and quit
m,n wq!	Force file write and quit
x	Save and quit
r new_file	Read new file into current session
! command	Execute single UNIX command
r ! command	Execute single UNIX command and insert output into current session
e!	Reinitialize current edit session, discard changes since last save
sh	Invoke subshell and let user enter commands
cd dir	Change current directory to dir

m and n are optional and can be . (current line - the default), $ (last line), number of line to act on, +number (act one line number of lines ahead), -number (act on line number of lines before), or /pattern/

Figure 6.16
ed and ex Editor Movement and Modification Commands

Key	Description
number	Go to line number specified
m,n d	Delete lines
m,n m toline	Move specified lines after toline
m,n co toline	Copy specified lines after toline
m,n t toline	Copy specified lines after toline
vi	Start visual mode
&	Repeat last substitute command
s/old/new/opt	Change old string to new on current or specified lines. opt is omitted for once per line, g for every occurrence, c to confirm before changing, and p to print all changes
g/expr/opt	Locate expression on current or specified lines opt is omitted for last occurrence, p for print, nu for print with line number. Other ed/ex commands can be used in place of opt:
g/expr/s//new/	Use g command to find expr and replace it with new string using substitute

m and n are optional and can be . (current line - the default), $ (last line), number of line to act on, +number (act on line number of lines ahead), -number (act on line number of lines before), or /pattern/

Figure 6.17
ex and vi Editor Configuration Commands

Key	Description
set	Set options (see Figure 6.9)
map key seq	Causes key to execute sequence of keys
map! key seq	Causes key to execute sequence of keys while in input mode
ab abbrev string	Causes string to replace abbrev as it is input. Expands abbreviation
unmap key	Remove key mapping
unmap! key	Remove input mode key mapping
unab abbrev	Remove abbrev mapping

These commands are usually placed in your $HOME/.exrc file but can be entered interactively.

SUMMARY

There are a number of editors that you can use under UNIX: visual, transitional, and line-oriented. Each has its place. It is up to you to determine which is best for your application. Personally, I use the transitional editors when I need to look at binary data or extremely long records. For programming I use vi. Once you learn the commands for any new editor, they are not quite so difficult as they would appear from their list of commands. Remember, at one time ISPF was difficult for you, but eventually you learned it and became comfortable with it.

CHAPTER 7

ACCOUNT CONFIGURATION

When you login to a UNIX system, the shell executes system and then user login configuration files. When you log onto the mainframe, it also executes configuration files. On the mainframe, account configuration is usually performed by the system programmer. Except for ISPF profiles, these files are usually not modified by the account owners due to their complexity and the tendency for forced standardization. Under UNIX, the system administrator will set up the stock, or standard, configuration files for your shell that can be modified. It is much more common for the account owner to modify his or her configuration files.

If you are happy with your environment, you can skip the material in this chapter. However, by setting the right parameters and creating command aliases, you can be more productive.

When you invoke a new shell (explicitly by using the command or by running a shell script), it executes the system and user configuration files. The shell differentiates between a login and non-login shell invocation and executes different configuration files for each. The files executed vary by the shell you are running as shown in Figure 7.1.

These files also perform the same function as the CONFIG.SYS and AUTOEXEC.BAT files under MS/PC-DOS: They configure the current environment. Many applications have their own configuration files that you can create or modify such as .exrc (for ex and vi), .netrc (for FTP), .plan (for finger), .project (for finger), .mailrc (for mail), and others.

Figure 7.1
Shell Configuration Files

Event	Bourne	Korn	C
Login	/etc/profile $HOME/.profile	/etc/profile $HOME/.profile ENV= $HOME/.kshrc	/etc/.login /etc/cshrc $HOME/.cshrc $HOME/.login
New Shell		ENV= $HOME/.kshrc	/etc/cshrc $HOME/.cshrc
Logout			$HOME/.logout

Figure 7.2
Bourne Shell Common Variables

Variable	Description
EXINIT	Defines options for ex and vi editors
HOME	The user home (login) directory
IFS	String of delimiters used to separate items in command lines
LOGNAME	Userid of current user
LPNEST	Default destination for print files when none is specified on lp or lpr command
MAIL	Name of mail file
MAILCHECK	Frequency, in seconds, that the shell checks for new mail. Default is 600
MAILPATH	Similar to PATH for mail to check for mail files
PAGER	Used to set program that man uses to page through documentation
PATH	Search path for commands and scripts
PS1	Shell prompt. Default is $
PS2	Continuation prompt. Default is >
SHELL	Default shell. Used when invoking script or by programs that allow shell prompts
TERM	Terminal type
TZ	Time zone

BOURNE SHELL .profile FILE

The following are some of the things I have in my .profile for Bourne shell:

```
export PATH=.:$HOME/bin:$PATH:     # look in current, my bin, then others

if [ -s "$MAIL" ]                  # check for waiting mail
then echo "You have mail waiting"
fi

export MAILCHECK=300               # check for new mail every 5 minutes

biff y                                     # expanded mail pending messages
mesg y                                     # enable messages

export APPVAR="some value"         # values required by applications

stty erase ^?                      # My emulater uses <DEL>
stty intr ^c                               # I like <^C> to interrupt

echo
/usr/games/fortune                 # witty saying
echo
echo
```

I customize my login to behave the way I prefer and do the things that I like to see first thing in the morning. If there is existing shell code, you may want to put yours after it. Figure 7.2 shows the common environmental variables for the Bourne Shell.

Using the `biff` and `mesg` commands as well as setting the MAILCHECK environmental variable are all similar to the TSO signon options mail and notice. To disable mail messages, you could set MAILCHECK to a very high number (29000 seconds for instance) and disable `biff` with the `n` (no) option. Using `mesg n` is similar to using `nonotice` under TSO.

KORN SHELL .profile AND ENV FILES

The .profile for a Korn shell is a little more complicated because the shell understands more commands:

```
export PATH=.:$HOME/bin:$PATH:     # look in current, my bin, then others

if [ -s "$MAIL" ]                          # check for waiting mail
then echo "$MAILMSG"
fi

biff y                                     # expanded mail pending messages
mesg y                                     # enable messages

export HISTSIZE=256                        # save 256 last command
export ENV=$HOME/.kshrc            # execute when invoking subshells
export MAILCHECK=300               # check for new mail every 5 minutes

export APPVAR="some value"         # values required by applications
    export JULIAN='date +%y%j'             # define julian date

    stty erase ^?                  # My emulater uses <DEL>
    stty intr ^c                           # I like <^C> to interrupt

    echo
    /usr/games/fortune                     # witty saying
    echo
    echo
```

Since the Korn shell can have another configuration file that is executed when the shell is invoked (non-login), I enable it by pointing the environmental variable ENV to the file. I also expand the default command history file to 256 commands instead of the default 128. In the file pointed to by ENV (.kshrc), I place those commands that I want to execute for each and every shell. That is where I place commands to affect every shell. My .kshrc looks something like:

```
# Command aliases
alias ll="ls -al"
alias psme="ps -ef | grep dhorvath"
alias psuser="ps -ef | grep -i "
alias cc="cc -qlist -qsource -qprint -v "
alias od="od -Ad –t c -t x "
alias pg=more
```

```
alias cookie="/usr/games/fortune"
alias fortune="/usr/games/fortune"
alias dfhigh="df -v | grep [8-9][0-9]%; df -v | grep 100% "
alias mybin="cd $HOME/bin"
alias myc="cd $HOME/c_stuff"
alias mycob="cd $HOME/cob_stuff"

alias cd..="cd .."
# set shell options
set -o vi                                   # vi command line editing
set +o bgnice                         # do not be nice with background
# set shell environmental variables
export PS1='[$LOGNAME@hostname]: $PWD:>>'
export PS4='[+$0:$LINENO]'
```

The alias commands ensure that my commands are set up the way I like them. Some of them are abbreviations for commands I use all the time (like `ll`), some are combinations of commands that I do not want to type repeatedly (`psme` and `dfhigh`), a few set the options for commands so they behave the way I prefer (`cc` and `od`). The last alias, cd.., makes my life easier if I miss the space bar when using the `cd ..` command—the alias translates `cd..` to `cd ..` (with a space). The `set` commands define options for the shell: `vi` command line editing and disabling bgnice (run background jobs at lower priority).

The last two commands define my command prompts. By enclosing the strings in single quotes, substitution does not occur until the prompts are displayed. My normal prompt looks like:

```
[dhorvath@hostname]: /u/dhorvath:>>
```

And my prompt when using `set -o xtrace` with a shell script (named jobs_1 run from the current directory, first line) looks like:

```
[./jobs_1+1]
```

The settings for prompts are up to you. Not surprisingly, I have even seen people put humorous phrases in their prompts. The contents of your .profile and ENV= are almost entirely up to you.

Figure 7.3 shows the common Korn shell environmental variables; we have discussed a number of these already.

C Shell .login and .cshrc Files

The C and Korn shell .profile and .login files perform the same function, executing once when you login. The C and Korn shell ENV= and .cshrc files also perform the same functions. The difference is the commands used and environmental variables set.

Figure 7.3
Korn Shell Common Variables

Variable	Description
CDPATH	Search path used by cd commands when given partial pathname
COLUMNS	Screen width
EDITOR	Fully qualified name of editor used for command line editing
ENV	Pathname to environment file (often set to $HOME/.kshenv)
EXINIT	Defines options for ex and vi editors
FCEDIT	Fully qualified name of editor used for fc editing. Default is /bin/ed
FPATH	Search path for automatically loading functions
HISTFILE	Name of history file. Default is $HOME/.sh_history
HISTSIZE	Number of commands to save in HISTFILE. Default is 128
HOME	The user home (login) directory
IFS	String of delimiters used to separate items in command lines
LOGNAME	Userid of current user
LPNEST	Default destination for print files when none is specified on lp or lpr command
MAIL	Name of mail file
MAILCHECK	Frequency, in seconds, that the shell checks for new mail. Default is 600
MAILMSG	Message to display when new mail is available
MAILPATH	Similar to PATH, but for mail to check for mail files
MANPATH	Similar to PATH, but for man to check for man page files
PAGER	Used to set program that man uses to page through documentation
PATH	Search path for commands and scripts
PS1	Shell prompt. Default is $
PS2	Continuation prompt. Default is >
PS3	Prompt for Korn shell select command. Default is #?
PS4	Prompt for set -o xtrace output. Default is +
SHELL	Default shell. Used when invoking script or by programs that allow shell prompts
TERM	Terminal type
TMOUT	Time out variable - number of minutes inactive before you are logged out
TZ	Time zone

```
set path=(. $home/bin $path )  # look in current, my bin, then others

mail -e                        # check for waiting mail

biff y                                 # expanded mail pending messages
mesg y                                 # enable messages

setenv APPVAR "some value"             # values required by applications

stty erase ^?                  # My emulater uses <DEL>
stty intr ^c                           # I like <^C> to interrupt

echo
/usr/games/fortune                     # witty saying
echo
echo
```

Figure 7.4
The C Shell Common Variables

Variable	Description
argv	List of arguments supplied with current shell invocation
autologout	Time out variable - number of minutes of inactivity before you are logged out
cdpath	Search path used by cd command when given partial pathname
fignore	List of filename suffixes to ignore when performing filename completion (like .o)
histchars	Set history substitution characters (defaults to ! and ^)
history	Number of lines of history to retain in memory
mail	Name of file that contains new mail
path	Search path for commands and scripts
prompt	Shell prompt. Default is %
savehist	Number of lines to save to $HOME/.history when user logs out
shell	Default shell. Used when invoking script or by programs that allow shell prompts
status	Exit status from previous command
term	Terminal type
time	Display time required by command if it is greater than this value
user	Userid

Figure 7.5
C Shell Settings

Setting	Description
echo	Echo commands (like set -o xtrace)
filec	Enable filename completion
hardpaths	Resolve all directories in path to remove symbolic links
ignoreeof	Disable logout through use of end-of-file (like set -o ignoreeof)
nobeep	Disables bell when filename completion results in multiple possible filenames
noclobber	Prevent overwriting of an existing file (like set -o noclobber)
noglob	Disable filename substitution (like set -o noglob)
nomatch	Return filename substitution pattern if pattern is not matched (instead of error)
notify	Notify immediately when background job ends (similar to set -o monitor)
verbose	Display command after history substitution takes place

The C shell makes a distinction between shell variables (available within the current shell) and environmental variables (available to subshells). The set command sets shell variables, setenv sets environmental variables. Some of these are automatically set by the shell and others you can modify. Figure 7.4 shows the variables commonly modified.

Many of the settings used with C shell also appear as shell variables but perform the same function as Korn shell flags. Figure 7.5 lists the C shell settings.

The $HOME/.cshrc file is executed every time a shell is started. An example follows:

```
# Command aliases
alias ll "ls -al"
alias psme "ps -ef | grep dhorvath"
alias psuser "ps -ef | grep -i "
alias cc "cc -qlist -qsource -qprint -v "
alias od "od -Ad –t c -t x "
alias pg more
alias cookie "/usr/games/fortune"
alias fortune "/usr/games/fortune"
alias dfhigh "df -v | grep '[8-9][0-9]%'; df -v | grep '100%' "
alias mybin "cd $HOME/bin"
alias myc "cd $HOME/c_stuff"
alias mycob "cd $HOME/cob_stuff"

alias cd.. "cd .."
# set shell options
set savehist=256                              # save 256 last command
set history=256                               # save 256 last command
```

This file performs the same function as the Korn shell ENV= file: It sets variables and settings for the current shell. The contents of these files are also almost entirely up to you.

C SHELL .logout FILE

The .logout file is executed after you issue the logout command from your login C shell. You can use it to clean up space, submit jobs, or perform other processing that you want to happen as you leave. A simple one might include a good-bye message:

```
echo
echo
echo "Have a good night..."
echo
echo
```

OTHER CONFIGURATION FILES

Many commands have their own configuration files that are stored in your home directory because they may be unique to you. The `ex` and `vi` editors use .exrc; the file transfer program (`ftp`) will use .netrc to automatically connect to another system and transfer files; `finger` uses .plan and .project to display more information about you; Internet programs like `rcp`, `rsh`, and `rlogin` use .rhosts to determine which user and system combinations can pretend they are you.

.exrc

This file is used by the `ex` and `vi` editors for configuration. It typically contains set commands to individualize your editing environment and may also include key mappings, which change the behavior of specific keys.

.netrc

The .netrc file is used by `ftp` to automate file transfers. When ftp is invoked with a system_name on the command line, it searches for the file $HOME/.netrc. If the file exists, it searches the file for an entry for that system. If it is found, it will execute the commands that follow. The next example automatically logs in and transfers the file new_directory/get_file:

```
macdef init
machine system_name login userid password userpswd
cd new_directory
get get_file
bye

# comment—macro ended by pressing <enter> twice.
```

The file must be set to a permission of 600 (no access other than owner) because it contains a user's password.

.plan

The .plan file is used by the `finger` command to display more information about the user. It tends to be tactical information such as current plans. Do not put anything in this file that you would not mind your boss (or his or her boss) reading.

.project

The .project file is used by the `finger` command to display more information about the user. It tends to be information about what you are doing on a longer term basis than what you put in your .plan. It might be the project team on which you are working or some description about your department. The same warnings about political correctness apply.

CHAPTER 8

THIRD-PARTY TOOLS

This chapter consists of 13 tables that are a survey of tools available on the mainframe. Where the mainframe tool is also available under UNIX, it is shown, when it is not, UNIX replacements are shown. The categories are fairly arbitrary and many of the tools fit in multiple ones.

This information is from CD-ROM searches, the Internet, magazines, and other sources. It is a survey, and therefore is far from containing every tool available. You should not consider a listing to be an endorsement of a particular product, as there are too many for me to have used but a small fraction. The tools are changing so fast that this list was outdated as soon as it was put on paper, but should provide you with an idea of what is available. Perform your own survey or search when you need a tool because odds are that it may be available by the time you need it. Because UNIX is becoming so popular and being used to host formerly mainframe applications, many vendors of mainframe tools are releasing those products for UNIX.

PROGRAMMING LANGUAGES

Figure 8.1
Programming Languages

Mainframe	UNIX	Vendor	Description
Ada	Ada	Rational Software, DEC	
APL	APL	ISVs	
BAL	as	Hardware Vendors and others	Most hardware vendors support as assemblers for their machines. Also available from ISVs
BASIC	BASIC	ISVs	Beginners All Purpose Symbolic Instruction Code
C, C++	C, C++	Hardware Vendors and others	C is usually supplied with each UNIX system. Each hardware vendor has its own version
COBOL	COBOL, MicroFocus COBOL, ACU-COBOL	IBM, DEC, MicroFocus, Acucobol, Inc., andothers	Many hardware vendors support their own COBOL languages. Micro Focus and Acucobol COBOL compilers are available for many platforms
FORTRAN	FORTRAN	IBM,DEC, andothers	Some hardware vendors support their own FORTRAN compilers. Also available from ISVs
Pascal	Pascal	DEC	
PL/I	Open PL/I	Liant	

4th Generation Languages, Application Generators, and Application Development Environments

Figure 8.2
4th Generation Languages, Application Generators, and
Application Development Environments

Mainframe	UNIX	Vendor	Description
	Art Enterprise	Inference Corp.	Application development tool that targets MVS and UNIX
	Pipes Platform	Peerlogic, Inc.	Application development environment that targets MVS and UNIX
AD/Advantage		Cincom Systems, Inc.	Application development environment. Creates portable programs for MVS and UNIX
CA-ADS	CA-ADS	Computer Associates, Inc.	4GL/Application development environment for CA-IDMS. Was known as ADS/O
CA-Ideal	CA-Ideal	Computer Associates, Inc.	4GL/Application development environment. Accesses DB2 and CA-Datacom/DB databases.
CA-Ramis	CA-Ramis	Computer Associates, Inc.	4GL
CA-Telon	CA-Telon	Computer Associates	Application generator for MVS and UNIX
CICS spII	CICS spII	Flexus International Corp.	CICS screen designer and driver code generator
COBOL spII	COBOL spII	Flexus International Corp.	Portable screen designer and driver code generator
EasyReporter	EasyReporter	Speedware Corp.	4GL
FOCUS	FOCUS	Information Builders, Inc.	4GL for MVS and UNIX
Forté Development Environment	Forté Development Environment	Forté Software, Inc.	4GL/application generator-generates for MVS and UNIX
Mantis	Mantis	Cincom Systems, Inc.	4GL/application development environment
Natural2	Natural2	Software AG	4GL for Adabas and DB2 databases
Nomad	Nomad	Must Software International	
Powerhouse	Powerhouse	Cognos	4GL
SAS	SAS	SAS Institute Inc.	Suite of tools. Was originally Statistical Analysis System, now considered a general 4GL

OTHER DEVELOPMENT TOOLS

Figure 8.3
Other Development Tools

Mainframe	UNIX	Vendor	Description
	lint	Hardware Vendor; Gimpel Software	Used to check C programs for fuzzy syntax (technically valid but bad practice). Usually comes with UNIX and third-party compilers. ISV versions available
	make	Hardware Vendor, Compiler Vendor, ISV's	Selectively compiles and linkedits program code when modules or include files change. Usually comes with UNIX and third-party compilers. ISV versions available
INSPECT	adb, sdb, dbx	Hardware Vendor, Compiler Vendor, ISV's	One or more versions come with UNIX. Also available with third-party compilers and ISVs
ISPF	SPF/UX	Uneclipse Software Systems	ISPF by IBM, transitional tools for UNIX by others
ISPF	Tritus SPF	Tritus	ISPF by IBM, transitional tools for UNIX by others
ISPF	uni-SPF	The Workstation Group, Ltd.	ISPF by IBM, transitional tools for UNIX by others
REXX	IBM REXX/6000	Tritus	REXX by IBM
REXX	uni-REXX	The Workstation Group, Ltd.	REXX by IBM. Also available via shareware
Xedit	uni-Xedit	The Workstation Group, Ltd.	Xedit by IBM, Xedit for UNIX by others

OLTP—CICS AND REPLACEMENTS

Figure 8.4
OLTP - CICS and Replacements

Mainframe	UNIX	Vendor	Description
	Encina	Transarc Corp.	OLTP; syntax is different from CICS
	Top End	NCR (AT&T)	OLTP that includes support for 3270 terminals and LU 6.2. Syntax different from CICS
CICS	CICS-6000	IBM	Available on the RS/6000, HP, Sun, and others
CICS	MTS	MicroFocus	MicroFocus Transaction Support - portable replacement for CICS; supports CICS syntax

Figure 8.5
CASE Tools

Mainframe	UNIX	Vendor	Description
	ADW	KnowledgeWare	CASE Tool - targets MVS and UNIX
	Bachman	Bachman Information Systems, Inc.	CASE Tool - targets MVS and UNIX
	CASE Suite	Intersolv, Inc.	CASE Tool - targets MVS and UNIX
	CorVision	International Software Group	CASE Tool - targets MVS and UNIX
	Erwin	Logic Works	CASE Tool - targets MVS and UNIX
	FOUNDATION	Anderson Consulting	CASE Tool - targets MVS and UNIX
	IEF	TI	CASE Tool - targets MVS and UNIX
	PacBase	CGI Systems, Inc.	CASE Tool - targets MVS and UNIX
ADW Repository	ADW Repository	KnowledgeWare /R&O Inc.	Repository for CASE tools, targets MVS and UNIX

CASE TOOLS

Most CASE tools were originally targeted at the MVS environment because that is where most of the business computing was occurring. The tools typically ran on a PC, although some were UNIX-based. The repository or encyclopedia that contained the global view of all models was mainframe-based for the tools that targeted the mainframe. The new direction for the tools is to target mainframe, UNIX, and client/server development with the repository stored on a server. The server can be a mainframe, a UNIX server, or a traditional server.

There certainly are other CASE tools than those listed in Figure 8.5—it is intended to be a survey of the most popular.

SOURCE CODE CONTROL AND CONFIGURATION MANAGEMENT

Figure 8.6
Source Code Control and Configuration Management

Mainframe	UNIX	Vendor	Description
	PVCS	INTERSOLV	Source code control for UNIX and PCs
	rcs, sccs	Hardware Vendor and ISVs	Source code control and configuration management that is included with most versions of UNIX
CA-PAN	CA-PAN/LCM	Computer Associates, Inc.	Source code control; versions for MVS and UNIX. Was known as Panvalet
CCC/Harvest	CCC/Harvest	Softool Corporation	Source code control and configuration management for MVS and UNIX
CCC/Manager	CCC/Manager	Softool Corp.	Configuration management for MVS and UNIX
Endevour	Endevour	Legent Corp.	Source code version control for MVS and UNIX

RELATIONAL DATABASES

Figure 8.7
Relational Databases

Mainframe	UNIX Tool	Vendor	Description
	Informix	Informix Software, Inc.	For UNIX and other platforms
	UniData RDBMS	UniData Corporation	For UNIX
Adabas	Adabas	Software AG	For MVS and UNIX
CA-DB:Star	CA-DB:Star	Computer Associates, Inc.	For MVS and UNIX
DB2	DB2/6000	IBM	For MVS and some versions of UNIX (AIX, HP-UX, others as time progresses)
Oracle RDBMS	Oracle RDBMS	Oracle Corporation	For MVS, UNIX, and other platforms
Supra	Supra Server	Cincom Systems Inc.	For MVS and UNIX

Figure 8.8
Other Databases and Data Access Methods

Mainframe	UNIX Tool	Vendor	Description
CA-Datacom/DB	CA-Datacom/DB	Computer Associates, Inc.	Production-oriented database
CA-IDMS	CA-IDMS for VAX and UNIX	Computer Associates, Inc.	Network database
VSAM	Encina Structured File Server (SFS)	Transarc	Replacement for VSAM that supports KSDS, RRDS, and ESDS under UNIX
VSAM	ISAM	Hardware Vendor, Compiler Vendor	ISAM is really a method with different product names that perform the functions. RRDS and ESDS VSAM type files handled by UNIX, KSDS (Indexed Sequential) handled by compilers

OTHER DATABASES AND DATA ACCESS METHODS

(See Figure 8.8.)

MIDDLEWARE / MIGRATION (ACCESSING DATA ON THE MAINFRAME FROM OTHER PLATFORMS)

Middleware is the term used for software used in the middle of application systems. In other words, between the application software and the network, database, and systems software. It is also used for software used to access legacy data. (See Figure 8.9.)

CODE TRANSLATION

Sometimes a decision is made to take code written in one language and get rid of it. But the functions the code performs cannot be thrown out, so as an alternative to manually rewriting the code, it can be translated to another language. (See Figure 8.10.)

SYSTEM UTILITIES

Some of the tools in this section are listed by generic names because they do not have mainframe equivalents or there are multiple tools from the vendor that perform the function: job scheduling, performance monitor, resource accounting, and system management software. (See Figure 8.11.)

UNIX Sorting—An Overview

The editors and other tools under UNIX may not work with data from applications converted from the mainframe or written in the typical mainframe style. The UNIX `sort` utility does not work unless the records have a <line feed> at the end and do not contain binary data. In addition, it was not designed to sort large volumes of data. It was created when a large disk drive was 30 MB. These are serious limitations and if you will be sorting large files, because the sort utility

Figure 8.9
Middleware / Migration
(Accessing Data on the Mainframe from Other Platforms)

Mainframe	UNIX	Vendor	Description
		Informix Software Inc.	Provides links to DB2 on the mainframe for Informix users under UNIX
	COBOL Direct Connect	UniData Corporation	Provides a set of data migration and I/O re-direction modules that allow ACUCOBOL-85 application programs to operate seamlessly and directly with the UniData RDBMS
	Picasso	WinGate Technology/ Intra-Sys	Creates GUI wrapper to 3270-based (CICS, IMS/DC, TSO, and other) applications through generated Visual Basic code
	SCALE Data Links	Symatec Corp.	Links PCs to DB2 and Oracle on mainframe. Provides links to other databases on and off mainframes
	Select*	Computer Corp. of America	Provides UNIX access to Model 204 databases on the mainframe
CICS (access)	Parts CICS Wrapper	Digitalk, Inc.	Provides routines for UNIX programs to access mainframe data by getting screens from CICS applications
Distributed Computing Environment (DCE)	DCE	IBM, DEC, other hardware vendors and ISV's	DCE is an effort of the Open Software Foundation that allows application interoperability and sharing across multivendor networks. Supplied by many hardware vendors with the operation system (including MVS and UNIX)
EDA/SQL	EDA/SQL	Information Builders, Inc.	Gateway between mainframe data and UNIX systems
IMS/DB	IMS TM 74	IBM	Allows UNIX access to IMS databases on the mainframe
Open Client for CICS		Sybase	Allows mainframe 3270 terminal users access to character-based applications running under UNIX
Open Server for CICS		Sybase	Provides routines for UNIX programs to access mainframe data by getting screens from CICS applications. Runs on MVS and client
SQL*Connect		Oracle	Provides link to DB2 and IMS/DB on the mainframe for Oracle users under UNIX. Runs under MVS
TransAccess	TransAccess	Netwise, Inc.	Enables Oracle running under UNIX to access IMS/DB, IDMS, DB2, Adabas, and VSAM data on the mainframe

will not work well. If you plan on sorting large volumes of data (over 300 MB), many of the COBOL internal sorts suffer serious performance problems.

The alternative is to purchase an external sort from a third-party software developer. Cosort claims to be available for UNIX and PC/MS-DOS; Opt-Tech Sort claims availability for SCO UNIX, Xenix, and C Source Code for PC/MS-DOS, Windows 3.x, Windows NT, and OS/2; SyncSort claims availability for AIX, HP-UX, Solaris, the mainframe, and others. Cosort and SyncSort support record-oriented (fixed sequential) and binary data that the UNIX sort does not.

Figure 8.10
Code Translation

Mainframe	UNIX	Vendor	Description
ASM370 (BAL)	ASM370 (BAL) to C translation	Micro-Processor Services, Inc.	Language translation services
ASM370 (BAL)	ASM370 (BAL) to COBOL translation	Micro-Processor Services, Inc.	Language translation services
COBOL	COBOL to C translation	Micro-Processor Services, Inc.	Language translation services
JCL	JCL to Korn Shell translation	IBS	JCL translation services
PL/I	PLI to C translation	Micro-Processor Services, Inc.	Language translation services
PL/I	PLI to C/C++ Code Translator	Solar Computer Exchange, Inc.	Language translation services and object libraries to support PL/I constructs under C++

I have seen SyncSort successfully used in the conversion of a mainframe application to UNIX. External (utility) and COBOL internal sorts were replaced with SyncSort sorts. The external sorts had to be replaced because they were fixed-length record-oriented without record separators and contained binary data. The COBOL internal sorts were replaced because of performance issues with large volumes of data. One particularly nice feature of SyncSort is the ability to sort ASCII data in EBCDIC order.

The EBCDIC character set is ordered lowercase alphabetic first, uppercase alphabetic next, and then numeric characters last. In ASCII sort sequence, numeric characters come first, then upper-case alphabetic, then lower-case alphabetic. The sort order matters if reports must look exactly the same in the mainframe and UNIX box. If the control breaks assume that letters come before numbers and they do not, then the processing will be incorrect. A sort ordering problem can be particularly difficult to debug. The UNIX sort utility will not sort in alternate character sets like SyncSort does.

The `sort` command that comes with UNIX works very well if you are working with text files. It can be used to sort, merge, and verify that files are sorted. For sorts, the input file(s) or stdin are read and the resulting output written to stdout. For merges, the input file(s) or stdin are read, merged together, and written to stdout. By default, the entire record is used as the key. It also provides the capability of sorting in dictionary order (ignoring special characters), mapping lowercase characters to uppercase for comparisons, and treating numeric fields as their value (sort as a number, not a collection of characters).

Figure 8.11a
System Utilities - Part 1 of 2

Mainframe	UNIX	Vendor	Description
ADSTAR Distributed Storage Manager (ADSM)	ADSTAR Distributed Storage Manager (ADSM)	IBM	ADSM provides the ability to backup from PC and UNIX systems through the disks and tapes on a mainframe
BookManager	BookManager	IBM	On-line documentation MVS and UNIX (AIX)
CA-TOP SECRET and CA-ACF2	CA-TOP SECRET and CA-ACF2	Computer Associates, Inc.	Security packages handling user, file, and resource access originally for MVS; moving to UNIX
CA-Unicenter	CA-Unicenter	Computer Associates, Inc.	Systems management software for MVS and UNIX
Data Archival	CA-Archival	Computer Associates, Inc.	Archives files
Data Archival	Hierarchy	Software Partners/32	Moves old files to tape but keeps entry in catalog like IBM HSM (Hierarchical Storage Manager)
Enterprise Performance Data Manager (EPDM)		IBM	Performance measurement for MVS and UNIX; runs under MVS
IMSL	IMSL	Visual Numeries	Mathematical library
Job Scheduling	AutoSys	Autosystems Corporation	Job scheduling for UNIX
Job Scheduling	Enterprise Control Station (ECS), Control-M	4th Dimension Software, Inc.	Batch job scheduling for single system (Control-M) and for multiple systems (ECS)
Job Scheduling	Express	Operations Control Systems	Job scheduling for UNIX
Job Scheduling	IBM Job Scheduler	IBM	Job scheduling for UNIX
Job Scheduling	Lights Out	Relational Data Systems	Data center management - lights out operations
Job Scheduling	Q Master	GD Associates, Ltd.	Batch job scheduling, print spooling, system performance measurement, and other functions for UNIX
Job Scheduling	UniQBatch	Primary Ltd.	Job scheduling for UNIX
MVS/NFS	MVS/NFS	J. Frank & Associates	Implementation of NFS (Network File System) for MVS - allows UNIX systems direct access to MVS disks
NewView	NetView/6000	IBM	Network management for MVS, UNIX, and other networks
Omegacenter/ Omegamon	Omegacenter Omegamon	Candle, Inc.	System performance measurement and management originally for MVS; moving to UNIX

Figure 8.11b
System Utilities - Part 2 of 2

Mainframe	UNIX	Vendor	Description
Operations Planning Control (OPC)	Operations Planning Control (OPC)	IBM	Job Scheduling for MVS and UNIX
Performance monitor		Legent	System performance monitors for MVS and UNIX
RDBMS tools	Platinum	Platinum Technology Inc.	Originally tools for DB2 - support, tuning, performance measurement, etc., now being distributed for UNIX-based RDBMS
Resource accounting	JobAcct	BrainTree Technology, Inc.	Job resource accounting for UNIX
Resource accounting	UNISOL JobAcct	Unisolutions	Job resource accounting and chargeback for UNIX
SecurID Card	SecurID Card	Security Dynamics, Inc.	Access security - front-line intrusion prevention for MVS, UNIX, and other platforms
Sort	Cosort	Innovative Routines International	Replacement for UNIX Sort Utility
Sort	Opt-Tech Sort	Opt-Tech Data Processing	Replacement for UNIX Sort Utility
Sort, SyncSort	SyncSort	SyncSort	Replacement for standard MVS sort. Conversion utility from MVS Sort syntax to SyncSort syntax provided
SpoolMate	SpoolMate	Unisom-Tymlabs	Print spooling across enterprise - MVS, UNIX, and other platforms
System management software	Ensign	Boole & Babbage	Systems management software for UNIX

The flags used by UNIX `sort` to specify sort parameters is cryptic and nothing like mainframe sort syntax. SyncSort includes a tool to convert from mainframe syntax to SyncSort UNIX syntax.

To perform a numeric sort on the second field of a colon separated file:

```
sort -t: +1 -2 input_file
```

Or:

```
sort -t: -k2,2 input_file
```

To sort using the second field numerically and then the first field in descending order of a colon-separated file:

```
sort -t: +1 -2 -n +0 -1 -r input_file
```

Or:

```
sort -t: -k2,2n -k1,1r input_file
```

The syntax for the `sort` command can be so difficult to work with that one of the examples in the AWK book is an `awk` program that builds sort commands. You definitely need to read the man page anytime you want to do anything more complicated than a one-key or entire record sort.

Replacement for SCRIPT—An Overview of Text Processing

The mainframe SCRIPT language is used to create documents by embedding processing commands within the text itself. It is a far cry from the WYSIWYG (What You See Is What You Get) word processors available on the PC today, where what you see on the screen matches what gets printed on paper. Before the advent of the PC, document preparation occurred three ways: manually on a typewriter, on a specialized multi-user word processing computer, and through embedded command languages.

The original justification for the purchase of the DEC PDP-11 computer at Bell Labs was for document preparation, not the development of an operating system (UNIX). This is a good example of serendipity on the part of management at that facility. They were convinced to purchase a computer to produce documentation and they ended up with one of the more successful operating systems.

The original embedded-command text processing system was RUNOFF, developed by J. E. Saltzer for CTSS at MIT during the 1960s. Most text processors trace their lineage back to this system including TeX by Don Knuth, Scribe by Brian Reid, mainframe SCRIPT, and the UNIX `roff`, `nroff`, and `troff`.

The first embedded-language text processing command under UNIX was `roff` (run-off). It was limited to producing simple documents on a line printer, but it was small, fast, and easy to use. The next text processor was `nroff` (next-run-off), written by Joe Ossanna. `nroff` was more flexible because it provided a programming language to allow users to format their documents. Instead of having a programmer develop code for every document format the users might need, they could create it themselves. After a typesetter was acquired, `nroff` was enhanced to handle multiple fonts, font sizes, and a larger character set that the typesetter supported. The new text processor was known as `troff` (typesetter-run-off). The `nroff` version will ignore any of the `troff` commands it cannot process such as those dealing with fonts or font sizes.

Many vendors have implemented versions of `roff`, `nroff`, or `troff` on their systems. DEC systems have DSR (Digital Standard Runoff), shareware versions are available for the PC, and the mainframe has SCRIPT. Even with the PC WYSIWYG word processors, there is a use for embedded-command text processors. Instead of an application having to perform formatting of text output, it can embed commands and pass the output to a text processor. The text processor then does the hard work of formatting the output. For regular reports, this is too much effort. For complex reports that include long descriptions or for things like form letters, it make more sense. Instead of the programmer making sure the output is formatted perfectly from within the program (making sure that full lines are printed), the text is just output with the commands to format and justify. Creating form letters from large databases (known as mail merging) is a good example of this.

UNIX on-line manual pages are free form text with embedded commands; when the man command is issued, it passes the appropriate file through `nroff`, which directs it to your screen.

Using `nroff` and `troff` commands to perform complex tasks can be difficult as an individual user. As a result, a number of macro packages (including those for manual pages, manuscripts, and memos) and other commands were developed. There are commands to format mathematical

Figure 8.12
Text Processing Commands,
Macros, and Pre-processors

Text Processors

roff	Original text processor. Not usually available anymore
nroff	Formats text for typewriter-like devices and line printers
troff	Formats text for typesetter or other device that supports multiple fonts
psroff	Formats text for postscript printers (runs troff and psc/psedit)
psc	Converts troff output to postscript (equivalent to psedit)
psedit	Converts troff output to postscript (equivalent to psc)
deroff	Removes nroff, troff, tbl, and eqn command constructs from files

Pre-processors

cw	Formats constant width text (program code examples) using troff
eqn	Formats mathematical text for the troff command. eqn file -flags | troff...
neqn	Formats mathematical text for the nroff command. neqn file -flags | nroff...
tbl	Formats tables for the nroff and troff commands
pic	Pre-processes troff command input to draw simple figures on a typesetter
refer	Finds and inserts literature references in documents
mm	Formats documents containing memorandum macros (uses nroff)
mmt	Formats documents containing memorandum macros (uses troff)
ptx	Builds permutated indexes for documents using mptx macros

Document Correction and Analysis

spell	Finds English language spelling errors
style	Analyzes the writing style of a document including readability, word usage, and verbs
diction	Analyzes the sentence structure of a document for unclear or wordy diction

nroff/troff Formatting Macro Packages

mm	Memorandum formatting macros
ms	Manuscript formatting macros (similar to me)
man	Manual page formatting macros
me	Manuscript thesis formatting macros (similar to ms)
mptx	Permutated index macros
mv	Slide and view graph formatting macros

equations, create tables, and perform simple picture drawing. In addition to the text processing (formatting) commands, there are commands to analyze the grammar of a document (`style` command), highlight lengthy sentences (`diction` command), and check English spelling (`spell` command). It is only within the past couple of years that the PC word processors gained this functionality.

Some systems have a file /usr/dict/papers or a subdirectory with the same name that holds multiple files. In either form, a bibliographical list of papers and books about UNIX and text processing are provided. The file(s) are in `nroff` format and must be processed before printing. If you are particularly interested in this topic, it would be worth your effort to determine if your system has this information.

Figure 8.12 shows the commands, macros, and pre-processors used for text processing under UNIX.

Figure 8.13
Communications

Mainframe	UNIX	Vendor	Description
3270 Emulation	3270 Emulation	IBM, DEC, Stratus Computers, Inc., others	Allows terminals connected to UNIX to access 3270 based mainframe applications. Versions also available for PCs
APPC LU6.2	APPC LU6.2	IBM, DEC, Stratus Computers, Inc., others	Advanced Peer-to-Peer Communications and Logical Unit 6.2
NDM (Connect: Direct)	Same	Sterling Software, Inc.	Originally known as NDM (Network Data Mover), now being marketed as Connect: Direct. Originally was just MVS, now available for UNIX and many other platforms
RJE	RJE	IBM, DEC, Stratus Computers, Inc., others	Remote Job Entry - 2780, 3780, and other protocols
SNA	SNA	IBM, DEC, Stratus Computers, Inc., others	System Network Architecture
TCP/IP	TCP/IP	Hardware Vendor and ISVs	Usually supplied with UNIX system; available from many vendors for many platforms. Shareware versions available
X.25	X.25	IBM, DEC, others	

If you are comfortable using SCRIPT on the mainframe, the transition to `nroff` or `troff` under UNIX will be easy. The commands may be slightly different, but the methods are the same.

COMMUNICATIONS

(See Figure 8.13.)

An Overview of File Transfer

The mainframe supports a number of tools for the transfer of datasets between systems. The traditional methods include NDM (Network Data Mover), now being marketed as Connect:DIRECT by Sterling Software and RJE (Remote Job Entry) where the data was embedded as SYSIN to a job that copied it to the appropriate remote dataset.

The Connect:DIRECT product provides connectivity between the mainframe and other systems. Mainframe-to-mainframe and mainframe-to-other architectures is supported. UNIX and the mainframe running MVS can communicate over LU6.2 (the UNIX system is assigned a SNA ID) and TCP/IP.

The most common networking method is TCP/IP which stands for Transmission Control Protocol/Internet Protocol which is the basis for the collection of computers known as the Internet in the media. Originally developed under contract to DARPA (department of Defense Advanced Research Projects Agency), TCP/IP is now available for most platforms on the market today. TCP/IP is available on the mainframe, UNIX systems, Personal Computers (under PC/MS-DOS, IBM's OS/2, and Microsoft Windows), DEC VAXen, and many others.

Like UNIX, TCP/IP has specific and generic meanings. Specifically, it is the name for a pair of networking protocols; generically, it has come to include a set of that work with TCP/IP including FTP, NNTP, SMTP, SNMP, `rcp`, `rlogin`, `rsh` (or `remsh`), and others. More detail is provided on this topic in Appendix F (Using TCP/IP Networks).

FTP stands for File Transfer Protocol and is used to provide a means of transferring binary or text files between machines. It includes mechanisms for filename translation, record separator translation between systems (some use <LF>, some use <CR>, and some use both <CR> and <LF> together), and ensures that the contents are transmitted properly. Some versions will also provide ASCII to EBCDIC and EBCDIC to ASCII translation.

`rcp` was originally a UNIX command that is now available with many TCP/IP packages. It is like the UNIX `cp` command in that it copies files. The difference is that it can copy files remotely (hence the prefix `r`) instead of just on the local system. The command allows you to specify the local and remote filenames, the user (file owner), and of course, node name (system address). Like FTP, `rcp` ensures that the contents of the file are transmitted properly.

UNIX provides user and system-level security in the use of FTP and `rcp`. Individual users can be allowed or prevented from using these commands. Individual nodes (systems) can also be allowed or prevented from transferring files to or from the local system. The `rcp` command requires the name of a user on the remote system, while FTP supports a mode known as anonymous where there is no user name required. FTP is often used to download files from servers on the Internet like shareware/public domain software, bug fixes from vendors, and documents.

UNIX also supports embedding text data as SYSIN to a command and the transmission of that command to the remote system. By using this mechanism, you are effectively performing a `rcp` command in two steps: moving the command file with the embedded text and then using the `cp` command to store the data local to the remote system.

Other Sources of Tools

Many of the tools that are part of commercially distributed versions UNIX began as user developed and supported software. They were not written by a vendor to be sold, but written by individuals and groups that saw a need and decided to fill it. Not to make money, just to fill the need. Much of the software for UNIX and the Internet were developed this way. Someone wrote it and started distributing it freely. At some point, it became part of UNIX. The Korn and C shells, ex and vi editors are good examples of this.

There are other names for user developed and supported software: freeware, shareware, and public-domain software. Each has different licensing requirements and levels of support. The term user refers to technical professionals who are not vendors, not to unsophisticated end users.

Freeware is software that is generally available for free, and probably has no support available, but you can always try to contact the author for help. If the source code is provided, you are usually free to make modifications but you are not allowed to sell the product to make a profit. If you consider modifying the software, contact the author and discuss it with him or her as he or she may already be making a similar change or would like to include your changes in the next release.

Shareware is software that you are welcome to try for free but a payment is expected by the author if you intend to continue using the product for more than about 30 to 90 days. Some commercial products are distributed as shareware so you can evaluate and then pay if it meets your needs. Some shareware became so popular it has become commercially distributed software. There are now commercial versions of emacs; the official version, maintained by the original author, is GNU-ware. The freeware rules regarding modifications and sale generally apply to shareware.

Public-domain software is code that someone wrote and then gave up all rights to (placed it in the public domain or ownership). You can use the software like freeware; you can copy, change, and even sell it for a profit. Do not expect any support. As a courtesy, you should not attempt to make a profit selling the code and should attempt to contact the original author before making any modifications.

Some of this software is covered under GNU Public Licenses (GPL) and Berkeley style licenses. Software covered by the GPL is referred to as GNU-ware. The GNU (GNU is Not Unix) project is sponsored by the Free Software Foundation (FSF), and is dedicated to developing and distributing user-supported software. If you acquire and use a GNU application, it is effectively freeware; if you modify the code or use it in another application, and then distribute it, you must be willing to release the source code to anyone who asks for it. This concept is also referred to as copy-left, a modified form of copyright, that promotes the growth of software instead of preventing people from copying source. Software covered by a Berkeley style license is also effectively freeware for someone using it. In addition, you use portions of the code and distribute it without having to provide free source code.

You can find user-supported software on the Internet. You can download software by using anonymous ftp to connect to servers that store them. There are companies that sell collections or compendiums of software that you can buy. When you do this, you are buying the distribution (the act of collection and duplication); if the software is shareware, you are still expected to send money to the author if you use the software. GNU-ware is available for free via ftp or you can pay FSF a fee for them to make a copy for you on a medium you can load into your system (i.e., various tape formats). The fee is not for the software, it is to cover the costs of the equipment (tape drives), the physical tape, and for operators to handle the duplication.

Many installations prohibit the use of non-commercial software for a number of reasons. One is the lack of support, another is the lack of someone to hold responsible (understood to mean sue) if there is a problem. There is also the fear of malicious code (Trojan horse, logic bombs, virus code). Even at companies with prohibitions, just about every UNIX system has some software that falls into this category. The `emacs` editor may come from a vendor or be user-supported; the popular scripting language `perl` (Practical Extraction and Reporting Language) is not available commercially.

There is a tremendous wealth of software available over the Internet. Whether you purchase a package or take advantage of user-supported software is up to you, your system administrator, and your organization's rules. But do not rule it out of hand for support and responsibility reasons: This is software that you can modify to meet your specific needs or fix yourself if it fails. These are options not available to you with commercial software.

Summary and Conclusion

The remainder of the book consists of appendices, information that may be very useful but is not central to learning a new operating system. Take a look at them as they may help if you actually move applications from the mainframe to UNIX in addition to moving yourself.

Hopefully this book has been helpful to you. It is a technology book designed to help move you (as opposed to an application or data) from the mainframe to UNIX. But do not stop with this book. UNIX (and networking) has many tools to learn and many features you might not encounter on a mainframe. You may have to invest some time and even some money for books (if you cannot convince your boss to pay) to learn but you will be rewarded. The rewards are not entirely financial (there are plenty of those), because there is a lot of value going home at night and thinking how you picked up some new trick to make your life easier.

UNIX has been compared to an erector set. If you ever played with them or similar building toys as a child, you probably remember how frustrating they were when you were getting started, but as you learned them, it got very exciting as you built the next fire truck or airplane or imaginary object. That is UNIX!

APPENDIX A

COMMON ERROR MESSAGES, CODES, AND UNIX SIGNALS

ERROR MESSAGES

Many of the common error messages were described with the commands that would produce them. Most commands and programs used under UNIX are written in the C programming language. One of the functions available with C is perror which displays a program-supplied message and then the error message assigned to the error encountered. The perror function is called after another function detects an error and returns the error code in the variable errno. These error codes have a mnemonic or variable name assigned to them; these mnemonics appear in the manual pages. The values assigned to the variables may vary between versions of UNIX, which does not cause conflicts because programs compare against the variable names. The C programming language header file (equivalent to a COBOL copybook) errno.h defines the values assigned to each variable. Since the operating system and programs use errno.h, there is consistency.

The typical form of an error message is as follows:

```
command: cause: error message
```

The command will be the command that encountered the error; it can also be the shell you are using (ksh, sh, csh). The cause is often the file or directory name being accessed; the message is telling you what caused the error. And finally, the error message is a short description of the problem.

Message	Meaning
Text file busy	The executable itself is used for swapping; program is running and cannot be changed until it is no longer running. Rename file and copy new version to original name
New password requires a minimum of 1 elapsed week between changes.	Password change—too soon after last
Killed or Process Killed	System ran out of virtual memory and started killing processes so it does not crash
bad status—be /no_such_directory	Usually from `find` command. Unable to find directory mentioned (may disk hardware problem)
arg list too long	Usually from `cp`, `mv`, or `rm` commands. Occurs when a command in the form mv /from/one/directory/some/where/*.file /somewhere/else. The first parameter is expanded—one entry per file in the directory with a fully qualified name. If there are too many, the list is too long. The maximum command line is approximately 4,096 characters

Message	Meaning
: not found	Command does not exist or was typed incorrectly
COMMAND THISISNO NOT FOUND	Command THISISNO does not exist or was typed incorrectly—TSO
cannot access /the/input/FILE	You do not have permissions to the directory that contains this file or the directory does not exist
cannot open /the/input/FILE	You do not have read permissions to this file or the directory that contains it
cannot create /the/new/FILE	You do not have write permissions to replace an existing file or the directory where you are trying to create a new one
no space on device	There is no more space for the file you are creating. The device (filesystem or quota) is full
File too large:	You exceeded a shell limit or quota
No such file or directory	You attempted to access (read, delete, execute, or create) a file or directory that does not exist. Check for typing error.
mv: cannot unlink /the/input/FILE	The `mv` command was unable to remove a link (delete the old file). You have read but not write permissions to the file or the directory that contains it.
ln: cannot link across file systems	You attempted to link a file that exists on a different filesystem than your current. You must create a symbolic link.
ksh: ulimit: exceeds allowable limit	You cannot increase your limits using `ulimit` unless you have root permissions. If you lowered your limits and want to raise them, you have to logout and login again.
rm: /a/file/to directory	You cannot delete a directory with the `rm` command. Use `rmdir` or `rm -r` instead
touch: cannot change times on /a/file /to/CREATE	You do not have write permission to an existing file or the directory that contains it
ksh: /a/file/to/CREATE: file already exists	You attempted to replace a file with noclobber enabled. Delete the file and then replace it or turn noclobber off
cannot access Directory /a	Directory does not exist
mkdir: cannot make directory /a/file/to	Directory already exists

Message	Meaning
mkdir: cannot access /a/file.	You do not have permissions to directory /a to create /file in
mv: cannot mv directories across file systems	You will have to create the directory in the new location, move all the files (using wildcards) to the new location, and then delete the old one. Or you could create a symbolic link connecting the original directory to its new location
find: cannot read dir /etc/fixes: Permission denied	You do not have permission to read the directory
man: nosuch: entry not found man: nosuch: no match found in database	The manual page you requested, nosuch, does not exist. Check your typing.
can't open yourfile in /usr/spool/cron/crontabs directory. No such file or directory	You do not have a crontab cron file so you cannot check the contents. Create one.
at: bad date specification	The time or date you specified for the `at` command was formed incorrectly. Check the manual page for correct format
ksh: my_who: permission denied	You do not have permission to execute my_who. Is it a new file that you forgot to make executable? If it belongs to someone else, he or she may not allow you to use the command.
ksh: c_stuff: bad number	When using the `let` command to perform arithmetic, you put spaces around the asterisk or did not escape it so the shell interpreted as a file wildcard.
ksh: +: syntax error	When using the `let` command to perform arithmetic, you put spaces around the plus sign.
[Extra characters at end of "#" command]	`vi`, `view`, and `ex` produce this message—your $HOME/.profile has comments on the pound sign <#> command. You can ignore this message because everything after the first # is ignored.
"filename" File is read only	`vi`, `view`, and `ex`: You attempted to save (:w, :wq, ZZ, or :x commands) a file that is read-only, either because of permissions or being in browse mode.
No write since last change (:quit! overrides)	`vi`, `view`, and `ex`: You attempted to quit without saving your changes. This message appears even if browse mode to remind you that you have changed something.
Cannot su to "userid" : Authentication is denied.	You did not provide the correct password to become the new user. You may not be allowed to become that user.

ERROR CODES

The following chart is based on the ANSI, POSIX, and X/Open standards that require certain values be stored in the C programming language header file errno.h. In some cases, the standards are enhanced or extended by individual vendors; some of the common ones are included. These values are used within the UNIX operating system to flag errors and can be detected by user programs.

Some of the values differ between versions of UNIX (primarily based on whether the version sticks to the standards or not). The errors 1 to 48 generally are the same between all versions of UNIX. The other actual values are not important since all programs should be using the header file and the error variable itself; they are shown for informational purposes.

Error Variable	Value	Description
EPERM	1	Operation not permitted (not super-user)
ENOENT	2	No such file or directory
ESRCH	3	No such process
EINTR	4	Interrupted system call
EIO	5	I/O error
ENXIO	6	No such device or address
E2BIG	7	Arg list too long
ENOEXEC	8	Exec format error
EBADF	9	Bad file descriptor (number)
ECHILD	10	No child processes
EAGAIN	11	Resource temporarily unavailable (no more processes)
ENOMEM	12	Not enough space (memory)
EACCES	13	Permission denied
EFAULT	14	Bad address
ENOTBLK	15	Block device required
EBUSY	16	Resource (mount device) busy
EEXIST	17	File exists
EXDEV	18	Improper link (cross-device or filesystem)
ENODEV	19	No such device

Error Variable	Value	Description
ENOTDIR	20	Not a directory
EISDIR	21	Is a directory
EINVAL	22	Invalid argument
ENFILE	23	Too many open files in system (file table overflow)
EMFILE	24	Too many open files (for process)
ENOTTY	25	Inappropriate I/O control operation (ìNot a typewriterî)
ETXTBSY	26	Text file busy
EFBIG	27	File too large
ENOSPC	28	No space left on device
ESPIPE	29	Invalid seek
EROFS	30	Read-only filesystem
EMLINK	31	Too many links
EPIPE	32	Broken pipe
EDOM	33	Domain error within math function
ERANGE	34	Result too large (not representable)
ENOMSG	35	No message of desired type
EIDRM	36	Identifier removed
ECHRNG	37	Channel number out of range
EL2NSYNC	38	Level 2 not synchronized
EL3HLT	39	Level 3 halted
EL3RST	40	Level 3 reset
ELNRNG	41	Link number out of range
EUNATCH	42	Protocol driver not attached
ENOCSI	43	No CSI structure available
EL2HLT	44	Level 2 halted
EDEADLK	45	Resource deadlock avoided or deadlock condition

Error Variable	Value	Description
ENOTREADY	46	Device not ready
EWRPROTECT	47	Write-protected media
EFORMAT	48	Unformatted media
ENOTSUP	48	Operation not supported (4.3 BSD)
ENOLCK	49	No record locks available
ENOCONNECT	50	No connection
ESTALE	52	No filesystem
EDIST	53	Old, currently unused (AIX errno)
EWOULDBLOCK	EAGAIN	Operation would block (AIX)
EWOULDBLOCK	54	Operation would block (4.3BSD)
EINPROGRESS	55	Operation now in progress
EALREADY	56	Operation already in progress
		ipc/network software argument errors:
ENOTSOCK	57	Socket operation on non-socket
EDESTADDRREQ	58	Destination address required
EMSGSIZE	59	Message too long
EPROTOTYPE	60	Protocol wrong type for socket
ENOPROTOOPT	61	Protocol not available
EPROTONOSUPPORT	62	Protocol not supported
ESOCKTNOSUPPORT	63	Socket type not supported
EOPNOTSUPP	64	Operation not supported on socket
EPFNOSUPPORT	65	Protocol family not supported
EAFNOSUPPORT	66	Address family not supported by protocol family
EADDRINUSE	67	Address already in use
EADDRNOTAVAIL	68	Can't assign requested address

Error Variable	Value	Description
		ipc/network software operational errors:
ENETDOWN	69	Network is down
ENETUNREACH	70	Network is unreachable
ENETRESET	71	Network dropped connection on reset
ECONNABORTED	72	Software caused connection abort
ECONNRESET	73	Connection reset by peer
ENOBUFS	74	No buffer space available
EISCONN	75	Socket is already connected
ENOTCONN	76	Socket is not connected
ESHUTDOWN	77	Can't send after socket shutdown
ETIMEDOUT	78	Connection timed out
ECONNREFUSED	79	Connection refused
EHOSTDOWN	80	Host is down
EHOSTUNREACH	81	No route to host
ERESTART	82	Restart the system call—used to determine if the system call is restartable
EPROCLIM	83	Too many processes
EUSERS	84	Too many users
ELOOP	85	Too many levels of symbolic links
ENAMETOOLONG	86	Filename too long
ENOTEMPTY	EEXIST	Directory not empty (AIX)
ENOTEMPTY	87	Directory not empty (4.3BSD)
EDQUOT	88	Disk quota exceeded
	89-92	Reserved for future use compatible with AIX PS/2
EREMOTE	93	NFS Item is not local to host

Error Variable	Value	Description
	94-108	reserved for future use compatible with AIX PS/2
ENOSYS	109	Function not implemented POSIX
EMEDIA	110	Disk driver—media surface error
ESOFT	111	Disk driver—I/O completed, but needs relocation
ENOATTR	112	Security—no attribute found
ESAD	113	Security—authentication denied
ENOTRUST	114	Security—not a trusted program
ETOOMANYREFS	115	4.3BSD RENO Too many references: can't splice
EILSEQ	116	Invalid wide character
ECANCELED	117	Asynchronous i/o canceled
		SVR4 STREAMS:
ENOSR	118	Temporarily out of streams resources
ETIME	119	I_STR ioctl (timer) timed out
EBADMSG	120	Wrong message type at stream head
EPROTO	121	STREAMS protocol error
ENODATA	122	No message ready at stream head
ENOSTR	123	Device or filedescriptor is not a stream
ECLONEME	ERESTART	This is the way we clone a stream…
		Convergent Error Returns
EBADE	50	Invalid exchange
EBADR	51	Invalid request descriptor
EXFULL	52	Exchange full
ENOANO	53	No anode
EBADRQC	54	Invalid request code
EBADSLT	55	Invalid slot
EDEADLOCK	56	File locking deadlock error
EBFONT	57	Bad font file fmt

Error Variable	Value	Description
		Shared library problems
ELIBACC	83	Can't access a needed shared lib
ELIBBAD	84	Accessing a corrupted shared lib
ELIBSCN	85	.lib section in a.out corrupted
ELIBMAX	86	Attempting to link in too many libs
ELIBEXEC	87	Attempting to exec a shared library
EILSEQ	88	Illegal byte sequence
ENOSYS	89	Unsupported filesystem operation
ELOOP	90	Symbolic link loop
ERESTART	91	Restartable system call
ESTRPIPE	92	If pipe/FIFO, don't sleep in stream head
ENOTEMPTY	93	Directory not
EUSERS	94	Too many users (for UFS)

UNIX SIGNALS

The following chart is based on the ANSI, POSIX, and X/Open standards that require certain values be stored in the C programming language header file signal.h. In some cases, the standards are enhanced or extended by individual vendors; some of the common ones are included.

Signals are used to communicate special events to programs from the operating system and from other programs. When using the kill command to cancel a program, a signal is generated telling the target program to end.

As with the table of error codes, some of the values differ between versions of UNIX (primarily based on whether the version sticks to the standards or not). The signals 1 to 19 generally are the same between all versions of UNIX, the other actual values are not important since all programs should be using the header file and the signal variable itself.

Mnemonic	Value	Description
SIGMAX	63	Maximum signal number, 0 is not used
SIGHUP	1	Hangup, generated when terminal disconnects
SIGINT	2	Interrupt, generated from terminal special char

Mnemonic	Value	Description
SIGQUIT	3	Quit, generated from terminal special char
SIGILL	4	Illegal instruction (not reset when caught)
SIGTRAP	5	Trace trap (not reset when caught)
SIGABRT	6	Abort process
SIGEMT	7	EMT instruction
SIGFPE	8	Floating point exception
SIGKILL	9	Kill (cannot be caught or ignored)
SIGBUS	10	Bus error (specification exception)
SIGSEGV	11	Segmentation violation
SIGSYS	12	Bad argument to system call
SIGPIPE	13	Write on a pipe with no one to read it
SIGALRM	14	Alarm clock timeout
SIGTERM	15	Software termination signal (from kill)
SIGURG	16	Urgent condition on I/O channel
SIGSTOP	17	Stop (cannot be caught or ignored)
SIGTSTP	18	Interactive stop
SIGCONT	19	Continue (cannot be caught or ignored)
SIGCHLD	20	Sent to parent on child stop or exit
SIGTTIN	21	Background read attempted from control terminal
SIGTTOU	22	Background write attempted to control terminal
SIGIO	23	I/O possible, or completed
SIGXCPU	24	CPU time limit exceeded (see setrlimit())
SIGXFSZ	25	File size limit exceeded (see setrlimit())
SIGMSG	27	Input data is in the HFT ring buffer
SIGWINCH	28	Window size changed
SIGPWR	29	Power-fail restart

Mnemonic	Value	Description
SIGUSR1	30	User defined signal 1
SIGUSR2	31	User defined signal 2
SIGPROF	32	Profiling time alarm (see setitimer)
SIGDANGER	33	System crash imminent; free up some page space
SIGVTALRM	34	Virtual time alarm (see setitimer)
SIGMIGRATE	35	Migrate process (see TCF)
SIGPRE	36	Programming exception
SIGVIRT	37	AIX virtual time alarm
SIGGRANT	60	HFT monitor mode granted
SIGRETRACT	61	HFT monitor mode should be relinquished
SIGSOUND	62	HFT sound control has completed
SIGSAK	63	Secure attention key
		Additional signal names supplied for compatibility, only
SIGIOINT	SIGURG	Printer to backend error signal
SIGAIO	SIGIO	Base lan i/o
SIGPTY	SIGIO	pty i/o
SIGIOT	SIGABRT	Abort (terminate) process—IOT Instruction
SIGCLD	SIGCHLD	Death of child signal (old)
SIGLOST	SIGIOT	Old BSD signal ??
		Valid signal action values
SIG_DFL	0	Use default signal handler
SIG_IGN	1	Ignore signal
SIG_HOLD	2	Not valid as argument to sigaction or sigvec
SIG_CATCH	3	Not valid as argument to sigaction or sigvec
SIG_ERR	-1	Error

APPENDIX B

HINTS AND TECHNIQUES

GDG PROCESSING UNDER UNIX

There are four Korn shell scripts in this section that will allow you to emulate Generation Data Groups (GDG). These will allow you to create a GDG base, create and use GDG members (including relative, G0000V00, and all modes), and delete GDG members. The GDG behaves like the mainframe with one exception—it does not track the +1 generation of a GDG within a job. On the mainframe, the +1 generation of a GDG is the same dataset throughout a job; if a second new generation is needed in the same job, it is referenced as +2. Using these scripts, you use +1 to create a new member, and if you use that member in another step, you reference it as bias 0. If you are converting mainframe JCL, you will have to pay attention to this detail.

The four scripts are gdg_idcm.ksh (replacement for IDCAMS), gdg_use.ksh (create and use GDG members), gdg_del.ksh (delete GDG members), and rcp_gdg.ksh (copy latest GDG from another system).

gdg_idcm.ksh

This Korn shell script is used to create an emulation of the mainframe GDG. It creates the base for the GDG that is used by gdg_use.ksh and gdg_del.ksh, which create and delete generations respectively. The syntax to create a GDG base is:

```
$ pwd↵
/u/dhorvath
$ gdg_idms.ksh NAME_OF.GDG 5↵
$ ls -al NAME_OF.GDG*↵
-rw-r--r--  1 dhorvath users        13 Feb 18 14:13 NAME_OF.GDG.gdgbase
$ more NAME_OF.GDG.gdgbase↵
5  0000 0000
$
```

The name of the GDG file is specified, followed by the maximum number of generations, which, in this case, is five. The shell script imitates the mainframe IDCAMS utility for GDG creation. The base file is created with the name of the GDG file with a suffix of .gdgbase, which contains information about the GDG: the maximum number of generations, the highest generation created or zero otherwise, and the lowest generation number in use. The highest generation will always be updated when a GDG is created and is used when accessing a GDG through a bias (0, +1, -1, etc.). The lowest generation in use is really a comment field and is not always updated.

The shell script follows and will work with most versions of the Korn shell.

```
#! /bin/ksh
# Handler for gdg's independent of any other routine.
# Run as follows:
#    gdg_idcams.ksh fully_qualified/file.name max_generations
#
#   Initialize variables
#
set +o xtrace
gdgbasename=".gdgbase"
goovoo=".G[0-9][0-9][0-9][0-9]V00"
typeset -L4 max_generation min_generation newgeneration oldgeneration
#
#   Determine bias and base file name
#
if [[ $# -eq 2 ]]
then
   max_generations="$2"
   basefile="$1"
else
   echo "improper form" >&2
   exit 10
fi
#
#   Determine if gdgbase file exists
#
gdgfilename="$basefile$gdgbasename"
if [[ -f $gdgfilename ]]
then
   echo "GDG control file (base) already exists.  Delete file first." >&2
   exit 15
fi

echo $max_generations " 0000 0000" > $gdgfilename
exit $?

exit 0
```

gdg_use.ksh

This Korn shell script is used to create new or access existing generations of a GDG. It will create a new generation and return the name with the .G0000V00 suffix with a bias of +1, return the latest name with the G0000V00 suffix with a bias of 0, and return prior version with a bias of -1, -2, etc. If a name with the .G0000V00 suffix is supplied, it will simply return that filename. If the base name of the GDG is supplied alone (no bias, no suffix), it will concatenate all members of the GDG together into a temporary file and return the name of that file. The concatenation occurs in the same order as the mainframe.

The one big difference between these routines and the mainframe GDG is the handling of generation bias. On the mainframe, once a new generation has been created with a +1 bias, it is referenced as the +1 bias throughout the job. When the job finishes, the +1 bias becomes the +0 bias. Using these routines, +1 always creates a new generation; +1 bias becomes +0 bias as soon as the command executes.

The syntax to create a new generation is:

```
$ pwd↵
/u/dhorvath
$ export dd_MYDDNAME=gdg_use.ksh NAME_OF.GDG +1↵
$ echo $dd_MYDDNAME↵
NAME_OF.GDG.G0001V00
$ ls -al NAME_OF.GDG*↵
-rw-r--r--  1 dhorvath users        0 Feb 18 14:29 NAME_OF.GDG.G0001V00
-rw-r--r--  1 dhorvath users       16 Feb 18 14:29 NAME_OF.GDG.gdgbase
$ more NAME_OF.GDG.gdgbase↵
5   0001   0000
$ gdg_use.ksh NAME_OF.GDG +1↵
$
```

An empty file was created with the name NAME_OF.GDG.G0001V00, which was also placed in the environmental variable dd_MYDDNAME for a COBOL program or other command to use. Essentially, this is a DISP=(NEW,CATLG,CATLG). The highest generation field of the gdgbase was updated to one. A second generation was created for further examples.

For a COBOL program or other command to use the latest generation, the bias of zero is used. To use a prior generation, a negative bias is used. Both are shown in the following example:

```
$ export dd_LATEST=gdg_use.ksh NAME_OF.GDG 0↵
$ echo $dd_LATEST↵
NAME_OF.GDG.G0002V00
$ export dd_PRIOR=gdg_use.ksh NAME_OF.GDG -1↵
$ echo $dd_PRIOR↵
NAME_OF.GDG.G0001V00
$ ls -al NAME_OF.GDG*↵
-rw-r--r--  1 dhorvath users        0 Feb 18 14:29 NAME_OF.GDG.G0001V00
-rw-r--r--  1 dhorvath users        0 Feb 18 14:35 NAME_OF.GDG.G0002V00
-rw-r--r--  1 dhorvath users       16 Feb 18 14:35 NAME_OF.GDG.gdgbase
$ more NAME_OF.GDG.gdgbase↵
5   0002   0000
$ gdg_use.ksh NAME_OF.GDG +1↵
$
```

If I want to access all generations at once, I leave the bias off as shown in this example:

```
$ export dd_ALLGDG=gdg_use.ksh NAME_OF.GDG↵
$ echo $dd_ALLGDG↵
```

```
/tmp/GDGcat.2173.960218.144037
$
```

If the full GDG name is specified (including the .G0000V00 suffix), the routine will return that name without any checking as shown:

```
$ export dd_MYGV=gdg_use.ksh NAME_OF.GDG.G0002V00↵
$ echo $dd_MYGV↵
NAME_OF.GDG.G0002V00
$
```

The shell script follows and will work with most versions of the Korn shell

```
#! /bin/ksh
# Handler for gdg's independent of any other routine.
# Run as follows:
#    export dd_DDNAME='use_gdg.ksh fully_qualified/file.name bias'
#
# where bias is 0/+0, 1/+1, or -n (-1 to whatever).  If bias is not specified
# it will attempt to smartly concatenate all members found (assuming that
# a gdgbase file was actually found).  If no gdgbase file was found, then
# this is a flat file and the name is passed as-is.
#
# @ @ @ @ @ @ @ @ @ @ @ @ @ @ @ @ @ @ @ @ @ @ @ @ @ @ @ @
#
#   Subroutines
#
GET_GDG_VALUES ()
{
   if [[ -f $gdgfilename ]]
   then
      if [[ -w $gdgfilename ]]
      then
         exec 3< $gdgfilename
         read -u3 generations max_generation min_generation
         if [[ $? -ne 0 ]]
         then
            echo "invalid gdg base file " >&2
            exit 20
         fi
         return 1
      else
         echo "gdg exists but bad permission" >&2
         exit 21
      fi
```

```
   else
      return 0
   fi
}
#
# @ @ @ @ @ @ @ @ @ @ @ @ @ @ @ @ @ @ @ @ @ @ @ @ @ @ @ @ @
#
#
#   Initialize variables
#
set +o xtrace
gdgbasename=".gdgbase"
goovoo=".G[0-9][0-9][0-9][0-9]V00"
typeset -RZ4 max_generation min_generation newgeneration oldgeneration
#
#   Determine bias and base file name
#
if [[ $# -eq 1 ]]
then
   bias=""
   basefile="$1"
else if [[ $# -eq 2 ]]
then
   bias=${2#[+]}           # strip off "+" from "+1" bias (if included)
   basefile="$1"
else
   echo "improper form" >&2
   exit 10
fi fi
#
#   Determine if gdgbase file exists
#
gdgfilename="$basefile$gdgbasename"
GET_GDG_VALUES; is_a_gdg=$?
if [[ $is_a_gdg -eq 0 ]]
then
#    this is not a gdg or does not exist, echo filename only and exit
   echo $basefile
   exit 0
fi
#
#   different processing for each bias type
#
#
```

```
#   bias = "": If name contains GnnnnV00, echo that name back directly.
#             (actually is-GDG test will fail because of GnnnnV00 and
#              will echo out the filename, so this code is extra...)
#              Otherwise, attempt to do a smart concatenation of all
#              generations in reverse order into a file "/tmp/f<pid><time>"
#              and echo *that* name back.
if [[ $bias = "" ]]
then
#     "handle no bias - check for GnnnnV00 or concatenate"
   if [[ $basefile = *"$goovoo" ]]
   then
      echo $basefile
      exit 0
   else
#        get list of GDG elements and concatenate them all into temporary file;
#         return the temporary name to be used.
      list_of_gdg_elements='ls -R -C $basefile$goovoo'
      temp_filename="/tmp/GDGcat."$$".'date "+%Y%m%d.%H%M%S"'"
      cat $list_of_gdg_elements > $temp_filename
      echo $temp_filename
      exit 0
   fi
#
#   bias = 0 : build a filename with the maximum generation and verify
#              that the file exists.  If so, echo filename back. Done!
else if [[ $bias -eq 0 ]]
then
   fullfilename="$basefile".G"$max_generation"V00
   if [[ -f $fullfilename ]]
   then
#        Bias 0, file name built, echo it and exit - we're done!
      echo $fullfilename
      exit 0
   else
      echo "Bias zero file does not exist - ERROR" $fullfilename >&2
      exit 30
   fi
#
#   bias = 1 : build the next filename (generation number), verify the
#              file does not exist, touch it, and then store the new
#              value back in the GDG control file.
else if [[ $bias -eq 1 ]]
then
#     handle +1 processing
   newgeneration='expr $max_generation + 1'
   fullfilename="$basefile".G"$newgeneration"V00
```

```
   if [[ -f $fullfilename ]]
   then
      echo "Bias +1 file already exists, ERROR " $fullfilename >&2
      exit 45
   else
#     Bias +1, filename built, save, clean up old, echo it and exit - we're done!
      oldgeneration='expr $max_generation - $generations + 1'
      min_generation='expr $oldgeneration + 1'
      if [[ $min_generation -lt 0 ]]
      then
         min_generation=0
      fi
      echo $generations " " $newgeneration " " $min_generation > $gdgfilename
      oldfullfilename="$basefile".G"$oldgeneration"V00
      rm -f $oldfullfilename
      touch $fullfilename
      echo $fullfilename
      exit 0
   fi
#
#  bias < 0 : build a filename with the maximum generation minus the
#             value of that bias and verify that the file exists.  If
#             so, echo filename back. Done!
else if [[ $bias -lt 0 ]]
then
#     handle -1...-n processing
   newgeneration='expr $max_generation + $bias'  # bias is negative
   fullfilename="$basefile".G"$newgeneration"V00
   if [[ -f $fullfilename ]]
   then
#        Bias -n, filename built, echo it and exit - we're done!
      echo $fullfilename
      exit 0
   else
      echo "Bias " $bias " file does not exist - ERROR" $fullfilename >&2
      exit 40
   fi
else
#
#  bias = ? : Unknown or invalid bias; just bail out.
   echo "Invalid GDG Bias " $bias >&2
   exit 35
fi fi fi fi

exit 0
```

gdg_del.ksh

This Korn shell script is used to delete an existing generation of a GDG. It can delete a specific bias (0, -1, -2, etc.), a specific generation if the .G0000V00 suffix is included, or will delete all generations if just the GDG name is specified. The syntax to delete the latest generation is:

```
$ pwd↵
/u/dhorvath
$ gdg_del.ksh NAME_OF.GDG 0↵
$ ls -al NAME_OF.GDG*↵
-rw-r--r--  1 dhorvath users       0 Feb 18 14:29 NAME_OF.GDG.G0001V00
-rw-r--r--  1 dhorvath users      16 Feb 18 14:35 NAME_OF.GDG.gdgbase
$ more NAME_OF.GDG.gdgbase↵
5   0001   0001
```

A bias of +1 is invalid since it is not possible to delete a generation not yet created. To delete a specific generation, the .G0000V00 suffix is used instead of the bias as shown:

```
$ gdg_del.ksh NAME_OF.GDG.G0001V00↵
$ ls -al NAME_OF.GDG*↵
-rw-r--r--  1 dhorvath users      16 Feb 18 14:37 NAME_OF.GDG.gdgbase
$ more NAME_OF.GDG.gdgbase↵
5   0000   0000
```

To delete all generations, only use the name of the GDG. All generations will be deleted but not the gdgbase file. All generations are gone after the following example:

```
$ gdg_del.ksh NAME_OF.GDG↵
$ ls -al NAME_OF.GDG*↵
-rw-r--r--  1 dhorvath users      16 Feb 18 14:39 NAME_OF.GDG.gdgbase
$ more NAME_OF.GDG.gdgbase↵
5   0000   0000
```

The shell script follows and will work with most versions of the Korn shell.

```
#! /bin/ksh
# Handler for gdg's independent of any other routine.
# Run as follows:
#    del_gdg.ksh fully_qualified/file.name bias
#
# where bias is 0/+0, 1/+1, or -n (-1 to whatever).  if bias is not specified
# it will delete  all members found (assuming that
# a gdgbase file was actually found).  If no gdgbase file was found, then
# this is a flat file and the name is passed as-is.
#
# @ @ @ @ @ @ @ @ @ @ @ @ @ @ @ @ @ @ @ @ @ @ @ @ @ @ @ @ @
#
#   Subroutines
#
```

```
GET_GDG_VALUES ()
{
   if [[ -f $gdgfilename ]]
   then
      if [[ -w $gdgfilename ]]
      then
         exec 3< $gdgfilename
         read -u3 generations max_generation min_generation
         if [[ $? -ne 0 ]]
         then
            echo "invalid gdg base file " >&2
            exit 20
         fi
         return 1
      else
         echo "gdg exists but bad permission" >&2
         exit 21
      fi
   else
      return 0
   fi
}
#
# @ @ @ @ @ @ @ @ @ @ @ @ @ @ @ @ @ @ @ @ @ @ @ @ @ @ @ @ @
#
#
#   Initialize variables
#
set +o xtrace
gdgbasename=".gdgbase"
goovoo=".G[0-9][0-9][0-9][0-9]V00"
typeset -RZ4 max_generation min_generation newgeneration oldgeneration
#
#   Determine bias and base filename
#
if [[ $# -eq 1 ]]
then
   bias=""
   basefile="$1"
else if [[ $# -eq 2 ]]
then
   bias=${2#[+]}
   basefile="$1"
else
   echo "improper form" >&2
   exit 10
```

```
fi fi
#
#   Determine if gdgbase file exists
#
gdgfilename="$basefile$gdgbasename"
GET_GDG_VALUES; is_a_gdg=$?
if [[ $is_a_gdg -eq 0 ]]
then
#    this is not a gdg or does not exist, echo filename only and exit
   echo $basefile
   exit 0
fi
#
#   different processing for each bias type
#
#
#   bias = "": Delete all generations in reverse order
if [[ $bias = "" ]]
then
#     "handle no bias - delete all"
#     get list of GDG elements and remove them
   list_of_gdg_elements='ls -R -C $basefile$goovoo'
   echo $generations " " $max_generation " " $max_generation > $gdgfilename
   rm -f $list_of_gdg_elements
   exit $?
#
#   bias = 0 : remove the current generation (max)
else if [[ $bias -eq 0 ]]
then
   fullfilename="$basefile".G"$max_generation"V00
   if [[ -f $fullfilename ]]
   then
      newgeneration='expr $max_generation - 1'
      if [[ $newgeneration -lt 0 ]]
      then
         newgeneration=0000
      fi
      if [[ $newgeneration -lt $min_generation ]]
      then
         min_generation=$newgeneration
      fi
      echo $generations " " $newgeneration " " $min_generation > $gdgfilename

      rm -f $fullfilename
      exit $?
   else
```

```
      echo "Bias zero file does not exist - ERROR" $fullfilename >&2
      exit 30
   fi
#
#   bias = 1 : Not allowed - error.
else if [[ $bias -eq 1 ]]
then
   echo "Bias +1 file deletion not allowed, ERROR " $fullfilename >&2
   exit 45
#
#   bias < 0 : delete that version.
else if [[ $bias -lt 0 ]]
then
#     handle -1...-n processing
   newgeneration='expr $max_generation + $bias'  # bias is negative
   fullfilename="$basefile".G"$newgeneration"V00
   if [[ -f $fullfilename ]]
   then
      rm -f $fullfilename
      exit $?
   else
      echo "Bias " $bias " file does not exist - ERROR" $fullfilename >&2
      exit 40
   fi
else
#
#   bias = ? : Unknown or invalid bias; just bail out.
   echo "Invalid GDG Bias " $bias >&2
   exit 35
fi fi fi fi

exit 0
```

rcp_gdg.ksh

The following script will rcp the lastest member of a GDG from another computer:

```
#! /bin/ksh
# Shell script to grab gdgbase from another system and use the
# information to figure out the latest generation and then
# grab that file.
#
set -o xtrace
typeset -Z4 gdgcurr
```

```
#--------------------------------------------------------------------
# pull over the gdgbase from the other box
#--------------------------------------------------------------------
rcp other_user@other_box:/path/name/FILE.gdgbase /tmp/$$.gdgbase
read gdglimit gdgcurr < /tmp/$$.gdgbase
#--------------------------------------------------------------------
# pull over GDG latest generation from other box
#--------------------------------------------------------------------
rcp other_user@other_box:/path/name/FILE.G$gdgcurr''V00 \
   /path/name/FILE.other_box
rm /tmp/$$.gdgbase
```

Converting ASA Formatted Print Output

UNIX does not provide a facility to print files that contain the ANSI printer control characters usually produced in output to be printed on the mainframe. To handle those files, the following program, filter_asa.c, has been provided. This program will run in two different modes. If an input file is specified, it will open that file, convert the ASA printer control to ASCII control characters, and write the output to stdout. If no file is specified, it will take stdin, perform the conversion, and write the output to stdout. In this way, it works as a filter with stdin being redirected through a pipe to use the output of another program.

The program can work on sequential files with a record length of 133 and no record separators or on line-sequential files with a record length of 134 and separator at the end of each record. This is done through the use of links. If the program name is filter_asa, it will process a sequential file. If the name is filter_line_asa, it will process line sequential files. If it runs as some other name, it will behave as though it were filter_asa.

Compile this program and save it as filter_asa. Then create a link with the name filter_line_asa. There will be only one copy of the executable but it will be referenced as two different names.

To use the program with an existing file:

```
$ filter_asa SEQUENTIAL_ASA_FILE | lp↵
        or
$ filter_line_asa LINE_SEQUENTIAL_ASA | lp↵
$
```

To use the program as a filter from another command, pipe the output of the first command into this program:

```
$ our_command | filter_asa | lp↵
        or
$ our_command2 | filter_line_asa | lp↵
$
```

filter_asa.c

```
#include <stdio.h>
#include <stdlib.h>
#include <errno.h>

/* compile this program and create a link:                              */
/*    filter_asa expects a sequential file DCB=(LRECL=133,RECFM=FBA)    */
/*    filter_line_asa expects a sequential file with <nl> on each line */

main(int argc, char *argv[])
{
   FILE *in_stream;
   char line[255];
   char in_file[255];
   int line_length;

   if (argc > 0 && strcmp(argv[1], "-?") == 0)
   {
      printf(" Usage is: \n  filter_asa [Mainframe_print_format_file] \n");
      printf("        or: \n  something | filter_asa \n");
     printf(" Usage is: \n  filter_line_asa [Mainframe_print_format_file] \n");
      printf("        or: \n  something | filter_line_asa \n\n");
      printf("        You should redirect output to a pipe or file to print\n");
      printf("        filter_asa expects a sequential file DCB=LRECL=133\n");
      printf("        filter_line_asa expects a file with record seperators\n");
      exit(99);
   }

   if (argc == 2)
   {
      strcpy (in_file, argv[1]);

      in_stream = fopen (in_file, "r");
      if (in_stream == NULL)
      {
         perror (" Unable to open input file:");
         exit(99);
      }
   }
   else
      in_stream = stdin;

   if (strcmp(argv[0], "filter_line_asa") == 0)
      line_length = 135;   /* line sequential */
   else
```

```
        line_length = 134;    /*  Sequential */

    fgets (line, 134, in_stream);

    while (!ferror (in_stream) && !feof (in_stream) )
    {

        line[133] = '\0';

        if (line[0] == '1')            /* new page */
        {
            printf ("\n\0x0C");
        } else if (line[0] == ' ')     /* single space */
        {
            printf ("\n");
        } else if (line[0] == '0')     /* double space */
        {
            printf ("\n\n");
        } else if (line[0] == '/')      /* triple space */
        {
            printf ("\n\n\n");
        } else if (line[0] == '+')      /* stay on same line */
        {
            ;            /* no op */
        } else if (line[0] != '-')      /* invalid ? */
        {
            errno = 0;
            fprintf (stderr, "%s: Invalid character in ASA control: %c\n",
                argv[0], line[0]);
        }

        printf ("%-132.132s", &line[1]);    /* print the data out */

        fgets (line, 134, in_stream);
    }
    printf("\n\0x0c");
    if (argc == 2) fclose (in_stream);
    exit 0;
}
```

MAINFRAME TAPE PROCESSING

When processing mainframe tapes under UNIX, there are a number of items on the tape that behave like files to UNIX. See Figure 2.6 for a graphic of these items.

To get a file from a tape, the physical mount is performed (by you, an operator, or the system administrator depending on the size of your installation), and a command is issued or program run that accesses the proper device. A plain tape, equivalent to a mainframe LABEL=(,NL) is no problem. Tapes with labels (LABEL=(,SL)—the default) are more difficult to process.

The dd command or something locally developed can be used. A dd command to read one file from a tape (with no conversion) is shown in the following example:

```
dd if=/dev/rmtX.1 of=disk_name bs=32767
```

This will copy the file from the tape to the disk file. Remember, for some versions of UNIX, /dev/rmtX.1 is the way to specify a tape drive so it does not rewind when the command is complete (AIX is one of them). If you keep issuing this command with new disk filenames, you will eventually read all the files off the tape. When you get two or three zero length files or get a read error, that is a good indication that all data from the tape has been read. Another way is to convert each file on the tape from EBCDIC to ASCII and check the information contained therein. The following dd command read and convert:

```
dd if=/dev/rmtX.1 of=disk_name conv=ascii bs=32767
```

This works for text files and files with binary data if all you want to do is scan the contents (to ensure you have the correct file) without processing it. See Appendix C (Data Conversion, ASCII and EBCDIC Charts) for more information on the dd command.

As shown in Figure 2.6, most mainframe tapes have volume labels (describing the tape itself), file labels (describing the file), and end-of-file labels. If a file does not fit on a single tape, an end-of-volume label is written, and the file label on the next tape notes that it is the second tape in the set.

UNIX does not give special meaning to labels. As far as it is concerned, tape labels are just more files on the tape, this is the same as coding LABEL=(,NL) on the mainframe. In processing a labeled tape, multiple files must be read to process the labels and actual data files.

The following example has four mainframe datasets stored on two tapes. The third dataset starts on the first tape and finishes on the second; the final dataset resides on the second tape. The original data was in EBCDIC and converted to ASCII using the dd command.

1. First Tape, First Header
   ```
   VOL1123456
   HDR1.1ST.DATASET.HERE12345600010001000400 YYJJJ000000000000IBM OS/VS 370
   HDR2F32111005354OJOBNAME1/STEPNO1      B    88638
   ```
2. Data file is here real name is GROUP.APP.PROGRM.NAME.1ST.DATASET.HERE
3. First Tape, First Trailer
   ```
   EOF1.1ST.DATASET.HERE12345600010001000400 YYJJJ000000000121IBM OS/VS 370
   EOF2F32111005354OJOBNAME1/STEPNO1      B    88638
   ```
4. First Tape, Second Header
   ```
   HDR1.2ND.DATASET.HERE12345600010002000400 YYJJJ000000000000IBM OS/VS 370
   HDR2F32111005354OJOBNAME1/STEPNO2      B    88638
   ```
5. Data file is here real name is GROUP.APP.PROGRM.NAME.2ND.DATASET.HERE (empty)
6. First Tape, Second Trailer
   ```
   EOF1.2ND.DATASET.HERE12345600010002000400 YYJJJ000000000000IBM OS/VS 370
   EOF2F32111005354OJOBNAME1/STEPNO2      B    88638
   ```

7. First Tape, Third Header
   ```
   HDR1.3RD.DATASET.HERE1234560001000300040 0 YYJJJ0000000000000IBM OS/VS 370
   HDR2F164480051240JOBNAME1/STEPNO3       B    88638
   ```
8. Data file is here real name is GROUP.APP.PROGRM.NAME.3RD.DATASET.HERE
9. First Tape, Third Trailer—tape crosses physical tapes
   ```
   EOV1.3RD.DATASET.HERE1234560001000300040 0 YYJJJ0000000005802IBM OS/VS 370
   EOV2F164480051240JOBNAME1/STEPNO3       B    88638
   ```
10. Second Tape, First Header
   ```
   VOL1654321
   HDR1.3RD.DATASET.HERE1234560002000300040 0 YYJJJ0000000000000IBM OS/VS 370
   HDR2F164480051241JOBNAME1/STEPNO3       B    88638
   ```
11. Data file is continued here real name is GROUP.APP.PROGRM.NAME.3RD.DATASET.HERE
12. Second Tape, First Trailer
   ```
   EOF1.3RD.DATASET.HERE1234560002000300040 0 YYJJJ0000000003558IBM OS/VS 370
   EOF2F164480051241JOBNAME1/STEPNO3       B    88638
   ```
13. Second Tape, Second Header
   ```
   HDR1.4TH.DATASET.HERE6543210001000400010 0 YYJJJ0000000000000IBM OS/VS 370
   HDR2F164480051240JOBNAME1/STEPNO4       B    88638
   ```
14. Data file is continued here real name is GROUP.APP.PROGRM.NAME.4TH.DATASET.HERE
15. Second Tape, Second Trailer
   ```
   EOF1.4TH.DATASET.HERE6543210001000400010 0 YYJJJ0000000000346IBM OS/VS 370
   EOF2F164480051240JOBNAME1/STEPNO4       B    88638
   ```

123456 is the VOLSER of the first tape, 654321 is VOLSER of second tape. YYJJJ is date tape was created. IBM OS/VS 370 is the system that created the tape. JOBNAME1 is the job and STEPNO1 through STEPNO4 is the job step that created the file. 12345600020003 in #10 and #12 (on tape 654321) shows that it is the second part (physical volume) of a file that began on tape 123456 and it is the third file written to this tape set (tape or collection of tapes). The datasetname stored in the header/trailers is the right-most 17 characters of the name, everything to the left is omitted. The numbers proceeding the IBM... are the number of blocks written to the tape in this file (in the EOF1 and EOV1 records). That is how we know that the dataset GROUP.APP.PROGRM.NAME.2ND.DATASET.HERE on line 5 was empty—(because the number was zero). The number after the F (for Fixed blocks) on HDR2/EOF2/EOV2 is the blocksize (32111 for the first and second, 16448 for the remaining datasets). The numbers before the JOBNAME is the number of the job that created the file (53540).

VOL1 is a volume header record (label)
HDR1 and HDR2 contain information about the file—at beginning
EOF1 and EOF2 contain information about the file—at end (matches to HDR1 and HDR2)
EOV1 and EOV2 contain information about the file—at the end of a physical volume when it takes more than one tape (matches to HDR1 and HDR2).

I was unable to find any software that would handle mainframe tape and datasets that cross physical tapes. That does not mean there are none, just that I (and co-workers) could not find them. If I knew there would be enough market demand for this type of product, I would develop the package myself. I have processed enough of these by hand, I think I could code it without great difficulty!

Comparing Sequential Files

The UNIX comparison commands, cmp, diff, etc., cannot handle the typical fixed record length sequential COBOL files. This is especially true if the files contain binary data. For line sequential files that contain text only, the UNIX commands work fine. You could convert the sequential files into line sequential or use the compare_data.c program below.

compare_data.c

This program takes the name of two sequential or line sequential files, the record length of the files, and the name of an output file. The two input files will be compared on a byte-by-byte and record-by-record basis. Any differences will be written to the output file in the format:

```
[1:recnum] Record from the first file
[2:recnum] Record from the second file
----------------------------^^^^^^^^^^^
```

The first line is the record from the first file with a 12-byte prefix showing that it is the first file and the record number within the file. The second line is the record from the second file with a similar prefix. The last line is a row of minus signs <-> with circumflexes <^> where there are differences. The program will send the following to stdout:

```
Records read in First  File file1 = 131
Records read in Second File file2 = 4177
Total records that differed = 4177
```

If there are any errors (missing files, unable to allocate buffers, unable to write to output), they will be written to stderr. If the files are different sizes, the program will report differences on every record in the larger file once the smaller runs out. The record number will not change on the smaller file.

Compile this program and save it as compare_data. If you get an error message that reports the macro TRUE is undefined, uncomment the line that looks like:

```
/*  #define TRUE  !FALSE */
```

by removing the first four and last two characters on the line.

To compare the files file1 and file2 with a record length of 32 and store the output in cmp_out, use the program as follows:

```
$ compare_data file1 file2 32 cmp_out↵
```

```
#include <stdio.h>
#include <memory.h>
#include <stdlib.h>
#include <string.h>
#include <errno.h>
```

```
/* compare_data.c - this program compares two files and puts */
/*                  the results in a comparison file with    */
/*                  flags to show where the records are       */
/*                  different.                                */


#define OUTPUT_PREFIX_SIZE 12
#define RECORD_SEP_LINE '-'
#define FALSE 0
/*  remove first 4 and last 2 characters on next line to uncomment */
/*  #define TRUE  !FALSE */

void display_usage(void);

int main(int argc, char *argv[])
{
   FILE  *file1, *file2, *cmp_file;
   int   loop_index, result = 0, lrecl = 0, outbuf_len = 0;
   long  diff_recs = 0, num_recs1 = 0, num_recs2 = 0;
   int   eof_in1 = FALSE, eof_in2 = FALSE, files_differ = FALSE;
   char  *inbuf1, *inbuf2, *outbuf, *sepbuf;

   if (argc != 5)
   {
      display_usage ();
   }

   /****************************************************************/
   /* Convert and validate record length                           */
   /****************************************************************/
   if ((lrecl = atoi( argv[3] )) == 0)
   {
      fprintf (stderr, "Invalid Logical Record Length = %s\n\n", argv[3] );
      display_usage();
   }
   /****************************************************************/
   /* Open input and output files                                  */
   /****************************************************************/
   if((file1 = fopen( argv[1], "rb" )) == NULL)
   {
      perror ("Unable to open first file");
      exit( errno );
   }
   if((file2 = fopen( argv[2], "rb" )) == NULL)
   {
      perror ("Unable to open second file");
```

```
      exit( errno );
   }
   if((cmp_file = fopen( argv[4], "wb" )) == NULL)
   {
      perror ("Unable to open comparison file");
      exit( errno );
   }
   /*************************************************************/
   /* Allocate buffers for input files, compare output, and      */
   /* comparison separator line.                                  */
   /*************************************************************/
   inbuf1 = malloc( lrecl );
   if (inbuf1 == NULL)
   {
      perror ("Unable to allocate buffer to read first file");
      exit( errno );
   }
   memset( inbuf1, 0, lrecl );
   inbuf2 = malloc( lrecl );
   if (inbuf2 == NULL)
   {
      perror ("Unable to allocate buffer to read second file");
      exit( errno );
   }
   memset( inbuf2, 0, lrecl );
   outbuf_len = lrecl + OUTPUT_PREFIX_SIZE;
   outbuf = malloc( outbuf_len );
   if (outbuf == NULL)
   {
      perror ("Unable to allocate buffer for output file");
      exit( errno );
   }
   memset( outbuf, ' ', outbuf_len);
   sepbuf = malloc( outbuf_len );
   if (sepbuf == NULL)
   {
      perror ("Unable to allocate buffer for output file (separator)");
      exit( errno );
   }
   memset( sepbuf, RECORD_SEP_LINE, outbuf_len );
   /*************************************************************/
   /* Read the first records from the two input files to setup   */
   /* for the comparison and read loops.                          */
   /*************************************************************/
   result = fread( inbuf1, 1, lrecl, file1 );
   if (feof( file1 ))
```

```
{
   fprintf (stderr, "First file empty\n");
   eof_in1 = TRUE;
}
else if (ferror (file1))
{
   perror ("Error reading first file");
   exit( errno );
}
else
{
   num_recs1++;
}

result = fread( inbuf2, 1, lrecl, file2 );
if (feof( file2 ))
{
   fprintf (stderr, "Second file empty\n");
   eof_in2 = TRUE;
}
else if (ferror (file2))
{
   perror ("Error reading second file");
   exit( errno );
}
else
{
   num_recs2++;
}
/**************************************************************/
/* Read loop.                                                 */
/**************************************************************/
while ( !eof_in1 || !eof_in2  )
{
   /**************************************************************/
   /* Compare the two records, character by character           */
   /**************************************************************/
   files_differ = FALSE;
   for (loop_index = 0; loop_index < lrecl; loop_index++)
   {
      if (*(inbuf1 + loop_index) != *(inbuf2 + loop_index))
      {
         files_differ= TRUE;                    /* yes, records differ */
         *(sepbuf + loop_index + OUTPUT_PREFIX_SIZE) = '^';
                                                /* flag byte different */
      }
```

```
}
if (files_differ)   /* write out records from each file and separator */
{
   memset( outbuf, 0, outbuf_len );
   sprintf( outbuf, "[1:%7.7d] ", num_recs1 );
   memcpy( outbuf+OUTPUT_PREFIX_SIZE, inbuf1, lrecl );
   result = fwrite( outbuf, 1, outbuf_len, cmp_file );
   if (ferror( cmp_file ))
   {
      perror ("Unable to write to output file (input 1)");
      exit( errno );
   }
   memset( outbuf, 0, outbuf_len );
   sprintf( outbuf, "[2:%7.7d] ", num_recs2 );
   memcpy( outbuf+OUTPUT_PREFIX_SIZE, inbuf2, lrecl );
   result = fwrite( outbuf, 1, outbuf_len, cmp_file );
   if (ferror( cmp_file ))
   {
      perror ("Unable to write to output file (file 2)");
      exit( errno );
   }
   /*  Separator line.  */
   result = fwrite( sepbuf, 1, outbuf_len, cmp_file );
   if (ferror( cmp_file ))
   {
      perror ("Unable to write to output file (separator)");
      exit( errno );
   }
   memset( sepbuf, RECORD_SEP_LINE, outbuf_len );

   diff_recs++;               /* count of differences */
}
/************************************************************/
/* Read first file records until EOF, then bypass.          */
/************************************************************/
if (!eof_in1)
{
   result = fread( inbuf1, 1, lrecl, file1 );
   if (ferror( file1 ))
   {
      perror ("Error reading first input file");
      exit( errno );
   }
   else if (feof( file1 ))
   {
      memset( inbuf1, 0, lrecl );
```

```
            eof_in1 = TRUE;
         }
         else
         {
            num_recs1++;
         }
      }
      /***********************************************************/
      /* Read second file records until EOF, then bypass.        */
      /***********************************************************/
      if (!eof_in2)
      {
         result = fread( inbuf2, 1, lrecl, file2 );
         if (ferror( file2 ))
         {
            perror ("Error reading second input file");
            exit( errno );
         }
         else if (feof( file2 ))
         {
            memset( inbuf2, 0, lrecl );
            eof_in2 = TRUE;
         }
         else
         {
            num_recs2++;
         }
      }
   }  /* end while */

   fclose( file1 );
   fclose( file2 );
   fclose( cmp_file );

   printf ("Records read in First  File %s = %d\n", argv[1], num_recs1 );
   printf ("Records read in Second File %s = %d\n", argv[2], num_recs2 );
   printf ("Total records that differed = %d\n", diff_recs );
}

void display_usage(void)
{
   printf ("Usage is: \n compare_data file1 file2 lrecl cmp_file\n" );
   printf("       where:\n");
   printf("              file1 and file2 are fixed length sequential or \n");
   printf("                                line sequential files.\n");
   printf("              lrecl is the record length of the original file\n");
```

```
    printf("             cmp_file will contain any miscompares.\n");
    printf("       The lrecl of the cmp_file is 12 higher than the input.\n");
    exit(90);
}
```

Converting Sequential Files to Line Sequential

Many COBOL files are in sequential format with a fixed record length. Each record is the same number of bytes and because they are the same size, there is no need for a record separator character. However, the UNIX tools cannot deal with data that does not have record separators. To help you out, there are two methods available depending on the file being converted: a single record or one-to-many records. A single record can be converted with the first method, which is quick and simple, or with the more complicated method used for larger files. A file that contains one-to-many records requires a more complicated conversion method because there may be multiple records.

Converting a Single Record Fixed Sequential File to Line Sequential

Since the UNIX commands are designed to work with line sequential files, fixed sequential files are difficult to work with. There is a simple way to convert a fixed sequential file that has only one record into a line sequential file that UNIX commands can work with. There are two different results: a new file and an environmental variable. The following example will create a line sequential file:

```
$ (cat sequential_file; echo "") > line_sequential_file↵
```

To create an environmental variable, use the following:

```
$ env_var=$(cat sequential_file; echo "")↵
```

To use this method with a UNIX command, such as a cut command to extract a specific field (through column numbers), you can use the following:

```
$ env_var=$((cat sequential_file; echo "")|cut -b129-134)↵
```

The echo command is very important here. It outputs a new line character, which is required to make the file line sequential.

add_newline.c

This program takes the name of the input sequential file, the name of a line sequential file to create, and the record length of the sequential file. The line sequential file will have a record length 1 byte higher than the sequential file to hold the record separator (the newline character). If any of the command line parameters are missing or invalid, the program will report the problem. If a file exists with name of the line sequential file, it will be replaced by this program without warning (unless there is a security violation).

Compile this program and save it as add_newline. To convert the file sequential_file with a record length of 32 to line sequential and save it as new_line_seq_file, use the program as follows:

```
$ add_newline sequential_file new_line_seq_file 32↵
```

```
#include <stdio.h>
#include <stdlib.h>
#include <errno.h>
#include <memory.h>

/* add_newline.c - this program appends a newline character */
/*                 to a sequential file making it line-     */
/*                 sequential.  It will work with binary    */
/*                 files but the other UNIX tools may not.  */
void display_usage(void);


int main(int argc, char *argv[])
{
   FILE *in_stream, *out_stream;
   char *input_buffer;
   char in_file[255], out_file[255];
   int lrecl;
   size_t bytes_read, bytes_written;

   if (argc == 0 || (argc > 0 && strcmp(argv[1], "-?") == 0) ||
       argc != 4)
   {
      display_usage();
   }

   strcpy (in_file, argv[1]);

   in_stream = fopen (in_file, "rb");
   if (in_stream == NULL)
   {
      perror (" Unable to open input file:");
      exit(99);
   }

   strcpy (out_file, argv[2]);

   out_stream = fopen (out_file, "wb");
   if (out_stream == NULL)
   {
      perror (" Unable to open output file:");
      exit(98);
   }
```

```
    if ((lrecl = atoi( argv[3] )) == 0)
    {
       printf( "Invalid Logical Record Length = %s\n\n", argv[3] );
       display_usage();
    }

    input_buffer = malloc( lrecl + 1 );
    if (input_buffer == NULL)
    {
       perror ("Unable to allocate buffer");
       exit( errno );
    }
    memset( input_buffer, 0, lrecl + 1 );

    bytes_read = fread (input_buffer, 1, lrecl, in_stream);

    while (!ferror (in_stream) && !feof (in_stream) &&
           bytes_read == lrecl)
    {
       input_buffer[lrecl] = '\n';
       bytes_written = fwrite (input_buffer, 1, lrecl + 1, out_stream);

       if ((bytes_written != lrecl + 1) || ferror (out_stream))
       {
          perror ("Unable to write to output file");
          exit (errno);
       }

       bytes_read = fread (input_buffer, 1, lrecl, in_stream);
    }

    if (!feof(in_stream) && bytes_read != lrecl)
    {
       fprintf(stderr, "File is not even multiple of %d bytes\n",
               lrecl);
       exit (96);
    }
    fclose (in_stream);
    fclose (out_stream);
    exit (0);
}

void display_usage(void)
{
      printf(" Usage is: \n  add_newline seq_file line_seq_file lrecl\n");
      printf("       where:\n");
```

```
     printf("            seq_file is a plain sequential file.\n");
     printf("            line_seq_file is the file to create.\n");
     printf("            lrecl is the record length of the original file\n");
     printf("      Adds new line character to end of sequential records\n");
     printf("      converting them from sequential to line-sequential\n");
     exit(90);
}
```

APPENDIX C

DATA CONVERSION, ASCII, AND EBCDIC CHARTS

DATA CONVERSION—AN OVERVIEW

One of the biggest problems with moving from a mainframe to a UNIX box is the character set translation. The mainframe uses EBCDIC while most UNIX systems use ASCII. Not only are the values different, but the general structure is different: EBCDIC uses 8 bits, ASCII officially uses 7. PCs implement Extended-ASCII using 8 bits with extra (or extended) characters; most UNIX systems use the standard ASCII.

If you are working in ASCII alone, there are no problems other than getting used to the sequence of characters (collating sequence or sort order). If you need to convert between ASCII and EBCDIC, it is much more complex. EBCDIC has more possible characters than ASCII; ASCII has some characters that EBCDIC does not. With the proper translation table, converting text or printable numbers (not binary) from one character set to the other is reasonably simple: Use the input character as a pointer into a lookup table to provide the character in the other. These conversion tables are available from vendors such as IBM, Microfocus, and Sterling (Network Data Mover), most of which are based on the conversion table used by the IBM file-transfer utility IND$FILE.

The conversion table in the example below (xlatecde.cpy) is based the aforementioned conversion tables and modified from project experience. The difficulty that was encountered with the standard conversion tables was that some characters were translated from multiple other characters. As an example, mainframe <!> and <|> might become ASCII <|> characters. The problem with that is if those characters have special meaning to your application, that meaning is lost. Also, the conversion back to EBCDIC (often done as a feed to other legacy applications) might not produce the desired results. When used consistently, the conversion table in xlatecde.cpy will translate properly between EBCDIC and ASCII in either direction. The subroutine contained in xlatecde.cbl uses these conversion table on records of up to 4096 characters in length in either direction. The buffers can be expanded if needed by your application.

Binary or packed numeric fields are another matter entirely. A 2 byte integer that contains hexadecimal 4040 on the mainframe has a decimal value of 16448. If the language being used on the UNIX box handles the binary field the same way as the mainframe (ANSI COMP standard), the field should not be converted from EBCDIC to ASCII. A straight conversion would change the hex 4040 (which happens to be two EBCDIC spaces) to hex 2020 (two ASCII spaces) with a decimal value of 8224. The value contained in the binary (COMP) field has changed and will have a serious impact on further processing! COMP-3 (packed) fields exhibit similar behavior; if they are converted, the values change and the results are incorrect.

The way around this problem is to convert the parts of the record that are not binary or packed and not convert the parts that are. Although not the most efficient method in terms of CPU usage, one way is to convert the entire record and then move the fields that should not be converted.

Figure C.1
Processor Byte Ordering

Byte Ordering	Byte Layout				Description
Little Endian	1	2	3	4	Least-significant byte first (DEC VAX)
Big Endian	4	3	2	1	Most-significant byte first (IBM mainframes)
PC Endian	3	4	1	2	Least-significant byte first, most significant word first in long (PCs)
PDP Endian	3	4	1	2	Least significant byte first, most-significant word first in long (DEC PDP - original UNIX)

This method is implemented in the example xlateuse.cbl below. The example reads in a record, calls the XLATECDE subroutine to convert the entire record from EBCDIC to ASCII, and then moves the binary and packed fields from the original (nonconverted) record into the converted record. That way, the fields that need to change are changed and those that do not, are not. It may take fewer CPU cycles if each display field is converted individually with the binary and packed fields moved unconverted between records. But this approach would result in much larger programs with many more calls to the XLATECDE subroutine: more code, more programmer time, more typing, and more opportunities for error.

If your tool (language) does not support the mainframe binary or packed field formats, the conversion becomes more complicated. You may want to create a program on the mainframe that writes the fields out as PIC 9 USAGE DISPLAY fields instead of USAGE COMP or USAGE COMP-3. DISPLAY fields are easy to convert—they are printable numbers and an EBCDIC <0> converts very nicely into an ASCII <0>. Where reformatting the mainframe dataset is not an option, it is then necessary to change the format of the binary or packed numbers into a format acceptable by the UNIX machine. This conversion is dependent on the hardware architecture of CPU within the machine. The byte ordering (highest value byte on the left or right) and position of sign bit vary depending on the architecture. Common byte order definitions are shown in Figure C.1.

If you need to convert from mainframe binary or packed fields yourself, check with your language vendor—as there may be technical hint sheets for your hardware because you are probably not the first to be doing the conversion. Because of the variety of hardware architectures and language tools, one could write an entire book on this one topic; an example subroutine (swapbyte.cbl) is provided for byte order swapping when moving binary fields from the mainframe to PC CPU architectures.

Figure C.2
dd Command conv Options

Option	Conversion Performed
ascii	EBCDIC to ASCII
ebcdic	ASCII to EBCDIC
ibm	ASCII to EBCDIC with a different conversion table (may match printers better)
lcase	Upper to lowercase
ucase	Lower to uppercase
swab	Swap every pair of bytes
sync	Variable to fixed record length (every record becomes the length from the ibs=)

The conversion can be any one of the above.

Simple Data Conversion with the dd Command

Most versions of UNIX include the dd command. The name of this command actually comes from the DD statement on the mainframe. It is used to copy a file from the input name to the output and perform a number of different conversions. It can convert from EBCDIC to ASCII, ASCII to EBCDIC, uppercase to lowercase, lowercase to upper, swap pairs of bytes, and even force every record to a specified record length. The ASCII/EBCDIC conversions are based on the 256 character standard in the CACM of November 1968. There is another ASCII to EBCDIC conversion known as IBM mode, which is not a real standard but is intended to better fit IBM printer conventions.

The dd command can be used to convert text files between ASCII and EBCDIC. The file must consist only of text; any binary data will converted as though it were text and will not have the same value in memory once converted.

The general form is:

```
dd if=infile of=outfile conv=conversion ibs=in_blksize obs=out_blksize
```

Or:

```
dd if=infile of=outfile conv=conversion bs=blksize
```

The if option specifies the input file, often the name of a device (device special file). The of option specifies the output file, and conv specifies the type of conversion to perform. Figure C.2 shows the valid conversion values.

The input and output block sizes default to the normal system disk block size (usually 512) and must be a multiple of the physical block size for the specified device. The bs option is used to specify both the input and output block sizes. As with ibs and obs, it must be a multiple of the physical block size for the specified device.

The rules are a little different for tapes. When working with mainframe tapes, I typically use a blocksize of 32767 (bs=32767) because that is the largest physical block available for a mainframe dataset. If the actual blocksize is smaller on the mainframe tape, the actual value will be used. In this case, the bs option is setting the maximum blocksize instead of a multiple of the actual.

Check the man page for dd on your system for specific options and conversions available.

DATA CONVERSION EXAMPLE PROGRAMS

All examples compile under Microfocus COBOL. The version information from the cob -V command:

```
version @(#)cob.c        1.58
PRN=2XCLY/ZZM:7a.1a.11.08
PTI=NLS
I see no work
```

The version information is also reported, from the rts32 command, as:

```
V3.2 revision 43 build 10/10/2 G; 05395. Run Time System 2XCLY/ZZ0/00000C
```

swapbyte.cbl—Byte Order Swap Function

This subroutine will swap the order of bytes in a binary field. It is coded for moving between mainframe and PC CPU architectures.

```
*****************************************************************
*  byteswap.cbl -  Swap even and odd bytes to solve the big/    *
*                  little endian problem when converting        *
*                  between different hardware architectures.    *
*                  Specifically coded for mainframe to x86 CPU.*
*                  This function accepts two parameters - the   *
*                  binary field to convert and the length of    *
*                  that field (must be multiple of 2).          *
*                                                               *
*****************************************************************
 EJECT
$SET ANS85
$SET MF
 IDENTIFICATION DIVISION.
 PROGRAM-ID.     BYTESWAP.
 AUTHOR.         David B Horvath, CCP (based on others' code).
 DATE-WRITTEN.   February 12, 1996.
 DATA DIVISION.
 WORKING-STORAGE SECTION.
 01  BY-2                            PIC S9(08) USAGE COMP.
 01  CURRENT-POSITION                PIC S9(08) USAGE COMP.
 01  TEMP-X-FIELD                    PIC X(01).
```

```
LINKAGE SECTION.
01  COMP-FIELD                        PIC S9(08) USAGE COMP.
01  COMP-FIELD-X                      PIC X(01) OCCURS 8 TIMES
                                      REDEFINES COMP-FIELD.
01  COMP-FIELD-LENGTH                 PIC 9(09).

PROCEDURE DIVISION USING COMP-FIELD, COMP-FIELD-LENGTH.
PROCESSING SECTION.
    DIVIDE COMP-FIELD-LENGTH BY 2 GIVING TALLY REMAINDER BY-2.
    IF COMP-FIELD-LENGTH > 8 OR
       COMP-FIELD-LENGTH < 2 OR
       BY-2 NOT EQUAL ZERO
        GO TO CONV-EXIT.

    PERFORM SWAP-BYTE THROUGH SWAP-BYTE-EXIT
       VARYING CURRENT-POSITION FROM 1 BY 2
       UNTIL CURRENT-POSITION NOT LESS THAN COMP-FIELD-LENGTH.

CONV-EXIT.
    EXIT PROGRAM.
    STOP RUN.

*******************************************************************
SWAP-BYTE.
    MOVE COMP-FIELD-X(CURRENT-POSITION) TO TEMP-X-FIELD.
    MOVE COMP-FIELD-X(CURRENT-POSITION + 1) TO
         COMP-FIELD-X(CURRENT-POSITION).
    MOVE TEMP-X-FIELD TO COMP-FIELD-X(CURRENT-POSITION + 1).
SWAP-BYTE-EXIT.
    EXIT.
```

xlatecde.cbl—Character Set Conversion Function

This subroutine performs translation from EBCDIC to ASCII or ASCII to EBCDIC based on the flag. It would be a simple matter to translate this from COBOL to C for processing of single characters or entire strings (buffers):

```
$SET ANS85 MF
*****************************************************************
*  xlatecde.cbl -  Translate from ASCII to EBCDIC or EBCDIC to *
*                  ASCII.  The input buffer is unchanged.      *
*                  flag = 1 for EBCDIC to ASCII                *
*                         2 for ASCII to EBCDIC                *
*                  maximum buffer size is 4096.  Output buffer *
*                  must be at least as large as input.         *
*                  RC   = 1 - buffer length =< 0               *
*                         2 - buffer length > 4096             *
*                         3 - invalid flag                     *
```

```
*                                                              *
*                  The algorithm is fairly simple - the current*
*                  character in the input buffer is used to    *
*                  subscript into the translation table.       *
*                                                              *
*                  Valid values are 0 - 255.  Since COBOL bases*
*                  its tables on 1 (1 - 256), the offset must  *
*                  be increased by 1 before using.  This takes *
*                  advantage of enhanced COBOL functionality   *
*                  which allows character splitting of a single*
*                  pic X() field.  If your COBOL does not      *
*                  support it, the input and output buffers    *
*                  can be redefined as tables.  You do not     *
*                  want to move the buffers around - this      *
*                  routine is called for each and every record *
*                  in a file and could have serious performance*
*                  issues.                                     *
*                                                              *
****************************************************************
     EJECT
 IDENTIFICATION DIVISION.
 PROGRAM-ID.     XLATECDE.
 AUTHOR.         David B Horvath, CCP (based on others' code).
 DATE-WRITTEN.   February 5, 1996.
 DATE-COMPILED.
*
 DATA DIVISION.
*
 WORKING-STORAGE SECTION.
 COPY "xlatecde.cpy".
*
 LINKAGE SECTION.
 01  XC-RETURN-CODE              PIC 9(2) COMP-X.
 01  XC-FLAG                     PIC 9(2) COMP-X.
 01  XC-BUFFER-LENGTH            PIC 9(9) COMP-X.
 01  XC-INPUT-BUFFER             PIC X(4096).
 01  XC-OUTPUT-BUFFER            PIC X(4096).
*
     EJECT
 PROCEDURE DIVISION USING XC-FLAG,
                          XC-BUFFER-LENGTH,
                          XC-INPUT-BUFFER,
                          XC-OUTPUT-BUFFER.
 XLATE-MAIN SECTION.
*
     MOVE ZERO TO XC-RETURN-CODE.
```

```
           IF XC-BUFFER-LENGTH NOT GREATER THAN ZERO
              MOVE 1 TO XC-RETURN-CODE
              GO TO XLATE-MAIN-EXIT
           ELSE IF XC-BUFFER-LENGTH GREATER THAN 4096
              MOVE 2 TO XC-RETURN-CODE
              GO TO XLATE-MAIN-EXIT.
      *
           MOVE XC-BUFFER-LENGTH TO BUFFER-LENGTH.
      *
           IF XC-FLAG EQUALS 1
               PERFORM XLATE-EBCDIC-ASCII THRU XLATE-EBC-ASC-EXIT
                       VARYING BUFFER-INDEX FROM 1 BY 1
                       UNTIL BUFFER-INDEX > BUFFER-LENGTH
           ELSE IF XC-FLAG EQUALS 2
               PERFORM XLATE-ASCII-EBCDIC THRU XLATE-ASC-EBC-EXIT
                       VARYING BUFFER-INDEX FROM 1 BY 1
                       UNTIL BUFFER-INDEX > BUFFER-LENGTH
           ELSE
               MOVE 3 TO XC-RETURN-CODE.
      *
       XLATE-MAIN-EXIT.
           EXIT PROGRAM.
      *
      * EBCDIC to ASCII Conversions.
      *
       XLATE-EBCDIC-ASCII.
           MOVE ZERO TO INPUT-WORD.
           MOVE XC-INPUT-BUFFER (BUFFER-INDEX : 1) TO INPUT-CHAR.
           ADD 1 TO INPUT-WORD.
           MOVE EBCDIC-ASCII-XLATE (INPUT-WORD) TO OUTPUT-CHAR.
           MOVE OUTPUT-CHAR TO XC-OUTPUT-BUFFER (BUFFER-INDEX : 1).
      *
       XLATE-EBC-ASC-EXIT
           EXIT.
      *
      * ASCII to EBCDIC Conversions.
      *
       XLATE-ASCII-EBCDIC.
           MOVE ZERO TO INPUT-WORD.
           MOVE XC-INPUT-BUFFER (BUFFER-INDEX : 1) TO INPUT-CHAR.
           ADD 1 TO INPUT-WORD.
           MOVE ASCII-EBCDIC-XLATE (INPUT-WORD) TO OUTPUT-CHAR.
           MOVE OUTPUT-CHAR TO XC-OUTPUT-BUFFER (BUFFER-INDEX : 1).
      *
       XLATE-ASC-EBC-EXIT
           EXIT.
      *
```

xlatecde.cpy—Copybook Used by xlatecde.cbl

This is the copybook used by xlatecde.cbl and contains the conversion tables. It would be a simple matter to translate this table from COBOL to C arrays for use by a C version of xlatecde.cbl:

```
***********************************************************
* Translation tables used to convert from ASCII to        *
* EBCDIC and from EBCDIC to ASCII.  These tables differ   *
* from the "normal" translation tables from IBM and       *
* other vendors because their tables map multiple    *
* characters to a single character preventing a clean     *
* two-way conversion for important characters like the    *
* vertical bar.                                           *
***********************************************************
*
* EBCDIC to ASCII Translation Table
*
 01 TRANSLATION-TABLES.
    05  EBCDIC-ASCII-VALUES.
        10  FILLER PIC X(16)
            VALUE X"00010203EC09CA7FE2D2D30B0C0D0E0F".
        10  FILLER PIC X(16)
            VALUE X"10111213EFC508CB1819DCD81C1D1E1F".
        10  FILLER PIC X(16)
            VALUE X"B7B8B9BBC40A171BCCCDCFD0D1050607".
        10  FILLER PIC X(16)
            VALUE X"D9DA16DDDEDFE004E3E5E9EB14159E1A".
        10  FILLER PIC X(16)
            VALUE X"20C9838485A0F28687A4D52E3C282BB3".
        10  FILLER PIC X(16)
            VALUE X"268288898AA18C8B8DE121242A293B5E".
        10  FILLER PIC X(16)
            VALUE X"2D2FB28EB4B5B68F80A57C2C255F3E3F".
        10  FILLER PIC X(16)
            VALUE X"BA90BCBDBEF3C0C1C2603A2340273D22".
        10  FILLER PIC X(16)
            VALUE X"C3616263646566676869AEAFC6C7C8F1".
        10  FILLER PIC X(16)
            VALUE X"F86A6B6C6D6E6F707172A6A791CE92A9".
        10  FILLER PIC X(16)
            VALUE X"E67E737475767778797AADA8D45BD6D7".
        10  FILLER PIC X(16)
            VALUE X"9B9C9DFA9FB1B0ACABFCAAFEE45DBFE7".
        10  FILLER PIC X(16)
            VALUE X"7B414243444546474849E8939495A2ED".
        10  FILLER PIC X(16)
            VALUE X"7D4A4B4C4D4E4F505152EE968197A398".
```

```
           10  FILLER PIC X(16)
               VALUE X"5CF0535455565758595AFDF599F7F6F9".
           10  FILLER PIC X(16)
               VALUE X"30313233343536373839DBFB9AF4EAFF".
      *
       05  EBCDIC-ASCII-TABLE REDEFINES EBCDIC-ASCII-VALUES.
            10 EBCDIC-ASCII-XLATE PIC X OCCURS 256.
      *
       05  ASCII-EBCDIC-VALUES.
           10  FILLER PIC X(16)
               VALUE X"00010203372D2E2F1605250B0C0D0E0F".
           10  FILLER PIC X(16)
               VALUE X"101112133C3D322618193F271C1D1E1F".
           10  FILLER PIC X(16)
               VALUE X"405A7F7B5B6C507D4D5D5C4E6B604B61".
           10  FILLER PIC X(16)
               VALUE X"F0F1F2F3F4F5F6F7F8F97A5E4C7E6E6F".
           10  FILLER PIC X(16)
               VALUE X"7CC1C2C3C4C5C6C7C8C9D1D2D3D4D5D6".
           10  FILLER PIC X(16)
               VALUE X"D7D8D9E2E3E4E5E6E7E8E9ADE0BD5F6D".
           10  FILLER PIC X(16)
               VALUE X"79818283848586878889919293949596".
           10  FILLER PIC X(16)
               VALUE X"979899A2A3A4A5A6A7A8A9C06AD0A107".
           10  FILLER PIC X(16)
               VALUE X"68DC5142434447485253545756586367".
           10  FILLER PIC X(16)
               VALUE X"719C9ECBCCCDDBDDDFECFCB0B1B23EB4".
           10  FILLER PIC X(16)
               VALUE X"4555CEDE49699A9BAB9FBAB8B7AA8A8B".
           10  FILLER PIC X(16)
               VALUE X"B6B5624F646566620212270237273 74BE".
           10  FILLER PIC X(16)
               VALUE X"7677788024158C8D8E41061728299D2A".
           10  FILLER PIC X(16)
               VALUE X"2B2C090AAC4AAEAF1B3031FA1A333435".
           10  FILLER PIC X(16)
               VALUE X"36590838BC39A0BFCA3AFE3B04CFDA14".
           10  FILLER PIC X(16)
               VALUE X"E18F4675FDEBEEED90EFB3FBB9EABBFF".
      *
       05  ASCII-EBCDIC-TABLE REDEFINES ASCII-EBCDIC-VALUES.
            10 ASCII-EBCDIC-XLATE PIC X OCCURS 256.
      *
        01 LOCAL-VARIABLES.
```

```
05 BUFFER-LENGTH          PIC 9(9) COMP-X.
05 BUFFER-INDEX           PIC 9(9) COMP-X.
05 INPUT-WORD             PIC 9(4) COMP-X.
05 FILLER REDEFINES INPUT-WORD.
    10  FILLER            PIC X.
    10  INPUT-CHAR        PIC X.
05 OUTPUT-CHAR            PIC X.
```

xlateuse.cbl—Program to Use xlatecde.cbl

This sample program uses xlatecde.cbl to convert records from EBCDIC to ASCII. For simple text files, it would be fairly easy to create a C program to read in records of a specified size and perform the translation (using a C version of xlatecde.cbl and xlatecde.cpy). The EBCDIC records contain binary (COMP) and packed (COMP-3) fields that should not be converted when converting the rest of the record:

```
$SET IBMCOMP MF NOFLAG
*****************************************************************
*  xlateuse.cbl  - Sample program that translates a record     *
*                  from EBCDIC to ASCII using xlatecde module. *
*                  An ASCII to EBCDIC would be the same except *
*                  the flag would be 2 instead of 1.           *
*                                                              *
*                  In this example, a buffer (record) of 512   *
*                  bytes is used; the maximum is 4096.         *
*                                                              *
*                  Special code is required for non-text fields*
*                  because they do not convert - a binary      *
*                  integer variable has a bit pattern that     *
*                  represents its value; if it was converted,  *
*                  the value would change.  Text fields (pic x *
*                  or pic 9 usage display) should be converted *
*                  since they contain the characters in EBCDIC *
*                  (or ASCII) form.                            *
*                                                              *
*****************************************************************
     EJECT
 IDENTIFICATION DIVISION.
 PROGRAM-ID USEXLATE.
 AUTHOR.          David B Horvath, CCP (based on code by others).
 DATE-WRITTEN.    February 5, 1996.
 DATE-COMPILED.
* EBCDIC to ASCII example with COMP fields.
 ENVIRONMENT DIVISION.
 CONFIGURATION  SECTION.
 INPUT-OUTPUT SECTION.
 FILE-CONTROL.
```

```
           SELECT FILEIN  ASSIGN TO UT-S-INFILE.
           SELECT FILEOUT ASSIGN TO UT-S-OUTFILE.
       DATA DIVISION.
       FILE SECTION.
       FD  FILEIN
           RECORDING MODE F
           LABEL RECORDS STANDARD
           RECORD CONTAINS 513 CHARACTERS
           BLOCK CONTAINS 0
           DATA RECORD IS FILEIN-RECORD.
       01  FILEIN-RECORD  PIC X(513).

       FD  FILEOUT
           RECORDING MODE F
           LABEL RECORDS STANDARD
           RECORD CONTAINS 513 CHARACTERS
           BLOCK CONTAINS 0
           DATA RECORD IS FILEOUT-RECORD.
       01  FILEOUT-RECORD  PIC X(513).
       WORKING-STORAGE SECTION.
      *---------------------------------------------------------------*
       01  END-OF-FILE-IND                 PIC X VALUE 'N'.
       01  I                               PIC 9(8) COMP.
       01  REC-COUNT                       PIC 9(8) VALUE 0.
       01  PIC9-DISP                       PIC 9(8) VALUE 0.
      * FOR USE BY XLATECODE.
       01  WS-CONVERSION-AREA.
           03  XLATE-RETURN-CODE           PIC 9(02) COMP-X.
           03  CONVERSION-FLAG             PIC 9(02) COMP-X.
           03  RECORD-LTH                  PIC 9(09) COMP-X.

      ***********************************************************
      *  record layout for input (unconverted) and              *
      *                     output (converted) records          *
      ***********************************************************
       01  EBCDIC-RECORD.
           05  ER-X-FIELD-1          PIC X(100).
           05  ER-COMP-FIELD-1       PIC S9(04) USAGE COMP.
           05  ER-COMP3-FIELD-1      PIC S9(09)V99 USAGE COMP-3.
           05  ER-X-FIELD-2          PIC X(92).
           05  ER-X-FIELD-4          PIC X(100).
           05  ER-X-FIELD-5          PIC X(100).
           05  ER-X-FIELD-6          PIC X(100).
           05  ER-X-FIELD-7          PIC X(13).
      *
       01  ASCII-RECORD.
```

```
     05  AR-X-FIELD-1          PIC X(100).
     05  AR-COMP-FIELD-1       PIC S9(04) USAGE COMP.
     05  AR-COMP3-FIELD-1      PIC S9(09)V99 USAGE COMP-3.
     05  AR-X-FIELD-2          PIC X(92).
     05  AR-X-FIELD-4          PIC X(100).
     05  AR-X-FIELD-5          PIC X(100).
     05  AR-X-FIELD-6          PIC X(100).
     05  AR-X-FIELD-7          PIC X(13).
*****************************************************************
*   MAIN BODY OF THE PROGRAM
*****************************************************************
 PROCEDURE DIVISION.
*****************************************************************
*  MAIN ROUTINE                                                 *
*****************************************************************
 0000-MAINLINE.
     OPEN INPUT  FILEIN
          OUTPUT FILEOUT.
     PERFORM 0500-INITIALIZATION.
     PERFORM 1000-PROCESS-EACH-RECORD
         UNTIL END-OF-FILE-IND = 'Y'.
     CLOSE FILEIN, FILEOUT.
     DISPLAY 'TOTAL RECORDS PROCESSED = ' REC-COUNT
     STOP RUN.
*****************************************************************
*  INITIALIZE PROGRAM DATA AREAS                                *
*****************************************************************
 0500-INITIALIZATION.
*    SET CONVERSION FLAG FOR EBCDIC TO ASCII CONVERSION         *
     MOVE 1 TO CONVERSION-FLAG.
     MOVE 513 TO RECORD-LTH.

*****************************************************************
* CONVERT EACH RECORD                                           *
*****************************************************************
 1000-PROCESS-EACH-RECORD.
     READ FILEIN INTO EBCDIC-RECORD
         AT END MOVE 'Y' TO END-OF-FILE-IND.
     IF END-OF-FILE-IND = 'N'
        ADD 1 TO REC-COUNT
        CALL 'XLATECDE'  USING    XLATE-RETURN-CODE
                                  CONVERSION-FLAG
                                  RECORD-LTH
                                  EBCDIC-RECORD
                                  ASCII-RECORD
```

```
        IF XLATE-RETURN-CODE NOT EQUAL ZERO
           DISPLAY 'TRANSLATION ERROR NUMBER ' XLATE-RETURN-CODE
           STOP RUN
        ELSE
           PERFORM 2000-MOVE-COMP-FIELDS
           WRITE FILEOUT-RECORD FROM ASCII-RECORD
        END-IF
     END-IF.
*****************************************************************
* HANDLE COMP and COMP3 FIELDS                                  *
*****************************************************************
 2000-MOVE-COMP-FIELDS.
     MOVE ER-COMP-FIELD-1  TO AR-COMP-FIELD-1.
     MOVE ER-COMP3-FIELD-1 TO AR-COMP3-FIELD-1.
```

xlateuse.ksh—Shell Script To Run xlateuse.cbl

This is a Korn shell script to run xlateuse.cbl:

```
#! /bin/ksh
# KornShell script to run xlateuse.cbl program
#
# If you are using another compiler, check the documentation
# on the proper form to run a program and define external filenames.
#
export dd_FILEIN="/top/next/next2/INPUT.EBCDIC"
export dd_FILEOUT="/top/next/next2/OUTPUT.ASCII"

# Use *ONE* of the following two xlateuse lines.
cobrun xlateuse              # Microfocus COBOL gnt or int code
xlateuse                     # Executable
```

ASCII and EBCDIC Chart

DEC	HEX	OCT	ASCII	EBCDIC
000	00	000	NUL	NUL
001	01	001	SOH	SOH
002	02	002	STX	STX
003	03	003	ETX	ETX
004	04	004	EOT	SEL
005	05	005	ENQ	HT
006	06	006	ACK	RNL
007	07	007	BEL	DEL
008	08	010	BS	GE
009	09	011	HT	SPS
010	0a	012	LF	RPT
011	0b	013	VT	VT
012	0c	014	FF	FF
013	0d	015	CR	CR
014	0e	016	SO	SO
015	0f	017	SI	SI
016	10	020	DLE	DLE
017	11	021	DC1	DC1
018	12	022	DC2	DC2
019	13	023	DC3	DC3
020	14	024	DC4	RES/ENP
021	15	025	NAK	NL
022	16	026	SYN	BS
023	17	027	ETB	POC
024	18	030	CAN	CAN
025	19	031	EM	EM
026	1a	032	SUB	UBS
027	1b	033	ESC	CU1
028	1c	034	FS	IFS
029	1d	035	GS	IGS
030	1e	036	RS	IRS
031	1f	037	US	ITB/IUS
032	20	040	SP	DS
033	21	041	!	SOS
034	22	042	"	FS
035	23	043	#	WUS
036	24	044	$	BYP/INP
037	25	045	%	LF
038	26	046	&	ETB
039	27	047	'	ESC
040	28	050	(	SA
041	29	051	)	SFE
042	2a	052	*	SM/SW
043	2b	053	+	CSP
044	2c	054	,	MFA
045	2d	055	-	ENQ
046	2e	056	.	ACK
047	2f	057	/	BEL
048	30	060	0	
049	31	061	1	
050	32	062	2	SYN
051	33	063	3	IR
052	34	064	4	PP
053	35	065	5	TRN
054	36	066	6	NBS
055	37	067	7	EOT
056	38	070	8	SBS
057	39	071	9	IT
058	3a	072	:	RFF
059	3b	073	;	CU3
060	3c	074	<	DC4
061	3d	075	=	NAK
062	3e	076	>	
063	3f	077	?	SUB
064	40	100	@	SP
065	41	101	A	RSP
066	42	102	B	
067	43	103	C	
068	44	104	D	
069	45	105	E	
070	46	106	F	
071	47	107	G	
072	48	110	H	
073	49	111	I	
074	4a	112	J	¢
075	4b	113	K	.
076	4c	114	L	<
077	4d	115	M	(
078	4e	116	N	+
079	4f	117	O	|
080	50	120	P	&
081	51	121	Q	
082	52	122	R	
083	53	123	S	

DEC	HEX	OCT	ASCII	EBCDIC
084	54	124	T	
085	55	125	U	
086	56	126	V	
087	57	127	W	
088	58	130	X	
089	59	131	Y	
090	5a	132	Z	!
091	5b	133	[	$
092	5c	134	\	*
093	5d	135	]	)
094	5e	136	^	;
095	5f	137	_	¬
096	60	140	`	_
097	61	141	a	/
098	62	142	b	
099	63	143	c	
100	64	144	d	
101	65	145	e	
102	66	146	f	
103	67	147	g	
104	68	150	h	
105	69	151	i	
106	6a	152	j	|
107	6b	153	k	,
108	6c	154	l	%
109	6d	155	m	_
110	6e	156	n	>
111	6f	157	o	?
112	70	160	p	
113	71	161	q	
114	72	162	r	
115	73	163	s	
116	74	164	t	
117	75	165	u	
118	76	166	v	
119	77	167	w	
120	78	170	x	
121	79	171	y	
122	7a	172	z	:
123	7b	173	{	#
124	7c	174	|	@
125	7d	175	}	'
126	7e	176	~	=
127	7f	177	DEL	"

DEC	HEX	OCT	ASCII	EBCDIC
128	80	200		
129	81	201		a
130	82	202		b
131	83	203		c
132	84	204		d
133	85	205		e
134	86	206		f
135	87	207		g
136	88	210		h
137	89	211		i
138	8a	212		
139	8b	213		
140	8c	214		
141	8d	215		
142	8e	216		
143	8f	217		
144	90	220		
145	91	221		j
146	92	222		k
147	93	223		l
148	94	224		m
149	95	225		n
150	96	226		o
151	97	227		p
152	98	230		q
153	99	231		r
154	9a	232		
155	9b	233		
156	9c	234		
157	9d	235		
158	9e	236		
159	9f	237		
160	a0	240		
161	a1	241		~
162	a2	242		s
163	a3	243		t
164	a4	244		u
165	a5	245		v
166	a6	246		w
167	a7	247		x
168	a8	250		y
169	a9	251		z
170	aa	252		
171	ab	253		

DEC	HEX	OCT	ASCII	EBCDIC	DEC	HEX	OCT	ASCII	EBCDIC
172	ac	254			215	d7	327		P
173	ad	255			216	d8	330		Q
174	ae	256			217	d9	331		R
175	af	257			218	da	332		
176	b0	260			219	db	333		
177	b1	261			220	dc	334		
178	b2	262			221	dd	335		
179	b3	263			222	de	336		
180	b4	264			223	df	337		
181	b5	265			224	e0	340		\
182	b6	266			225	e1	341		NSP
183	b7	267			226	e2	342		S
184	b8	270			227	e3	343		T
185	b9	271			228	e4	344		U
186	ba	272			229	e5	345		V
187	bb	273			230	e6	346		W
188	bc	274			231	e7	347		X
189	bd	275			232	e8	350		Y
190	be	276			233	e9	351		Z
191	bf	277			234	ea	352		
192	c0	300		{	235	eb	353		
193	c1	301		A	236	ec	354		
194	c2	302		B	237	ed	355		
195	c3	303		C	238	ee	356		
196	c4	304		D	239	ef	357		
197	c5	305		E	240	f0	360		0
198	c6	306		F	241	f1	361		1
199	c7	307		G	242	f2	362		2
200	c8	310		H	243	f3	363		3
201	c9	311		I	244	f4	364		4
202	ca	312		SHY	245	f5	365		5
203	cb	313			246	f6	366		6
204	cc	314			247	f7	367		7
205	cd	315			248	f8	370		8
206	ce	316			249	f9	371		9
207	cf	317			250	fa	372		
208	d0	320		}	251	fb	373		
209	d1	321		J	252	fc	374		
210	d2	322		K	253	fd	375		
211	d3	323		L	254	fe	376		
212	d4	324		M	255	ff	377		EO
213	d5	325		N					
214	d6	326		O					

APPENDIX D

HARDWARE COMPARISONS

Like the mainframe, UNIX systems consist of three main parts: CPU, memory, and peripherals. There can be from one to many CPUs in a box, varying amounts of memory, and many different peripherals. The peripherals supported included hard disks, various tapes, CD-ROM disks, printers, and terminals.

On the mainframe, the typical disk drive is a model 3380 or 3390 with a maximum storage per volume (or drive) of 1.98 GB and 2.94 GB respectively. Each unit contains multiple volumes 7.56 GB and 11.34 GB respectively. These drives are large, expensive, and highly reliable. Most UNIX systems use physically smaller and less expensive disks. To a certain extent, the cheaper drives are less reliable; but those problems are reduced through the use of RAID. RAID stands for Redundant Array of Inexpensive Disks, and in its simplest form is called RAID 0 or disk mirroring. For each logical disk, there are two physical disks; if one fails, the second is used until the failed drive is replaced. The theory is that the two inexpensive disks and controlling hardware are cheaper than one expensive disk and by providing the redundancy, are as reliable if not more so. This has proven to be a popular concept for now IBM is selling RAID devices for mainframes.

There are other levels of RAID (one through five) that include combinations of mirroring, striping (putting portions of files on multiple drives), bit-level striping (eight drives are used, each byte written to the device is split into one bit per drive), bit-level striping with error correction (additional drives are used to store additional bits which ensure data integrity). With mirroring, there is generally a better read response time than a single drive because the data can be read from each physical disk independently. However, there may be a degradation of write response time because of the additional overhead. The other levels of RAID are designed to improve both the read and write response times. Mirroring and the other RAID levels improve the availability of data. In other words, if a device fails, the data is immediately available from the duplicate disk. There is no need to retrieve files from the last backup.

RAID is not without its own problems. There is additional operating system and hardware support required. When a failed device is replaced, the process of synchronizing it with the active disk can impose significant overhead on the system. Until a failed device is replaced, the redundancy may be lost, resulting in the loss of data and system availability if the spare also fails. But based on the popularity, the benefits (cost, speed, and availability) of RAID far outweigh its problems.

On a typical UNIX box, a single physical disk will range from 1 to 4 GB. There are still some smaller disks available, but with the prices coming down rapidly, more home computer users have more than 1 GB of disk storage, so the business UNIX machine should not have anything smaller than 1 GB. The access times of these disks vary from 8 to 15 ms using a SCSI (Small

Computer System Interface) or SCSI-II connection to the disks. Each SCSI board or channel can support up to 15 devices including hard disks, tapes, scanners, and CD-ROM drives.

Because of the wide range of boxes which UNIX will run, it is hard to determine the total capacities that a typical UNIX system would include. It can run on a home PC, engineering workstations, servers, and mainframes. Since you are probably already familiar with the mainframe, it will be excluded except for comparisons; servers are highlighted because they are the most common replacement for mainframes. A server can be based on Intel or proprietary chips, and as a programmer, you may not be able to tell the difference because the behavior of UNIX and the shell you use is fairly independent of the underlying hardware architecture.

The top-end IBM mainframe, the ES/9000-9X2, comes standard with 536 MB of memory, multiple 2 GB virtual address spaces, 32 channels (128 maximum), and a total of 10 central processing units in a two-sided (five CPU each) configuration. A high end UNIX box, on the other hand, from one vendor supports up to 2 GB of memory, a total of 48 bits for addressing virtual storage (281 Terabytes—281,000,000,000,000 bytes), and up to four CPUs. It is unlikely that this system will use that much virtual memory since it can only support 8.3 TB of disks.

Another high-end UNIX box supports up to 2 GB of memory, a total of 43 bits for addressing virtual storage (8.7 Terabytes—8,700,000,000,000 bytes), and up to 12 CPUs. It supports a maximum of 20 TB of disk storage. A third vendor's powerful UNIX box supports up to 2 GB of memory, a total of 32 GB of virtual storage, and up to eight CPUs. The documentation states that it supports up to 947 GB of disk storage. The actual maximum may really be 1.9 TB because a larger disk has been released since the documentation.

You can purchase round tape (reel-to-reel), cartridge (3490), 4mm, 8mm, optical jukebox, tape silo, 3.5 inch floppy disk, and CD-ROM drives for UNIX boxes and mainframes. I doubt you will see a mainframe create a floppy, but it is possible. It does make sense to have one on a UNIX box because there are commands to access disks created by MS/PC-DOS computers and the environments are often physically close together.

At this time, UNIX boxes will not replace mainframes for all applications because of raw data throughput and connected devices. They do, however, provide a good base for moving selected applications from the big iron.

The CPU inside a computer can belong to one of two different design philosophies. CISC (Complex Instruction Set Computer) is the design used by mainframe and most PC (Intel) designers; there are many instructions built into the CPU including such complex constructs like string copy or table lookup. The other philosophy, RISC (Reduced Instruction Set Computer) is based on the idea of fewer built-in instructions that are optimized to run very quickly. Instead of having a string copy, a RISC chip would have a basic move or copy instruction that the programmer would enclose in a loop to copy an entire string. The RISC CPU can run at a very high clock speed because the instructions are highly optimized but do less; a CISC CPU might run at a slower clock speed, but one instruction might do the work of hundreds of RISC instructions. The RISC speed numbers might sound impressive but remember that for every instruction that a CICS CPU might execute, the RISC may be executing hundreds or thousands.

I would have liked to include specific configurations and performance comparisons, but the difficulty in getting copyright permissions combined with the speed at which the information changes prevented it.

APPENDIX E

C SHELL—AN OVERVIEW

The C shell was originally developed as a replacement for the Bourne shell by Bill Joy at Berkeley. The syntax is similar in many ways to the C programming language and includes features for interactive use that are missing from Bourne.

Figure E.1 shows the command line options that can be used when invoking the C shell.

Figure E.2 shows the characters that have special meaning in the C shell (known as metacharacters).

Figure E.3 shows the syntax of C Shell variable substitution.

Figure E.4 shows the characters used creating patterns for filename matching. These are similar to those used with Korn shell.

Figure E.5 contains the arithmetic and comparison operators in the C shell.

Figure E.6 shows the test operators for files available in the C shell.

The C shell does not support a vi or emacs style command history and editing like the Korn shell does. Instead, it provides means of retrieving prior commands, editing, and then executing them. It has its own edit language, but less ability to see the command being changed (visually). Figure E.7 shows the available command history commands.

Figure E.1
C Shell Command Line Options

Option	Description
-b	Break from shell command line option processing. Other options placed in argv
-c	Read commands from file named as next argument. Other options placed in argv
-e	Exit if command returns non-zero status
-f	Fast startup - do not read .login or .cshrc
-i	Force interactive - get commands from stdin even if not connected to a terminal
-n	Interpret but do not execute commands
-s	Accept commands from stdin
-t	Accept and execute a single command
-v	Verbose. Set verbose variable
-V	Verbose but set before executing .cshrc
-x	Echo commands before execution
-X	Echo but set before executing .cshrc

Many of these options are available as set commands as shown in Figure 8.5.

Figure E.2
Characters with Special Meaning in C Shell

<table>
<tr><th>Meta-
character</th><th>Description</th></tr>
<tr><td>#</td><td>Comment</td></tr>
<tr><td>:</td><td>Null statement (No Op). Used where a statement is required but none is desired</td></tr>
<tr><td>&</td><td>Run process in background</td></tr>
<tr><td>cmd1 | cmd2</td><td>Pipe stdout of first commands into stdin of second</td></tr>
<tr><td>cmd2 |& cmd2</td><td>Pipe stdout of stderr of first command into stdin of second</td></tr>
<tr><td>cmd1 || cmd2</td><td>Execute cmd1; if it fails, execute cmd2</td></tr>
<tr><td>cmd1 && cmd2</td><td>Execute cmd1; if it fails, do not execute cmd2</td></tr>
<tr><td>;</td><td>Separate commands to run at same level</td></tr>
<tr><td>(cmd1; cmd2)</td><td>Run commands as separate subshell and group output</td></tr>
<tr><td>'...'</td><td>Do not perform substitution on string contained within single quotes</td></tr>
<tr><td>"..."</td><td>Disable substitution of filenames</td></tr>
<tr><td>set var=`cmd`</td><td>The command is executed and any output stored in variable</td></tr>
<tr><td>\char</td><td>Escape meaning of char - use as character, not as special meaning or operator</td></tr>
<tr><td>\</td><td>Continue on next line <|>, <()>, <">, <'>, and <`> will not continue without <\>.</td></tr>
<tr><td><<</td><td>Here document redirection</td></tr>
<tr><td>></td><td>Redirect stout to file; create new file even if one exists</td></tr>
<tr><td>>!</td><td>Redirect stdout to file and truncate even if noclobber set</td></tr>
<tr><td>>&</td><td>Redirect stderr and stdout to file</td></tr>
<tr><td>>&!</td><td>Redirect stderr and stdout to file and truncate even if noclobber is set</td></tr>
<tr><td>>></td><td>Redirect stdout - append to file; produce error if file does not exist and noclobber is set</td></tr>
<tr><td>>>!</td><td>Redirect stdout - append to file; no error if file does not exist and noclobber is set</td></tr>
<tr><td>>>&</td><td>Redirect stderr and stdout to file</td></tr>
<tr><td>>>&!</td><td>Redirect stderr and stdout to file; no error if file does not exist and noclobber is set</td></tr>
</table>

Figure E.3
C Shell Variable Substitution

Form	Description
$var	Substitute value contained in var
${var}	Substitute value contained in var; use when appending text to var
$var[index]	Substitute value contained in array var at index position. Range [m-n] and all [*]
$#var	Substitute number of words in variable
$0	Substitute the name of the file being executed
$1...$9	Command line arguments. Equivalent to argv[n]
$*	All command line arguments; equivalent to argv[*]
$?var	Returns one if var is set and zero if not
$$	Process id of shell running script
$<	Substitute the contents of input line from stdin. Used to read from keyboard
$status	Equivalent to $? in Korn shell

Figure E.4
C Shell Filename Matching Patterns

Character	Description
*	Match zero or more characters
?	Match any single character
[...]	Match any single character in list or range
~userid	Home directory of user
{str1, str2 ...}	Match to each string

Figure E.5
C Shell Operators

Operator	Description
(...)	Grouping - use to override order of operations
~	Bitwise not - ones complement
!	Logical not
* / %	Multiplication, division, and remainder (Modulo)
++ --	Increment and decrement (change by one)
+ -	Addition and subtraction
<< >>	Bitwise shift left and right
< > <= >=	Less than, greater than, not greater than, not less than (numeric only)
== != =~ !~	Equals, not equal, filename pattern (wildcard) match, filename pattern mismatch
&	Bitwise And
^	Bitwise Exclusive Or (XOR)
|	Bitwise Or
&&	Logical And
||	Logical Or

Operators are shown in order of precedence; operators at same level are performed left to right.

Command history and substitution is available for use from the keyboard or from within commands. To show the arguments from the last command, you could use the following `echo`:

```
echo !*
```

The C shell provides two different forms of the if statement. The first allows one command and only one command. On the same line as the if itself, the second form allows one to many commands after the if. It also supports, but does not require, an else. It also allows stacking of if statements as else if statements.

The first form is:

```
if (expression) command
```

Figure E.6
C Shell File Test Operators

Operator	Description
-r file	Returns true if file is readable by user
-w file	Returns true if file is writable by user
-x file	Returns true if file can be executed or, if directory, searched by user
-e file	Returns true if file exists
-o file	Returns true if file is owned by user
-z file	Returns true if file exists with a length of zero (empty)
-f file	Returns true if file is a plain file (not pipe, directory, or link)
-d file	Returns true if file is a directory

Figure E.7
C Shell Command History Manipulation

Operator	Description
!number	Get the command you entered at number and execute
!-number	Get the command number times ago and execute
!!	Get last command and execute
!string	Get the last command that begins with string and execute
!?string	Get the last command that contains string and execute
!*	Get all the arguments of the last command (but not the command itself)
!^	Get the first argument of the last command
!$	Get the last argument of the last command
!:number	Get the argument number from the last command
^old^new	Get the last command and change old string to new and execute
:	Word designator separator. The commands above appear before this separator
0	First word (command)
number	Word at number (nth argument)
^	First argument on line. Equivalent to using 1 to select word at number
$	Last argument on line
%	Word matched by last ? search
num1-num2	Range of words. -num2 defaults to 0-num2
*	All arguments
num*	Range of words: num-$
num-	Range of words from num to $ minus 1
s/old/new/	Used as a suffix to get command to change old string to new and execute
:h	Remove trailing pathname
:r	Remove trailing suffix in form of .xyz
:e	Remove all but suffix
:t	Remove all leading pathnames
:&	Repeat previous :s command
:g	Apply change (:gs/.../.../ or :g&) to first occurrence in each word
:p	Print new command but do not execute it
:q	Apply quoting to the substituted words preventing further substitution
:x	Similar to :q but break into words at each whitespace (no multiple word quoting)

The one command can be a goto causing one-way branching. The second form, with optional else if and else statement, is as follows:

```
if (expression) then
        ...
else if (expression) then
        ...
else
        ...
endif
```

If you have no statement to go after an if or an else (including else if), you can use the null statement <:> to fulfill the requirement of at least one statement.

The C shell also supports a switch statement. The switch command contains the name of the variable being used for selection; each case statement contains a string or pattern that will be matched with the variable. When a match occurs, all commands will be executed until a breaksw (break switch) command is found at which time the switch will be concluded. There is one special case, default, that behaves like the else of an if—when nothing else matches, it executes. The switch can be used to replace many stacked if/else if combinations and is useful for menu selection. The following is a typical switch statement:

```
switch (string_var)
        case string1:
                ...
                breaksw
        case string2:
        case string3:
                ...
                breaksw
        default:
                ...
endsw
```

The C shell provides three structured loops: while, foreach, and repeat. The while executes the command in its body until the expression is no longer true. The expression is checked before the body is executed, so the loop contents might not be executed. The while loop looks like:

```
while (expression)
        ...
end
```

The foreach statement steps through the values specified, once through the loop for each, until they are all used. Like the Korn shell for statement, to make a loop go from one to five, you have to specify all the numbers (1 2 3 4 5). Both the while and foreach can contain break and continue statements to modify the normal behavior of the loop. The break statement causes the loop execution to terminate immediately. The continue statement causes the remaining commands in the loop body to be skipped and return controlled to the top where the test occurs or next value is assigned. The following is the structure of a foreach:

```
foreach var (values)
        ...
        if (end_expression) then break
        if (skip_rest_expression) then continue
        ...
end
```

The third structured loop is the repeat. The repeat will execute a single command for count number of times. There can be one and only one command that is repeated as shown:

```
repeat count command
```

The C shell supports one feature not available in the Korn shell: the goto. The one restriction is that the label (target) of the goto must be physically after the goto in the shell script. The goto and label look like the following:

```
goto label
        ...
label:
```

The `jobs`, `fg`, `bg`, `kill`, and `nohup` commands in the C shell behave much like they do for Korn. Respectively, they display running background jobs, move a background job to the foreground, move a suspended job to the background, send signals to running processes (generally to kill them), and run processes that will not be terminated by the HUP (hangup) signal.

As with some versions of the Korn shell, <^Z> will suspend a foreground process in C shell; once suspended, `fg` and `bg` can unsuspend it.

The filename matching (wildcarding) is almost identical in behavior between Korn and C shells. Regular expression expansion is a little different. For example, if the expression is not contained within single <'> or double <"> quotes, it will be expanded into matching filenames. In the Korn shell, the expansion takes place only for filenames. The `ls` command behaves exactly the same way, the regular expression used with `grep` may need to be quoted under C shell.

The `shift`, `echo`, `umask`, and `exit` commands within shell scripts work exactly the same. The `ulimit` command in Korn is replaced by the `limit` command in C shell.

As shown in Chapter 8, C shell `alias` commands are a little different from Korn. The environmental variables are different, so the `set` or `setenv` command is required when setting a variable equal to a value or other variable.

The shells behave exactly the same way when it comes to executing shell scripts and binary executables (compiled program). If the first line is #! /bin/shell_name, a sub-shell is created and it executes the commands in the shell script. If the file is a binary executable it will be executed by the current shell. There is one minor difference though. To execute a script in the current shell (like when you want to re-execute your Korn .profile after changing it), you use the source command instead of the Korn <.>. The following will run your C shell .login in the current shell:

```
% source .login↵
%
```

In order for you to execute a program or shell script (without using source), you must, of course, have execute permissions. You need read, not execute permissions, to run a shell script using source because your current shell reads the commands in the specified file and executes them. Korn and C shells behave the same way in this matter, only the command name changes.

The way math is handled in C shell is substantially different from Korn. Not only are there additional operators (++, – –, and others), but the command to perform calculations is different. The @ command performs arithmetic. The following example shows C shell arithmetic:

```
% @ vvv=3 + 5↵
% echo $vvv↵
8
% @ vvv = 3 + 4; echo $vvv↵
7
% @ newv = 3 + 2 * 5; echo $newv↵
13
% @ newv = (3 + 2) * 5; echo $newv↵
25
%
```

Use the parentheses to change order of operation.

There are many subtleties to the C shell just like the Korn shell; if you will be using the C shell, get one of the good books on the subject. Check the man page. Try out different exercises.

APPENDIX F
USING TCP/IP NETWORKS

TCP/IP

The name, TCP/IP, much like the name UNIX, has multiple meanings. At the simplest level, it refers to a pair of protocols for communications. In a more generic sense, it refers to all the tools, commands, and communications protocols that are related to the more specific name TCP/IP. TCP stands for Transmission Control Protocol and IP stands for Internet Protocol.

Development of the protocol began in the late 1960s as a project funded by the U.S. Department of Defense Advanced Research Projects Agency (DARPA, or more commonly at the time, ARPA). It was originally developed to allow researchers to communicate with each other and provide a proving ground for a network that could survive a nuclear war. The original network was known as ARPAnet or Arpanet and is the precursor to the Internet that is so often mentioned in the media.

To a large extent, the suite of TCP/IP tools and the Internet as a whole has evolved through committees; not with the normal bland result of the typical committee, but with innovative solutions. The committees were not like traditional committees in that they did not necessarily meet at a single location on a regular basis. Instead, they have been groups of people who communicated via electronic mail and their results were open to the community as a whole. The people involved were strongly motivated and committed to seeing the results.

Most of the documents related to TCP/IP and the Internet are communicated through RFC (Request for Comment) specifications. As the name implies, they are initial suggestions from the formal committee that the community can comment on. Often the comments are used to improve the specification. The formal specification for TCP is RFC 793: Transmission Control Protocol; for IP, it is RFC 791: Internet Protocol.

Before the concepts developed for the Arpanet, networking computers together generally involved direct connections between boxes. The connection might be direct if the machines were close, over a leased telephone line if the machines were remote and needed full-time connections, or even dial-up for remote, part-time connections. The problem was that they were one-to-one connections; each machine had to be connected to another, there was no facility for multiple machines to connect to the same line or communications channel. Figure F.1 shows the old network layout. Although the data is shown as flowing one-way only, it can actually move both ways.

As the technology progressed, store-and-forward, routing, and ethernet became available. Originally, to get some data (mail, programs, payroll data) from computer A to computer C, there would have to be a connection between the two, even if they were on opposite sides of the

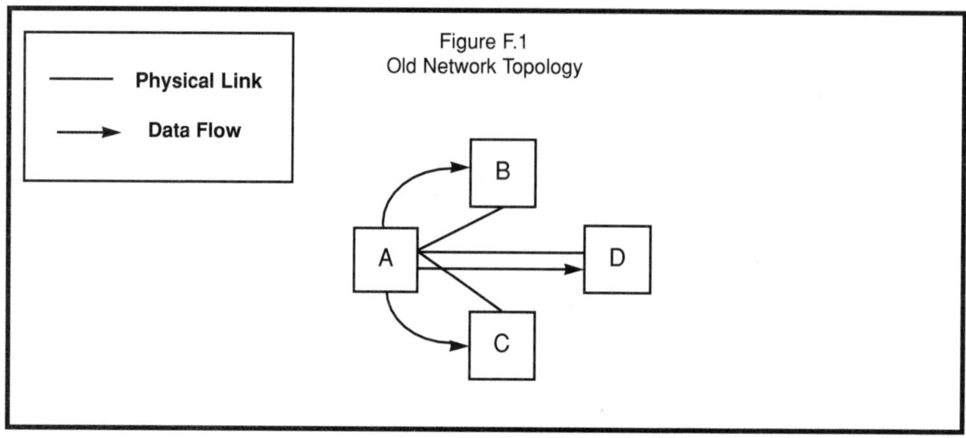

Figure F.1
Old Network Topology

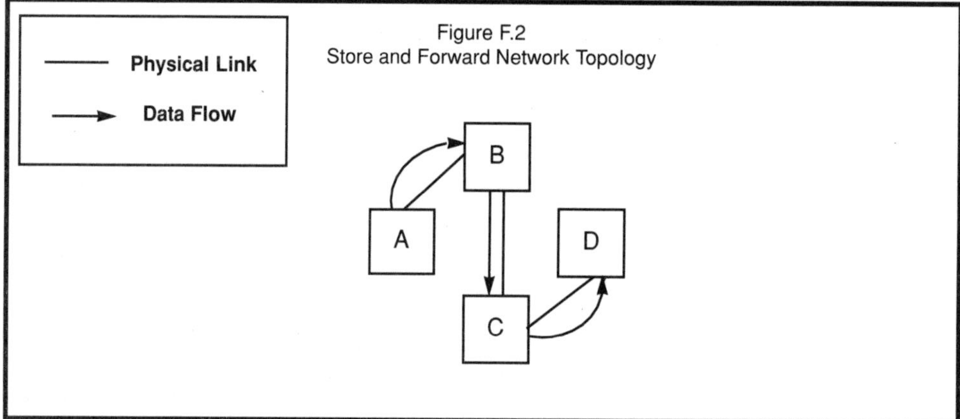

Figure F.2
Store and Forward Network Topology

country. With store-and-forward, computer A might connect to B, which connects to C, but even if the connection was not active at a specific time, the data would be held and forwarded when the connection was made.

UUCP, UNIX-to-UNIX Copy Program, is based on this technology. During its peak, it was possible to UUCP mail or data from one end of the country to the other with each system making local calls to the next. The network was informal and provided on a volunteer basis by individuals, universities, and businesses. It was not perfect because member systems came and went, but it was able to handle missing systems and connections and route data over different routes. With the Internet inexpensively available, the UUCP network is beginning to deteriorate. Figure F.2 shows store and forward networks.

Routing is the capability for data to take have multiple paths from one point to another. If the link between system B and C was not available but the links between B and D, D and C were, then the data could use the longer link. Figure F.3 shows routing and how it handles failed links.

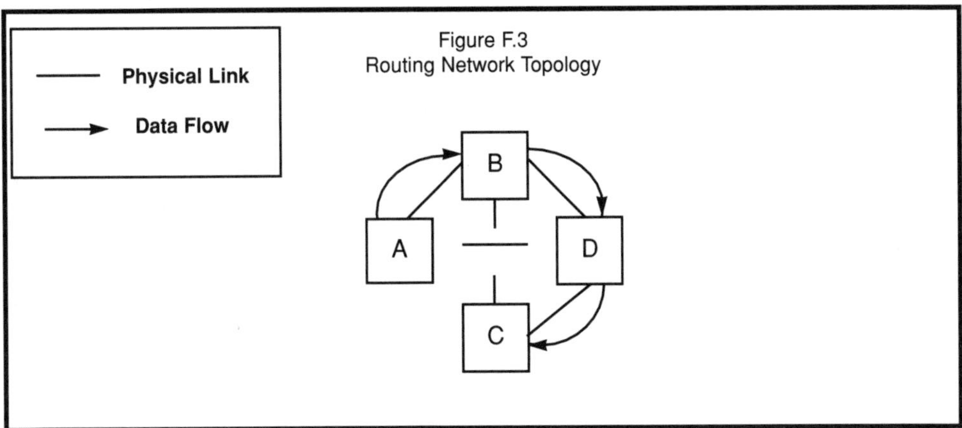

Figure F.3
Routing Network Topology

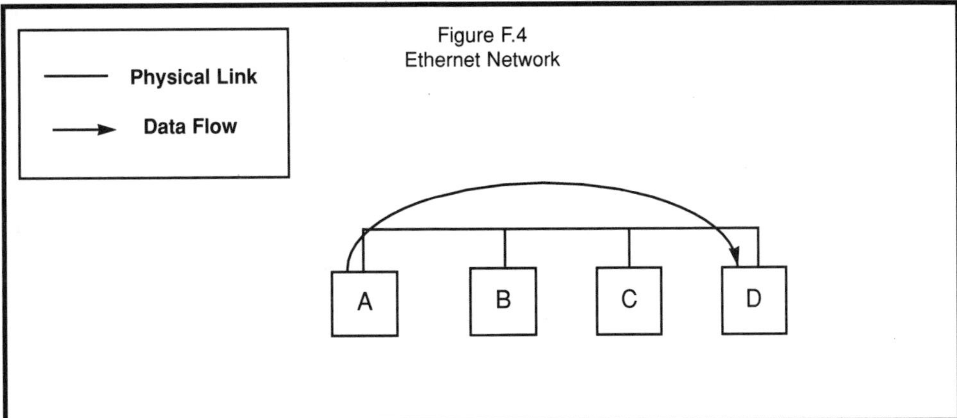

Figure F.4
Ethernet Network

The technology has evolved further with things like ethernet where multiple systems are on the same line and all traffic travels over that common line. There can be multiple networks with interconnections for data to move between them. Systems can be on multiple networks or have multiple paths at one time although it is not mandatory. Figure F.4 shows a simple ethernet network.

With connections between networks, there are gateways. There are hardware devices known as routers; the difference between that and the hardware known as a gateway are becoming less and less. The terms router and gateway are becoming interchangeable. In general, a gateway is the connection between one network and another. The gateway can be between internal (corporate) and external (the Internet and others) network, or it can be between multiple networks (NFSnet, Milnet, NYsernet, etc.). The Internet itself is really a series of smaller networks gatewayed together. The smaller networks themselves may be broken down into smaller networks. The name, Internet, is a combination of Inter (connection between) and net (network).

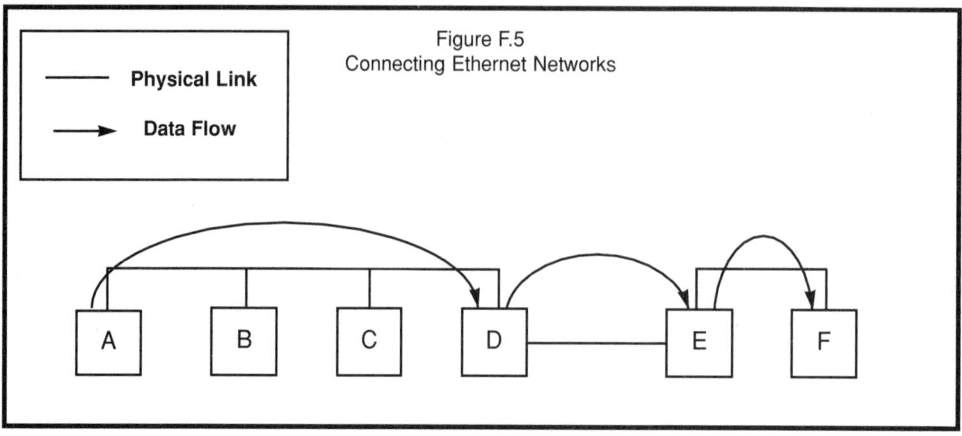

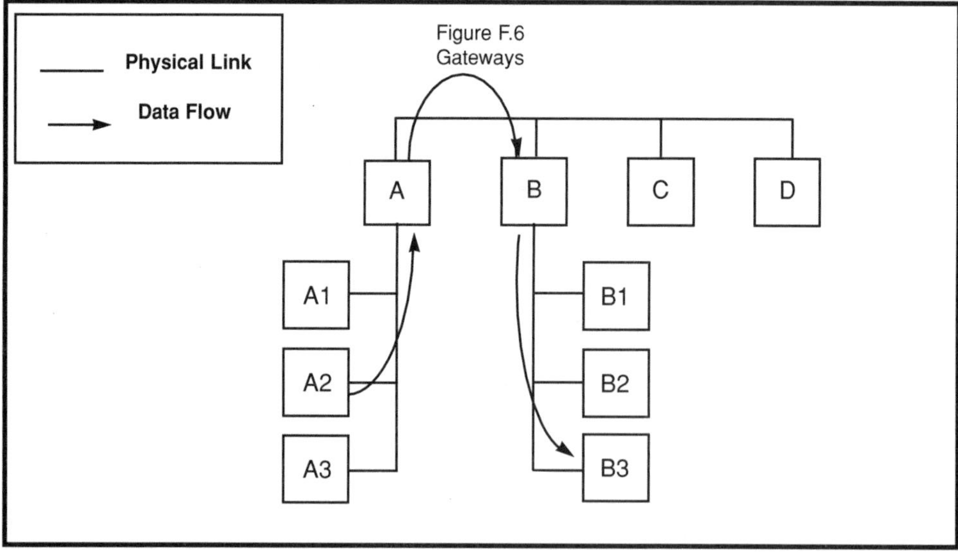

Figure F.5 shows connected ethernet networks.

Figure F.6 shows gateways with ethernet networks. The real distinction between a gateway and a router is that a gateway connects multiple networks together, acting as an interface between one set and another. It performs such functions as routing of transactions, address translation (multiple addresses to a single machine), and datagram filtering (preventing certain types of actions on the network below).

There are other physical network media besides ethernet that allow similar architectures or topologies. In addition, many networks are connected to multiple other networks, which provides redundancy with the routing technology able to find a path when the primary link is not available.

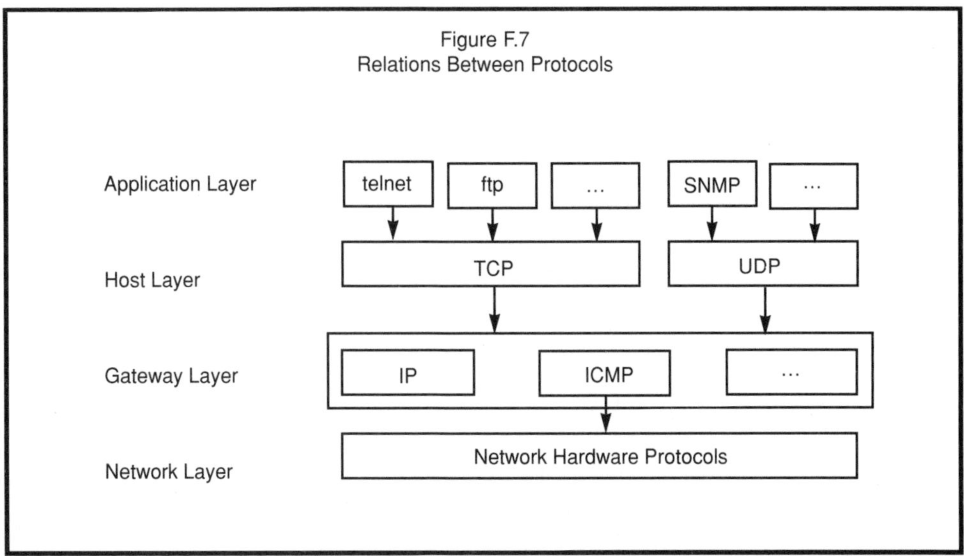

Figure F.7
Relations Between Protocols

TCP/IP are a pair of layered protocols; an application passes data to TCP, which passes it to IP; IP passes the data over the physical connectivity layer. Figure F.7 shows the relationship between the layers. As a user of TCP/IP, you do not need to be concerned with the layers, but it is useful to know the relationship and terminology.

In the process of data moving between the layers, it is broken up into packets, known as datagrams in TCP/IP terminology. The process of converting application data to datagrams is known as data encapsulation because the data is contained within the control information of the lower layers. One application data block may result in many datagrams because of size limitations. Because of the way datagrams can move through the network, it is possible for the second datagram to reach the destination before the first. It is the job of TCP to ensure reliable communications and combine the datagrams back into the original application data format at the recipient machine.

IP adds its own header to the TCP datagram by encapsulating the original data and the TCP header. Its main purpose is to route datagrams from one machine to another; TCP tells IP where to send it (the address of the machine). IP routes the datagrams by determining the best way to get them to their destination. There may be multiple paths between points and it tries to find the shortest path. Each time a datagram has to go through a host, it is known as a hop. IP does not verify that the data arrived, it only sends it out.

TCP verifies that the data got to its destination by maintaining a conversation mode between the two machines. It also ensures that the data arrived correctly without being corrupted. If the data is corrupted or does not arrive, TCP will resend the datagram. This continues through the whole time the application is communicating over the network or until TCP decides the connection is too unreliable to continue.

Figure F.8
TCP/IP Services

File Transfer	ftp command (uses FTP - File Transfer Protocol) rcp command which performs a remote copy (cp) between two machines
Remote Login	telnet command which connects a user to another machine tn command - another name for telnet tnvtXXX command (XXX can be 100, 320, etc.) telnet that emulates vt terminals tn5250 command - telnet emulating IBM 5250 terminal for connection to AS/400 tn3270 command - telnet that emulates IBM 3270 terminal for mainframe rlogin command which connects a user to another machine
Electronic Mail	mail command SMTP - Simple Mail Transport Protocol
RemoteExecution	rsh command - executes remote shell commands remsh command - another name for rsh rexec command - executes a single command on remote system rcmd command - executes remote shell commands in background RPC (Remote Procedural Call) allows one system to call functions on another NFS (Network File Server) allows remote systems to mount disks on local

The handshaking that TCP performs causes a fair amount of overhead, but it ensures reliable communications. Another protocol UDP (User Datagram Protocol), does nothing to ensure that data reaches the other end correctly, but forces the application to perform those tasks. But as a protocol, it has much less overhead than TCP. It also uses IP.

The physical or hardware layer may process each datagram further by breaking it into smaller pieces, applying headers, checksums, addresses. All of this is transparent to TCP and IP. An interface like x.25 has a maximum of 128 bytes for data; if the datagram is larger (including the TCP and IP headers), it will be split into smaller pieces. Other physical media have their own limits.

TCP/IP has expanded from a research and military network and is available for just about every system being manufactured today, from the PC to workstations to server/minicomputers to mainframes to supercomputers. TCP/IP, because it is available for so many platforms, provides a common method of communications enterprise-wide.

TCP/IP, when being used as the name for a suite of tools, includes file transfer, remote login, electronic mail, and remote execution. Figure F.8 shows the commands for each of the TCP/IP services.

It is truly based on the client-server paradigm—portions run on each machine where it is appropriate. The application program (or a command such as telnet) is the client and the system being connected to is the server. The server runs programs to communicate with the client code. Under UNIX, the server programs run as daemons—programs that are system related background processes. Figure F.9 lists the common TCP/IP daemons. Some, like inetd, run all the time, others, like telnetd, are loaded as needed.

Figure F.9
Common TCP/IP Daemons

Name	Purpose
inetd	Services Internet (TCP/IP) requests. Runs other daemons based on service type
named	Name server daemon. Translates system names to addresses
routed	Routing daemon. Performs routing; gated may be used instead
gated	Advanced Routing (Gateway) daemon. Provides additional protection; can act as firewall
nfsd	NFS server daemon. Provides disk drives to other systems
mountd	NFS mount daemon. Provides mount requests
nfsiod	NFS I/O daemon. Used by client system to connect to servers
timed	Time daemon. Uses NTP (Network Time Protocol) to synchronize time on systems
xntpd	Advanced time daemon. Uses XNTP protocol
rwhod	Remote who daemon. Provides information on system for rwho and ruptime commands
pppd	PPP daemon. Processes incoming PPP connections
lpd	Printer daemon. Processes remote printing requests
httpd	HyperText Transport Protocol daemon. Used for World WIde Web requests
fingerd	Processes finger requests
ftpd	Processes ftp requests
ntalkd	Processes talk requests
rshd	Processes remote shell requests (rsh, remsh, and rcmd)
rexecd	Processes remote exec requests (rexec)
telnetd	Processes telnet requests
tftpd	Processes tftp requests
uucpd	Processes uucp over TCP/IP requests
rpc*	Process remote procedure call requests. Execute functions called by other machines
sendmail	Processes incoming mail. Uses SMTP (Simple Mail Transport Protocol)

IP is designed to run over high-speed permanent connections. For dial-in, part-time connections, there are protocols that perform functions similar to IP: SLIP and PPP. SLIP stands for Serial Line IP and PPP stands for Point-to-Point IP. The primary difference between the two protocols is that SLIP is designed for a single system and PPP is designed to behave as a gateway, routing datagrams between one network and another. A network can consist of just one system. Figure F.10 lists the TCP/IP related protocols.

IP, SLIP, PPP, and ICMP are low level protocols. TCP and UDP are the next layer, and most of the other protocols use TCP or UDP. The file transport protocol (FTP) actually uses TCP, the trivial file transport protocol actually uses UDP. These third-level, application-specific protocols, are referred to as services. The protocols are defined in the file /etc/protocols, services in /etc/services.

Each of the networking protocols has a protocol number assigned to it so the lower layer (IP for instance) knows where to route the data (TCP or UDP). The translation table is /etc/protocols. The application protocols or services also have an identifying number known as a port and the protocol it uses (TCP or UDP). On some commands, you will see an option for port number or id, which is used to specify the service being used. The default usually works fine, although some systems use an alternate number to identify the service for internal reasons.

Figure F.10
TCP/IP Related Protocols

Protocol	Description
FTP	File Transfer Protocol
TFTP	Trivial File Transfer Protocol
NNTP	Net News Transfer Protocol
SMTP	Simple Mail Transport Protocol
SNMP	Simple Network Management Protocol
NTP/XNTP	Network Time Protocol and Extended Network Time Protocol
TCP	Transport Control Protocol
UDP	User Datagram Protocol
IP	Internet Protocol
IPv6	Internet Protocol, the next generation. Also known as IPng
PPP	Point-to-Point internet Protocol - routing IP over modem
SLIP	Serial Line IP - IP over modem
ICMP	Internet Control Message Protocol
RIP	Routing Information Protocol (used by routed or gated)

TCP/IP Tools and Commands

When you are working with the TCP/IP suite of tools, there are two ways you can specify a system address: system name (node name) and numeric address. Internally, the numeric address is used. The translation is a process known as name lookup and is performed through the /etc/hosts file for small internal networks and a Domain Name Server (DNS) for larger internal networks and the Internet.

TCP/IP Addresses

The DNS is basically a list of systems and their IP addresses. The IP address is currently 32 bits broken down into 4 bytes (referred to as octets because some systems have bytes that are not 8-bits wide). When an IP address is written or used with a command, the form is 198.76.168.9.

There are four classes of networks determined by the maximum number of systems that can be connected. Class A networks are identified by the first bit of the first octet set to zero; the next 7 bits identify the network. There can only be 126 networks with 16,777,216 hosts on each. Class B networks have the first two bits set to 10 with the next 14 bits used for the network id: 128.1 through 191.254. There can be 16,384 networks with 64,516 hosts each. Class C networks have the first three bits set to 110 and use the next 21 bits for the network: 192.1.1 through 223.254.254. There can be 2,097,152 networks with 254 hosts on each. Host numbers above 223 are reserved for future use.

Most of the class A and B addresses have been assigned and the class C addresses are running out fast. At the present time, an organization that has more systems than would fit in a class C network is being assigned multiple class C network addresses. Because the addresses are running out so fast, a new numbering scheme has been adopted: IPv6 or IPng which is a 64-bit addressing scheme; effectively an extension of the 32-bit standard. The difficult part for the designers was handling the current 32-bit addresses while implementing the new standard—not everyone will be able to change their software at the same exact time.

Figure F.11
Common Domain Names

Domain	Purpose
.edu	Educational organizations (colleges, school districts, technical schools, etc.)
.com	Commercial enterprise (a company or corporation)
.net	Network organization (Internet provider)
.mil	Military
.gov	Governmental
.org	Other. Some organization that does not fit the other categories
.uk	Systems in the United Kingdom
.ca	Systems in Canada
.au	Systems in Australia
.nz	Systems in New Zealand
.de	Systems in Germany (Deutschland)
.us	Systems in the United States not belonging to three-letter domains (often home systems)

Using the Internet host name is much easier than remembering four three-digit numbers because it usually contains a mnemonic meaning in the form of computer.organization.domain. The domain is typically a two or three character abbreviation for the type of organization to which the systems belong. Figure F.11 shows a survey of the domain names. Additional ones will be coming soon (.firm, .rec, etc.).

Technically, all systems in the United States should belong to the .us domain, but because the Internet began in the United States, the three-letter domain names were assigned to organizations here. I have sent electronic mail to people outside the United States that had three-letter domain names (mostly .com). In those cases, the company for which they work (who provides them Internet access) is based in the United States. The company extends its internal network to other countries. Some of the large computer manufacturers work this way.

The next level is the organization name. It could be the company, network provider, branch of government or military, or educational institution. The next level is the name of the host within the organization. Some organizations provide a single address (organization.com) and internally transfer or route datagrams to the proper computer system internally. If the organization breaks things down further internally, there may be multiple names instead of one host name. One company splits addresses based on the internal network involved so the address looks like computer.network.company.com. Another might break it down by internal organizational lines: computer.division.company.com. There is no requirement to do this, it just makes administration easier and in some cases, makes the address easier to remember.

There are also some common hostnames that you should be aware of. Like the splitting of organizations, these are naming conventions, not requirements. Figure F.12 shows some of the common host names. Again, these are conventions but not all organizations follow them.

If someone gives you his or her electronic mail address, it generally will be in the form theirname@host.organization.domain. That person's name could be in the form first_last, first.last,

Figure F.12
Common Host Names

Host	Purpose
ftp	Source of files through ftp command
www	Source of HTML documents through HTTP
gopher	Searched by Gopher Internet search engines
archie	Searched by Archie Internet search engines

firstlast, FMlast, or something similar. The way you read it is their name at host dot organization dot domain.

Enough about the background on how the Internet works, and how the addresses are put together, it is time to look at the commands you use with TCP/IP.

TCP/IP COMMANDS

The commonly used TCP/IP commands are shown in Figure F.13.

Check the man pages on your system for more information or one of the books listed in Appendix G.

OTHER INTERNET TOOLS

There are a number of other tools for accessing data over TCP/IP networks and the Internet. The World Wide Web is accessed through a Web Browser, which is simply a tool that processes HTTP and documents written in HTML (HyperText Markup Language). The web is not an independent network, it is just an artificial structure imposed over the existing Internet. Some sites have separate machines to act as web servers (usually with the www. prefix), others have a single machine that performs multiple purposes such as web server, student homework, etc. Because one machine can have multiple addresses, the same physical machine may be known by multiple names (one with and one without the www. prefix).

HTML is similar to the runoff family of text processing languages except it has links to other documents and files that may be on the same or different systems. You can start in one place, step through several links, and end up looking at material from the other side of the world. This navigation all occurs through hyper text. The web browser does the communications and displays the material for you. Like ftp, a web browser is just another program that communicates with servers over the network. Most browsers are graphical in nature since the web includes graphical material (pictures, drawings, and even video). Of course, there are character-only versions for people using older terminals that do not display any graphics and are severely limited ways of browsing the web.

Internet Relay Chat (IRC) is another structure imposed over the network. The IRC is similar to a Citizens-Band radio. People join groups (like channels) and hold multiway communications via keyboard. The machines are not directly connected, but each person is connected to an IRC server. Multiple people may be connected to the same server and the servers communicate with

Figure F.13
TCP/IP Tools and Commands

Command	Purpose
telnet, tn	Use telnet protocol to connect (to login) to another system Most PC emulators emulate vt100 terminals; most UNIX versions can also emulate the vt100
tn3270	Telnet command emulating a mainframe terminal
tn5250	Telnet command emulating an IBM AS/400 system terminal
tnvt320	Telnet command emulation a vt320 terminal (advanced vt100)
rlogin	Connect and login to another system. Usually does not emulate terminals
rsh, remsh	Remote shell allowing execution of commands or jobs on another system Output is returned to local system (and your terminal)
rexec	Remote shell allowing execution of one command on another system Output is returned to local system (and your terminal)
rcmd	Remote shell allowing execution of command or job on another system Output is not returned to local system
ping	Determines if specified system is connected to the network (and is up and running). It also can tell you how long a character takes to travel between the local and remote systems
rcp	Remote file copy. Acts like the cp command between two systems
ftp	File Transfer Program that uses the File Transfer Protocol to move files between systems. A system may allow anonymous logins (no need for a userid on the remote system) for the distribution of files and programs

each other so it appears that everyone is directly connected to each other. The whole purpose of IRC is to hold conversations, or, as the name implies, allow people to chat with each other. Like ftp and www, you need a program to communicate. There are character and graphical interface versions of IRC available.

I-phone or Internet-Phone has been a frequent topic in the media recently. It is software for using the Internet like a speaker phone or semiprivate CB radio. The software takes advantage of the capabilities of sound cards attached to each PC to input and output speech, but because most sound cards can only input or output, not both at the same time, the conversation can only occur one way at a time. Because of the way data moves over the Internet, there may be delays in the transmission of blocks of speech. Instead of hearing the other person immediately (or after a small fraction of a second delay if you are talking to Australia) on a regular telephone, there can be delays of several seconds or more.

Normal telephones are full-duplex, meaning both parties can speak at the same time. Most radios (CB) are half-duplex—only one can talk at a time. Most Internet phone software is half-duplex due to the sound card limitations. You might wonder how you can make calls all over the world for the cost of a local call (to your Internet provider). It is possible because the network is turned on all the time—the phone lines are always open. The cost for the network is already being paid for whether it is used or not. Think of it another way: The long distance telephone companies have networks of phone lines throughout the country. They are not used all of the time, some have to be held in reserve for line breakage and peak times. The phone lines are there, they are maintained, and they cost the company money, used or unused.

The Internet is similar. The major difference is that many more people have telephones than have access to the Internet. You cannot call someone who does not have a telephone, just as you cannot call someone over the Internet if he or she doesn't have access or the right software. It is because of this that the phone companies are unhappy with Internet telephones. Basically they provide the caller with the equivalent of practically free phone calls. This whole area may become regulated or charged much like current long distance calls. Only the future will tell.

There are also older ways of communicating over the Internet; electronic mail is one of them. It is similar to regular paper mail (often referred to as snail mail or Usnail or similar names) where you create something and send it to the recipient. Once he or she receives it, he or she reads it at his or her convenience and may reply. Both text and converted binary files (see uuencode and uudecode) can be sent through e-mail—programs, pictures, and word processing documents are all specially formatted files that you can think of as being binary. One word of caution: e-mail is much more public than paper mail; so think of it as a postcard. Just about anyone who handles it can read it although most will not bother to spend the time. Although there are laws regarding privacy of e-mail, to a large extent, that only regulates the government and not individuals. There are tools to enhance the privacy of your e-mail; PGP (Pretty Good Privacy by Jeff Zimmerman) is one of them (it encrypts your mail in a form that only the recipient can read). Or at least that is the theory. It could prevent your boss or spouse from reading your mail, but it probably would not prevent a governmental agency if they really wanted to.

Another older form of communications that goes over the Internet is netnews. At one time, netnews traveled exclusively over UUCP networks between UNIX machines and others that ran UUCP programs. Now most traffic travels over the Internet. Netnews is a global bulletin board. You post a note and people may respond. They can respond with other postings or they can send you e-mail about it. The postings (and response postings) are public; e-mail replies are private from the standpoint that the world is not reading them.

There are new Internet tools being developed constantly. If they fill a need, they become popular and remain around for a while; if they do not, they quietly die off. Some tools fill needs that slowly disappear. It is during only the past few years that Internet connections became affordable for the private individual. UUCP, for example, provides a means for any technically competent person to send e-mail and access netnews. Now that Internet access is cheap and (relatively) easy to use, however, the UUCP networks are falling into disuse. They filled a need that is ceasing to exist.

SNA—IBM Systems Network Architecture

Most mainframe applications are accessed through terminals generically known as model 3270 terminals. The terminal may be a 3178 or 3179 or some other model, but they all talk the same language as the original model 3270 terminals. On the mainframe, VTAM (Virtual Terminal Access Method) communicates with these terminals. It handles data routing, sets up the packets to send to the terminal, and translates the incoming packets for applications. This is known generically as LU2 (Logical Unit 2) and is a component of SNA. As the name implies, SNA is an architecture, not a specific product. It is a collection of products, tools, and protocols much in the same way TCP/IP refers to more than just a protocol.

A 3270 terminal can be emulated through the tn3270 command on a UNIX system or PC. The emulator understands and processes the same control sequences as a real terminal but the data is transmitted using TCP/IP protocol. A user terminal session can connect to the mainframe through SNA gateways and by running TCP/IP on the mainframe.

SNA gateways talk to the mainframe using SNA protocols and connect to a routed TCP/IP network using TCP/IP. Each device on the TCP/IP network communicates using the TCP/IP protocols; to the mainframe, it is communicating through SNA protocols. The gateway system performs the translations. The data to the mainframe application is encapsulated in TCP/IP datagrams between the user device and the gateway. The downside to gateways is the additional equipment required that must be maintained and administered. When it becomes too busy, new gateways must be added.

Using IBM MPTN (Multiprotocol Transport Network), the mainframe runs TCP/IP and telnet servers that pass the data through VTAM to the individual application the user connects to (like CICS or IMS/DC).

IBM 3745 and 3712 controllers can now support TCP/IP directly and will act as network routers within the TCP/IP network. Not only will they gateway between the mainframe and the TCP/IP network, they will also route transactions for the network.

SNA also supports other logical units including 0, 1, 3, and 6.2. LU0 is used for unformatted data much like UDP in TCP/IP. LU1 is used for printing. LU3 is used for RJE (Remote Job Entry) stations that can include card readers, card punches, printers, and a console. In reality, most RJE stations are now implemented as software on other systems with logical card readers and punches—jobs for the mainframe are sent to a queue that looks like a card reader to the mainframe.

LU6.2 is becoming much more common and is used for Inner Process Communications (IPC) using APPC (Advanced Peer-to-Peer Communications), CPI-C (Common Programming Interface—C language), and ENHAPPC (Enhanced APPC). Basically, they are a set of Application Program Interfaces (API) for program-to-program communications. Because the API code is at such a low level, they are rarely used by application programs. Instead, they are wrapped in other code and used through function libraries known as middleware. CICS can run on top of LU6.2, providing mainframe data access to applications running on other systems.

APPENDIX G

REFERENCES, READING LIST, OTHER SOURCES

TRAINING

Local colleges (credit and non-credit)

Your local college is a great place to start. Many offer college credit courses in UNIX, C, C++, networking, and other topics that are important to the market. In many organizations, funding for training and travel expenses is difficult to find, but funding for college courses is still available. You may have to take the course on your own time and get a decent grade, but you can get your employer to pay for it. In many of the evening schools, the courses are taught by local professionals who end up teaching what they were working on during the day. Personally, I teach C at a local community (junior or county) college; I enjoy it and feel I really help my students.

USER GROUPS AND CONFERENCES

USENIX 'YY, The USENIX Association, 2560 Ninth Street, Suite 215, Berkeley, CA 94710 USA, office@usenix.org, 510-528-8649/f:5738. Usenix Conference Office, Lake Forest, CA, 714-588-8649, conference@usenix.org

UniForum 'YY, The Interface Group, http://www.uniforum.org, 800-255-5620/408-986-8840

SANS (System Administration, Networking, and Security) Conference 'YY, by Sage (USENIX) and FedUNIX, 719-599-4303, sans@fedunix.org

Open Computing & Server Strategies Conference, Meta Group Inc., 203-973-6715

Software Development 'YY, 800-441-8826

DECUS 'YY, Digital Equipment Computer User Society, 800-DEC-US55.

Unix Expo 'YY

IBM Technical Interchange 'YY, 800-872-7109 or 617-893-2056

You can also use the learn command that comes with some versions of UNIX.

There is also a UNIX course available via World Wide Web at http://cuhhca.hhmi.columbia.edu/classes/unix.html, and a C++ class at http://uu-gna.mit.edu:8001/uu-gna/text/cc/index.html

Figure G.1 shows some of the newsgroups in netnews (discussion groups over the Internet) related to UNIX.

Figure G.1
Newsgroups

Newsgroup	Topic Area
comp.os.unix	UNIX operating systems
comp.os.aix	IBM AIX flavor of UNIX operating systems
comp.os.bsd	BSD UNIX operating systems
comp.sys.3b1	AT&T 7300/3B1/UNIX PC systems
comp.sys.acorn	Acorn and ARM-based systems
comp.sys.amiga.*	Amiga systems
comp.sys.apollo.*	Apollo systems
comp.sys.att	AT&T older systems (prior to AT&T/NCR merger)
comp.sys.cdc	Control Data Corporation systems
comp.sys.convex	Convex systems
comp.sys.dec	DEC systems
comp.sys.hp.*	HP systems
comp.sys.ibm.pc.*	Intel x86-based systems
comp.sys.intel	Intel built x86-based systems (and often PCs)
comp.sys.m68k	Motorola 68000 chip-based systems
comp.sys.mac	Apple Macintosh systems
comp.sys.mips	MIPS chip-based systems
comp.sys.ncr	AT&T/NCR systems
comp.sys.next	Next systems
comp.sys.powerpc	PowerPC chip-based systems
comp.sys.pyramid	Pyramid systems
comp.sys.sequent	Sequent systems
comp.sys.sgi	Silicon Graphics Iris systems
comp.sys.sun	Sun Microsystems systems
comp.sys.unisys	Burroughs, Convergent, Sperry, and Unisys systems

and many others!

Books

1996 UNIX Business Software Directory, CBM Books, 800-285-1755 or 215-643-8105.

A Quarter Century of Unix, Salus, Addison-Wesley Publishing Company, 1994, ISBN: 0-201-54777-5, U$26.95

Building Internet Firewalls, Brent Chapman and Elizabeth Zwicky, O'Reilly & Associates, Inc., 1995, ISBN 1-56592-124-0.

Data Link Protocols, Uyless Black, Prentice Hall PTR, 1993, ISBN 0-13-204918-X.

Ethernet Tips and Techniques, Byron Spinney, Prentice Hall PTR, 1998, ISBN 0-13-755950-X.

Firewalls and Internet Security, Cheswick/Bellovin, Addison-Wesley Publishing Company, 1994, ISBN 0-201-63357-4.

How to Manage Your Network Using SNMP: The Networking Management Practicum, Marshall Rose and Keith McCloghrie, Prentice Hall PTR, 1995, ISBN 0-13-141517-4.

The HP-UX System Administrator's "How To" Book, Marty Poniatowski, Prentice Hall PTR, 1994, ISBN 0-13-099821-4.

IBM International Technical Support Centers, *MVS to AIX Application Migration Cookbook*, GG24-4375-00.

Internetworking with TCP/IP, Volume I, Principles, Protocols, and Architecture, 3rd ed., Douglas E. Comer, Prentice Hall PTR, 1995, ISBN 0-13-216987-8.

IPng and the TCP/IP Protocols, Stephen A. Thomas, Wiley, 1996, ISBN 0-471-13088-5.

Learning the GNU Emacs, Debra Cameron and Bill Rosenblatt, O'Reilly & Associates, Inc., 1992, ISBN 0-937175-84-6.

Learning Perl, Randal L. Schwartz, O'Reilly & Associates, Inc., 1993, ISBN 1-56592-042-2.

Learning the Korn Shell, Bill Rosenblatt, O'Reilly & Associates, Inc., 1993, ISBN 1-56592-054-6.

Learning the UNIX Operating System, Grace Todino, John Strang and Jerry Peek, O'Reilly & Associates, Inc., 1993, ISBN 1-56592-060-0.

Learning the vi Editor, Linda Lamb, O'Reilly & Associates, Inc., 1990, ISBN 0-937175-67-6.

Local and Metropolitan Area Networks, William Stallings, Macmillan, 1993.

Managing Internet Information Services, Cricket Liu *et al.*, O'Reilly & Associates, Inc., 1994, ISBN 1-56592-062-7.

Networking Personal Computers with TCP/IP, Craig Hunt, O'Reilly & Associates, Inc., 1995, ISBN 1-56592-123-2.

Newnes UNIX Pocket Book, Steve Heath, ISBN 0-7506-2073-0, Newnes/Butterworth-Heinemann Ltd. I do not know if you will find this book in the U.S. I picked up my copy at a conference in Cannes, France in 1994. I carry this one with me all the time.

O'Reilly & Associates reference set—O'Reilly & Associates, Inc., 707-829-0515—excellent learning books.

Practical Internetworking with TCP/IP and UNIX, Carl-Mitchell/Quarterman, Addison-Wesley Publishing Co., 1993, ISBN 0-201-58629-0.

Practical UNIX and Internet Security, Simson Garfinkel/Gene Spafford, O'Reilly & Associates, Inc., 1996, ISBN 1-56592-148-8.

Running Linux, Matt Welsh/Lar Kaufman, O'Reilly & Associates, Inc., 1995, ISBN 1-56592-100-3, U$24.95.

SNMP Application Developer's Guide, Robert L. Townsend, Van Nostrand Reinhold, 1995.

SNMP, SNMPv2, and CMIP: The Practical Guide to Network-Management Standards, William Stallings, Addison-Wesley, 1993, ISBN 0-201-63331-0.

STREAMS Modules and Drivers for UNIX System V, Release 4.2, The UNIX System Group, UNIX Press, Prentice Hall PTR, 1992.

TCP/IP Illustrated, Volume I: The Protocols, W. Richard Stevens, Addison-Wesley Publishing Company, 1994, ISBN 0-201-63346-9.

TCP/IP Illustrated, Volume II: The Implementation, W. Richard Stevens, Addison-Wesley Publishing Company, 1994, ISBN 0-201-63354-X.

TCP/IP Network Administration, Hunt, O'Reilly & Associates, Inc., 1992, 0-937175-82-X.

The Awk Programming Language, Alfred V. Aho, Brian W. Kernighan, and Peter J. Weinberger, Addison-Wesley Publishing Company, ISBN 0-201-07981-X.

The C Programming Language, Brian W. Kernighan and Dennis M. Ritchie, Prentice Hall PTR, ISBN 0-13-110163-3. The second edition (Prentice Hall PTR, 1989, ISBN 0-13-110362-8) includes information on ANSI C.

The C++ Programming Language, 2nd ed., Bjarne Stroustrup, AT&T Bell Laboratories, Addison-Wesley Publishing Company, 1991.

The Complete Idiot's Guide to UNIX, John McMullen, Alpha Books, 1995, ISBN 1-56761-511-2.

The Device Driver Interface/Driver-Kernel Interface (DDI/DKI) Reference Manual for UNIX System V, Release 4, UNIX Press, Prentice Hall PTR, 1992.

The Internet Book: Everything You Need to Know About Computer Networking and How the Internet Works, Douglas E. Comer, Prentice Hall PTR, ISBN 0-13-890161-9.

The Internet Connection: System Connectivity and Configuration, Carl-Mitchell/Quarterman, Addison-Wesley Publishing Co., ISBN 0-201-54237-4.

The KornShell Command and Programming Language, Morris I. Bolsky and David G. Korn, Prentice Hall PTR, ISBN 0-13-516972-0.

The Simple Book: An Introduction to Networking Management, 2nd ed., by Marshall T. Rose, Prentice-Hall PTR, 1996, ISBN: 0-13-451659-1.

The UNIX and X Command Compendium, Alan Southerton, Edwin C. Perkins, Jr., ISBN 0-471-01281-5, John Wiley & Sons, Inc. Listing of most UNIX commands with entries for each option categorized by shell, UNIX version, and type (skill level) of user—comes highly recommended by a UNIX guru I know.

The UNIX Programming Environment, Brian W. Kernighan and Rob Pike, ISBN 0-13-937681-X, Prentice Hall.

The UNIX-Haters Handbook, Garfinkel/Weise/Strassmann, International Data Group (IDG Books), 1994, ISBN 1-56884-203-1. Foreword by Dennis Ritchie.

Total SNMP, 2nd ed., Sean Harnedy, Prentice Hall PTR, 1998, ISBN 0-13-646994-9.

UNIX in a Nutshell, Gilly, O'Reilly & Associates, Inc., 1992, ISBN 1-56592-001-5.

UNIX Network Programming, by W. Richard Stevens, Prentice Hall PTR, 1990, ISBN 0-13-949876-1.

UNIX System Administration Handbook, Evi Nemeth, Garth Snyder, and Scott Seebass, Prentice Hall PTR, ISBN 0-13-933441-6.

UNIX System V Release 4 Programmer's Guide Networking Interfaces, The UNIX System Group, UNIX Press, Prentice Hall PTR, 1992, ISBN 0-13-020645-8.

UNIX System V Release 4 Programmer's Guide: STREAMS for Intel Processors, The UNIX System Group, UNIX Press, Prentice Hall PTR, 1991, ISBN 0-13-879461-8.

UNIX, Quick!, Andrew Feibus, CBM Books, ISBN 1-878956-01-9.

Using the Korn Shell, Rosenblatt, O'Reilly & Associates, Inc.

When You Can't Find Your UNIX System Administrator, Linda Mui, O'Reilly & Associates, Inc., 1995, 1-56592-104-6, U$19.95. Acts as second book to *Learning the UNIX Operating System*.

Zen and the Art of the Internet, Brendan P. Kehoe, Prentice Hall PTR, ISBN 0-13-010778-6.

MAGAZINES/NEWSPAPERS

/AIXtra, IBM, Department 40-B3-04, P.O. Box 9000, Roanoke, TX 76262-9989.

AIXpert "A publication for AIX developers," Gloria Hardman, Editor, AIXpert, IBM Corporation, Mail Stop 36, 472 Wheelers Farms Road, Millford, CT, USA 06460, hardman@rhqvm21.vnet.ibm.com

DEC Professional, Cardinal Business Media, 708-564-1385, FX 708-564-9002.

HP Professional, Cardinal Business Media, 708-564-1385, FX 708-564-9002.

IBM Internet Journal, Cardinal Business Media, 708-564-1385, FX 708-564-9002 (networking—mainframe to mixed platform).

INTERNETWORK, Cardinal Business Media, 708-564-1385, FX 708-564-9002 (networking—mixed platform).

MIDRANGE Systems, Cardinal Business Media, 708-564-1385, FX 708-564-9002 (AS/400 and RS/6000).

Open Computing, Subscription Services, P.O. Box 570, Hightstown, NJ 08520-0570.

RS/Magazine, Computer Publishing Group, 320 Washington Street, Brookline, MA 02146, 617-739-7001 FX 617-739-7003, http://www.cpg.com

RS/The PowerPC Magazine, Circulation Department, Computer Publishing Group Inc., 1330 Beacon Street, Brookline, MA 02146, 617-739-7001 circ@cpg.com. Free to qualified subscribers, $60 US otherwise.

SunExpert Magazine, Computer Publishing Group, 320 Washington Street, Brookline, MA 02146, 617-739-7001 FX 617-739-7003, http://www.cpg.com

SysAdmin, R&D Publications, Inc., 1601 W. 23rd Street, Suite 200, Lawrence, KS 66046-2700, 913-841-1631, approximately $40 per year.

UNIX Review, P.O. Box 420035, Palm Coast, FL, 32142-0035.

GLOSSARY

$HOME	Special environmental variable that points to your login directory.
/etc/group file	Contains information about groups, the users they contain, and passwords required for access by other users. Some systems put the password in a shadow group file to protect from attacks.
/etc/motd file	Message Of The Day—information the system administrator feels is important for you to know.
/etc/passwd file	Contains user information and password. Some systems actually put the password in a shadow password file to protect from attacks.
arguments	See parameters.
ARPA	See DARPA.
ASCII	American Standard Code for Information Interchange. The code used to represent characters in memory for most non-mainframe computers.
AT&T UNIX	Original version of UNIX developed at AT&T Bell Labs, later known as UNIX System Laboratories. Many current versions (or flavors) of UNIX are descendants from this. BSD UNIX was derived from early AT&T UNIX and is the other major direction.
background	Programs usually running at a lower priority and with their input disconnected from the interactive session. If they require input and stdin is not redirected to a file or another program, they will wait.
batch	Also known as a background process under UNIX.
batch queue	Where jobs are submitted for processing. Under UNIX, some system administrators create batch queues, on other systems, use the cron, crontab, and at commands—or a 3rd party tool.
binary data	Information stored using entire character set. May include printable and control characters because it is the same bit pattern as used in memory to store the information. When in memory, it can be directly manipulated by the CPU because it is in native format. This data causes problems with UNIX tools

	because it can represent special characters that match end-of-file or the record separator. Known as COMP fields in COBOL. COBOL COMP-3 fields (packed data) cause the same problems as COBOL COMP fields.
binary fields	See binary data.
Bourne Shell	The original standard user interface to UNIX; supports programming.
BSD UNIX	Version of UNIX developed by BSD. Many current versions (or flavors) of UNIX are descendants from this. AT&T UNIX is the other major direction.
C	Programming language developed by Brian W. Kernighan and Dennis M. Ritchie. UNIX is written using C. The C language is highly portable and available on many platforms.
C Shell	A user interface for UNIX; supports programming. Written by Bill Joy at Berkeley.
CASE	Computer Aided Software Engineering. A suite of tools designed to assist in the development of software. It has not yet lived up to the marketing hype.
catalog	This is the means used on a mainframe to store the location of a dataset anywhere in the system. The dataset can be stored on a hard disk or tape. So long as it is in the catalog, the programmer does not need to know which specific volume contains the dataset. It also contains information about the structure of the file (information from the DCB). Loosely equivalent to a UNIX directory.
CD-ROM	Compact Disk-Read Only Memory. Computer readable data stored on the same media as a musical CD. Large capacity, inexpensive, slower than a hard disk, cannot be written to by most computer users. There is equipment that allows the recording of these disks (CD-R, CD Recordable) and other formats that can be written to once or many times.
characters, alphabetic	The letters A through Z and a through z. Can be represented using ASCII or EBCDIC.
characters, alphanumeric	The letters A through Z and a through z, the numbers 0 through 9. Can be represented using ASCII or EBCDIC.
characters, control	Any non-printable characters. The characters at the beginning of the interchange codes have special meaning such as controlling devices, separating records, and ejecting pages on printers. Can be represented using ASCII or EBCDIC.

characters, numeric	The numbers 0 through 9. Can be represented using ASCII or EBCDIC.
characters, special	Any of the punctuation characters or printable characters that are not alphanumeric. Include the space, comma, period, and many others. Can be represented using ASCII or EBCDIC.
CICS	Customer Information Control System. OLTP tool for the mainframe.
CMS	Code Management System. The primary guest operating system under VM that provides an interactive program development environment.
command line editing	The ability to take a previous command, modify it, and re-execute it without typing it in from scratch.
command line parameters	Used to specify parameters to pass to the execute program or procedure. Equivalent to EXEC PARM=. Also known as command line arguments.
COMP	See binary data.
COND=	Used to control execution of steps within a job based on return codes from prior executed programs and PROCs. The Korn shell variable $? contains program return codes which value can be saved and tested.
configuration files	Collections of information for commands and programs. Also sets up user session when using shell configuration files.
configuration files, shell	For Bourne shell: /etc/profile and $HOME/.profile For Korn shell: /etc/profile, $HOME/.profile, and ENV= file For C shell: /etc/.login, /etc/cshrc, $HOME/.login, $HOME/.cshrc, and $HOME/.logout
CPU	Central Processing Unit. The guts of the computer—the calculation and logic controller. Some systems will contain multiple Central Processing Units. If the system manufacturer also makes the CPU, it is referred to as proprietary. If another company makes the CPU, it is considered open (like the CPU used in a PC).
daemon	A system related background process that runs with the permissions of root and services requests from other processes.
DARPA	(U.S. Department of) Defense Advanced Research Projects Agency. Funded development of TCP/IP and ARPAnet (predecessor of the Internet).

datasetname — The name of a file on the mainframe; see filename.

datasets — Name for files on mainframe; see files.

DB2 — Data Base/2. Relational database for the mainframe from IBM.

DCB — Data Control Block. Specifies information about a mainframe dataset including record format, record length, and block length.

DD — Data Description. No direct UNIX-standard equivalent; many COBOL compilers will look for and environmental variable in the form $dd_DDNAME (that contains the filename) for SELECT FD-NAME ASSIGN TO UT-S-DDNAME.

device file — File used to implement access to a physical device. Provides consistent approach to access of storage media under UNIX—data files and devices like tapes are implemented as files; to the programmer, there is no real difference.

directory — It is a collection of files. The directory itself is a file that contains a list of files contained within it. The root (/) directory is the top level and every other directory is below it. A directory may contain other directories which are referred to as sub-directories.

directory navigation — This is the process of moving through directories. The directory you are in is your current working directory. The directory you get when you log in is your default directory. You can move up and down through the tree structure with the `cd` command.

DISP= — Dataset disposition processing—what to do before the step is run, what to do when it is done, and what to do if the step fails. Because UNIX does not provide this functionality, it must be mimicked programmatically:

NEW—Default behavior if no file; use UNIX touch to create empty copy.

OLD—Must code shell script test for existence.

MOD—Default behavior if file exists.

CATLG—No real equivalent under UNIX (no catalog).

KEEP—Default behavior under UNIX.

DELETE—Must explicitly use `rm` command

UNCATLG—No real equivalent under UNIX; `rm` command deletes.

DNS — Domain Name Server—converts the name of a machine on the Internet to the Internet address (numeric).

DOS	Disk Operating System. Disk based operating system. MS-DOS and PC-DOS are the Disk Operating Systems for the Personal Computer. MS-DOS is the version Microsoft sells, PC-DOS the version IBM sells. Both are based on Microsoft code.
DSN	See datasetname.
EBCDIC	Extended Binary Coded Decimal Interchange Code. The code used to represent characters in memory for mainframe computers.
ESA	Extended System Architecture. Operating system that worked with the extended system architecture of some machines to allow more real and virtual memory with multiple sets of 2 Gb address spaces.
ESDS	Entry Sequenced Data Set. See VSAM.
ethernet	Networking hardware where all computers are connected to a single line and all traffic is available to every machine. The traffic includes an identifier of the recipient who is the only machine that bothers to pay attention to it.
EXEC PARM=	Used to specify parameters to pass to the execute program or procedure. Under UNIX, these are known as command line arguments—place the parameters on the command line (after the program name or shell script to execute).
EXEC PGM=/PROC=	Used to specify program or proc (procedure) to execute. Under UNIX, there is no distinction—just enter the name of the program or shell script to execute.
expression	It is a constant, variable, or operands and operators combined.
fifo	See pipe, named.
file compression	The process of applying mathematical formula to data resulting in a form of the data that occupies less space. A compressed file can be uncompressed (lossless) resulting in the original file.
file, indexed	A file based on ISAM or VSAM KSDS.
file, line sequential	A file with record separators. May be fixed or variable length; UNIX tools can handle these files because it can tell when the record ends (by the separator).
file, sequential	A file without record separators. Typically fixed length but UNIX does not know what that length is and does not care. The mainframe breaks the records down for you.
filename	The name used to identify a collection of data (a file). Without a pathname, it is assumed to be in the current directory.

filename, fully qualified	The name used to identify a collection of data (a file) and its location. It includes both the pathname and name of the file; usually the pathname is absolute. See also pathname and pathname, absolute.
files	A collection of information. Under UNIX there are device, directory, pipes, links, and plain files. A plain file is usually a data file or executable program. See also pipe. See also link.
filesystem	Is a collection of disk storage that is connected (mounted) to the directory structure at some point (often at the root). The storage is also referred to as a disk partition. It is similar to a SMS storage group.
flags	See options.
foreground	Programs running while connected to the interactive session.
fseek	Tool used by UNIX to locate data inside a file or filesystem. It accepts a parameter that can hold a value of +2 to -2 Billion. This function, used by the operating system, system tools, and application programs, is the cause of the 2 Gb file and filesystem size limitation.
GDG	Generation Data Group. Method of providing for child-parent-grandparent relationships of files on the mainframe. No direct UNIX equivalent; see Appendix B (Hints and Techniques) for GDG replacements.
here document	See SYSIN, Embedded.
HPO	High Performance Option.
HTML	HyperText Markup Language—describes World Wide Web pages.
i-node	Describes a file and where it is stored. A directory contains a cross-reference between the i-node and pathname/filename combination. Also known as inode.
ICMP	Internet Control Message Protocol—part of TCP/IP.
IDCAMS	Mainframe utility to create and delete VSAM and GDG files. Third-party tools may have utilities to manipulate ISAM files; see Appendix B (Hints and Techniques) for GDG replacements.
IEBGENER	Mainframe utility used to copy files. Use UNIX `cp` command.
IEBPTPCH	Print/Punch utility on the mainframe. Use UNIX `lp` or `lpr` command.

IEFBR14	The worlds smallest utility. All it does is return control to the operating system on the mainframe. But as a result, all file operations specified in the JCL take place. Use UNIX touch or rm command.
IKJEFT01	The program that is TSO—it can be run in a batch job to execute TSO commands in batch. Use UNIX `ksh`, `bsh`, `sh`, or `csh` command to invoke a sub-shell.
IMS	Information Management System. Older, hierarchical database for the mainframe from IBM.
IOF	Input/Output Facility. See SDSF.
ISAM	Indexed Sequential Access Method. On mainframe systems, VSAM replaced it. On UNIX and other systems, ISAM refers to a method for accessing data in a keyed and sequential way. ISAM to most mainframe professionals refers to the product IBM replaced with VSAM.
ISPF 0 (User Parameters)	Used to set session environment. Under UNIX, commands are put in .profile, .kshrc, .login, .cshrc, or .logout depending on the shell you are using. The vi editor configuration is stored in .exrc.
ISPF 1 (Browse)	Use UNIX view (or `vi -R`), uni-SPF 1 (browse), or SPF-UX 1 (browse) command.
ISPF 2 (Edit)	Use UNIX vi or emacs, uni-SPF 2 (edit), or SPF-UX 2 (edit) command.
ISPF 3.1 (Library)	Use the UNIX `mkdir`, `rmdir`, `mvdir`, `cd`, or `ls` command to manipulate subdirectories with act to replace mainframe library datasets (PDS).
ISPF 3.2 (Dataset)	Use the UNIX `touch`, `rm`, `>` *`filename`*, `ls`, or `df` command to manipulate files.
ISPF 3.3 (Copy/Move)	Use the following UNIX commands: `cp` to copy, `mv` to move, `ln` to link (create another name for the same file), or `mvdir` to move a directory.
ISPF 3.4 (Dataset List)	Use the UNIX `ls`, `df`, `du`, or `find` command to get information about files.
ISPF 3.x (Search-For)	Use the UNIX `grep` command to search the contents of files; use `find` to locate the files themselves.
ISPF 3.x (Super-Compare)	Use the UNIX comparison commands: `diff`, `cmp`, and `bdiff`.

ISPF 4 (Foreground Jobs) — Running commands and jobs in the foreground is normal shell mode; you can also use uni-SPF and SPF-UX foreground menus.

ISPF 5 (Background Jobs) — To run a command in the background under UNIX, you add an ampersand <&> after the command, or you can force a foreground command into the background by suspending it and using the `bg` command. Using the `cron`, `crontab`, and `at` commands mimic batch processing; uni-SPF and SPF-UX provide background menus.

ISPF 6 (Command) — Running commands and jobs in the foreground is normal shell mode.

ISPF Browse/Edit profile command — See ISPF 0 (User Parameters).

ISPF HELP — Used to get information about commands and their syntax. UNIX provides `man` and `apropos` commands—on-line manual pages.

ISPF SDSF/IOF — See SDSF.

ISPF/PDF — Interactive System Productivity Facility/Program Development Facility. A menu based mainframe tool for developing programs, manipulating datasets, and supporting production.

ISV — Independent Software Vendor. Generic name for software companies that do not build hardware.

JCL — Job Control Language. Statements used to control the running of programs on the mainframe. It specifies files, sizes, programs, execution order, resource limits, and error handling. Replaced with shell scripts.

job — Collection of work submitted for batch processing on the mainframe. May consist of one or more steps. Written in JCL. Also used for background processes under UNIX. Known as a process under UNIX.

JOBLIB DD — Used to specify location of programs and procedures. Replaced with UNIX path—where the shell searches for scripts (jobs/PROCs) and programs to execute.

kernel — The core of the operating system that handles tasks like memory allocation, device input and output, process allocation, security, and user access.

keys, big — These are keys on the mainframe that perform a function instead of displaying a character. They require the CPU to take control and perform the function: the <enter> key causes the operating system to input the current screen and perform any appropriate processing.

keys, special	These are keys that perform a function instead of displaying a character. These functions have names: the end-of-file key tells the UNIX that there is no more input; it is usually the <^D> key.
Korn Shell	A user interface for UNIX; supports programming. Written by David G. Korn and will run scripts written for the Bourne Shell.
KSDS	Key Sequenced Data Set. See VSAM.
LAN	Local Area Network. A collection of networking hardware, software, desktop computers, servers, and hosts all connected together within a defined local area. A LAN could be an entire college campus.
link file	File used to implement a symbolic link producing an alias on one filesystem for a file on another. The file only contains the fully qualified filename of the original file.
link, hard	Directory entry that provides an alias to another file that is in the same filesystem. Multiple entries appear in the directory for one physical file without replication of the contents.
link, symbolic	Directory entry that provides an alias to another file that is in another filesystem. Multiple entries appear in the directory for one physical file without replication of the contents. Implemented through link files; see also link file.
logical unit	Logical Units—networking protocols for the mainframe. See LU0, LU1, LU2, LU3, or LU6.2.
LU0	Logical Units—networking protocols for the mainframe. Unformatted data, similar to TCP/IP UDP.
LU1	Logical Units—networking protocols for the mainframe. Used for printing.
LU2	Logical Units—networking protocols for the mainframe. Used for interactive terminals (3270 type).
LU3	Logical Units—networking protocols for the mainframe. Used for Remote Job Entry (RJE) terminals that can include card readers and punches, printers, and consoles. These may be real or logical devices that are internal to a UNIX system.
LU6.2	Logical Units—networking protocols for the mainframe. Used for inner process communications (IPC).
Mainframe	Large scale computer from any one of a number of manufacturers. However, in general usage, a mainframe is a large scale computer manufactured by IBM. Any usage in this book refers to an IBM system.

man page	On-Line reference tool under UNIX that contains the documentation for the system—the actual pages from the printed manuals. It is stored in a searchable form for improved ability to locate information.
manual page	See man page.
memory	The stuff that contains executing programs and the data they are actively working on. Was made out of magnetic cores for old systems, now made on silicon chips.
memory, real	The amount of storage that is being used within the system (core or silicon).
memory, virtual	Memory that exists but you cannot see. See also virtual.
Meta-character	A printing character that has special meaning to the shell or another command. It is converted into something else. For instance, the asterisk <*> is converted by the shell to all the files in the current directory.
MFT	Multiple Fixed Tasks. Old mainframe operating system that could run a fixed number of programs at any one time.
MPTN	MultiProtocol Transport Network—IBM networking protocol to connect mainframe to TCP/IP network.
MVS	Multiple Virtual Storage. Operating system that allowed for multiple virtual memory address spaces.
MVT	Multiple Variable Tasks. Old mainframe operating system that could run a varying number of programs at any one time.
NFS	Network File System—means of connecting disks that are mounted to a remote system to the local system as if they were physically connected.
Null Statement	A program step that performs no operation but to hold space and fulfill syntactical requirements of the programming language. Also known as a NO-OP for no-operation performed.
OLTP	On-Line TeleProcessing. Programs and infrastructure used to process transactions interactively at a high rate. CICS is the most popular mainframe OLTP and is available for UNIX; there are other OLTP tools.
operator	Meta-character that performs a function on values or variables. The plus sign <+> operator adds two integers.
options	Special indicators that control the behavior of a command. Sometimes called flags. The `-l` option to the `ls` command

produces a long listing of files in the current directory. Without it, only the names are shown. These are used on the command line. See also parameters.

OS Operating System. Mainframe operating system that was not disk or tape based. Used as prefix to many operating system names.

parameters Data passed to a command or program through the command line. These can be options (see options) that control the command or arguments that the command works on. Some have special meaning based on their position on the command line.

parameters, positional See parameters.

pathname The means used to represent the location of a file in the directory structure. If omitted, the current directory is implied.

pathname, absolute The means used to represent the location of a file in a directory by specifying the exact location including all directories in the chain including the root.

pathname, relative The means used to represent the location of a file in a directory other than the current by navigating up and down through other directories using the current directory as a base.

PDP Personal Data Processor—computer manufactured by Digital Equipment Corporation. UNIX was originally written for a PDP-7; it gained popularity on the PDP-11 model. Both were mini-computers. DEC also produced other members of the PDP series.

PDS Partitioned Data Set. File that consists of a collection of smaller files. Also referred to as a library. A typical PDS might contain source code or executables. Similar to a sub-directory in UNIX; also similar to an archive except that on the mainframe all tools can access the members of a PDS; most UNIX tools cannot access the members of an archive.

pipe A method of redirecting the output of one program to become the input of another. The pipe character <|> tells the shell to perform the redirection. In general, it is stdout redirected to stdin except when named pipes are used.

pipe file See pipe, named.

pipe, named Performs expanded function of a regular pipe—redirecting the output of one program to another. Instead of connecting stdout to stdin, the output of one program is sent to the named pipe (implemented through a special file known as a pipe file or fifo) and another program reads data from the same file. The operating system ensures the proper sequencing of the data. Little or no data is stored in a pipe file; it acts as a connection between the two.

PPP — Point-to-Point Internet Protocol—routing protocol over serial link (modem).

printer control, ANSI — See printer control, ASA.

printer control, ASA — In general, printers on mainframes are controlled through the use of printer control that is known as ASA, ANSI, or FORTRAN control characters. These characters occupy the first byte sent to the printer and are not printed. A space causes the printer to advance to next line before printing. A zero causes the printer to advance two lines before printing. A minus sign <-> causes the printer to advance three lines before printing. A plus sign <+> causes the printer to print over the current line (not advancing). A one causes the printer to advance to top of next page.

printer control, ASCII — Most non-mainframe printers use ASCII printer control—special characters cause the printer to act. The formfeed character causes the printer to advance to top of next page. A newline character causes the printer to advance to the next line before printing. Anything else keeps it on the same line.

printer control, mainframe — See printer control, ASA.

PROC — Collection of JCL in separate source module that is run by a job by JCL like a subroutine in other programming languages. Equivalent to one shell script called by another—no special distinction from other shell scripts.

process — A discrete running program under UNIX. The user's interactive session is a process. A process can invoke (run) and control another program that is then referred to as a sub-process. Ultimately, everything a user does is a subprocess of the operating system.

PROCLIB DD — See JOBLIB.

QDAM/BDAM — Queued Direct Access Method and Basic Direct Access Method. Older methods of accessing relative or direct access datasets on mainframe. Largely replaced with VSAM RRDS now.

redirection — The process of directing a data flow from the default. Input can be redirected to get data from a file or the output of another program. Normal output can be sent to another program or a file. Errors can be sent to another program or a file.

regular expression	A way of specifying and matching strings for shells (filename wildcarding), `grep` (file searches), `sed`, and `awk`.
RFC	Request For Comment. Document used for creation of Internet and TCP/IP related tools and protocols.
root	This is the user that owns the operating system. The processes of the operating system run as though a user, root, signed on and started them. The root user is all powerful and can do anything they want. For this reason, they are often referred to as a super-user. It is also the very top of the directory tree structure.
routing	The process of moving network traffic to machines on different physical wires; also decides which path to take when there are multiple connections between the two machines. It will also send traffic around transmission interruptions.
RPC	Remote Procedural Call—the ability to call functions or subroutines that run on a remote system from the local one.
RRDS	Relative Record Data Set. See VSAM.
RS-232	Hardware standard for the connection of serial devices like terminals, printers, and modems to each other and to computers.
scripts	A program written for a UNIX utility including shells, AWK, sed, and others. Also see shell scripts.
SDSF	The Spool Display and Scroll Facility. SDSF and IOF are mainframe utility that allow the user to: view output of jobs in hold queue or waiting to print; display status and running output of executing jobs; display jobs in input queue; cancel jobs (input/output/hold queues) and executing, purge output printing or on hold queue; and alter output routing and print output on printer. Use UNIX lpstat, ps, who, vmstat, or iostat command.
shell	The part of UNIX that handles user input and invokes other programs to run commands. Includes a programming language.
shell scripts	A program written using a shell programming language like those supported by Bourne, Korn, or C shells.
signal	Used to communicate special events to programs by the operating system and other programs. Also see Appendix A (Common Error Messages, Codes, and UNIX Signals).
SLIP	Serial Link Internet Protocol—Internet over a serial link (modem).
SNA	System Network Architecture—IBM networking architecture.

stderr	The normal error output for a program; the screen by default. Can be changed by redirection. Functionally equivalent to mainframe SYSERR, SYSOUT, or SYSPRINT. See also redirection.
stdin	The normal input for a program; the keyboard by default. Can be changed by redirection. Functionally equivalent to mainframe SYSIN. See also redirection.
stdout	The normal output for a program; the screen by default. Can be changed by redirection. Functionally equivalent to mainframe SYSOUT or SYSPRINT. See also redirection.
STEPLIB DD	See JOBLIB.
sticky bit	A status flag on a file that tells UNIX to keep a copy of the file in the page file when it is executed for the first time. This implies that the file will be used frequently (commonly used program or frequently accessed directory are examples).
stream	A sequential collection of data. All files are streams to the UNIX operating system. To it, there is no structure to a file—that is something imposed by application programs or special tools (some COBOL compilers include ISAM).
sub-directory	See directory.
sub-process	See process.
substitution	See variables, substitution.
super-user	See root.
SVS	Single Virtual Storage. Operating system that used virtual memory as one single address space.
SYSIN	See stdin.
SYSIN, Embedded	In mainframe jobs, input data to programs can be included with the JCL and read through //SYSIN DD *. The << redirection operator, known as here document, performs this function under UNIX.
system administrator	The person who takes care of the operating system and user administrative issues on non-mainframe systems. Also called a system manager although that term is much more common in DEC VAX installation. The equivalent name on the mainframe is system programmer.
system manager	See system administrator.
system programmer	See system administrator.

TCP/IP	Transport Control Protocol/Internet Protocol. Pair of protocols and also generic name for suite of tools and protocols.
text processing languages	A way of developing documents in text editors with embedded commands that handle formatting. The file is fed through a processor that executes the embedded commands producing a formatted document.
TOS	Tape Operating System. Very old mainframe operating system that was tape-based. It had a short history.
TSO	Time Sharing Option. The interactive user interface for mainframe computers running MVS.
TSO HELP	Used to get information about commands and their syntax. UNIX provides man and apropos commands—on-line manual pages.
UDP	User Datagram Protocol—part of TCP/IP.
UNIX	A popular operating system often compared to a construction toy. Name is not an acronym even though it should be all capital letters. The name is a play on a predecessor operating system MULTICS.
UUCP	UNIX-to-UNIX-Copy-Program. Early informal network for the transmission of files, email, and netnews.
variables, attributes	The modifiers that set the variable type. A variable can be string or integer, left- or right-justified, read-only or changeable, and other attributes.
variables, environmental	Places to store data and values (strings and integers) in the area controlled by the shell. These variables can be local to the current shell or available to a sub-shell (exported).
variables, substitution	The process of interpreting an environmental variable to get its value.
virtual	Part of a disk is used as a paging file and portions of programs and their data are moved between it and real memory. To the program, it is in real memory. The hardware and operating system performs translation between the memory address the program thinks it is using and where it is actually stored.
VM	Virtual Machine. Operating system that provided each user with the impression they had their own private computer. Each user could run a different guest operating system (MVS, DOS, CMS). Useful when converting between operating systems (DOS to MVS) or between versions of the same operating system.

VS — Virtual Storage. Denoted operating system that could treat the disk as an extension of memory allowing more and larger programs to execute at any one time.

VSAM — Virtual Sequential Access Method. IBM replacement for ISAM. Provides keyed access (KSDS—Key Sequenced Data Set), sequential access (ESDS—Entry Sequenced Data Set), and relative or direct access (RRDS—Relative Record Data Set). See ISAM.

VSE — Virtual Storage Extended. Enhancement to mainframe DOS to use virtual memory. The DOS/VSE operating systems are primarily used on 4300 series systems.

VTOC — Volume Table Of Contents. The listing of all datasets on a mainframe disk. See also catalog. Equivalent to UNIX filesystems.

wildcard — Means of specifying filename(s) where the operating system determines some of the characters. Multiple files may match and will be available to the tool. UNIX and ISPF support wildcards.

XA — eXtended Architecture. Operating system that worked with the extended address architecture of some machines to allow more real and virtual memory to a maximum of 2 Gb.

INDEX

A

B

C

D

E

F

G

H

I

J

K

L

M

N

O

P

Q

R

S

T

U

V

W, X, Y, Z